Society, Politics and Development in North East India

About the Editors

Dr. Asok Kumar Ray (B.1951) obtained his M.A. and Ph.D. Degrees in Political Science from Burdwan University, West Bengal and taught Political Science at degree level in Manipur. He has extensively worked on the political systems of the highlander tribes of the northeast. He has authored three books. Also, he has co-edited seven books. Besides, he conducted a FAO-Forestry Study on Marketing of NTFP in Bihar and M.P. He has to his credit about one hundred research papers presented in different national and international seminars. Many of his research papers have been published in different academic journals and books.

Dr. Satyabrata Chakraborti (b.1943) obtained his M.Sc. and Ph.D. degrees in Anthropology from Calcutta University. He retired from Anthropological Survey of India, Government of India, as the Deputy Director in January 2003. He studied the problems of some marginal tribes as well as some peasant and urban communities in West Bengal, Kerala, Karnataka, Andhra Pradesh, some parts of North-East India and Andaman. He also served as the Visiting Faculty in Arunachal University, Vidyasagar University, West Bengal and Lal Bahadur Sastri National Academy of Administration, Mussoorie.

Dr. Chakrabarti has authored, edited, co-edited eleven books and published more than fifty research papers.

SOCIETY, POLITICS AND DEVELOPMENT IN NORTH EAST INDIA

Essays in Memory of Dr. Basudeb Datta Ray

Edited by
Asok Kumar Ray
and
Satyabrata Chakraborty

CONCEPT PUBLISHING COMPANY, NEW DELHI-110059

Cataloging in Publication Data—DK
Courtesy: D.K. Agencies (P) Ltd. <docinfo@dkagencies.com>

Society, politics and development in North East India :essays in memory of Dr. Basudeb Datta Ray / edited by Asok Kumar Ray and Satyabrata Chakraborty.
p. cm.
Basudeb Datta Ray, 1925-2008, founder secretary of North East India Council for Social Science Research; contributed articles.
Includes bibliographical references.
Includes index.
ISBN 13: 9788180695728
ISBN 10: 8180695727

1. India, Northeastern—Civilization. 2. India, Northeastern—Social life and customs. 3. India, Northeastern—Social conditions. 4. India, Northeastern—Economic conditions. 5. Economic development—Government policy—India, North-eastern. 6. Women in development—India, Northeastern. 7. Tribes—India, Northeastern—Social life and customs. I. Datta Ray, B. (Basudeb), 1925-2008. II. Ray, Asok Kumar, 1951- III. Chakrabarti, S. B. (Satya Brata), 1943-

DDC 954.1 22

ISBN-13: 978-81-8069-572-8
ISBN-10: 81-8069-572-7

First Edition 2008

Published and Printed by
Ashok Kumar Mittal
Concept Publishing Company
A/15-16, Commercial Block, Mohan Garden
New Delhi-110059 (INDIA)

Phones : 25351460, 25351794
Fax : 091-11-25357103
Email : publishing@conceptpub.com

Dr. B. Datta Ray
(1924-2008)

Contents

Preface ix
A Brief Profile of Prof. Basudeb Datta Ray xi
List of Contributors xv
Introduction xvii

PART I
SOCIETY AND CULTURE

1. Archaeological and Architectural Remains: Testimony of Cultural Interactions of the People of North-East India 3
Jayanta Sarkar

2. Folklore and Development: Are they Antithetic? 15
Soumen Sen

3. Tribal Identity, Culture and Politics: The North-East Indian Perspective 30
Rajat Kanti Das

4. Culture and its Impact on Human Personality 39
Bobby Mahanta

5. Global Concern(s): Indigenous People/Tribes vis-à-vis Non-Tribes 47
R. K. Bhattacharya and *Kumkum Bhattacharya*

6. Dormitories in the Life of the Wanchos of Arunachal Pradesh 62
Sarit K. Chaudhuri and *Nokkai Wangsaham*

7. Marriage that was in Manipur 76
Oinam Ranjit Singh

8. Student/Youth Movement with Special Reference to North-East India 89
S.B. Chakrabarti

9. Society and Politics in Manipur 99
Ksh. Bimola Devi

10. Women's Movements in Conflict Situation in Manipur 108
Th. Binarani Devi

11. Impact of North East Indian Tribal Values and Culture on the Hill Region's Socio-Economic Development in the Pre-plan Period 115
J. B. Ganguli

12. Society, Culture and Development 118
Xavier Pfokrehe Mao

13. Family as the Primary Agency of Education: Among the Poor Khasis of Shillong City 122
Gita Pyal

14. Gender Dimension of Social Sector Development in Manipur 128
Asha Thokchom

15. Bio-Social Diversity among Caste Populations of Assam 139
Debashis Basu

PART II
DEVELOPMENT

16. Between South and Southeast Asia: Recasting India's Northeast in the Age of Globalization 149
Samir Kumar Das

17. Institutional Reforms, Governance and Growth: A Case Study of North-East India 166
Asok Kumar Ray

18.. The Coming of Tea in the Brahmaputra Valley 175
Keya Dasgupta

19. Land Administration in the Char Areas of Assam: The Task Ahead 190
Gorky Chakraborty

20. Some Aspects of Sustainable Socio-Economic Development in North Eastern Region of India — 210
P. C. Dutta

21. Tourism in North East India: Exploring the Paradise — 243
Elangbam Nixon Singh

22. Urbanization in Meghalaya — 264
Surojit Sen Gupta

23. Urbanisation among the Tribals of Tripura — 280
Malabika Das Gupta

24. Some Aspects of Urbanizations and Economic Development in Bodoland: A Perspective of Kokrajhar Town — 295
Sujata Bhadra

25. A Glimpse at the Distribution and Concentration of Farm Land Holdings in North Eastern India — 307
A.K. Neog

26. Centrally Sponsored Schemes for Upliftment of Rural Economy of North East India: An Analysis — 316
A. Rajmani Singh

27. Women Development & Sex Ratio: Treading between North and North East India — 329
Paulavi Das

28. Empowerment of Women Through Information and Communication Technology — 337
Jahitha Begum and *M. Vakkil*

29. Ecosystem Enrichment and Livelihood Management: An Endeavour for Synthesis towards Symbiotic Sustainability — 342
Kaustubh Lahiri

Index — 355

Preface

Bringing out a volume to felicitate Prof. Basudeb Datta Ray—the Founder Secretary of North East India Council for Social Science Research, Shillong, a public intellectual and a great visionary—for his life time dedication to the cause of promoting social science research and providing an academic platform to the scholars and researchers working in and on the otherwise difficult areas of the region, was a long cherished dream of all the members of the Council and the well-wishers of Prof. Datta Ray. "We had the desire to felicitate Dr. Basudeb Datta Ray with this book. Unfortunately, his sudden demise on 14th April, 2008 did not allow us to do so. This book is therefore dedicated in memory of Dr. Basudeb Datta Ray and is handed over to his wife, Smt. Minati Datta Ray.

Dr. S.B. Chakraborti, Dr. A.K. Ray and Dr. B.J. Deb took the initiative as convenors of this project. All the members of the Council gave full moral support to this initiative and within a short period of time a good number of research papers was made available for this volume. Those who could not send papers gave constant moral support and encouragement to go ahead.

The contents of this book are well researched and thought provoking. These have raised and addressed multi-dimensional issues of society, culture and development in the northeastern region. Academic value apart, this book gives food for thought to the development thinkers and the policy-makers. This book, we hope, will be a befitting tribute to Prof. Datta Ray.

On behalf of the Convenors, all members of North East India Council for Social Science Research, Shillong and all the well-wishers including Mr. A.K. Mittal of Concept Publishing Company, New Delhi, we do hereby dedicate this book in memory of late Prof. Basudev Datta Ray for his life-time contribution and commitment for the cause of social science research in North East India.

On behalf of the Convenors and all the members of North East India Council for Social Science Research, we express our deep sense of gratitude for the moral commitment of Concept Publishing Company, New Delhi for bringing out this book in a very short time.

A Brief Profile of Prof. Basudeb Datta Ray

S.B. CHAKRABARTI

The North East India Council For Social Science Research (NEICSSR) has built up its sustained intellectual tradition bit by bit over more than the past three decades since 1974. This diligently pursued academic forum has been instrumental in systematically mobilizing and activising a huge band of upcoming committed social researchers, social workers and social thinkers belonging by and large to the North-East region. The long list of publications regularly brought out so far based on the modestly organized seminars (twice a year on average) would speak eloquently on the extra ordinary achievement of this Council.

The most vital role has been cardinally played by late Dr. Basudev Datta Ray, M.A., B.T, LLB, Ph.D. Born on 10.3.1924 in Bankura (now West Bengal), he was primarily rooted to Barisal, the then East Bengal and now Bangladesh where he completed his early education and had spent childhood days upto the age of sixteen. His otherwise colourful life during the pre-independence period remained mostly unknown and unfamiliar to the great many friends and admirers. He became involved in the struggle for India's independence at the age of twelve. His close association with the revolutionary group known as "Jugantar" gave him a perennial source for gaining enough courage and confidence in moulding his political outlook for achieving the cherished goal. He was detained in jail for a long time first in 1941 and then between 1943-46 and stayed as political detinue in Calcutta and Delhi. He fully utilized his stay there in the stimulating company of a number of co-prisoners who were the illustrious sons of the country in those days. He prepared himself for higher education as well as wrote innumerable pieces of poems. A few of the selected such poems found the light in printed form entitled "Agami Dupur-O-Chander Kalanka" in 2003.

After release from the jail Dr. Datta Ray gradually completed his higher education; he obtained M.A. degree in economics in 1949 from Calcutta University. Subsequently he got his other degrees, namely B.T, LLB and Ph.D. from Gauhati University. He was actively involved in the Economic and Political Research Department of the All India Congress Committee when Pattavi Sitaramiya was the president. At this juncture he suddenly decided to leave Delhi and came down to Shillong in 1950 with a teaching assignment in St. Edmund's College.

It is in Shillong that his new phase of life began. He served in the Department of Economics till 1962 and then shifted to Political Science Department as the head. He remained there till his retirement in 1985. In between he was the Director, Faculty of Post Graduate Studies in Political Science from 1965-72. This P.G. department was located in St. Edmund's College which was subsequently closed down with the coming of North-Eastern Hill University, Shillong. Side by side with teaching he tried to organize Assam Political Science Association and Shillong Political Science Association in mid 1960s. He also organized another academic body known as Inter-Disciplinary Forum which remained active till 1973. Then emerged the NEICSSR in 1974 ushering in a new era for unified and inter-disciplinary social science research in North-East India. With the co-operation of a group of committed colleagues he became the Founder Secretary of the Council—a position which he is still holding at the age of eighty five. Along with this continuous pressure of the Council Dr Datta Ray also shouldered the heavy responsibilities of a secondary school and a women's college in Shillong. He was the Project Director of Indian Council For Social Science Research for two important research works, namely Crime Perspective in North-East India and Tribal Occupational Mobility, both published in 1984 and 1986. This apart he is credited with a number of academic publications-research articles and edited volumes of which a few important ones are appended here. Before I conclude this brief profile of late Dr Basudev Datta Ray I must mention with sincere regards for his wife Mrs. Minati Datta Ray, whom married on 11.2.1953. She is equally a competent academic collaborator, but for whose constant help, encouragement and sacrifice late Dr Datta Ray perhaps could not be able to firmly stick to his mission. Last but not the least, to my mind, this elderly couple's compounded challenges of life have been continuously made easier by the spiritual strength provided by Viswanath, their physically depended son, through his meaningful non-verbal communications, invisibly sensitizing the nerves of his parents for faithfully carrying out their tasks in hand. It is but perfectly natural that we should all share our concern for late Dr B. Datta Ray and his family through this Volume.

Some of the important publications of Prof. Dutta Ray are listed below:

- Assam Secretariat-1874-1947. An Administrative History of North East India.
- Tribal Identity and Tension in North East India.

Edited Books

- Emergence and Growth of Middle Class in North East India.
- Social and Economic Profile of North East India
- Shifting Cultivation in North East India
- Agricultur in the Hills: A Study of Meghalaya
- Tribal Occupational Mobility
- Crime Perspective in North East India
- Social and Political Institutions of the Hill People of North East India.
- North East India—2000.
- Reorganisation of the North East India.
- An Agenda for North East India.

Co-edited Books

- Urban Development in North East India.
- Population, Poverty and Environment in North East India.
- Sociological Constraints in Industrial Development in North East India
- Dynamics of Tribal Society in North East India.
- Dynamics of Power Relationship in North East India.
- Pattern and Problems of Population in North East India.
- Female Emancipation: Focus North East India.

A Collection of Bengali Poems Entitled

- Besides he has to his credit innumerable research papers and articles of Public interest published in regional newspapers of North East India.

List of Contributors

A.K. Neog, Directorate of Economics & Statistics Department of Agriculture & Cooperation, Ministry of Agriculture, GoI.

Asha Thockchom, Y.K. College, Wangjing.

Asok Kumar Ray, Scholar.

Bobby Mohanta, Research Scholar, NEHU, Shillong.

Debasish Basu, Anthropological Survey of India, Shillong.

Gita Pyal, St. Peter's College, Shillong.

Gorky Chakraborti, Doom Dooma College, Assam.

J.B. Ganguli, Former Vice Chancellor, Tripura University.

Jayanta Sarkar, Scholar, Kolkata.

Juhita Begum , Scholar, Chennai.

Kaustav Lahirti, Surendranath College for Women, Kolkata.

Keya Dasgupta, Centre for Studies in Social Sciences, Calcutta.

Ksh. Bimola Devi, Manipur University, Imphal.

Kumkum Bhattachariya, Viswa Bharati University, West Bengal.

M. Vakil , Scholar, Chennai.

Malabika Dasgupta, Scholar, Kolkata.

N. Wangsang, Research Scholar, Arunachal Institute of Tribal Studies, Rajiv Gandhi University, Itanagar.

Nixon Singh, Assam University , Diphu Campus, Assam.

O. Ranjit Singh, Kha-Manipur College, Manipur.

P.C. Dutta, Hailakandi College, Assam.

Paulavi Das, Indraprastha College for Women, Delhi.

R.K. Bhattachariya , Former Director, Anthropological Survey of India.

R.K. Das, Vidyasagar University, West Bengal.

Rajmani Singh, Manipur University, Imphal.

S.B. Chakraborti, Former Deputy Director, Anthropological Survey of India.

S.K. Choudhury , Reader, Rajiv Gandhi University, Itanagar.

Samir Kumar Das, University of Calcutta.

Soumen Sen, Former Professor, NEHU, Shillong.

Sujata Bhadra, Janata College, Assam.

Surojit Sengupta, St. Edmund's College, Shillong.

Th. Binarani Devi, G.P. Womens' College, Imphal.

Xavier Pfokrehe Mao, North Eastern Hill University, Shillong.

Introduction

This book is a collection of essays in memory of late Dr. Basudev Datta Ray, Secretary of North East India Council for Social Science Research, Shillong. The research articles are drawn from inter-disciplinary fields of social science and touch upon the multiple contours of society, culture and development in northeast India. The issues and concerns raised by the authors of these articles are of immense significance in the specific socio-economic and development contexts of northeast India. The scholars and researchers working on and in this region have shown anxieties and raised the criticalities of socio-cultural issues in the region vis-à-vis development. This book is planned in two parts: Part I deals with society and culture of northeast India and Part II deals with development issues thereof.

The northeast India in general exposes a paradox of cultural insulation and protectionism on the one hand and cultural exchanges, sharing and crosscuts with cultures of other regions on the other. This paradox to a large extent impacted the process of social formation and community imagination in different ethnic groups in this region. This paradox also attributed to articulate cultural politics or ethnic politics in this region. As such we have two types of historiographic sources to understand and analyse society and culture of northeastern region of India. One is the vast array of folk culture, archaic traditions and pristine socio-cultural institutions. The other is the more tangible archaeological and architectural remains found in different parts of northeast India. The first type of historiographic source is insulated in nature and is confined within the local society in which pristine content provides a shield for self-defence against the onslaught of the so-called outside world. It is true that industrialization and modernization have destroyed many properties of archaic cultural and social institutions although the majority of the people in this region still cling to those for their social existence and recognition at least in form though not in content. This gives rise to tradition-modernity antithesis on northeast India. But as the forces of modernization are becoming stronger and stronger, the very survival and recognition of the community are becoming difficult unless the latter become flexible enough to cope up with the challenges of modernization.

Jayanta Sarkar traced the testimony of cultural interactions of the people of northeast India as evidenced in the archaeological and architectural remains found in northeast India. It is generally believed that the people of this region by and large remained least affected and were insulated by the cultures of other people in other parts of the country, primarily because of lack of adequate communication facilities till the recent past. On the other hand ethnic migrations from the neighbouring regions became historical fact in this region. Such migrants brought with them not only tradable goods in this region but also brought cultural packages to build up cultural relations between neighbouring countries and this region. They did the bridging function between the local and the outside world and built up strong foundations of cultural relations between the neighbouring countries and regions. This led to a process of cultural metamorphosis in this region. There are glimpses of these on some archaeological sites and architectural characters, as observed in the temple archaeology and old architectures of Assam, archaeological remains of Arunachal Pradesh, temples and monuments of Manipur and in the Archaeology of Meghalaya, Tripura and Nagaland. These bear the testimony of cultural interactions of the people of northeast India with outside cultures and show that the people of these apparently difficult terrains had actually experienced impacts of other cultures, particularly of eastern India together with some religious faiths during the medieval historical period. Contributions made in the spheres of art, architecture and culture by the people of Orissa and Bengal helped evolve a unique combination of local creativity with the artistic styles of Orissa and Bengal. Most of the archaeological and architectural activities of this region also received patronage from the rulers of the plains of northeast India. While these were happening in the plains of this region, the hills of this region were relatively insulated and remained largely unaffected. The hill people of this region could thrive within their self-contained cultural boundaries. The archaeological remains also suggest intrusion of Hindu religion in its art and cultural forms in different parts of northeast India. In some cases association of Muslim architecture with Hindu art forms and sculptures is also found. Northeast India also exhibited interesting confluences of the Tantric and the Vaishnavite cults. All these confluences and interactions produced cultural synthesis, secularization of society and religious syncretism in the northeastern region of India.

Folklore, the archaic cultural expression of the people living in nature has been subject to both conservative and progressive discourses in the history. According to the conservative view, folklore is pushed back as a result of technology and civilizational changes- a view that prevailed till the first half of the 20th Century. It was the Marxist theory of dialectical and historical materialism that gave a new treatment to folklore and initiated a brake in the erstwhile conservative thought. The literature on this was first developed in Russia and then in other parts of the world. The Contexualists of the US also got disenchanted with the conservative view, although they did not agree with the Marxist view. A similar trend was found in Europe that rejected the view that folklore is quaint. The mid-20th Century folklore scholarship therefore found no antithesis between folklore and technological civilization. Folklore was rather seen as having adaptive potential in the situation of change. Prof. **Soumen Sen** with this sketch of folklore, stands for the complementarity of folklore with modernity. He considers tradition as a transitive series and denies folklore as quaint and irrelevant. From such standpoint Prof. Sen deals with cultural identity and cultural politics in the northeast India.

He contends the view that 'development destroys folklore' around which many socio-political movements of the region have evolved. In the northeastern region there is a tremendous sense of insecurity of culture and folklore in the face of modernization and globalization. This sense of insecurity provides the rationale for cultural protectionism in this region. But on the other hand the growing opening of the region to the outside world through education and information technology is bringing about fast changes in many traditional art and cultural forms including folklore. In this situation the Nehru- Elwin Policy of protectionism, once criticized by the political leaders including the tribal leaders and the anthropologists, needs re-assessment in the light of the current socio-cultural situation in the tribal areas of the region. This in turn demands re-assessment of the strategies for development in this region. It is true that in the changing context, no culture can remain static and uncontaminated. Therefore utility of folklore lies in negotiating with the factors of changes and in coping up with the changes that are taking place in the region. In this way, folklore and development can become complementary to each other.

The archaeological and architectural evidences and from the progressive treatment of folklore of the respective authors have broken the 'isolation myth' prevailing in the psyche of the rank and file of the northeast India.

Prof. R.K. Das found that the tribal identity in the northeast crystallized with ethnic identity in the pluri-cultural situation. International boundaries influenced the greater territorial and even trans-territorial identity formations in this region. Cultural affinity had a great role to play in such formations that often led to intra-ethnic conflict and consequent politicization of culture. The concept of cultural relativism therefore could not remain uncritical, nor the region could build a proto-type of 'cultural type'. In this region there are cases when some tribes even adopted the identity of other tribes. The northeastern scenario in such situation resembles to R.S. Naroll's concept of 'cultunit' whereby the tribal people of Manipur, for example, became a subject group of a linguistically diverse state. On the other hand there is a growing trend to transcend the 'cultunit' status towards nation state status and a shift of emphasis from a pure 'cultural model' towards the nation-state-based model. Within the nation state model again there are other critical trends including the degree and extent of inter-dependency within the nation state and extreme claim for sovereignty by some section of the tribal groups. The latter however is a difficult proposition in the face of the authoritative Indian state. Despite, those who could assume power by defying the authoritative state, in turn, exercised power over the group and acted for a political struggle aspired by the people. In such case alignment of the ethnic groups with a distinct cultural base and their political organizations produced some kind of solidarity-oriented action. But the complex nature of society, local boundary systems, regional and national alliances, tension between change and preservation of cultural identity, resistance and development, shared cultural practices and so on in the northeast came in the way of typical culture-based politics. While the lives of the tribal people of this region are rooted largely in their cultures, merging individual craze for wealth and power hit at the roots. On the other hand bureaucratic corruption, administrative and military repression let loose by the Indian state have de-essentialized culture and reduced sincere participation of the people in public affairs. To come out of this, as some people think, it needs re-negotiation with their identities that are forced upon them by the Indian state.

On the other hand, **Bobby Mohanta** found evidence of 'cultural pattern' that emerged in Assamese culture as a result of confluence of diverse folk cultures based on agricultural economy. As such the northeast as a region became a home for diverse cultures, nature-friendly traditional technologies and enduring social institutions that were shaped by the tribal and non-tribal population alike. While the indigenous communities still retain a great deal of pristine culture, tradition, knowledge, technology and social institutions, expansion of transport and communication, exchange of ideas and views on academic platforms, change in habitat pattern and global economy make way for greater cultural diversity and national integration. But ironically re-negotiating the identity of the people of the northeast that was forced upon them by the Indian state on the one hand and the more polite and civility of approach of national integration on the other not only created hiatus at the empirical level but also shaped and re-shaped the attitude of the people of this region towards the Indian state vis-à-vis their cultural identities.

According to **R.K. Bhattachariya and Kumkum Bhattachariya** a multi-ethnic society of India became a universal concern from the time of colonial rule. The colonials constructed both the terms 'Tribes' and 'Indigenous People' at different points of time. The other terms like 'Adivasi' 'Vanavasi', Janajati' etc. also came up as contending terms. In recent years the term 'Indigenous People' has become more popular among the more educated tribes. The democratic divide, thus created, is widened by the affirmative action of the Indian state that blocked the process of tribe-caste and caste-sanskritization continuum and state formation. At the global context, the terms 'fourth world' and 'Indigenous People' as used as an attempt to confederate the tribes did not much impact India. In fact, as the authors argue, there seems to be no historical and factual support to the concept of 'Indigenous People' except when we define such people with 'ecological niche' criterion. Besides, in the Indian context, lack of appropriate definition of the term, the polarized power structure, dominant and minority differentiations, elite manipulation of the term and the instrumentality of the term in the international conventions are not unknown. On the other hand socio-political changes and external forces made the term ambiguous and made the exclusive tribal movements problematic. Nevertheless 'Indigenous People' became an ideological ammunition in the hands of the elites in reshaping their identity and gave them an agency to negotiate with others and made it important in transforming the local and global perspectives.

S.K. Choudhury and N. Wangsam dealt with structural-functional implications of the dormitories in the lives of the Wanchoo tribe in Arunachal Pradesh. The speciality of the Wanchoo dormitory is that unlike the others, the membership in it is permanent. Thus once a member, always a member. Therefore Wangchoo dormitory is not identical to any other youth dormitory systems prevailing among other tribes of the region. There are separate male and female dormitories among the Wanchos. The male dormitory is known as *Paa* and the female one is know as *zipsum hum.* While there can be more than one dormitory in one village, the size of the same may vary according to the number of households in the village. Besides, there is Chief's Dormitory which has a separate structure. There are different membership criteria, norms, taboos and rituals in both the male and the female dormitories. For the male dormitory there is a distinct ground plan and distribution of space. Inside the *Paa* there are different items and arrangements for common use. The girl dormitory on the other hand is not so structured although it is a socially sanctioned institution. The functional domain of male dormitory is varied. It deals with the issues and concerns of common interest. It is both a culturai and a communicative space wherein different socio-political, cultural and religious decisions are taken. Male dormitory also acts as village court to deal with petty cases of conflict among the members of the dormitory. It guards the village from enemy attacks and at the same time is a space for knowledge building, learning, and for working together. It is also the "lovers' point" for the young boys and girls.

In today's changing context such dormitories are facing

erosion. The authors have expressed worries about it and raised the question whether revival of these institutions is possible that can yet remain functional in addressing many contemporary issues facing the Wanchoo tribe?

O. Ranjit Singh dealt at length with the history and origin of the family and marriage in Manipuri society taking the cue from the "Mother Right" propounded by Bechofen, Bancroft and Morgan. He sketched the history of transition from the state of promiscuity through different regulatory forms of sexual behaviour to the present state of monogamy including the organization of family and the institution of marriage. This process of social formation corresponded to the revolutionary changes in the productive forces and production relations. These changes happened with the threshold of agricultural civilization that culminated in feudalism. Monogamous family and marriage superseded the state of "Mother Right" and brought about discordant patriarchal institution in stead. This state of social and institutional formation did not take place simultaneously in all the societies because of different stages of development of the productive forces and production relations in different societies. In case of Manipur, Dr. Singh traced the origin of different family structures and marriage practices including polyandry and polygamy parallel to monogamy and traced out the once existing matriarchal practices in Manipur. He also identified different forms of marriages in Manipur including marriage by capture, marriage by elopement and arranged marriage. Along with this came up the practice of bride price and clan exogamy. Though marriage among the Meiteis became an institution with religious character attached to it, in the semi-feudal society of Manipur monogamy, considered sacrosanct, could not mature into an ideal institution. Polygamy became very common but luxuriant practice among the kings, nobles and the rich people. The practice of polygamy also seeped into the practice of the common people though polygamous persons came to be treated with hatred and abhorrence in general.

S.B. Chakraborti while dealing with the youth movement in northeast India stated that in the absence of capital, the emerging middle class and the educated elites conveniently used ethnicity and the primordial cultural assets of different kinds both in the colonial and in the post-colonial times to assert their political demands and aspirations. The Bengal Renaissance had much to do with the rising middle class consciousness and the rising youth movements in Assam. The involvement of the students in the freedom movement in the early part of the 20th Century made the city of Calcutta the hub from where the message of the movement spread out to some parts of Assam. After Independence the youth movement oscillated more towards the issues of ethnic mobilization, cultural autonomy, control over local resources, foreigners' issue, linguistic and regional identity, industrialization and so on. The emergence of AASU and Gana Andolan among the student communities in Assam was a pointer to these changes. In Arunachal Pradesh, the All Arunachal Pradesh Students Union flagged the issues of refugees, border dispute with Assam, trade license to non-Arunachalese, infiltration of foreign nationals and heralded the movement for reviving the indigenous faith known as *Donya Polo'*. The student organizations of Meghalaya, Nagaland and Manipur got involved in socio-political issues. In Manipur, the women community built a chequered history of women movement. The All Manipur Students' Union established in 1946, fought for primary school education and for restoration of human rights in the state. The Mizo Students' Union got involved in state politics. The Young Lushai Association and the Young Mizo Association in Mizoram, Jaja Siksha Samiti and Gana Mukti Parishad in Tripura mobilized the youth for educational advancement and social transformation. The TUJS, an organization of the tribal youth in Tripura virtually matured into a regional political party.

As student and youth movements can not be de-linked Dr. Chakraborti found two distinct aspects in these movements. One is to consider such movements as necessary parts of the larger political movement and the other is to assess these movements in terms of the specific situations in the region. Two other emerging areas of student and youth movements in this region, according to the author, are: creative production in the fields of art including performance art & literature and political extremism. It is true that the student and the youth movements of this region have encountered different phases of ideological, social and political trauma. Later, liberalization and globalization have eroded the community. In such situation student and youth movements in this region need to look into the global, national and regional forces operating in the society in order to widen understanding of the problem of the region in a macro perspective and to bring about social transformation.

Prof. Bimola Devi gave a chronological account of the socio-political happenings in the state of Manipur. She said that the heterogeneity of ethnic and community groups influenced the social and political processes in the state. Back to the social history of Manipur in 33 A.D. she unveiled the feudal character of the state with the hegemonic authority of the kingship institution, theologically backed by the mandarin class represented by the Brahmin and the Brahma Sabha. Both these institutions were responsible for dividing the people socially and economically, so that the poor and the common people were virtually reduced to the status of slaves in Manipuri society. With the coming of the British colonials the economic condition of the people started to further worsen due to oppressive taxation system and other bad practices of the colonial rulers on the denizens of Manipur. There were series of movements led by the women community against the British and even the royal scion like Hijam Irabot spearheaded social and political movements against the British. These movements led to the emergence of some form of democratic governance in the 1930s. After 1947 a constitutional monarchy was institutionalized in the state for a short period till this institution was ended with the Accession Agreement of Manipur with the Union of India. Later as a Part- C state, Manipur was kept under the virtual hegemonic rule of the Chief Commissioner. The upgradation of Manipur as a full-fledged state in 1972 was another landmark. But immediately after this, different kinds of social and political movements appeared in the state and made the socio-economic situation volatile until AFPSA-1958 was imposed on the state. This situation made further intensification of socio-political crises in the state. This scenario provoked the women community in Manipur to fight against this draconian act. A fresh lease of conflict arose in the 1990s first between the Kukis and the Nagas and then among different ethnic groups in the state. The mushrooming of the underground outfits among different ethnic groups let loose political turmoil and social instability. In this process a section of the new middle class played authoritative role.

Th. Binarani Devi pictured women's' movement in the state of Manipur from the colonial to post-colonial period. The two major women's movements in Manipur, one in 1904 and the other in

1939, against the British bear testimony of historic struggle of women against the system of forced labour (Lallop) and against the export of rice from Manipur to outside by the Marwari traders. From the time of Accession of Manipur to the Union of India to the subsequent state violence in the 1970s, 1980s and 1990s the rights and peaceful living of the common people were adversely affected. Imposition of AFSPA-1958 and other draconian laws in the state worsened the civil lives of the people. These events ignited women movements in different parts of the state. The organized movements of the women agencies against the police and military atrocities including rape and custody-killing culminated in an unrobed protest march of the women organizations in 2004 in the heartland of Imphal. The peaceful Hunger Strike by Sharmila against the imposition of AFSPA in the state is another landmark in the history of women's movement in Manipur. Many women organizations and state level networks of Manipur came together to fight against state-sponsored violence in Manipur.

The women community of Manipur has a greater role in ensuring economic subsistence of the households. Reduced livelihood options led them to work in unorganized sectors with untold sufferings and indignity. Under these circumstances, the author feels, the women community needs to reaffirm its solidarity and to commit for organized liberation movement in order to achieve a just and developed society.

Prof. J.B. Ganguli examined the impact of tribal values and culture on the northeast India's hill region's socio-economic development. Taking the cue from Max Weber's " The Protestant Ethics and the Spirit of Capitalism" (Which fore-grounded the role of protestant ethics in economic development), Prof. Ganguli found conspicuous absence of the value systems in the economic practices of shifting cultivation that prevails in most parts of northeast India. Characterized mainly as subsistence or stationary, shifting cultivation economy could not become accumulative economy congenial for economic development and growth.

Within the larger equalitarian values with no caste-like division of labour, sex-based division of labour gave the women predominance in agrarian activities in northeast India. This division was not obviously on the basis professional skill. This factor also kept production at lower level. Prevalence of slavery and slavery-linked economy could hardly promote human enterprise that could produce surplus for accumulation.

Prof. Xavier Mao presented a critique of the concept of culture on development in the northeast India. He too found the Weberian thesis of "Protestant Ethics and the Spirit of Capitalism" irrelevant in the multi-religious, multi-cultural and multi-ethnic make up of the northeastern region. Physical vastness of India, lack of exchange and communication and lack of mutual trust and understanding hindered the process of development in the northeastern region. The apprehension of influx of outsiders and professionals from outside also stood in the way of development. The secular democratic principle of the Indian constitution could do little to change the scenario. Prof. Mao in such circumstances called for the pro-active roles of the enlightened citizens, teachers and student leaders in creating a new culture free of all inhibitions and complexities with a view to bring about development in the region.

Gita Pyal made a study of family as the primary agency of education among the poor Khasis of Shillong city. Such poor people are those who faced serious livelihood crises in their respective villages and hence migrated to the Shillong city in such of livelihood. Despite having a huge body of formal schools and other institutions of education for the children in Shillong city, the poor Khasi people adhered to the traditional family roles in educating (including religious education) and socializing the children, particularly the girl children. The poor Khasis in Shillong city failed to access formal institutions of education because of poverty, denial of social opportunities, rich-poor divide in the Khasi society and denial of equal opportunities in the missionary and private schools.

Though the parental roles in educating the children differ between the father and the mother in the family-based education practices of the poor Khasis in Shillong city, the children learn different coping strategies and survival education only from the family. But in the era of globalization, the focus of education is being laid on human resource development. Family-based education does not fit in with the emerging need of human resource development. At the policy level therefore not only investment in education and health needs be increased but also more opportunities need be extended to the children of the poor Khasis in the city for institutional education. Education should not be the blessed privilege of the affluent society alone. The poor children should also benefit from education in order to bring about an egalitarian society.

Asha Thokchom examined gender dimension in social sector development in Manipur. To her social sector development is not just about human capital formation and human development; it also refers to value component of social sector development like freedom, gender equality, nationalism etc. In terms of indicators of development like per-capita income, male and female literacy, sex ratio, Maternal Mortality Rate, Infant Mortality Rate and poverty reduction, Manipur exhibits a better profile. Total expenditure on social sector increased over the years in the state and the trends in annual plan outlays showed an increasing trend. However, viewing through gender lens, the gender planning including scheme-wise break-up of child welfare and women welfare, Grant- in- Aid to Manipur Social Welfare Board, total state plans and total sponsored schemes etc. seems to be top-down and welfarist in approach. In terms of HDI Manipur ranked 4th in 1981 but in 1991 it declined to 9th. The 2001 HDI ranking is not available but the human condition is found worsening in the state. Female literacy rate in Manipur is higher than that of India. But remarkable male-female literacy gap, non-accessibility of women to basic education, lack of awareness about woman education and pre-mature marriage of girls stand on the way. The unemployment rate among the women is higher than the men in the state, work participation rate is also lower among women. By the 'life expectancy rate at birth' and IMR indicators also Manipur exhibits a better trend. But the incidence of HIV/AIDS among the male and female population is an increasing area of concern. The status of Manipur, in terms of availability of safe drinking water and sanitation both in the urban and rural areas, is lower than the All-India status. As water is basically a woman issue, it affects the woman community most. The BPL population in the state consists by and large the women and children. The people of Manipur still lack better access to social infrastructure. Thus the social sector expenditure needs to focus on improving social infrastructure for ensuring better quality of living to the people.

Debasis Basu has studied the Gene Differentiation and genetic distance at 'ABO Locus' among eight caste populations of northeast India. The study brought out the distribution of gene frequencies of *p, q* and *r* alleles of ABO system respectively and found O allele to be proportionality higher over other alleles among the caste group populations in reference. The estimate of G_{ST} has been calculated for eight caste populations that show the total and average gene diversities among the caste populations of northeast India. It is found that the magnitude of inter –populations gene diversities is very small within castes and that no significant gene flow taking place among them. He also studied genetic distance among the sample caste groups. In the Hindu Varnashram system the Brahmins are located in the higher strata of the social hierarchy, followed by Katila, Baishya, Kumar, Jogi, Koch, Hira and Kaibarta. The study shows that Katila and Kumar together show minimum genetic distance making a cluster next to Brahmin and Kaibarta which together make a large cluster of four populations. Other studies show that Brahmins, Kaibartas, Katilas (and Muslim) of Assam form a loose cluster. The other two clusters i.e, Hira and Baishya are genetically close and Jogi and Koch together form the second cluster. The maximum genetic distance between Brahmin and Hira confirms their respective positions in the traditional social hierarchy.

Part II of the book deals with the issues of development in the northeast. In the development sector the complexities and criticalities are many more. These range from the policy issues at the micro, meso and macro levels; institutional issues; regional imbalance in development; income and employment generation; infrastructure building; land issue; social policies; supply of goods and services; redistribution; gender issues & women development to the issues of governance and environmental sustainability.

Prof. Samir Kumar Das presented a critique of the Look East Policy and expressed worries that while India may develop under the Policy, the northeast India may not. Under the globalization regime the Look East Policy banked upon the historic-cultural contiguity of the northeastern region and the contiguity of cultural heritage of the South Asian region as a whole. This factor has been officially proclaimed and has become a foreign policy asset for global trade flow across the countries of South Asia. While this policy has brought the northeastern region of India to the limelight, it has produced much hopes and promises for the people. Much of the literature on Northeast's claim to benefit from India's Look East policy is devoted to an analysis of the economic rationality. But in fact the impact of the policy on northeastern region is not that hopeful and rather it might spell disaster to the region unless it is appropriately designed. The ethnic considerations in this region are more likely to blur the imperatives of economic rationality and are less aligned with the appropriate design of a possible policy. It is also doubtful, the author says, how the region would be able to derive trade related gain when India's trade with the South East Asia is primarily of maritime nature. The instrumentality of cultural affinity in exploring Asian market would therefore de-essentialize the normative elements, if any, of historico-cultural contiguity of South and South East Asia. It would rather cater to the expanding foreign markets in this region.

Prof. Das has shown concern as to how the Look East Policy can be appropriately designed in order to address some critical but specific and largely overlapping issues of borders (trans-border integration), citizenship (through trans-border politics of recognition) and labour migration (across the region).

In the present policy context borders are seen more as gateways for trade and commerce and less as traditional boundaries. In the same context the very reality of trans-border movement of the ethnic people for being with their kinsmen, independent of trade relations, often remains silent. In fact the ethnic insurgencies in this region are predicated on the recognition of the region's geographical and cultural continuities with the neighbours as well as continuities within the region. If therefore history of nation state and international borders separated the ethnic groups in this region, the author found alternative possibilities contra-history of reenacting them. Double citizenship is another problematic as it itself may not be the right solution in the face of ethnic situation in the region. It can however be viewed as a strategy and experiment with the concept can be made without destroying the nation-state order. Lastly, the illegal migrants (in Assam mainly) who work as cheap labour got enfranchised which is difficult to detect and deport. They may continue to be so in the era of globalization. In such situation the 'work permit' system for immigrant labourers may be able to address the problem. But it requires improved bilateral relation of India with Bangladesh in particular. The author sees that globalization supersedes the same old border control regime and the sooner its anachronistic character is realized, the more the Northeast as a region can benefit from Look East Policy. Otherwise, the region might lose out yet again to 'the overall framework' of Indian foreign policy.

Asok Kumar Ray dealt with the issue of institutional reforms programme against the backdrop of 'Growth Theory' under globalization. Institutional reforms, as we know, have happened at three levels: micro, meso and macro implicating the community, state and the international bodies respectively. The reforms at different levels have been geared primarily towards establishing and securing market and trade regime of the global political economy. The institutional reforms at all levels (which includes the Look East Policy at macro level), have their respective instrumental roles in facilitating the entry of FDI, market induced economy and in ensuring safety of FDI and market infrastructure in the countries of investment. For that, the whole range of institutional reforms also includes supranational institutions in order to secure safety, efficiency, effectiveness and 'Pareto Optimal' growth. In this process the supranational institutional and adjudicative bodies stymied the sovereign sphere of the Indian state and the regions within the Indian state. Unfortunately, despite all the promises made by the Look East Policy, liberalizing the market economy did not go parallel to labour migration and human resource mobility not only within the region but also across the regions. Eventually, the trade-off between institution and growth on the one hand and denial of redistribution and subsistence on the other hand could not be ignored. Looking from the wide angle of the WTO Rules on Trade and Services that are embodied in the GATS, the services that are traded can be classified in four modes: 'cross-border service'; 'Consumption Abroad'; 'Commercial Presence' and 'Movement of Natural Persons'. Among these the last one, called Mode-4, has remained non-negotiable. This gave rise to a renewed framework of conflict. While insurgency retards private investment and growth, lack of employment and social opportunities arising out of such growth model lead to new lease of unrest. Another paradox arose out of the soft approach of micro-community institutions and social capital on the one hand and the rational choice of force on the other, in the growth process in this region that trivialized political analysis of the regional insurgency and criminalized the entire community. The institutional reforms process in this region had to adapt to security-linked development strategy and gave highly subsidized package to FDI. This scenario invalidated the hypothesis of institution-growth binary in this region and this in turn gave rise to subaltern globalization that became manifest in the region in different ways.

Prof. Keya Dasgupta raised the issue of space in colonized territories that were organised and constantly re-organized within global 'modernizing ' forces. At each phase, new points and areas have joined the operational space in a sequence of stages of spatial organization. The spatial concepts are characterized by movements, migrations, trade network, river-road-railway nodes, indigenous areas, service and market areas, administrative areas and so forth. Though the colonial economy and society were based primarily on mines and plantations, several new elements were introduced in the region's spatial structure. The export oriented tea plantation economy impacted the wider spatial structure and marked the distinction between wastelands and lands for cultivation. The tea plantation had access to both types of land and the wastelands were kept as special preserves of commercial plantation of tea against conventional plantation. The trade and export-oriented plantation economy significantly affected the wider spatial structure and gave a different notion of economy, society and polity. The land tenure system for wastelands made it separate from that under traditional cultivation. The wastelands were the special preserves for tea plantation where traditional cultivation was denied. This plantation economy in the Brahmaputra valley stymied subsistence cropping and diluted the concept of agricultural labour on the one hand and invited cheap labour from outside to work in exploitative and sub-human working condition in the plantation sector on the other. Plantation economy also took over the local or regional trade circuits, however small. This created networks for export-oriented economy. Extension of transport and communication infrastructure was made along road, rail and waterways, mainly in commercial interest. The urban centers and the nodes in the spatial structure of the region primarily emerged as administrative centers and for organizing services for the exploitation of the produce of the hinterlands without any production function. These centers became distinct units in the spatial frame of the Brahmaputra valley. Agency houses, auction houses and depots of Calcutta mainly catered to the traffic of the indentured labour for overseas plantation. Besides the housing layouts were designed in such a way as to maintain the hierarchical order as well as to ensure governance. Transformation of space therefore became both political and ideological under colonial regime. Space in colonial countries like India became a conjecture of diverse and heterogeneous smaller spaces the vestiges of which are still found in the region. Plantation and eventual transformation happened in the organization of space in Brahmaputra exemplifies this.

Prof. Gorky Chakraborti pointed out that in Assam the colonials made large-scale settlement of the people from outside on the wastelands of Assam and engaged them in plantation, mineral and railway industries. This made the wastelands economically profitable to the colonials. The revenue policy was made in such a way as to hard press the indigenous people and to give large-scale relief to the European Planters. Secondly, the British made settlement of labour coming from East Bengal to Assam with a view to engage them in making the wastelands including the 'Char' areas cultivable. He focused his arguments on the Char lands of Assam and the colonial rationale for wasteland use and for bringing these areas under the preview of the sovereign authority of the colonials. This broke the concept of community stewardship attached to land and brought in the concept of land as a tradable property. The vast areas of the so-called wastelands that were not so far revenue-yielding, were transformed into revenue-yielding lands. The colonials used rational choice of force and used the jurisprudential principle of *'res nullius'* and *'terra nullius'* to dispossess community stewardship. This also destructed the notion of lands based on the principle of *'lex loci rei sitae'* and such principle led the colonials to declare the "no-mans-lands as wastelands. Human habitation on wastelands since then depended on the colonial interests. Different land legislations and land revenue administration on Char areas of Assam were also governed by the colonial interests. During the colonial period there was virtually no concrete legislative protection of the Char lands. In the post-colonial period also we found conspicuous silence of the state government on the issue concerning legislative protection of the Char lands. Cadastral survey of the Char areas was not done thoroughly even after Independence. This silence often invited conflict between the users of Char lands and between them and the government. The rights and entitlements of the Char dwellers were not adequately addressed. As cadastral survey was not done, or even wherever it was done, three different patterns of land revenue settlement namely: *touzi, ek chonnai* and rarely *meady* settlements were found. Such arrangements did violence to distributive justice for the Char dwellers. This scenario destabilized the lives of the Char dwellers and brought their lives under constant flux. Ironically the Char lands have neither natural stability nor adequate legislative protection from the government. What is worse is that these areas are often seen as the abode of suspicious persons.

In order to accord due recognition to the toil of the Char dwellers and to usher in development, some broad and tangible policy suggestions are made by the author, that can really go to the benefit of the Char dwellers and can allow to live them with dignity and security.

Prof. P. C. Dutta while discussing the issue of sustainable development in northeastern India, found that the macro context of development created regional imbalance and skewed income distribution in the developing countries. Growing demographic pressure on the economy, weak social provisioning, shrinking social opportunities and high environment cost had pointed critical fingers at the equity issue. The Millennium Development Goal under the New Economic Policy has raised hopes and aspirations for wealth creation and more social opportunities. But in the northeast Indian context unequal resource distribution, rapid and unplanned urbanization made the rural and the urban poor more vulnerable and belied many hopes and promises thus made. He pointed out that the northeastern region lags behind in the New Economic Policy Regime. Increasing unemployment, involuntary migration of outsiders in the region, poor housing, water and sanitation and poor health care infrastructure featured poor social development scenario in this region. By other indicators of social development the region has not achieved much. Although the region has higher literacy rate than the national average, per-capita income remained lesser than the national average. The agro-forestry sector in this region is under crisis. Poor industrial infrastructure including power infrastructure led to poor performance of manufacturing and processing industries. This eventually reduced the number of large and medium industries in the region. Tea industry, the major industry in the region is also facing downward trend. Inadequate banking services and falling credit-deposit ratio further discouraged development in this region. Lastly corruption and growing governance problems in this region are largely responsible for poor investment and growth in this region.

The only alternative for sustainable economic development in the region, according to Prof. Datta, is to promote small-scale industries in the region so as to increase employment and income opportunities for the people. The Khadi and Village Industries Corporation has a great role in training, production and marketing of goods produced in small-scale industries. This needs improved institutional support of small-scale industries (and agriculture). There is also need for population control. Setting up of educational and technical institutions for creating better human resources and enhancing employment opportunities can address the issue of sustainable development. Governments of the northeastern states need to take bigger poverty alleviation programme and gender – sensitive social security schemes in order to ensure better socio-economic opportunities and to remove structural inequalities in the northeast Indian society.

Prof. Nixon Singh made a case for promotion of tourism in northeastern region of India in view of the growing importance of this sector in economic growth and revenue generation. The geographical location of this region, beautiful flora and fauna, natural beauty and attractive landscape, biodiversity, cultural variety, art including performance art, rich tradition and heritage, crafts and textiles of this region are attractive to the tourists and have huge market potential by way of tourism promotion. In the backdrop of the World Tourism Organization's Vision 2020, Prof Singh identified the recent trends and the emerging issues in promoting this sector in the region. Tourism industry not only provides services and products but also gives scope to enormous and diverse ranges of activities and increased employment opportunities including self-employment and income generation. Extension of communication and electronic media can make the sector more promising. The northeast can largely benefit largely through preservation and conservation of the tourist assets. At the social level tourism has the highest potential to promote universal brotherhood and solidarity. A realistic approach through planned tourism and cultural-environmental tourism can lead tourism industry towards sustainability. The Look East Policy may be made instrumental in promoting tourism industry by improving connectivity, appropriate social and economic infrastructure, development of wayside amenities along the Asian Highway and feeder routes, public-private partnership and community-base tourism so as to attract not only the tourists from the other parts of the country but also those from the foreign countries. Tourism planning needs to focus on cost effectivity and inter departmental coordination. However the region has certain vital limitations in tourism promotion. These are lack of infrastructure and investment, governmental instability, land issues, Protected Area and Restricted Area Permits and so on. But the prospects are evident from Governmental attention towards the northeastern region, institutional support of the DoNER Ministry, the North Eastern Council, international and transnational connectivity of this region, support from Asian Development Bank, opportunities for promotion of cross border tours and potential for private sector investment. This needs long term and integrated planning of both physical structure and natural resource endowments. It also needs governmental will and public-private partnership. In this direction Prof. Singh put forward a set of actionable recommendations that could be of use to the policy makers and the planners.

Surojit Sengupta studied the urbanization dynamics in Meghalaya. He first dealt with the conceptual aspects of urban sociology that includes the process and determinants of urbanization and then discussed the urban hierarchies of India and various Classes of towns in the states of India. The uneven nature of urban growth, administrative categorization of urban areas, decline of small towns and growth of larger cities and many other anomalies in the urbanization process became great concerns. In Meghalaya, urbanization and urban growth scenario are characterized by 'push factor', migration, influx and immigration. At the same time the urban areas became concentrations of the rich people. All these taken together led to more urban pathology rather than urban health. The study shows increasing growth rate of urban population, relatively stagnant Class status of towns, increase in number of statutory towns over the decades, changing ranking of districts in terms of percentage of urban population and the overall trend in urbanization over the last century.

Increased urbanization caused pressure on available urban infrastructure and urban civic amenities. It created social and political tensions and led to the growth of urban poverty. The

Shillong Master Plan became ineffective. The Town and Country Planning was not extended on time. The Autonomous District Councils did not accord assent to urban development. All these taken together created more problems than solutions. The economy of most urban centers of Meghalaya is tilted towards commercial and service sectors with very little diversification in other sectors of the economy. Absence of private sector investment is another factor for low urbanization in Meghalaya. Under this situation, Sengupta felt that the urban policy of the state needs to gear up productivity and employment. Infrastructure needs to be built with community participation in urban planning and the urban policy needs to be based on distributive justice.

Prof. Malabika Dasgupta found low urbanization among the tribal population in Tripura. Though there are district-level variations in the tribal population as a percentage of the total urban population, the tribal people of Tripura have limited urban presence and there is considerable gap between urbanization as such and urbanization of the tribals in all the four districts of Tripura. Demographic profile of the households and higher male migration to the tribal areas might have been responsible for lower level of urbanization among the tribes. Lack of employment opportunities in the urban areas, agro-based occupational patterns, low literacy, poor urban amenities for the tribal people, urban locations in the plain areas, alienation of landed property of the tribals acquired during the royal regime, threat of ethnic violence in the urban areas and lesser choice of the tribal people to live in urban areas are the factors responsible for low urbanization and increasing ruralization among the tribal people of Tripura. Prof. Dasgupta suggested inclusive policy measures by way of improving education and employment opportunities, improving urban amenities and rural-urban connectivity for the tribal people. Setting up of urban center close to the tribal inhabited interior areas and overcoming the psychological impediments of the tribal people to become urbanized are also suggested by Prof. Dasgupta.

Prof. Sujata Bhadra analyzed the trends of urbanization in Kokrajhar town in Bodoland of Assam. In the context of globalization Kokrajhar town exhibits more pathology of urbanization. There is increasing pressure of population, inadequate urban infrastructure and civic amenities, growing violence against women, trafficking, increasing trend of migration, corruption etc. in the town. In the agricultural sector, the production in the Kokrajhar Master Plan Area is very much meager as it is a town where very little production of major crops can be traced. Industrial set ups and industrial infrastructure in the town are not adequate enough for new entrepreneurship. The skewed land-use pattern, low employment generation potentials, informalization of labour, inadequacy of trade and commercial infrastructure, poor transportation and traffic hazards, cramped and crowded terminals etc. feature the town of Kokrajhar.

As remedial measures, Prof. Bhadra suggested quite a few points including diversion of agricultural working force and land to other sectors for balanced economic development, proper urban planning, improved road infrastructure, road safety and road safety-education to the people, roadside plantation, management of vehicle terminals, reduction of crowd, construction of bridge on river Gaurang for better connectivity, appropriate land-use and building market infrastructure.

Mr. A.K. Neog analyzed the trend of inequality in farmland holding in the states of northeast India by examining the endowments, farm size and farm practices. He used Gini Coefficient Ratio to examine concentration in holding. He found conspicuous inequality in share of holding vis-à-vis area operated and inter-class unequal distribution in holdings. The Gini Coefficient of concentration of operational holdings show that except in Arunachal Pradesh and Manipur, in all other states of the northeastern region there is a trend towards falling. The inferences that he drew from this study are: according to 2001 Census 81% of the total farm holding are marginal and small and 42.5% of operational area are marginal and small; there is inter class unequal distribution of land holdings; the degree of land inequality during 1990-91 and 200-01 is declining both at All India level and at regional level except in Arunachal Pradesh and Manipur; the degree of concentration is lower in the region than the All- India average; the tribal dominated states are categorized as non-land record states where community based ownership largely prevails. The author is however of the view that a Lower Gini Concentration Ratio with glaring inter-class inequality in land distribution might be misleading inference. Therefore in formulating policy, he thinks, the planners and policy makers need to keep the above scenario in view.

Prof. Rajmani Singh made a critique of the different centrally sponsored schemes of government for income & employment and rural development in northeast India. He found that the top down approach of the above schemes disable the people at the bottom to derive benefit out of those. Lack of access of the poor to the benefits of the schemes, lack of effective and efficient utilization of funds allocated for development, lack of transparency on the part of the policy makers and implementers and lack of people's participation are responsible for poor response of the centrally sponsored schemes in northeast India. The findings of his study on the centrally sponsored rural development schemes like SGSY, PMGSY, Special Accelerated RD Programme for NEI and NREGA show improper beneficiary selection; absence of baseline surveys; involvement of political leaders; bureaucratic red-tapism in the process of selection of beneficiaries; weak coordination among the functionaries of rural development & inadequate staffing; low bank access of the people; inadequate financial assistance; lack of governance; delay in delivery; poor rural infrastructure; under utilization and improper use of allocated funds and finally lack of people's participation.

To overcome these, Prof. Singh gave some concrete suggestions. These include plan for rural infrastructure; harnessing the central non-lapsable pool to build infrastructure and to undertake other economic development activities; harnessing the central grants for info-tech infrastructure and utilize them in right direction; developing agro-based, horticulture-based, forest-based small scale industries and eco- tourism. He also suggested use of Export Development Fund for setting up marketing development infrastructure and SEZ and gearing up of self-employment and entrepreneurship-oriented education policy. He felt that the state governments and local self-government institutions of this region should be pro-active and sensitive in the approaches towards rural development.

Prof. Paulavi Das raised the issue of women development and the skewed sex-ratio in the two social contexts of the north and the northeast India. The phenomenon of 'missing girls', sexual violence against women and sex-based discriminations are very much visible in the patriarchal structure of the Indian society. These phenomena are depicted both in the classical tradition as well as in the modern technology practices. The successive Census Reports unveiled the fact of adverse sex ratio in different parts of India. In the north India the sex ratios in 1921 and 1951 Census Reports were severely low, even lower than the All-India average. In contrast northeast India showed a better trend. Prevalence of matrilineal system in some parts of the northeast, higher involvement of the women in socio-economic activities and relatively improved status of the women did not allow so much of gender-based violence, female infanticide and other gender based discriminations in the northeast Indian society. This might have also contributed to better sex ratio in the region. On the other hand the rigid patriarchal structure of northern India became highly oppressive for social existence of women and excluded them from private and public spheres of life. These culminated in pre-natal sex determination, sex-selective abortion and other kinds of violence against women.

On the other hand better trend of sex ratio in the northeast also owes to higher participation of women in social services and to the emergence of women organizations working for the cause of women development. There is also fare increase in educational status and professional skill of the women community in the northeastern region that did not take place in the conservative north Indian societies. Hence it is the duty of the activists, social reformers, NGOs and the government to take initiatives for development and progress of women in northeast India.

Professors Jahita Begum and M. Vakkil have shown how ICT can be instrumental in empowerment of women. While more and more women are now-a-days opting for ICT as career, they are also creating knowledge society. Media network at local, national and international levels has also facilitated information dissemination, networking and mutual sharing among the women communities in different regions. The role in Internet has become more significant in this regard. Electronic communication, community radio, video and print media are highly promising for improving the lives of the women at the grassroots. In order to really empower the women through ICT, gender equality, participation, mobilization and organization of women need to be encouraged. Considering the role of ICT in poverty eradication and entrepreneurship development both in the rural and in the urban areas, women's access to ICT and inclusive ICT policy need be pursued. It is also important to address the issue of structural inequality and gender based discrimination in the society. This can be done through education, training and awareness campaign and through creation of women role models in training and management. At the social policy level again affirmative action is needed to bring the women in senior level management roles in the regulatory bodies.

ICT infrastructure in the northeast is yet to strengthen and spread widely. Weak infrastructure and restrictive ICT connectivity in this region need to be addressed adequately so as to mainstream the women of this region and to empower them. Northeast India has quite a number of vantage points. The youth community in this region is better equipped with English language, they have good communication skill in English language, the girls of this region are more exposed to public spheres and corporate sector is interested to promote ICT industry in this region. The DoNER Ministry also has earmarked a good budget for promotion of ICT in this region. Concrete efforts need to be made to tap the human resources of this region and to bring the women at the forefront of ICT boom in this region.

Prof. Kaustav Lahiri dealt with sustainable development with Ecological Dimension of Sustainability and focuses on the overall viability and health of ecological systems in terms of a comprehensive, multi-scale, dynamic, hierarchical measure of 'resilience', 'vigour' and 'organization' in the context of northeast India. In Development Management, the three foundations of sustainability namely, economic, environmental and social are of immense significance. Prof. Lahiri talked of an inclusive growth model steered by symbiotic sustainability and balanced use of assets with community aspirations. Common pool resources in this situation assume importance. In terms of selected indicators *Percentage of Persons Living Below Poverty Line* (PPL) and *Primary Product Export Share* (PPES), India's inherent condition and her global status show relevance to livelihood planning through ecological orientation. He examined growth dynamics of the northeast region by Macro spatial Economic Impact on ecology Infra Structure. Considering the ecological vulnerability in the northeastern region, Prof. Lahiri gave some valuable recommendations and showed how ecosystem oriented Management can cultivate Livelihood Prosperity for North East India.

Development in the northeast is on the cross-roads. The process of colonization of the region and the resources thereof started long ago. The situation, according to one view, has worsened in recent times and no amount of institutional reforms could address the situation effectively. According to the other view there are new opportunities for development in the region provided the region can cope up with the changing contexts. But development is as such not only about development of physical infrastructure and policy co-option. It is basically about redistribution, distributive justice to the vulnerable section of the society, environmental sustainability, balanced growth of urbanization, transparency and accountability in the development administration and abolition of class-based discriminations. Over and above enhancement of employment and income opportunities need be positioned at the center place of development.

Part I
Society and Culture

1

Archaeological and Architectural Remains: Testimony of Cultural Interactions of the People of North-East India

JAYANTA SARKAR

It is a common notion that northeast India comprising Assam, Arunachal Pradesh. Manipur, Meghalaya, Mizoram, Nagaland and Triupra remained secluded to a considerable extent from the rest of the country till the advent of the British rulers in the 19th century and more particularly till the Independence of India. However, a retrospective look into the historical accounts of this region reveals instances of migrations of different ethnic groups to this region from the neighbouring countries like China, present Myanmar and Bangladesh. Ethnic groups from Southeast Asian countries also came to this part of India in different phases. Many of them settled down in the hills, while the Ahoms and a few others entered the Brahmaputra valley and made the place their homeland.

The Ahom who ruled the valley for nearly 600 years from 1228-1826, brought many other people from the plains of Bengal and adjoining states. They had marginal interactions with the hill people by way of trade. The people in the hills thus faced least disturbance from the inhabitants of the valley. On the other hand, in many areas, they had some sort of trade relations beyond the present international boarder (Sarkar 1982).

The archaeological findings and the architectures of the

temples built in the region before the inroad of the colonial rulers indicate that the area had attracted people of diverse cultures from beyond this difficult geographical region. In order to explore the nature of cultural contacts that once prevailed between the people of this relatively unexposed terrain and those of the plains of India or of beyond the present international border, I would like to look into the available information on the archaeological remains unearthed in the region and also on the architectural styles of some of the temples.

Archaeology and Architecture of Assam

As already stated Assam has a long history of Ahom rule. Besides this long period of rule by the Ahom kings, the present state of Assam had many other kingdoms like those of the Kachari and Chutiyas. This area also remained a passage for migration of many ethnic groups from several countries of Southeast Asia. The rulers of Assam made valuable contribution towards development of art through their archaeological constructions. Many important archaeological specimens have been found in Assam, mention may be made of a few.

A frieze of a temple near Tezpur has three *sikaras* carved in bold relief of the Vesara type; ruins of ancient city also near Tezpur, including a huge stone architecture containing three dimensions of bold relief of three Buddhist *chaityas* of the Nepali temple pattern, Sidheswari at Soalkutchi near Guwahati; ruins of vast temples near Yogijan in Hojai; that of innumerable temples depict architecture of Nagara type in the Kopili and Jamuna river valleys (Bose, 1970 : 320). One of the most important architectural remains, perhaps the earliest one is the *Dah Parvatiya* near Tezpur shows existence of temples dedicated to both Vishnu and Siva (5th-6th century AD) which have affinity with the Gupta School of Art. The plinth molding from Tezpur ruins show that the sculptors from Assam employed the same motivations on figures as in other parts of north India. The ornamentation bear close resemblance to those from Orissa. The present temple on the Nilachal hill near Guwahati is one of the *pithasthans* in India and is an important sacred center of in the north-east India. The *sikara* of the temple is a combination of *Nagera* and *Vesara* types (*Ibid*).

There was a Buddhist shrine at Hajo centering round the

present Hayagriva temple. The ruins prove that the place was a center of worship of the various deities including Sun God, Vishnu, the Buddha and the deities of Tantric and Buddhist religions. The images of the elephant engraved at the base of the present *matha* are similar to those of the Kailasha temple at the caves of Ellora. The temple ruins of Pingalesvara and Madana Kamdeva near Guwahati show that these are of Tantric and Buddhist traditions. The Kapila and the Jamuna valleys contain a large number of ruins of temples and sculptures which have resemblance of Orissa architecture. (Barkakati 1969 : 69).

According to experts the temples of Assam have similarities with those of north India in conception and techniques. The stone cultures, rock-carvings, architectural remains etc. that have been discovered at different places prove beyond doubt the influence of the art and architecture of north India. According to Dikshit the affinity of the Assamese temples would seem to be more with the schools of Bihar and Orissa than that of the Pala art of Bengal (*Op cit.*: 72-73).

The remains found in Bhubanesvara Siva located at Bhubanpahar in Çachar-Manipur border suggest that this important pilgrimage center in Cachar developed in three different phases. During the first, cultural activities flourished around it. In the second phase sculptures were perhaps associated with the Tripuris or Tipras an Indo-Mongoloid people who subsequently built a kingdom in present Tripura state. The third and final phase of sculptures of this temple is probably associated with Buddhism as some images have manifest associated with the Buddhism (Singh and Sengupta 1991 : 162-164).

The Kamakhya temple at Guwahati, the Kechaikhati temple at Sadiya and the Mahadeva temple at Bergaon and the Sakta temples in North Lakhimpur bear proofs of the extent of Tantric influence in Kamrupa (Bose 1970 : 228).

Archaeological Remains in Arunachal Pradesh

The high hills of Arunachal Pradesh have no archaeological/ historical sites that may be accounted for as place of cultural interaction. However, in the foothills a few such sites like Ita fort near Itanagar, the capital of the state in lower Subansiri District, Malinithan near Likabali in Lower Siang District, Bhismaknagar near Tezu in Lohit District and Mud fort in Dibang Valley have been found by the historians and archaeologists.

The archaeological evidences are not clear enough to establish the date of construction of Ita fort. Raikar opines that the bricks of the fort are typically mediaeval and pre-Ahom as well. The mud fort in Tezu is a rectangular earthwork (1200' by 1150') with ditches on either side having a cavalier in the center. It belongs to the mediaeval period. Bhismaknagar has both brick works and earthen ramparts. It is an elongated circular shape as prescribed by the Sanskrit text and the construction is also as per the canons of classical fort architecture. It dates back to 8th to 16th century A.D. (*Op cit*. Dutta Choudhury 1991 : 78).

The archaeological site of Malinithan is situated in the Lower Siang District adjoining Assam where a few granite figures of Surya, Indra, Ganesha, Kartikeya, Durga and Lakshmi have been found in the ruins. The place is associated with the Krishna legends. It is believed that Krishna and Rukmini (daughter of King Bhismak) rested on their way to Dwaraka from Bhismaknagar. They were received by Shiva and Durga (Parvati) as guests and were offered garlands. At this Krishna addressed Parvati as Malini and from then the place came to be known as Malinithan or Malinisthan, the abode of Malini. The total absence of brick distinguishes Malinithan from most of the other archaeological sites in Arunachal Pradesh.

According to an expert the granite figures indicate the high technical accomplishment and their stylistic with the Eastern School of the Palas. These clearly indicate the extension of the mediaeval Eastern Indian art tradition to the foot hills in the north eastern region of the country (Billorey 1976 : 124).

Besides the figures already mentioned the scholars noticed frequent occurrence of *maithuna* figures in various postures. While these findings led them to assume that these erotic cultures suggests survivals of Tantricism of the fertility cult of the tribal society, upholding the Mother Goddess as the procreative power of nature, the occurrence of a beautifully carved bull suggests the place as a center of Saiva worship. The resemblance in the architectural pattern of the Malinithan temple with that of Dah Paravatiya temple located near Tezpur tempted the scholars to infer existence of probable influence of culture that developed around Tezpur on the north bank of the River Brhamaputra.

Chakravarty, who did intensive study of the archaeological remains found in Arunachal Pradesh, thinks that the occurrence of Lion-on-elephant motifs, which was also found in Dimapur ruins in Nagaland, the higher parts of a female figure, the figures like Ganapati on mouse, Kartikeya seated on the peacock, Surya standing on a chariot drawn by seven horses, Indra seated on Airavata, Lakshmi as being anointed by two elephants from sides clearly suggest that the locality had one time under the influence of Indian art and culture and had close relation with the Orissa School of Architecture of mediaeval period (Chakravarty 1976 : 5).

The architecture and art of Tawang monastery in Kameng District located about 10,000ft above the sea level shows its relation with the Tibetan art form. Buddhism entered among the Monpa and Sherdukpen tribes inhabiting this area some time in the eighth century with the famous monk Padmasambhava (Sarkar 1975 : 17). The religion then spread among the people of this area by subsequent visits of the monks from Tibet in phases. On the eastern part of the state the monasteries depict resemblance with the architectural designs of Myanmar having influence of Hinayana Buddhism that entered in the region with the migration of the Khamti from the Irravaddy valley in 17th century A.D. (Sarkar 1987).

Temples and Monuments at Manipur

Temples and monuments are very few in this state. The Vishnu temple at Vishnupur is considered to be built during 15/16th century A.D. Scholars are of the opinion that the temples of Manipur have influence of the Bengali and Southeast Asian architecture. The remains of the archaeological sites suggest that Manipur had influences both from Southeast Asia and plains of India. The *stupa* type of temple of Krishna and other monuments at Imphal and Lansthabha monuments (19th century A D) indicate the influence of both Buddhist and Vaishnavite Hindu architecture (Singh 1988 : 68-70).

The important temples of Manipur are of Lord Krishna, temple of Hanuman Thakur, Thangal General, Sanamai, Lemimapoapa, Keirungba and of Sri Gobinda. At the beginning of 18th century many temples were constructed by different architects to promote the newly introduced Hindu religion in the state. The Thangal

General temple is similar to the Islamic architecture of the mediaeval period. Out side the temple complex there are four Bengali hut type replicas (Bahadur and Gunindro 1991 : 163-66).

Archaeology of Meghalaya

A number of archaeological and historical remains have been found in the present state of Meghalaya. Remains are mainly confined to the eastern and northern Khasi-Jaintia Hills. Engraving of both human and animal are dominant. Life size portraits of worriers or parts such as human skulls, feet and footprints are also prominent. Carvings of animal figures like elephants at Rtiang, Rhino at Nongkhlieh, elephant at Syndai, horse at Mawrong, other figurines such as frogs, snakes, etc. are found which focus kind of art conception lived in this area. Most of the sculptures are confined at Bhoi and Jaintia areas while they become fewer in other parts of Khasi Hills. The sculptures found at the ancient capital of Mahadem kingdom in the Bhoi region of Khasi Hills suggest that the carving on the stone has similarity with the Chinese designs. Bareh opines that the sculptures symbolize the once close and intimate relations with China (Bareh 1981 : 42-43). One of the most important sites explored in Meghalaya is Bhaitbari near Phulbari in Garo hills. Some of the terracotta pieces found in the area are Siva, Dragon, Ganesha, Manasa, Kartikeya, male human figures, etc. According to scholars the sculptures from Bhaitbari are akin to the Pala and Sena period, especially in the facial treatment and the existence of *Jata Mukuta* on Ganesha's head. The culture may be assigned to the 10th to 12th century A.D. (Deva Choudhury 1996 : 158-161).

Archaeology of Mizoram

Nothing much is available on the archaeological remains in Mizoram. An engraved image of Lord Buddha, with those of dancing girls on either side, was found at a site near Mualcheng village of Lunglei town. The site also has another stone slab on which some human footmarks and a few implements like spearhead and *Dao* are engraved. It is assumed that some visiting Buddhists from the nearby Chittagong Hill Tracts were responsible for the Buddha engraving.

Archaeology of Nagaland

Remains of fortress have been found at Dimapur which was constructed during the Kachari kingdom. The Rengma Naga people of the place were brilliant sculptors who made stone inscriptions of arrow. At the ruins of the fortress oblong or 'V' shaped stone pillars of the Kachari have been found which closely correspond to the similar 'V' shaped posts protruding from the roof of a house of a wealthy Angami Naga. All the megalith remains found within the fortress were originally of the Nagas although these were erected under the Kachari Hindu symbolism. Similar patterns of stones were noticed at Chmukedima in foothills on the Dimapur—Cachar road which indicate that the megalithic culture of the Naga had influenced their neighbouring people (Bareh 1970 : 22-23).

Archaeology of Tripura

The archaeological evidences found in the state show the presence of Buddhism and various tribal religions at one time or other in its history. The major archaeological findings are distributed at Unakoti, Pilakpathar, Lungthung and Bilonia. The sculptures at the sites, in general, appear to depict mythological anecdotes in relief. The discovery of Siva images in different forms at Unakoti and its neighbourhood indicates that the place was initially a Siva pilgrimage. However, many other images and rock-cut sculptures found in this area also indicate that other religious sects like Sakta, Tantric, Bajrayanis and Nathayogis, etc. did not lag behind in the art rock carving at Unakoti (Menon 1975 : 67). Unakoti is considered as one of the most sacred pilgrimages in eastern India. Quite a large number of images of Boddhisattva and Buddha and at least one image of Ganesha found at Pilakpathar, suggest that the Buddhist monastic establishment might have extended in this area since a very old period, either in the form of Vihara or monastery. Finding of stone image of Ganesha and Narasingha and an image of Sakti having eight hands also suggest that the place was a center of multi-religious activity of different sects under the rule of different kings. A number of terracotta temple-plaques and ceilings with depiction of *stupa* and Buddhist creeds had also been found at this place. The plaques depicting Kinnara and charging boar deserve special mention as they are stylistically related to the terracotta plaque found at Moynamoti of Bangladesh not too far from Pilakpathar (Menon 1975 : 66 & 390).

A closer study of the temples of Tripura reveals the existence of a group of temples on the east of Mahadev Bari. These are classified as Mahadev Bari group, Gunabati group and the Luk-Palani Jhulan group. The temples of the south bank of river Gomati are instances of this type. Some temples had audience chamber resembling the Jagamohana temple of Orissa. All the temples of Tripura are of the *Challa* type *(Dochalla, Charchalla)*. In this sphere Bengali style had exerted great influence upon architecture of Tripura temples. *Charchalla* roof with an evolved *stupa* structure on it is the characteristic feature of these temples. *Challa* temples with *stupa shirsha* (top) are nowhere found in India. Considering the number of temples built in the same designs some scholars categorize this style of religious architecture as 'tribal style'. They also associate *Challa* temples with super *shirsha* as 'a happy and affectionate combination of Brahmanical and Buddhist idioms of expression of religious architecture' (Banerjee 1968 : 6). According to the scholars Tripura style not only depicts the Hindu and Buddhist idioms of architecture, but also combines the Muslim design to enrich aesthetically. The corner buttresses of Tripura temples are the evolved forms of Muslim *minars* (Lahiri 1971 : 93-97). Paucity of archaeological evidences from Tripura proper makes it difficult to say anything about the condition of Buddhism or Hinduism in Tripura during the early centuries of Christian era. Ickono-plastic art recovered from this land provide data about the prevalence of these folds since the earlier part of 7th century A.D. (Gan Chaudhuri 1985 : 31-32).

Discussion: A quick appraisal of the archeological sites found in the northeast India, and the art and culture that are depicted on such relics lead us to infer the followings:

(a) The people of the plains of northeast India, be they are of Brahamaputra or Barak Valleys or of plains of Tripura had experienced interactions with those of the neighbouring areas of Bengal, Orissa, Bihar and even of central part of India during the mediaeval period. In historical past the local dynasties like the Chutiya or the Kachari had established contacts with the art and culture of the people of Bengal, Orissa and Bihar as is apparent from the temple architecture found in the plains of north-east India. The Ahom who ruled the Brahamaputra valley for about six centuries, though originally belonged to the great Tai culture, in course of time absorbed many traditions relating to art, architecture and culture of the people of the neighbouring states. Contribution made in these spheres of art, architecture and culture by the people of Orissa and Bengal helped in evolving a unique combination of local creativity with the artistic styles of Orissa and Bengal. The archaeological ruins indicate that in the past creativity in the form of art and architecture received patronage from the rulers of the plains of northeast India. Under their encouragement the tradition of the Hindu art and culture of the neighbouring regions influenced the artistic expressions of this region.

(b) Distribution of temples, monuments and such other relics of archaeological importance suggest that the Hindu religion together with its associated art and culture penetrated even up to the foothills of Arunachal Pradesh. However, in certain areas of Cachar we can find the association of the Muslim architecture with the Hindu forms of art and sculptures.

(c) The plains of this region remained a meeting ground of many artistic activities of the neighbouring eastern part of India. Over the years these styles of art were maintained by those people who belonged to different cultural milieu of southeast Asia. This was a unique cultural synthesis that encouraged development of art and culture of one type in a completely different cultural milieu.

(d) The art and culture in the plains of northeast region played a significant role in the secular life of the people. The symbolic meanings and aesthetic values as observed in the Ita fort, Mud fort at Tezu, Bhismaknagar, Tezpur, Shivsagar, animal figures in the remains of Khasi and Jaintia Hills and so on provided ample evidences that the arts were practised also for expression of aesthetic creativity with imagination and speculation which are secular components of life of the people of northeast region. During the mediaeval period culture of the plains of this region showed a tremendous power of tolerance, coexistence of different form of religious faiths like Buddhism, Hinduism, Islam and local religions of the tribes.

(e) The plains of this region also experienced influence of Tantric cult. The art and architecture depicted at religious centers like Kamakhya temple indicate development of art and culture associated with this faith in close collaboration with the local people who originally migrated from various parts of southeast Asia along with their own traditional religious beliefs. The development of Vaishnavism and its related artistic expressions could find a very important place in the life and culture of the people of Brahamaputra and Manipur valleys.

(f) While the plains of northeast India had established relations with other parts of India in historical past, the various populations who made the hills of this region their homeland remained almost unaffected from the art and artistic imagination of the plains. These populations with the tradition of migration from different countries of southeast Asia could nurture their own art and related performances in accordance with their own wisdom. Their traditional art and cultural activities, however, did not diffuse to other cultural areas as by tradition, these groups maintained their own respective cultural boundaries and any encroachment in other's jurisdiction used to invite enmity.

(g) It is also apparent from the findings that while the entire plains of this region had some traces of historical remains including the foothills of Arunachal Pradesh, surprisingly no noteworthy information of any such relics has been reported from the present Mizoram, the reasons for which remain a subject of speculation.

(h) There are a few areas where people had brought architecture along with a religion like Buddhism from the neighbouring countries. Thus we find the presence of Mahayana and its associated artistic expressions in the hill region of Kameng and Hinayana Budhhism in Lohit Districts and in the states of Tripura and Mizoram. This is an example of unique co-existence that continued to

> profess ones own religion without affecting communities of other faiths, their art, culture and different traditions.

In view of what have been discussed above it may not be totally inappropriate to infer that in spite of some sort of geographical distances of the northeast from the rest of India that apparently existed till the British entered in the region and more so till the independence of India, the people of the valleys and plains of the region had established cultural relations, as evident from the findings of the archaeological and architectural remains. In fact these establish beyond doubt that the rulers of the different dynasties in reality had appreciation for the art, architecture and culture of the people of other parts of the country. They also adopted many of the religious beliefs of the Hindus that again inspired the local people to assimilate the artistic creations, particularly of Orissa and Bengal.

REFERENCES

Bahadur Mutua & Baonam Gunindro, Cultural Evolution of Manipur, *Manipur Past and Present* (ed) Naren Sanajaoba, New Delhi: Mittal Publishers, 1991.

Banerjee Adris, *Temples of Tripura*, Varanasi: Prithivi Prakashan, 1968.

Bareh H, *Gazetteer of India*, Nagaland, Kohima District, 1970.

Bareh H, Folk Art of the Khasi People, *Inaugural Issue*, State Museum, Meghalaya, 1981.

Barkakati S. *Assam*, New Delhi: National Book Trust, India, 1969.

Bhattacharya Priyabrata, Art and Archaeology in Tripura, *The Land and its People* (ed) Jagadish Gan Chaudhuri. Delhi: Leeladevi Publications, 1980

Billorey Iconographic Study of some sculptures from Malinithan. *Resarun*, Shillong: Arunachal Pradesh Research Department, 1975.

Bose, Nirmal Kumar, *Assam in the Ahom Age*. Guwahati: Sanskrit Pustak Bhandar, 1970.

Cakravarty L. N, Malinithan, *Resarun*, Shillong, Research Department Arunachal Pradesh, 1975.

Chowdhury, J.N., *Arunachal Panorama*, Shillong: Directorate of Research, Arunachal Pradesh, 1982.

Deva Choudhury, Nishipada, *Prehistory of Meghalaya and Social Formation in Khasi and Jaintia History*, Mimeograph, Shillong: Directorate of Art and Culture, State Museum, Meghalaya, 1996.

Dutta Choudhury, S. *Gazetteer of India, Arunachal Pradesh, Subansiri District*, Shillong: Govt of Arunachal Pradesh. 1991.

Gan Chaudhuri, J, *Place Names, Anthology of Tripura* (ed) J. Gan Chaudhuri. New Delhi: Inter India Publications, 1985.

Lahiry Kartik, Temple Architecture; Tripura *Pines*, Academic & Cultural Quarterly, Vol, Part-1. Shillong: Literary and Cultural Cooperative Society. 1971.

Menon, K.D. *Tripura District Gazetteer*, State Edition, Agartala: Government of Tripura. 1975.

Sarkar Jayanta, Economic System and Social Change in Arunachal Pradesh, *Economies of the Tribes and their Transformation* (ed) K.S. Singh Delhi: Concept Publishing Company, 1982.

Sarkar Jayanta, *Society, Culture and Ecological adaptation among three tribes of Arunachal Pradesh*. Calcutta: Anthropological Survey of India. 1987.

Sarkar Niranjan, Introduction of Buddhism among the Monpas and Sherdukpens, *Resarun*, 1975, Shillong: Directorate of Research, Government of Arunachal Pradesh, 1976.

Singh Jaiprakash and Gautam Sengupta, *Archaeology of North Eastern India* (ed) New Delhi: Vikas Publishing House Private Ltd., 1991.

Singh, O. K. *Religion and Culture of Manipur*, Delhi: Manas Publications, 1988.

2

Folklore and Development: Are they Antithetic?

SOUMEN SEN

There was a time when folklore was perceived as quaint, the relic of the past. This perception swayed folklore scholarship throughout the 19th Century and even in the early part of the 20th. The term "Folklore" itself was coined in 1846. Before that cut-off date it was variously known in different European countries such as popular antiquities in England and *Volkskunde* in Germany. Even the change in nomenclature did not alter the mindset of the investigators and their attitude towards the cultural traits other than their own, i.e, the culture of the non-metropolitan segment of the population. William Thoms suggested 'a Saxon compound-folklore' as a good replacement of popular antiquities. His perception of the material—the cultural trait of the people—was not in any way different from the prevailing one. While suggesting the good Saxon Compound-folklore, the lore of the people—he was confident in garnearing the few ears which were remaining scattered over that field from which our *forefathers* might have gathered a goodly crop (Thoms-1846, emphasis added). He conceived the lore of the people (folk) as the manners, proverbs etc. of the olden times.[1]

This perception, the accepted one throughout the 19th century both pre and post 1846 England, was the typical one that prevailed upon folklore scholarship in the whole of Europe, wherever agendas of folklore research were taken up by scholars and was consolidated at a time when scientific-technological conquest made significant inroads in European reality and social life. Grimm brothers, Jacob and Wilhelm, whose collection of German fairy tales (*marchen*) and interpretation of Teutonic mythodology, that happened in the first and second decades of the 19th Century and are considered as pioneering work not only in *Volkskunde* but in international research as well substantiated the notion that folklore represented the cultural expressions and ideology of a people living in nature, following the habits, manners etc. of the olden times and untouched by changing realities under the impact of technical discoveries and development processes. Wilhelm Grimm wrote about the *marchen*: "for only where avarice and the rattling wheels of machinery stupefy, any other though does not think that one can dispense with them; they endure where a secure, customary order and lifestyle still prevail, where the connection between human emotions and surrounding nature is still perceived and the past is not torn from the present".[2] Such ideas were however criticized in the later part of the 20th century in such words: 'Volkskunde, which begun under the sign of such declarations, was pushed into ever narrower concerns in course of the spread of technology and more seriously into an increasingly questionable attitude towards reality. The moral appeal of the Romantic era in the face of danger turned more and more into insincere zeal against reality (Bansinger-1990:9), significantly though, this notion continued, not only in Europe but in other countries as well, to dominate folklore scholarship till the first of the 20th century, with cracks developing since the 30s of that century. But before that change of attitude that had happened initially through Marxist intervention in post-revolution Russia and came to be known partially and perhaps reluctantly accepted by European and American scholarship at a much later date, the 19th century concepts dominated folklore research. Even in a 1931 encyclopaedic entry on folklore, Ruth Benedict, the American Anthropologist-folklorist wrote that in the modern civilized world folklore is no more a living trait. (Benedict 1931), indicating that it is in, but not of, our times. This is surely an echo of a declaration from Andrew Lang, a leading personality of the English Folklore Society (Estd. in 1878), who considered folklore only quaint and developed the theory of survival. He wrote: "The student of folklore is thus led to examine the usages, myths and ideas of *savages*, which are still retained in rude enough shape, by the European *peasantry*... In proverbs, riddles and nursery tales and superstitions, we detect the *relics of a stage of thought*, which is dying out in Europe, but which still exists in many parts of the world. (Lang-1884 : 11 emphasis added). Lang further says that the form of study called folklore can be compared with Archaeology, since the concerns of both the field of studies are the collections and study of the relics of the past. He says, "There is a science, Archaeology, which collects and compares the material relics of old races, the axis and the arrow heads. There is a form of study, folklore, which collects and compares the similar but immaterial relics of old races, the surviving superstitions and stories, the ideas which are *in our times but not of it*. Properly speaking, folklore is only concerned with the legends, customs, belief of the folk, of the people, of the classes which have least been altered by education, *which have shared least in progress*. But the student of folklore soon finds that these *unprogressive classes* retain many of the beliefs and ways of savages (*Ibid*: 11. Emphasis added).

These tendencies in folklore studies that prevailed till the third decade of the last century since the days of Grimm brothers or Lang and company and the trends of folklore research generated by such tendencies, have failed miserably in placing folklore formations in appropriate spaces in the processes of social formation and changes in social reality. This awareness came in a big way only in the 5th and 6th decades of the last century though the first signs were noticed in the 3rd decade of Russian folklore scholarship. That happened because of their commitment to the Marxist concept of dialectical and historical materialism, based upon an inevitable logic of social-technological processes determining the cultural constructs and institutional order. That folklore formation inevitably depends upon this process was underlined emphatically by the Russian folklorists. However their ideas did not percolate beyond Russian borders immediately for the then prevailing international politics. The Marxist perception of folklore came to be known in the outside world only in 1950 when Y. M. Sokolov's book "Russian Folklore" was translated in English and published in New York. In this book the Marxist principles of folklore studies were emphatically pronounced: Folklore is an echo of the past, but at the same time it is also the vigorous voice of the present, since it has been always a reflection and a weapon of class struggle (Sokolov 1950). Vladimir Propp is the best known Russian folklorist in the outside world after his book *Morphologia Skazki* was translated in English (Morphology of Folktale) and published in the USA in 1958. A good crop of his essays relating to the historicity of folklore was translated in English and published much later (1984). Propp, in his collection of essays, underlined a few principles in understanding the historicity of folklore and said that a proper study should show what happens to old folklore under new historical conditions and trace the appearance of new formations. All genres of folklore therefore can be studied from the standpoint of a broad conception of history. (Propp 1984). Needless to say that this 'broad conception of history' is based upon the Marxist concept of dialectical and historical materialism. Propp has further to say that creation of folklore is not an arbitrary process; it is governed by laws, which scholarship must explain and these laws are obviously linked with socio-economic contradictions.

Not that the Marxist viewpoints were immediately accepted in the Euro-American folklore circles, except a group of social and art historians here and there, including a few from India, such as D.D. Kosambi, who had studies folklore, particularly mythology, to traverse a new path in historiography. But that a fresh awareness about the inadequacy of old-fashioned dogmas in truly interpreting folklore material, was slowly emerging, is evident from almost a massive paradigm shift in folklore scholarship in the late 50s and early 60s of the last century. A group of folklorists in USA, later came to be known as Contexualists, had almost dramatically revised the earlier notion about the *folk, folklore* and research. While appreciating the contribution of the Marxists, in re-defining folk as working class including both rural peasantry and the factory workers, though not accepting the Marxist interpretation of folklore in an evolutionary framework in its totality, Alan Dundes, one leading Contexualist, candidly declared: 'if modern folklorists accepted the nineteenth century definition of the folk as illiterate, rural, backward peasants, then the study of such folk might well be strictly a salvage operation......' (Dundes: 1980 (1977). This perception surely came from awareness that both 'folk' and 'lore' need to be placed in proper spaces in the stages of social change and development. In an earlier essay his concern for re-defining 'folk' and revisiting 'folklore' has been expressed in the following words: 'An equally fallacious view is that folklore was produced by a folk in the hoary past and the folklore still extant today consists solely of fragmentary survivals. According to this incorrect view, the folk of today produce no new folklore; rather contemporary folk are forgetting more and more folklore, and soon folklore will have died out completely (Dundes 1965 : 2)'. Unfortunately we are not yet fully free from the influence of the erroneous 19th century dogmas and many of us still consider folklore studies as salvage operation to preserve the authenticity of all kinds of folklore before they die out. We, in such attempts, deny or undermine the vigourous potency of folklore for adjustment with epochal changes. Authenticity is always linked with spaces, time and change, and tradition, a name conveniently given to a concept of pastness of the past, is actually a transitive series of constructs.

At a time when Contexualists in USA were working in re-defining both folk and folklore, relating them with the processes of social change and development, similar voices were heard from the European countries. Hermann Bausinger, from the land of *Volkskunde* expresses an anxiety parallel to that of Dundes and other Contexualists and the Marxists before them, when he says, 'The transition from pre-industrial peasant culture to folk culture of the technological age has been noted by *Volksunde*. Generally the folk culture of the more or less recent past has not been studies in and for itself, but was mainly investigated for survival of earlier historical stages' [Bausinger 1990 (1961 : 3)]. That such assessment of folklore scholarship of the recent past and of the initial years of its growth was slowly and gradually taking shape is evident in Melville J. Herskovits' 1945 Presidential Address at the 57th annual meeting of the American Folklore Society wherein he categorically said 'If we refuse to consider the folk as quaint........... folklore becomes a field concerned with realities of life and not with the relics of the dead past (Herskovits 1946 : 99)'. Inspired by such perspective, the new generation of folklorists of the mid-twentieth century categorically declared that 'technology is not stamping out folklore; rather it is becoming a vital factor in the transmission of folklore and it is providing an exciting source of inspiration of new folklore' (Dundes 1980 : 17)

The important element in these arguments is the relationship between folklore and modernity—modernity in terms of literacy and technological growth. The contrast between folklore and modernity is based upon perception that modernism is positivistic, technocratic and rationalistic and identified with a rational planning of socio-economic orders. Folklore viewed as the expressive behaviour of the pre-modern folk, identified as rural peasants and semi savage communities who refuse to adopt and adapt, feeling comfortable in a quaint world of existence, is seen to be at the opposite end of the spectrum. The resultant argument then is that folklore needs to be salvaged, pre-modern conditions need to be protected and development programmes resisted, lest it dies out with pre-modern conditions. The adaptive power of folklore in situation of change is ignored. The basic fallacy lies in the perception that folklore is non-technological and non-rationalistic. What we forget however, is that the process of rationalization itself through technology shifts and modernism stems from pre-modern setting. What we really fail to realize is that folklore is a dynamic component of human culture with the capacity to adopt to social and cultural changes.[3]

(2)

The historical issue which in no way can be overlooked or neglected is that folklore is deeply rooted in the history of ideas and folklore categories. It is concerned with particular mentalities of the groups (folk) in particular epochs, and it produces specific cultural expressions based on specific social foundations. This happens in both the so-called *a-historical* and *historical* phases of life. The shift or transformation of one phase to the other also follows a course and a logic of history. It may be a gradual growth or, at times, dramatic turn.

From such a viewpoint and logic of history, folklore, development and socio-economic growth are not contradictory terms. Though the conventional mindset does not approve of such a logic and maintains that folklore is, by and large, a historical, it is the realization (in part perhaps) in current folklore research. This research does not subscribe to the view that folklore and modernity are two opposite concepts. Though may be accused of repetition of what I narrated in the first section, I am to reiterate that an anxiety has been expressed from different quarters, particularly in our country that development planning including industrialization may affect the tranquility of folklore and folklore may die out. The traditional patterns of earning a living, the customary systems of existence etc. may face extinction. These anxieties often forced leaders to resist modernization through the process of industrialization. Folklorists though do not take part in active resistance, subscribe at the same time to the theory that modernization and industrialization are antagonistic to folklore and folk life. Such a thesis almost touches a romantic naiveté, glorifies folklore with organic instinctiveness and simplicity and idealizes the traditional life. It talks of natural environment, the 'genius' of folk communities, the tradition-steeped peasant life etc. That tradition is not always a time honoured body of knowledge and values but is in constant state of disarray, about to disintegrate under different kinds of pressures, social and environmental, resulting in the process in readjustment and invention, is conveniently forgotten. Tradition in true perspective needs to be viewed as a 'transitive series' (Ramanujan: 1991 xiviii), a 'scale of forms' engaged in continuous and dynamic dialogic relations between the past and the present. In such a perspective tradition is viewed not as a cultural given but as a cultural construct (Ben Amos: 1990 : viii), reflecting epochal socio-economic changes. True, it may face the pressures of disintegration under pressure of change.; people may strive to restore and maintain it in new rituals, customs and other expressive forms of folklore, but at the same time, if necessary, may construct, even invent, new strands. The categories of culture as *literate and non-literate, refined or crude, modern or traditional, elitist and folk,* among other categories such as *grand and little, or margi and Deshi,* are only analytical groupings that help understand the process of cultural growth in historical spaces. Life is an expression through time and social change and tensions. Culture is the other name for this experience and it varies through time. Tradition therefore need not be perceived as simply a survival, as is usually done. If it is a qualitative marker as something representative of social group, it is not to be seen as quaint, but as a system, with a key, the key of selection, to an ordering process. For a movement form one scale of form to another, potential for adoption of available elements into contemporary systems is essential. No tradition can pass into contemporary culture without a selection. If it fails the test of selection, it gives way to a new cultural construct providing vitality to the uniqueness of an ethno-specific culture.

When we talk of ethno-specificity of culture including folklore, we come to a related issue—the issue of cultural identity, which is in sharp focus in culture and politics of northeast India for the last few decades. The important connection between identity and folklore can never be denied. Since the relationship between members of a group, or of a community determines the collective identity, folklore is the most important source of its construction., articulation and perpetuation. This is because it prepares the cultural symbols, the essential features of an identity system. A definition of folklore as a 'function of shared identity' (Bauman 1971 : 32) states this premise very well.

Hence the talk of retention at any cost of the cultural symbols of ethnic groups, articulated and perpetuated through the genres of folklore, for the retention of the identity system itself. There is an anxiety, obviously in the northeastern setting, that any development process in modern terms, disturbs and even destroys the identity of a group, retained through ages through folklore. Any northeast watcher is aware of this anxiety. Almost every socio-political movement in different parts of the region (both peaceful and militant) since the Sixties through Eighties of the last century, either for self-determination or for reinstement of the lost rights and position revolves round this syndrome. Even after the attainment of their rights, the establishment of states, the leaders of the scheduled tribes in particular, resisted the usual processes of development and modernization. They were distinctly articulate in propagating the preservation of their 'age-old tradition'—the customary laws, kinship regulations, land holding patterns, etc. While reading the manifestoes of parties, both regional and national, for 1983 Meghalaya Assembly elections (ten years after the coming up of the state), I had found that almost all of them, pledged for retention of the cultural identity of the people and that there would be no intervention in their traditional ways of life. In spelling out the programme of development in the agrarian sector, the two regional parties, the All Party Hill Leaders Conference and the Hill State Peoples' Democratic Party discouraged any programme of land reforms and assured their clients that the management of lands would follow the customary tradition of land tenure. Indian National Congress was conspicuously silent on this issue. Only the Communist Party of India suggested some measures for land reforms to vitalize the agrarian sector. On the issue of industrialization none of the parties except the Communist Party of India preferred any kind of broadbased programme. Their call was only for vitalizing the cottage and small industries sector, but that also without affecting the demographic factor, security and identity.[4] Significantly there was no declared industrial policy of the Govertnment of Meghalaya, though by that time it was in existence for more than a decade. The reason for the lack of enthusiasm for development and modernization of the economy and society, on the part of the political parties and government, is well known. There was a fear—genuine or perceived that industrialization and modernization would affect the tranquility of the 'tribal' life and would create an identity crisis. The net result is, obviously, the perpetuation of a static economy.[5] It is known how the project for extension of railways upto Byrnihat inside Meghalaya was resisted and abandoned due to this fear.

Unfortunately in India, customary culture and folklore including mythology, the traditional way of life etc. have been used and are used even today to resist the development programmes for reasons other than developmental. As I have discussed in the first section that there was (and is even today in some quarters, including Folklorists) a perception that folklore and development (modernization) are two antagonistic terms. This perception and the fear that modernization will 'mutate the ethnic and symbolic identities' still persist. In a 2006 article, Temsula Ao narrates this fear: 'the cultures of North East India are already facing tremendous challenges from education and modernization. In the evolution of such cultures and the identities that they embody, the loss of distinctive identity markers does not bode well for the tribes of the region. If the trend is allowed to continue in an indiscriminate and mindless manner, globalization will create a market in which Naga, Khasi or Mizo communities will become mere brand names and commodity makers stripped of all human significance and which will definitely mutilate the ethnic and symbolic identities of a proud people. Globalisation in this sense will eventually reduce identity to anonymity. (Ao: 2006 : 7).

A question may be asked, however, whether the French, German or even the Indians, to name a few, have all lost their identity during the last few hundred years or so when industrialization and so called modernization got consolidated. But fear is fear; anxiety is anxiety; these can not be erased easily.

Talking about the Mizo society in the present day contexts, Margaret Ch. Zama tells us a different 'story': 'In Mizo context, the clarion call by YMA regarding the dress code, behaviour, disapproval of marriage outside the community, expressions of concern and fear over assimilation and hybrid and so on, have not quite succeeded in stemening the flow of change and transformation. This has been facilitated by exposure to movement of peoples, inter-state travels, the internet and yes, the IT revolution too, which is beginning to have its impact on governance and higher education amongst other things. Even traditional dance forms and indigenous handloom designs have not escaped this transition. To cite an example, the popular 'Cheraw' or bamboo dance has mutated through the years to introduce more intricate steps, and the traditional '*Puanchei*' and *Kawrchei*' enhanced and upgraded, so to say, for the purpose of appearing as attractive and colourful, if not more so, than other cultural groups from other states. So sometimes changes are caused by reasons as innocuous as the desire to 'keep up with the Joneses'. Again traditional handloom designs of the Mizo *Puan* (wrap around woven cloth) and shawls have undergone their share of changes and borrowings from outside their region, to respond to market demands. The need for co-existence and space sharing are to be taken up with a more serious note by cultures of the northeast without compromising on traditional values or endangering territorial boundaries. After all, culture and traditions are alike in that they are both created by human beings and human experience. They are subject to change with the passing of time, though this could well be a subject for further debate (Zama: 2006 : 11).

Yes, let the debate go on as it has been going on since the days of Indian independence. Remember Nehru-Elwin philosophy for development and Nehru's 'Panchsil' for tribal development! They caught the imagination of many at that time. It is perhaps not required to elaborate on those principles since they are pretty well-known to every northeastern watcher. But it must be said that despite the genuineness of their concern for tribal way of life and ingenuity of their strategies for development, both Nehru and Elwin in a way suffered from romantic idealism. The contradiction between the 'protective aspects' and 'development aspects'[6] should have been more objectively assessed. This did not happen. It is therefore not surprising that Elwin preferred to call himself 'Philanthropologist' than a professional anthropologist. Nehru's idealism also received a boost in the company of such a philanthropologist. At that point of time itself when he declared his concept of 'National Park' with the implication that the 'tribal' people should be provided space so that they could live their own lives according to 'own genous' Elwin was severely criticized by political leaders and professional anthropologists alike. The famous statement of Ram Manohar Lohia that Elwin was treating tribals as domestic cattle is a pointer. Elwin, however, revised this position later when he realized the unfortunate connection of Expression 'National Park' (Elwin: 1964).

Both Elwin and Nehru were criticized by 'tribal' leaders as well, as in their assessment both were guilty of preference for segragation of the tribal communities. Barriter Pakem writes, 'concluding our observations on the tribal policy of Nehru, we may, therefore, say that it is nowhere near his idea of middle course' between the two extremes of assimilation-segregation. In the assimilation-segregation continuum Nehru's policy rather tilted heavily towards the side of segregation. This is more true in the case of the hill people of North East India........(many had severely attacked the policy and equated it with the old British policy of segregating the 'tribal people' (Pakem: 1992 : 97)

This 'assessment of Nehru's policy for tribal development follows, perhaps, the assessment of the current socio-cultural situation in the so-called tribal areas of the northeast, which, in turn follows a demand for re-assessment of the strategies for development. L.S. Gassah writes, "A large number of tribes in North East India have now undergone a period of transition. During this transitional period, many changes have taken place due to the process of modernization and other allied forces. It is high time now for the decision-makers and planners of the country to think in terms of these changed circumstances for the betterment and upliftment of the tribals of North East India'. (Gassah: 1992 : 106)

We have seen earlier that modernization in the shape of industrialization etc. and reforms in the age-old socio-political and cultural systems, were firmly resisted, both in the social and political spaces, in the fear that such process would disturb and erode the identity and exclusiveness of a culture. The situation has changed in recent years. I have quoted Gassah who feels that there should be a change in the policy and strategies for development keeping in view the process of modernization that has already happened in the tribal areas of the northeast. We have read Margaret Ch. Zamas's story of the Mizo situation. She is quite emphatic in asserting that over emphasis on ethnic identity has encouraged cultural myopia (Zama: 2006 : 11). Anil Boro, a folklore scholar from Bodoland, says, the question of identity and its uniqueness in the present context are tricky. Those who vouch for distinct identity and cultural purity forget that identity like any other practice in a society, is an evolving concept except that in a symbolic form it connotes the ethnic, linguistic and cultural markers and differences. Although mutations are facts of life, all that is called essential and unique in defining an identity is because of exclusion from of others, not as something self-evidential. Under a globalised cultural space, the larger question is, can unique identities remain pure and uncontaminated? To speak the truth, that is not possible because each community keeps on learning from other communities and thus the process of acculturisation continues. Keeping in mind the utilitarian value, a community adopts new ideas and practices. While a culture makes some re-adjustment in adopting the new, the new is re-shaped to be appropriated by a host culture. It is also true identity already, always hybridized (Boro: 2006 : 12).

If these are the experiences of the tribal leaders and scholars of the region, they are, perhaps, not different for other communities world-wide. The fact is: folklore, iderntity, tradition etc. are never static. Adjustments and inventions, spontaneous and organized and design constructs are results of an inbuilt mechanism of folklore formations, what I emphasized in the first section of this essay.

A question follows: how tradition, ethnicity, identity, authenticity of culture etc. can be preserved for all time without resisting the process of change? Either you remain where you were, or face the challenges of change. I have though and found through my study and research in folklore, that essentials are never destroyed, even if mutated. There lies the vitality of folklore which can comfortably negotiate with factors of change. New formations in the altered social environment, technological shifts do not always threaten the old ones, rather enrich them. 'Folk' and 'lore' therefore need be placed in a specific cultural space in specific social formations in the historical context. We must accept a reality, abandoning all kinds of romantic idealism and glorifications of age-old, authentic tradition, that folklore enriches itself through mutations and new formations in the spaces of change in social foundations. In this perspective, folklore, tradition, identities, etc. are to be viewed not as culturally given but as culturally construct in different phases of developmental history.

Folklore and development are therefore not antithetic but rather complimentary to each other. Folklore has, throughout millenniums, always have met the challenges of change successfully. It has an inbuilt mechanism of adaptation in new situation. The threat of extinction, both imaginary and real, has been countered with alterations in available genres and new formations.[7] Development and technology, far from being a hindrance, has always infused life and colour to folklore formation.

NOTES

1. Part of the text of Thom's letter, published in 'Athenium' of London on 22 August 1846 under a Pseudonym Ambrose Merton, quoted in Dundes ed. 1965: ' Your pages have so often given evidence of the interest which you take in what we in England designate as popular antiquities, or popular literature (Though by-the-be it is more a lore than literature, and would be most aptly describes by a good Saxon compound, Folklore—the lore of the people—that I am not without hopes of enlisting your aid in garnering the few ears which are remaining scattered over that field from which our forefathers might have gathered a goodly crop.
2. Quoted in Bausinger, 1990 : 8.
3. For a detailed discussion on the status of folklore in the modern world, see Chapter 1 of my book on Khasi-Jayantia Folklore, 2004.
4. See my essay in P.S. Dutta, 1986.
5. For a detailed discussion see my paper in Raha and Coomer, 1989.
6. See the Report of the Scheduled Areas and Scheduled Tribes Commission, 1961, of which Elwin was the chief architect.
7. For a discussion on this aspect with adequate example, see my paper-2007.

REFERENCES

Ao, Temsula (2006). 'Identity and Globalization: A Naga Perspective', Indian Folklore Serial No. 22. Special Issue on 'Globalization and Tribes' of North East India, Guest editor, Kailas C. Baral.

Bauman, Richard (1971). "Differential Identity and Social Base of Folklore" Journal of American Folklore. 85: 31-41.

Bausinger, Hermann (1990). 'Folk Culture in the World of Technology'. Tr Elke Dettmer, Bloomington, Indiana University Press.

Ben-Amos, Dan (1990). 'Foreword' in Folk Culture in the World of Technology, Herman Bausinger.

Benedict Ruth (1931). "Folklore". Encyclopaedia of Social Sciences, Vol: 6, London, MacMilan.

Boro, Anil (2006). 'Globalisation and Local Cultures: The Tribes of North East India' Indian Folklore Serial No:22.

Dundes Alan (1965). 'The Study of Folklore', Englewood Cliffs, New Jeresy, Prentice Hall.

Ibid. (1977). "Who are the Folk', Frontiers of Folklore, Edited by Wiliam Bascom, AAAS Selected Symposeum No:5. Included in Alan Dundes 1980, Interpreting Folklkore, Bloomington: Indiana University Press.

Elwin, Verrier (1964). 'The Tribal World of Verrier Elwin', New Delhi.

Gassah, L.S. (1992). Nehru's Approach to Understanding Tribal Life and Culture with Special Reference to 'North East India', in C.D. Tripathi and B. Datta Ray (eds), Jawaharlal Nehru and the Disadvantaged, NEICSSR, Shillong.

Herskovits, M.J. (1946). 'Folklore After a Hundred Years: A Problem of Redefinition'. Journal of American Folklore, 59.

Lang, Andrew (1884). 'The Method of Folklore' in Customs and Myths, London: Longmans Green & Co.

Pakem B. (1992). 'Jawaharlal Nehru's Tribal Panchsilla and the Hill People of North East India' in Tripathi and B. Datta Ray (eds), Jawaharlal Nehru and the Disadvantaged, NEICSSR, Shillong.

Propp, Vladimir (1984). 'Theory and History of Folklore' Tr, Ariadua Y & Richard P. Marth, Manchester University Press.

Ramanujan, A.K. 1991 (1994). 'Folklores From India', New Delhi, Penguine.

Sen, Soumen (1986). 'Election Manifestoes of Parties in Meghalaya' in P.S. Dutta Ed. Electoral Politics in North East India, New Delhi, Omsons.

Ibid. (1989). 'Development in A Tribal Setting: A Case of Meghalaya' in Tribal India Problem Development Prospect, Vol 1 Eds, M.K. Raha & P.C. Coomer. New Delhi, Gyan Publishing.

Ibid. (2004) 'Khasi Jayantia Folklore: Context, Discourses and History' Chennai, National Folklore Support Centre.

Ibid. (2007). 'Folklore in the Third World Countries in the Age of Mega Urbanization' in Urbanization and Multi-Ethnic Society. (IVAES Inter-Congree Proceedings, Vol. 2) Eds., Buddhadev Chaudhury and Sumita Chaudhuary, New Delhi, Inter India Publications.

Sokolov, Y.M. (1950). 'Russian Folklore', New York: MacMilan.

Thoms, William (1946). 'Leter to the Editor', Athenaem No:982, August 22. Included in Alan Dundes, The Study of Folklore 1965.

Zama, Margaret (2006). 'Globalization and the Mizo Story' Indian Folklore Serial No. 22.0

3

Tribal Identity, Culture and Politics: The North-East Indian Perspective

RAJAT KANTI DAS

In the context of North-East India tribal identity continues to draw our attention, which for the tribes has become a matter of considerable importance. Frankly speaking, it is almost habitual on the part of observers of this phenomenon to find a reference of it to 'tribalism' which is more or less synonymously used with 'ethnicity'. While analysing the African situation, Stephen Katz (1980) equates 'ethnicity' with 'tribalism' when he states:

> "In the African literature 'ethnicity' has replaced 'tribalism for purposes of respectability, although it theoretically pertains to the same thing".

Even after conceding the fact that the North-East Indian tribal situation may not be directly comparable to the African situation, one cannot help noticing the unmistakable manifestation of tribal identity as an expression of ethnic identity in North-East India, which sometimes cuts across community line. Obviously, tribal identity crystallized into 'ethnic identity' in a situation marked by pluralism, cultural hybridization and greater interplay of political variables. The question of tribal identity has multiple dimensions and can never be seen in isolation. As an expression of ethnic identity, it signifies the process of self-identification along ethnic line, though strict adherence to an ethnic boundary is practically impossible today. This undoubtedly paves the way for increasing use of symbols as a justification for their transcendent existence. Symbols as expressive forms create 'fables of identity'. Keeping aloft the banner of 'tribalism' by the operators of those, in the North-Eastern states of Mizoram, Manipur; and Nagaland having international boundary with Myanmar, it may be possible to identify the different stages at which the identity operates. At the first instance, the search for identity may be limited to a single tribe only. This is tribal identity with an independent expression. Secondly, a number of tribes may come together in their search for a mutually acceptable identity-marker. Attempts in this direction are not new. Thirdly, there are identity-reckoners at a broad regional level, which do not necessarily remain operative within the limits of the state. These involve ethnic identity, which, though invokes mutual affinity between the tribes in unison, also lays stress on alignment. The question is why and how do they forge an alignment? In simple terms, they have been trying to work out a concept of 'wholeness' by giving up the position of 'archaic localism' in favour of a larger territorial integrity. This concept of wholeness is constructed with the sole intention of carrying it in future, reducing the present to 'a politically charged existence'. This is an expression of 'cultural power', which is exercised when groups negotiate their respective boundaries. In contrast, 'social power' is exercised when groups are in conflict with each other. Under conditions of plurality, the distinctiveness of culture makes sense. It continues to be so as long as a society has 'a language of argument' by which contests for power are converted into 'the moral judgements'. There is no denying the fact that a historically enduring relationship involving different tribal groups will invariably focus on culture. The members of a particular group work out a 'cultural model' which is shared and socially distributed. Culture is thematic and its theme is shared by the members of a social group, which implies that an individual's publicly enacted behaviour has a cultural content in it. But in the wake of violence imparted through ethnic conflict and separatist movements carried out by some of the major tribal groups of North-East India, it may be difficult to accept unconditionally and uncritically the concept of cultural relativism. Though the wholeness pervading a tribal society could only be located in the past, there have now been attempts by the tribals themselves to carry it to the future. But only ideas about cultural wholeness could be brought forward. Almost every tribal community now has an association run by the educated and culture-conscious people to document, preserve, cultivate and reinterpret the customary practices and beliefs with a view to justify their continuance in a form that is relevant from community point of view. These could be projected as a reminder of the community's standing in the midst of surrounding communities. Ultimately, the whole effort touches upon the question of identity, in the present situation, not all ideas about culture are empirically defensible. Some of the ideas are not even mutually comprehensible. One might add that in the modern power structure the 'social actors' are differentially placed in terms of accumulation of economic wealth, authoritative control or ability to apply coercive force. Naturally, their response to culture will not toe the same line. What is apparent today is that the use of culture is related with political exigencies, interests and future expectations of the variously placed social actors. Their endeavour is to arrive at some sort of a consensus in this regard on the realization that the choice exercised by an individual cannot totally culture-free.

II

While there may not be much doubt about the validity of culture as being able to manifest the melting pot character of the society, there are doubts about its applicability in all situations of cultural and ethnic pluralism without undergoing change either in its form or meaning. It has to be admitted that structurally the North-East Indian tribes are not at the same level, some of the tribes were nothing more than clans or sub-tribes at the beginning. Murdock's (1953) equation of a tribe with a species is worth mentioning here. He considers communities of the same tribe equivalent in the absence of geographic or dialectic barriers to communication or diffusion.

> "We therefore propose to define a culture as including all local cultural variants exhibited by communities within a particular geographical area which speak mutually intelligible languages and have essentially similar forms of economic adjustment"

At the structural and functional level, the tribes of Manipur give an impression that they actually belong to a limited number of 'culture types'. A 'culture type', according to Murdock, is

> "a single unquestionably distinctive culture or group of cultures which differ from one another to a degree not significantly greater than the local variation to be expected in the culture of any homogeneous society of substantial geographic extent."

There are difficulties in applying Murdock's definition of 'culture type' to the tribes of Manipur in the contemporary situation. In a sense, no single tribe in Manipur can claim to possess 'cultural homogeneity' as a mark of cultural distinctiveness. Actually, in terms of 'cultured-type' only few identity labels could be recognized. These are (i) Naga, (ii) Kuki and (iii) Mizo. Today, these terms can hardly fit in the 'culture type' model. The focus has now shifted to power relations or more precisely, on 'codes of power' as devised, created and manipulated by the 'social actors'. The generic terms are now suggestive of an emerging power structure marked by political superordination and subordination. The example of the Maring may specifically be cited here. Earlier, the Maring held an 'independent' status without in any way swamped by the Naga (Tangkhul) or Kuki (Thadou) group of tribes. The fact that the Maring could preserve their territorial integrity in the face of frequent onslaught from the powerful Naga or Kuki tribes speaks volume of their sustaining capacity.

But during the post-independence stage, with the formation of the state-based political system, the tribal politics got realigned and the Marings also became a party to it. They gave up their 'independent' status and found a place within the Naga fold. By adopting 'Naga' identity, they could create more political space for them. Two factors directly contributed to their change in identity—the spread of Christianity among the Marings, the movement being led by the Tangkhul Naga Church leaders and the increasing contact of the Marings with the members of the underground Tangkhul Naga outfit, who used to take a shelter in the Maring villages when they were on the run. Following change in their identity, their perception about traditional culture had also changed in the sense that some of the customary practices were not only questioned but a few were altogether discarded. For example, after getting converted to Christianity they gave up the practice of wearing their hair long and confined in a bunch like a horn rising from the front of the head, which had formed an important element in their social and ritual life. The lesson one gets from this is that culture is more about the way people perceive it and search for alternate meaning. Goodenough's (1964) observations on culture may seem quite meaningful in this context,

> "Culture is not a material phenomenon, it does not consist of things people, behaviour or emotions. It is rather an organization of things. It is the form of things that people have in mind, their mode of perceiving, relating, and otherwise interpreting them."

A simple custom-cum-location approach may not be able to reveal the complexities of the situation. Can language prove handy in ascertaining inter-community relations to greater effect? Naroll (1964) has included culture content in the form of language and role of the state in his definition of the 'cultunit'. He defines 'cultunit' as

> "a group of territorially contiguous people who not only are domestic speakers of mutually intelligible dialects but also belong to the same state of contact groups."

Naroll has also specified four sub-types of the 'cultunit', such as—(i) the stateless (ii) the linguistically homogeneous state, (iii) the ruling group of a linguistically diverse state, and (iv) the subject group of a linguistically diverse state.

The tribal groups of Manipur approach more closely the fourth unit primarily because of their acceptance of Meitei as a 'lingua franca' and tacit recognition of the 'ruling group' status of the Meitei. The Meitei as the majority group also represent the 'ruling group' if not in letters but in spirits. Being the dominant community they have more representation more control and more say in the state governments. All of these have something to do with the demographic and situational advantages they enjoy over the tribal groups. Clearly the role of nation or state in the functioning of a tribe is well accepted. What is, however, more in evidence is that the tribes today are not exclusively limited to a 'cultunit' status. They are on their way to find an entry into the nation-state which initiates power process and systems into action and pervade the tribal institutions centering around a functioning society's culture. This calls for a shift in emphasis from a purely 'cultural model' to nation or 'state-based models of the political' since nations or states seem to be more appropriate for the study of political variables. There has now been a tendency to use 'nation' or 'state' interchangeably but this does not give a correct picture because nationalism can flourish in the absence of a state. It thrives on the issue of people's wholehearted participation in their own affairs. Not only that, states can be founded on 'principles other than nationalistic ones'. But the state here may not be understood in conventional terms. It is thought to be people-centric where power will rest with the people themselves who will decide the areas in which they want to develop a relation of interdependence with a particular nation (including India) and to what extent. Clearly the emphasis is more on the principle of sovereignty. Both the extremes occur in North-East India in one form or the other.

III

However, the ability of tribal society to withstand external instrusion of modern forms of authoritative control exercised by the dominating force at the national level may not got unnoticed. It all depends on the degree of ethnocentrism and the intensity of ethnic passion harboured by the hardcore elements, who very often succeed in carrying with them the less vocal common people. The result is, those who have assumed power in open defiance to the state, 'act on the actions of other people and exercise their power over the group.' By personifying the interests of the community they belong to and speaking on its behalf, when they are called upon to do so, the common people create an impression that they are only too willing to get along with the movement initiated by a politically charged activists who are out to install a new political order in their own terms that would be able to fulfill the wishes, as aspirations, community interests and cultural ethos of the people at large. A situation of political conflict and competition has developed in North-East India, which is reflected in the struggle for assessing identities in a given territory or, even in 'non-territorial networks'. Here the participation of tribes is almost total. Very often, they indulge in practicing a type of "rational per petuative nativism", which lays stress on the cultural items or symbols to justify the existence of their society as a separate entity.

In the present situation a tribe may be understood as an ethnic group with a distinct cultural base, but politically organized with a view to produce solidarity-oriented action among the members. Demographic character, territorial integrity, linguistic affiliation may contribute to prepare the ground for ethnic and cultural base to take a firm root, but ultimately it is left to the members of a community to define their own social environment and decide upon their future course of action. Admittedly, the behaviour of a people relating to orientation depends on an array of cross-cutting ideas and events. It appears that the orientation of thought and action of individuals or groups they belong to finds expression in the political will to organize for gaining access to power structure. Politics to the North-East Indian tribes do not represent an absolutely separate sphere. Activities modeled in accordance with cultural rules can set the pattern of a political process. Such a course of action has become necessary partly because of the growing internal class and gender differentiation and partly because of the conflict generated between the local boundary system on the one hand and regional and national alliances on the other. A proper understanding of the current situation may be sought by unveiling a series of tensions "between change and the preservation of cultural integrity; between resistance to development and the selective adoption of innovations to maintain a degree of culture and ecological balance; between shared cultural practices and significant heterogeneity…" (June Nash, as quoted by Escobar 1995). There has been a growing realization on the part of indigens of North-East India that over the years they have been made almost totally dependent on the national government and that they only serve and protect the interests of the national political establishment thereby loosing their own identity and self-esteem. Most of them feel that they have been forced to accept identities as devised and decided upon by the national government(s) by taking advantage of their economic plight and political instability. By any means, they would like to attain a position of strength economically and politically, which would provide them with the opportunity to challenge and re-negotiate the identities worked out unilaterally without their full consent. But what about the individual craze for money and economic wealthy and lust for political power? Do they not strike at the root of community cohesive structure built around a common culture? There is a general acceptance of such actions on the ground that these have some social effects or credibility. They have a role to play in building social wealth. A number of people rally around them for getting services, benefits, which have a social purpose. One is immediately reminded of Adam Smith's (1976 : 1776) concept of the operation of the 'invisible hand' which operates at psychological and economic levels to promote the conditions of wealth. In such a case, culture may take a backseat or, the reverse may still hold true culture will continue to function as the unifying force. After all, the tribes of North-East India are still rooted to their culture in a big way either as participant-performers or as 'interpreter-analysts', which have a telling effect on the pattern of social relations and lend substance to human experience and thought process. Akos Ostor probably strikes the right chord when he observes:

> "The cultural (symbolic, meaningful) are not mere expressive 'aspects' in opposition to society nor do they 'reflect' the basic social morphology. Rather, they form our awareness of society both as participants and interpreter-analysts. By culture we do not mean a concrete edifice abstracted out of society, rather the constitution of approaches to society, the forming of ideologies and social structures, the relations among indigenous categories, elements and units articulate into larger wholes in different places at different times."

The critical focus thus falls on the users of cultural ideas who could use them to good effect creating new alliances and preserving the existing ones. The ultimate aim is to ensure group's wholehearted participation in public affairs which has so long been denied to it by the state-controlled bureaucratic and administrative mechanism relying heavily on the Armed Forces to quell public demonstration of anger and discontent against injustice and oppression. The allegation that the Indian State in its present form could manifest its presence in North-Eastern region through corrupt or dubious practices, at times administrative highhandedness and, above all, through military operations may be difficult to be dismissed outright.

REFERENCES

1. Donan, Donald (1999). *History, Power, Ideology*, Berkeley : University of California Press.
2. Edgar, Andrew and Peter Sedgwick (Eds.) (2004). *Key Concept in Cultural Theory:* London, Routledge.
3. Escobar, Arturu (1995). *Emerging development: the making and unmaking of the Third Worlds.* Princeton University Press.
4. Goodenough, W. (ed.) (1964). *Explorations in Cultural Anthropology.* New York: McGraw-Hill.
5. Herzfeld, (1999). *Anthropology*, New York Blackwell.
6. Jenks, Chris (1993). *Culture: Key Ideas* London; Routledge.
7. Katz, Stephen. 1980. *Marxism, Africa and Social Class: A Critique of Relevant Theories.* Centre for Developing Area Studies, Montreal: McGraw-Hill University Press.
8. Monagham, John & Peter Just (2000). *Social and Cultural Anthropology*, Oxford.
9. Murdock G.P. (1953). *Social Structure.* New York: The Free Press.
10. Naroll, R.S. (1964). On Ethnic Classification, *Current Anthropology* 5.
11. Nash, Juan (2001). Globalization and the Cultivation of Peripheral Vision *Anthropology Today*, Vol. 17, No. 4.
12. Ostork, Akos (1984). *Culture and Power*, New Delhi: Sage.
13. Vincent, Jones (2002). *The Anthropology of Politics* London: Blackwell.

4

Culture and its Impact on Human Personality

BOBBY MAHANTA

Culture is an important factor for human resource development in any country. The Department of Culture operates a number of schemes of Government of India for preserving and promoting the cultural heritage of the country. It also has a network of subordinate & attached offices besides a number of other autonomous institutions/organizations, such as Archaeological Survey of India, Anthropological Survey of India, National Archives, Museums, Libraries, Academies, etc. in the field of Art & Culture. During 1999-2000, Rs.165 crore and Rs.185 crore have been allocated to the Department of Culture. Planning Commission has allocated Rs.185 crore for the schemes of Department of Culture under Annual Plan 2000-01. During 1999-2000, the Department's activities have increased in the North Eastern States including Sikkim.

In order to know and understand the culture prevalent in any particular society, it is very important that one understands the meaning of the word Culture. The English term "Culture has been derived from the Latin word 'Cultura' (root word being 'cult') which means an improved condition. Culture, therefore, is nothing but an improvement of human life and personality. It is culture that makes man superior to other living beings. Culture thus adds quality to human personality. Ottaway writes: "Culture is entirely dependent on the interaction of individual with the social environment, and has to be learnt from the social group." While defining culture Allport has stated that "Culture is the ground from which the personality emerges." It shows that the elements of personality are determined by the culture while culture itself is the outcome of various values of the past and present. E. B. Taylor has rightly remarked on the term culture in the on-going words: "Culture is defined as the complete whole which includes knowledge, belief, art, morals, law, custom and any other capacities and habits acquired by man as a member of society." Truly, culture is a treasure of the acquired qualities by men. It is a system of life which is the result of many centuries. Culture is the progressive growth into humanization and liberalization of the human spirit. It aims at enhancing the capacity of man for joyful pursuit of some fundamental ideas. Culture signifies man and his relationship with the social environment. The way he talks, behaves, respond, eat etc. reveals the type of personality he acquires.

Culture is an integrated system of learned behaviour patterns which are characteristic of the members of a society and which are not the result of biological inheritance. Culture is not instinctive either. It is learned. Culture is the creation of man. It includes all that the group conceives to modify his innate endowments and to meet the innate urges. As a new born baby grows older, he acquires different ideals, attitudes and values through imitation and social contacts. These experiences contribute to the formation of his personal culture. Culture emanates from man and gives a direction and purpose to his life. It extends the range of individual efficiency and his power of action. It supplements the man's native endowments and provides him with an additional extension of his anatomical apparatus. Man being a social being adopts the behaviour patterns from the surrounding in which he lives. He learns and adopts whatever he considers desirable for his survival. A term cultural pattern is used to describe the ways of behaviour associated with any permanent need or function in the social life. The way the food is eaten in different societies shows the pattern of their culture. Take for example the Indians, who eat food with their hands and fingers whereas the English people use the spoon, fork, and knife. All these represent the pattern of culture existing in the two different societies. The need is, however the same, eating food. Hence, we may say that different societies have different cultural patterns. Language, literature, rearing up of the young, values in the society, myths, customs, ideologies, beliefs and faiths—all are different cultural patterns existing in different societies. The cultural patterns are transmitted from one generation to another. Each generation is free to modify these and to transmit these to the next generation. This transmission is a continuous process.

Culture plays an important role in socializing the individual, and the ways, quality and direction of socialization differ from society to society. Every society has its own ethos that is communicated to the individual in many different ways. In other words, different societies have distinct cultural patterns establishing the different identities of different nations. To cite an example of one of the cultural patterns of north east India—the Assamese Culture—we need to know that during the ancient times, culture was mainly based on agricultural life. With the advent of Aryans, India became rich in culture, which immensely influenced the Assamese people. Assamese culture is composed of diverse elements. This included the culture of the various tribes living in Assam such as the Bodos, Rabhas, Dimasas, Tiwas, Misings and Deuris. These diverse elements sowed the roots of the present day culture of Assam, a culture which enriched Indian culture since the time immemorial and will enrich it in times to come.

The northeast culture certainly has an important identity in Indian society. It graces and adorns Indian culture which is 'Unity in diversity'. The richness of the Northeast culture has historically been acknowledged. This region of India is the home of many rich cultures, nature-friendly traditional technologies and enduring social institutions. These have been shaped and nurtured by many tribal and non-tribal social formations in different parts of the region. Among the indigenous communities, there are more than 120 Scheduled Tribes, most of whom are traditional inhabitants of the hill regions, which make up over 70 percent of the total area. Despite impressive social and economic changes, the indigenous communities, tribal and others, still retain a great deal of the pristine elements of their age-old life-styles. Nearly every indigenous community can be considered as a repository of a distinctive body of knowledge, cultural traditions, social institutions and technologies, which have evolved over a long period of time. Wisdom and knowledge embedded in the socio-cultural life of the people of this region are often astounding and the identity of the north eastern region in the cultural map of India is distinctive.

To make our present century rewarding, we should all realize that the development of social character is a must. This can be achieved by drawing the individual into the whole community. It is the unity in human diversity, which enriches the socio-cultural heritage of any society. The socio-cultural episodes of the North East India comprising the states of Assam, Arunachal Pradesh, Manipur, Mizoram, Meghalaya, Nagaland, Tripura and Sikkim can contribute much towards the greater interest of unity in diversity of our nation.

Ralph Linton has pointed out three ways in which the individual can participate in culture:

- In the first place he participates universally in culture, that is, he adopts the habits, ideas and emotional patterns that prevail among the adults of that particular group.
- In the second place, the individual specifically participates in some specific organization or specific group of people.
- Finally, in the third place, the individual's participation in culture turns to the alternative elements in which he adapts those elements which are found only in a small number of individuals.

George H. Mead expresses the opinion that in adopting his culture the individual's ego passes through three stages analogous to the three stages of education:

- In the first stage, the individual imitates other people around himself, normally unconsciously. He is found smiling at others. In childhood, the infant acquires his culture through imitation.
- In the second stage, the children imitate different individuals in society in their play. Play of this kind introduces many different kinds of qualities in the child's personality.
- The third stage of acquiring culture is the stage of games where the individual learns to control his behaviour. In the social environment of the playground, the individual cannot behave willfully, since he has to conform to the

norms. Hence, he gradually begins to adopt the ideals, principles, and beliefs of his group. These individuals are called as cultured individuals.

Types of Culture

Material culture includes all those man-made things and objects which human society has created for its physical welfare in times of peace and war. Items such as clothes, utensils, homes, roads, ornaments, television, radio, various machines, gadgets and various means of transport and communication are some examples of material culture.

Non-material culture includes all those ideals, attitudes and values which modify the behaviour of an individual. Language, literature, art, music, customs and traditions etc. are some examples of non-material culture.

As the scientific inventions and technological advancement are progressing rapidly, material aspect of culture is going ahead and its area is being greatly widened. The modern society is gradually adopting more and more these techniques and scientific achievements in their day to day style of living, while the non-material aspect of culture has been left far behind. The vast difference between the material and the non-material culture is known as cultural lag. It is education which can bridge the gap by eliminating this cultural lag and by inspiring the general people to march on the path of progress and modernization.

Impact of Culture on Human Personality

Personality as defined by Allport is a dynamic organization within the individual of those psycho-physical systems that determine his unique adjustment to his environment. In Eysenck's definition, personality is the more or less stable and enduring organization of a person's character, temperament, intellect, and physique, which determine his unique adjustment to the environment. It includes everything about a person. It is a complex blend of a constantly evolving and changing patterns of one's unique behaviour, emerged as a result of one's interaction with one's environment and directed towards some specific ends. Human personality is formed in the type of society he lives in. The society to a great extent influences the personality of the individual because it is the place where he relates with different kinds of people; their ways of living, habits, thoughts etc. and gets an impact on his own personality. He learns in the process of adapting and adjusting with the surroundings he comes across. Education is responsible for bringing about an all-around development in humans personality. Man lives in the society and he has to adjust himself according to the conditions available in that particular society. This process of adjustment results in culture. Personality is developed in the educational institutions, family and in the society. In short, many of the individual differences are the results of cultural differences. Ottaway has said: "Children who are born and grow up in New Guiena instead of England quite clearly acquire a different culture. But those who are born and grow up in France or in Russia equally acquire different culture". A culture is good if it has some utility to the individual as well as to the society. If it does not fulfill this purpose, it decays and dies out in the long run. It may be borne in mind that mutual give and take among different cultures is also an essential conditioning process.

The personality of an individual is manifested through his pattern of behaviour. The behaviour is in turn profoundly influenced by the culture of his group. Anthropologists have found differences in the basic behaviour patterns of individuals belonging to different cultures and those differences of behaviour correspond to differences in culture. One can find the clear imprint of Indian culture on an Indian and the imprint of Western culture on an European or American. Similarly, the culture of the people living in the North East India is very much influenced by the area they live in. It will definitely vary from one state to another. Thus, the culture Nagaland differs from that of Meghalaya, Manipur, Mizoram and so on. Again, a Manipuri girls who is brought up in Manipur will differ from a Manipuri girl who is brought up in Tripura or Sikkim. Further a girl from Sikkim brought up at Mizoram or any other state will to a great extent be influenced by the surrounding where she lives and vice-versa.

Education and culture are intimately connected. The cultural pattern of a society conditions its educational pattern. For example, if a society has a spiritual pattern of culture, then its educational procedures will emphasize the moral and eternal values of life. On the other hand, if the cultural pattern of a society is materialistic, then naturally its educational pattern will be shaped for the attainment of material values.

Culture brings progressive growth and liberalization of the human spirit. It aims at enhancing the capacity of man for joyful pursuit of life. The child's cultural education begins at home. The parents and other members of the family educate the child through traditions, customs, values, belief, etc. Again, it is in the family that the child first learns to distinguish between right and wrong. The various impressions impinging upon his mind in the family environment help to make the child acquire culture. The child imitates the behaviour of their adults, brothers, and sisters. Next to home is the educational institution which plays an important role in developing the personality of the child. Through text-books the educational institutions acquaint the child with values, mores, ideas, customs, etc. Various extra-curricular activities in the form of games of different kinds, songs, dances, discussions, tours and field trips etc., are also intended to impart culture to their students. Children should not only be taught about their own culture, but they should also be taught to appreciate other cultures. Personality of the individual will be reflected on his behaviour and response towards other culture. In the plural society, it is essential to develop positive outlook toward the different cultures. This will enable the individual to organize the society for peaceful co-existence.

The development of human personality also depends on how one makes use of his leisure time. Thus, one of the important aspects of cultural education is learning the proper use of leisure. Hence, children's should be educated to use their leisure for cultural attainments through literature, music, art, self-development, social service, etc.

Various state, national and international seminars, debate, quiz, and other academic programmes aim at preserving and propagating the cultural heritage of the people. Like any parts of the country, the North East States of India also organizes various programmes for the students, teachers, scholars and the public in general. One among many other programmes is, the National Seminar which is conducted twice in every year by North East India Council for Social Science Research (NEICSSR). Participants from any part of India assemble at Shillong and make their valuable contribution towards the nation. Such programmes make positive and valuable contribution towards nation-building and national integration. Expanded transport and communication systems are facilitating mobility and information exchange. The need to deal constructively with the cultural diversity is rapidly felt in the present context of social life. Socio-cultural exchanges are growing as a result of change in the organization of the world economy.

REFERENCES

1. Gazetteer of India, Meghalaya District Gazetteer, Khasi Hills District, Government of Mehalaya, Arts & Culture Department (1991). Meghalaya, Shillong.
2. Culture & Religions of Assam (2002). Edited by Kuriala Chittattukalam sdb, Omsons Publications, New Delhi.
3. Assamese Culture as Reflected in the Mediaeval Assamese Literature, (1999). edited by Aunima Bharali, Lawyer's Book Stall, Guwahati, Assam.
4. The Background of Assamese Culture, edited by Rajmohan Nath, Dutta Baruah & Co., Gauhati.
5. Foundations in Sociology of Education, edited by Yogendra K. Sharma (2003). Kanishka Publishers, Distributors, New Delhi.
6. Philosophy and Sociology of Education (2003). Edited by R.N. Sharma, Surjeet Publications, Delhi.
7. Teacher and Education in the Emerging Indian Society (Vol. 2), (2003). edited by Biranchi Narayan Dash, Neelkamal Publications Pvt. Ltd., New Delhi.
8. Encyclopedia of North-East India (Vol.1), Arunachal Pradesh, edited by H.M. Bareh, Mittal Publications, New Delhi, 2001
9. Encyclopedia of North-East India (Vol.2), Assam, edited by H.M. Bareh, Mittal Publications, New Delhi, 2001
10. Encyclopedia of North-East India (Vol.4), Meghalaya, edited by H.M. Bareh, Mittal Publications, New Delhi, 2001.
11. Encyclopedia of North-East India (Vol.5), Mizoram, edited by H.M. Bareh, Mittal Publications, New Delhi, 2001.
12. Encyclopedia of North-East India (Vol.6), Nagaland, edited by H.M. Bareh, Mittal Publications, New Delhi, 2001
13. Encyclopedia of North-East India (Vol.5), Mizoram, edited by H.M. Bareh, Mittal Publications, New Delhi, 2001
14. Enclyclopaedia of North-East India-Assam, edited by H.M. Bareh, Mittal Publications, New Delhi, 1985.

5

Global Concern(s): Indigenous People/ Tribes vis-à-vis Non-Tribes[1]

R. K. BHATTACHARYA and KUMKUM BHATTACHARYA

Preamble

In this paper we have consciously tried not to look at the concept of the indigenous people as only a political one. One reason for this is as social scientists we are more comfortable in taking a long and objective view of issues concerning the indigene. The other reason is the ground realities in our country, India, where it is not a pressing need to look at people in isolation. India is a multiethnic plural society. The use of the word 'global' in the title may seem to point to a wide spectrum of universal concern(s) about indigenous people; however, it will be pertinent to set the parameters within which our discussion shall be confined. There should not be any doubt that our attempt is to understand and present the situations in India in global perspective.

The concept of indigenous people in India emerged in very recent past. It was during the last phase (in the '30s) of British rule in India, when the exercise of scheduling was begun and sections

[1] A version of this paper was presented in the International Conference on "Indigenous Peoples: the Trajectory of a Contemporary Concept" organized by the Development Studies, Uppsala, Sweden, 2000. The authors are grateful to Dr Peter B. Andersen, Associate Professor, Department of Cross-cultural and Regional Studies, University of Copenhagen, Denmark for his suggestions and valued comments.

of people were classified as Scheduled Castes (SC) on the basis of their being educationally, economically and socially deprived. Besides, certain communities were termed as tribes since the last quarter of the nineteenth century. The British tended towards inclusion of tribes in the category of indigenous people describing them as autochthones or indigenes (Dalton 1872; Risley 1891, 1915). Thus colonialism constructed the indigenous categories in India. It is pertinent to remember that the colonialists brought with them the idea of tribe, which was fallout of colonization of the Americas and Australia. It was in America and Australia that the dichotomy between the categories of people was so noticeable and this dichotomy formed the basis of the primary opposition between tribes and non-tribes. Such colonial notions created the category of indigene among the population of the colonised land.

There is some confusion in the connotation of the Indian term, *adivasi,* which if literally translated means original inhabitant (apparently neutral connotation of the word). However in usage it has a pejorative connotation meaning "primitive". The suffix *adi*, also means 'ancient' or 'of the past'. (In this kind of time based classification, it is not clear 'ancient' to what or who—this too has pejorative undertone implying less developed in terms of culture/ civilization). Therefore, the term *adivasi* has at least three meanings ('original inhabitant', 'primitive' and 'ancient'). But of the three, the latter two come more into everyday interactions with others (non-*adivasis*) than the first having a neutral meaning. Thus, in social interactions and exchanges, the *adivasi* are not perceived to embody the not so neutral connotation of the term, whereas the connotation of original inhabitant (or autochthones) has got political tones. The notions that are associated with the tribes are in concordance with the ideas and connotations of the dominant sections of the non-tribes towards *adivasi.* The term *janajati* is a more Sankritized term for the tribes, often used in written text rather than in oral form. *Vanavasi* is another term for them meaning forest dwellers (this creates its own image of 'pristine' people who we tend to view rather romantically). In recent years, the English term or usage, "indigenous people" has become popular among educated tribes, and the Indian or the local term *adivasi* has come to be used by the elite among the tribes who claim the status of autochthones. Wider acceptance of the term indigenous people by the literates of the tribes has lent the usage more positive shades of meaning than the restrictive use of the homegrown word *adivasi*. The English term has engendered a sense of pan-world brotherhood as if such people are in harmony with each other in terms of their needs, urges, and in terms of ways of meeting those needs. This obviously does not stand the test of reality. From the above discussion, it becomes clear that looking at the concept politically would leave little scope for utility, reasonableness and acceptance of the concept in the background of day-to-day interaction of people in the multiethnic and plural society of India.

Introduction

Indian society (rural society in particular) is a composite collective of communities. In a plural and democratic society like India, the indigenous people, if any could be so designated, are a minority, and yet a part of the composite social set-up. Andre Beteille (1998 : 187) has cogently highlighted the issue by stating, "...tribes had coexisted in close and sometimes intimate association with other types of social formation for centuries". In the Indian sub-continent, tribal people who fit in well within the ambit of the indigenous have, since times immemorial, lived side by side with peoples who do not fit in the same bill. In the contemporary situation, this composite social system is bound by an electoral democracy and the "highest common factor of their wants... the economic factor" (cf. Furnivall 1967 : 449). These two forces operating both at group and individual levels, locally as well as extra-locally, mainly guide the day-to-day interactions.

As has been argued in the preamble, scheduling certain categories brought in constitutional and statutory division of this composite society. This division was further reinforced after independence in the fifties by scheduling the tribes as well as certain castes in the lower hierarchy in line with the colonial classification of Scheduled Tribe and Scheduled Caste. Later, other backward communities (OBC) were included in the schedule. There were certain discrepancies in the use of the markers for identifying these categories. There were communities who were economically, educationally, and socially deprived but were not included in this scheduling, e.g., the backward groups among the Muslims (e.g., Abdal, Dafali, Jolha, Lal Begi, Patua, Shah, Fakir). The exclusion of these groups of the Muslims from this scheduling happened because of objections raised by the Muslim elites. Conversely, communities (e.g., Sunri, Nadar) that did not fulfill the above criteria in terms of their economic and social position were included in the schedule. Noble sentiments and moral principles guided the scheduling for the execution of plans and for effecting affirmative action through positive discrimination. This created hiatus between scheduled and non-scheduled population. The provisions of affirmative action and positive discrimination have drawn more distinct lines between the scheduled people and others for the simple reason that avenues of mobility to overcome rank stigma in the caste-ridden hierarchic Indian society (Dumont 1972) are blocked not socially but by act of law.

Tribes in India do not technically belong to the caste system; however, they are accorded a peripheral position in the social hierarchy. The age-old pattern of mobility from one status to another through the process of absorption of tribes into the Hindu castes (Risley 1915: 75-76, 1891: 506; Radhakrishnan 1965: 29; Bose 1949: 22, 1953: 156-170, 1972: 12) and mobility of castes through sanskritization (cf. Srinivas 1962) and state formation (Sinha 1962) have been thwarted by the constitutional provision of scheduling. In the traditional system, mobility was achieved for a larger section of a community under more collective leadership. At present, however, constitutional provisions catalyse the mobility of a few projected leaders who have mustered mass support from their respective communities. The mass often remains as a support base without receiving any or only very small benefits. The mass involvement has been sustained because of the promise of benefits from the constitutional provisions though they are yet to be realized in reality by a large section of the people. The other reason for this mass support and involvement is the change that has already occurred in their needs and aspirations because of increased exposure to the majority culture through mass media and formal education. Their awareness about the lifestyle of the elite leadership and mobility have impacted changing aspirations and needs of the communities. Besides, the mass is sometimes coerced to support various rank enhancement efforts.

Like scheduling of tribes in India, not long ago in the global context, there was discussion about a "fourth world", that is to say, the world of the tribes, but such discussion did not earn much dividend in India. The concept of fourth world failed to draw the attention of the tribal mass and had no scope of immediate benefit while scheduling provided hope of direct benefit. The idea of fourth world was a political movement. The new term 'indigenous people' is another attempt to confederate tribes in the global context.

Now we would like to analyse the concept of 'indigenous people' specifically in the Indian context. India has experienced successive migrations over a long period of time. This has molded the social history and led to the admixture of the population in India. In a survey (1985-1993) of the Anthropological Survey of India, which covered the entire gamut of communities (total 4,693) in the country, not a single community could claim to be real autochthones of the region in which they are found (Singh 1992: 3 & 4, 103). Almost all of them have a history (oral or written) of migration into the area they occupy now. Often, the land of origin may be mythical as in the case of the Santhals.

In this backdrop, facts and realities do not support the political concept of indigenous people in India. We propose that it would be more appropriate in the context of the Indian sub-continent to use location-centric niche criteria to define those populations occupying special ecological areas and displaying styles of life in tune with the niche, rather than grouping them under the term 'indigenous'. Certain populations are considered as relatively permanent occupants of particular locations. Their traditional way of life has developed over a long period of time and this has come to be considered suitable to those locations i.e. ecological niches, e.g., communities like Sauria Paharia, Apatani, Shompen, Jarawa. It is possible for these communities to sustain themselves in the particular niches that they inhabit through their economic practices and concomitant lifestyles; e.g., swidden cultivation of the Sauria Paharias, terrace cultivation of the Apatanis, and the Shompens and Jarawas with their hunting and gathering. These groups on their part seem to have resisted the influence of the dominant groups and their economic practices. The locally dominant groups do not find the traditional resource management practices of the niche populations attractive. There are however some exceptions. This may account for the fact that a number of niche populations have been left more or less undisturbed till the recent past thereby strengthening their belongingness to the niche. It may be pointed out that ecological niches are located more on the fringes of those areas occupied by the dominant communities (Kroeber 1952 : 392). Besides, the niche populations perceive themselves as not being contemporary and as being unable to meet the challenges of modernity (Xaxa 1999).

Academically, the positive imputation of the concept of indigenous people lies in the historical significance of the knowledge that is provided in the chronicle of human settlement as it provides insight into the forces of human migration and evolution of different cultures in different places. It also imparts information for interpretation of the cultural and social artifacts of people and allows academics to place them in time and location. There is also a noble and moral aspect of the concept of indigenousness if looked at in the following manner. It seems that the early/first settlers belong to the part of mother earth that they occupy while those who have come to be their neighbours or have forced themselves on them as intruders in these already occupied territories, behave as if they possess the newly acquired habitation. It is this difference between belonging and possessing, the difference in mindset expressed in the greed for exploitation of resources (Bhattacharya and Bhattacharya 2003), which is important to note. In the light of the above, there is a need to straighten the pitch for people (niche populations) as they seem to be continually subject to encroachment of physical space. In addition, they experience encroachment of ideas, values and norms in respect of their relation with their habitat that has been beautifully expressed in the oft-quoted words of Chief Seattle.

Concept of Indigenous People (IP) and Formation of Interest Group

It is evident from the body of anthropological and sociological writings that the term "tribe" has not been cogently defined. As a result, scholars and administrators have used their own understanding in the presentation of ethnographic or other accounts of the categories of people marked as tribes in the Indian context. Scholars and others transcending the polemics of definition have by and large accepted the constitutional identity of people as tribes (Scheduled Tribe) as a valid classification. Similarly, the concept of the indigenous people skirts the issue of definition and its use reveals overt politicization.

Concept of the indigenous people in the Indian context is nebulous. After all, we must ask, indigenous to what? Is it in the context of the nation state society of India? Boundaries of nation state society keep changing and have already gone through many changes. In consequence, the question of being indigenous to changing limits becomes difficult to resolve. Keeping recent history in perspective, it was not very long ago that India extended beyond her present borders and that people shared history, culture and polity. More than the question of indigenousness, it is the polity of times and places that envelopes the fact of inclusion and exclusion of groups/communities from the ambit of this concept. In this connection, attention may be drawn to communities that inhabit areas that fall within or are adjacent to international boundaries and also people who occupy small niches within the nation state. There is also the issue of acceptance of the status of any one group by its neighbours in relation to their own status in the plural situation. Along with status, there is the issue of the functioning power structure, which is normally polarised, giving rise to dominant and minority differentiations. The dominant section will normally find it difficult to accept movement(s) launched by the minority section(s) or the movements launched for them that disturb the status quo of plurality and the composite nature of the social system.

The constitutional provisions for affirmative action and positive discrimination seem to have given the minority or marginalised people the impetus to question the status quo. In this they have been aided to some extent by the transformation from a social identity, whether part or not, of a plural society to the acquisition of a political identity. As this process of transformation gains momentum, it gives rise to the formation of an elite (cf. Miller 1969). The members of the elite have equipped themselves to avail of the provisions and benefits constitutionally earmarked for their communities, which they come from. They form the core body of the interest group (for explanation of interest group see Glazer and Moynihan 1975, Bhattacharya and Bhattacharya 1996 : 59). This interest group is always in search of "ideological ammunition" (Beteille 1998 : 191) for strengthening their claim to special status. In this attempt it is observed that it is not for long that the interest groups are left to fend for themselves, leaders among non-tribes coalesce in terms of their interests with them. The coalition depends on acceptability of the elite of the tribe by the non-tribe as well as the negotiating capabilities of the former with the latter.

What is the significance of the idea of indigenous people except for the information it provides regarding the history and chronology of human settlement in a particular place? The consequence of the counter-productive concept of indigenous people is the precipitation of selfish and narrow aims and objectives in providing ideological support to interest groups. The argument can be taken a step further—the formation of interest groups may breed two kinds of attitudes—one of support to the idea and cause of the indigenous, and the other of the rejection of the idea of the indigenous. Of the two, the former may assume parasitical characteristics of depending and surviving on the idea of the indigenous—almost like Dante's 'counsellors of fraud' in Nether Hell!

To use another one of Dante's allegory in his description of the first circle of Hell or Limbo the indigenous people may be seen as being buffeted by the cross-winds of their history over which they may or may not have had much choice or control and global interest and concern for them over which they have no choice or control altogether. However, a certain section among these "indigenous people" take on the strategy of being hand in glove with those from non-indigenous people in response to need for mutual support. This helps in emergence of interest groups working sometimes to their own advantage but sometimes being at odds with real issues and concerns.

The members of the interest group have the privilege of accessing the knowledge of extraneous concepts and interpreting them in support of their aims. However, the mass as discussed in the introduction, which supports the interest group, requires to accept the interpretations that are made on their behalf. These interpretations and appropriations may not always be in tandem with the felt needs and aspirations of the mass. Rather, there is a sense of discontentment that is manifested in various ways, sometimes in aberrant behaviour and sometimes in the clamour that is raised for certain issues that may not be central to conditions that they may face in their day-to-day lives. The mass certainly cannot be expected to be able to internalise or even relate to the international conventions of the International Labour Organization

(1994), the United Nations draft declaration on rights of indigenous people (1991), etc., that have been adopted from time to time. It would only be a kind of delusion that all have had much impact on the masses of the indigenous populations. The phraseology of these conventions and the draft are alien to them and these populations would require the help of interpreters to understand it. But interpreters may add/subtract from meaning/intent according to their understanding and projection of provisions. At best, these international conventions are of use to the elites who are working to apportion for themselves a share in the collective pie (Bhattacharya and Bhattacharya 1996). It may be through their efforts that there would be a percolation in gains, either directly by forcing change or indirectly through emulation at individual or micro levels. There is no doubt that the interaction and connection of the elite or the interest group with international forums yields 'benefits'; thus there seems to be an 'advantage' in positing local concerns in a wider orbit of influence and awareness.

The Backdrop of the Emerging Identities of the Indigene

For this section of the paper, we are going to discuss the background situation in which the socio-political identity of the peoples who are designated as "indigene" is emerging and the changes that are occurring in the ideas such people have about the non-indigenous population and vice-versa. We shall also discuss the strategies of confronting this situation by the dominant people—the so-called non-indigenous.

In the Indian context there are different categories of the population, which may claim the identity of being indigene or autochthons. One category is area specific (e.g.: Chattisgarh, the erstwhile Vananchal that has now gained the status of the state of Uttaranchal and Jharkhand); another category is scheduling as a tribe (e.g.: Mizo, Naga and such others); and there is another category of belonging to the same linguistic group (e.g.: Bodo). We would like to clarify that there are around 427 tribes (recorded as scheduled) of various numerical strengths spread throughout the country. All of them do not claim special treatment as indigenous people. We are restricting the discussion to those who have rallied round this concept in order to derive advantages from their special situations. The categories that have been mentioned have themselves gone through processes of change in the recent past in response to the present.

The Jharkhand movement (for detail of the genesis and transformation of the movement see Basu 1994 and Sen 1976, Panchbhai 1983) that started as a tribal movement in the states of Bihar, Madhya Pradesh, Orissa and West Bengal during the 1930s became an area-specific movement in which non-tribes have also acquired the identity of being considered autochthons. This was an outcome of the difficulties encountered in separating the non-tribes from the tribes and vice-versa in the context of their composite character. It was not certain that the movement could succeed if it would leave out a large population of non-tribes or rather a large section of their composite social existence. The history of the Jharkhand movement is a pointer to a mechanisms of consolidation of disparate groups under one umbrella of the indigene. Similarly, although the Nagas had warring relation among themselves, they have now conglomerated across language and other socio-cultural divisions in order to derive benefits of being indigenous.

There was no tribe known as the Bodo. The people who are now identified as the Bodo belong to the same linguistic group (a Tibeto-Burman language family) with different dialects. Sharing this common cultural artifact, common language helped them bring together different groups who shared the same ecology and collectively experienced deprivation. Some groups who did not share the language but were perceived to be in opposition to the dominant linguistic group, the Assamese, were included in this movement for realization of commonly felt needs (Mukherjee and Mukherjee 1976). The members of the Bodo movement feel strongly about the primacy of their settlement and their identity as autochthons. Those who were responsible for their exploitation and minority status are seen as latter-day comers. This second group was the foil against which their existing condition sharpened into focus. In comparison to the other claimants of indigenous status, the leaders of the Bodo movement feel that they have woken up rather late (ibid.) to the disadvantages of their situation as indigenes.

Disparate social groups in India function under a common political system. This has the potential of sharpening the differences among them as well influencing their actions on the perceived differences. One of the factors responsible for this may lie in the weakening of traditional structures of societies in the face of increasing extra-local pressures of polity, of economics and of modernization. In an attempt to redefine the functions of traditional institutions, there may be a resurgence of re-shaped, re-oriented traditional systems as defense mechanisms to deal with modernization and other perceived threats (Beteille 1970; Kothari 1970; Bhattacharya 1998). These instances underline the importance of going beyond the debate on the concept of indigenous people and the necessity of focussing on the study and the chronicling of movements and changes. These examples suggest that the concept of the indigenous people is, at best, ambiguous.

That the issue of the definition of indigenous people is ambiguous becomes especially clear in the Indian context. More mileage can be accrued if the issue, which shows indication of being sustained by sections of society, is probed and explored for understanding how different sections of the Indian population are affected by the nomenclature of the "indigene". The few movements that we have mentioned are areas of intense economic activity (considering the amount of money involved in sustaining the movements), and it therefore seems that the sustaining power of a movement depends more on economics than on social awareness.

Being defined as solely indigenous in nature makes these movements problematic: there are too many extraneous forces of interest, need and recourse of coming into public notice that shape them from within and without. This contributes to the "unequal" and "partisan" appreciation, appropriation and response to change. We cite here the example of a group living in the Andamans—Jarawa. The Jarawas are a monolingual hunting gathering community belonging to the Asiatic Negritos (for details on the Jarawas see Sarkar 1990). They are unaware of much of the modern world. In various national and international fora, issues regarding them have been raised. The issues include their land rights, laws of trespass (outsiders straying into their territory) and other rights (caused due to their endangered nature; the population being only 256 as per Expert Committee Report on the Jarawas, 2004) related to the fact of their indigenousness. Although the Jarawas are not even aware of the rights and provisions of other indigenous people, attempts have been made to thrust these on them without giving them a choice to choose their own course of life. Observations of the team of the Anthropological Survey of India working on the Jarawa problems and issues reveal that the Jarawas show a natural tendency to avail themselves of the resources utilized by their neighbours, a section of the mainstream population (for detail refer to Mukhopadhyay, Bhattacharya and Sarkar 2002). It is becoming increasingly difficult to contain them in their indigenous resource base at the present moment despite the fact that contact with the outsiders is posing to be a source of potential danger to their health.

Discussion

The above analysis is a dispassionate probe into the process of change within otherwise marginalized people in India, but there remains the gray area of the concept of indigenous people. The point that we would like to make is, however nebulous or debatable the concept of indigenous people is, it must be accepted that certain groups of people have taken it on, or have been given this identity and that they are part of certain movements or are expected to be part of these movements. The leaders have armed themselves with this "ideological ammunition" in the context of reshaping their identity and have also acquired the necessary charisma to attract more of their own group as well as other groups of people to their "causes". In this way they seem to have acquired powers of agency and negotiation vis-à-vis their own and the others.

To see the other side, in the event of affirmative action and positive discrimination reaching the target group, albeit in a trickling manner, the emerging elites among the target groups have equipped themselves to avail of the major benefits. They are not defined by their ethnicity alone but by their membership in a class at times cutting across boundaries of their individual social categories. It is in this context that we would like to assert that it will be of little purpose to remain at the level of defining or debating on the concept of indigenous people, rather it would help in enriching knowledge if the process of emergence of such categories that are active is recognized. They are also playing a role that is important in understanding and studying the nation (India) in process. India is a large country that is rhetorically united but in reality sustains enormous diversity and constitutes peoples who have the capacity to live with each other. The strength of this nation lies in its diversity and plurality. In this diversity the ancient, the modern and the post-modern exist side by side. The emergence and convergence of common goals, intentions and interests inevitably would take time. Comparable situation can be observed in the writings of B.K. Roy Burman (1969, 1971). The movements are voices raised in consequence of converging tendencies but the diversions are created by extraneous forces (within economy, in interest group formation and its strengthening) that act both from within and outside.

To sum up, it becomes evident that the debate on the concept of indigenous people can be interminable in terms of reasoning and logic because it has so many dimensions and because there are so many arguments for and against the issue. These do not seem to be able to take the issue to any logical resolution. There can be no doubt however about the importance of this issue as it is a part of a process of transformation in local as well as global perspectives. It behoves upon the scholars, administrators, planners and the others concerned to put in efforts in understanding the dynamics of such politico-social movements and processes for the furtherance of knowledge and for comprehending the subtleties of collective responses to change and transformation.

In all these efforts let there be sharing of the honours and recognition of insights gained from all that have guided the search for knowledge. Let us look at the gestalt of situations in which the relative strengths and weaknesses of aspects of people can be seen not in isolation but as part of the world as a whole. Therefore at least in the case of India, which has a composite society, this need not be so daunting a task.

REFERENCES

Basu, Sajal (1994). *Jharkhand Movement—Ethnicity and Culture of Silence*, Indian Institute of Advanced Studies, Simla.

Beteille, Andre (1970). "Caste and Political Group Formation in Tamilnadu", in Rajni Kothari (ed.) *Caste in Indian Politics*, Delhi: Orient Longman Ltd. pp 259-298.

———,——— (1998). "The Idea of Indigenous People", *Current Anthropology*, 39, 2, April. pp. 187-191.

Bhattacharya, Kumkum (1998). "History, Reality and Relevance: Study of Indian Villages", *The Visva-Bharati Quarterly*, 7, 2, July-September. pp. 57-64.

Bhattacharya, R. K. and Bhattacharya, Kumkum (1996). "Santhal Identity in Transition", in K.K. Chakravarty (ed.) *Tribal Identity in India: Extinction or Adaptation!* Indira Gandhi Rashtriya Manav Sangrahalaya, Bhopal, India, pp. 58-65.

Bhattacharya, Kumkum and R.K. Bhattacharya (2003). "Tribes –State of Mind?" in *Journal of the Indian Anthropological Society*, Vol. 38, Nos. 2 & 3 pp. 159-165.

Bose, Nirmal Kumar (1949). *Hindu Samajer Gadan* (in Bengali), Visva-Bharati Library, Calcutta.

——,——— (1953). *Cultural Anthropology and other Essays*, Calcutta, Indian Associated Publishing Co. Ltd.

——,——— (1972). *Some Indian Tribes*, National Book Trust, India, New Delhi.

Dalton, E. T. (1872). *Descriptive Ethnology of Bengal*, Calcutta, Government Printing Press.

Dumont, Louis (1972). *Homo Hierarchicus*, Paladin, London.

Furnivall, J. S. 1967, *Netherlands India, A study of Plural Economy*. Library of Congress Catalogue Card Number: 39-20815. First Published 1939.

Glazer, Nathan and Moynihan, Daniel P. (1975). *Ethnicity*, Massachusetts, Harvard University Press.

Kothari, Rajni (1970). *Caste in Indian Politics*, Delhi, Orient Longman Ltd.

Kroeber, A. L. 1952, "The Ancient Oikumene", *The Nature of Culture*, Chicago University Press, USA. p. 392.

Miller, Beatrice D. (1969). "Revitalization Movements: Theory and Practice—As evidenced among the Buddhists of Maharashtra", in M.C. Pradhan, R.D. Singh, P.K. Misra and D.B. Sastry (ed.) *Anthropology and Archaeology: Essays in Commemoration of Verrier Elwin*, New Delhi, Oxford University Press, pp. 108-126.

Mukherjee, D.P. and Mukherjee, S.P. (1982). "Contemporary Cultural and Political Movements among the Bodos of Assam", in K.S. Singh (ed.) *Tribal Movements in India*, Vol. 1, Delhi, Manohar, pp. 253-280.

Mukhopadhyay, K, R.K. Bhattacharya and B.N. Sarkar(eds.) (2002). *Jarawa Contact: Ours with them and theirs with us*. Kolkata, Anthropological Survey of India.

Panchbhai, S. C. (1983). "The Jharkhand Movements among the Santals", in K.S. Singh(ed.) *Tribal Movement in India*, Vol. 2. Delhi, Manohar Publications, pp. 31-52.

Radhakrishnan, S. (1965). *Hindu View of Life*, London, Unwin Books.

Risley, H.H. (1891). *The Tribes and Castes of Bengal*, Calcutta, Bengal Secretariat Press.

———, —— (1915). *The People of India*, Calcutta and Simla, Thacker, Spink and Co.

Roy Burman, B. K. (1961). "Meaning and Process of Tribal Integration in a Democratic Society", *Sociological Bulletin.* No. 10, pp. 30-40.
———, —— (1970). "Sociology of National Integration", *Journal of Indian Anthropological Society,* 5, pp. 41-56.
Sarkar, Jayanta Kumar (1990). *The Jarawa,* Calcutta, Seagull Books.
Sen, Jyoti (1976). "The Jharkhand Movement", in K.S. Singh (ed.) *Tribal Situation in India,* Indian Institute of Advanced Studies, Simla, pp. 432-437.
Sinha, S. C. (1962). "State Formation and Rajput Myth in Tribal Central India", *Man in India,* 42, 1 January-March, pp. 35-80.
Srinivas, M. N. (1962). *Caste in Modern India and other Essays,* Bombay, Asia Publishing House.
Xaxa, Virginius (1999). "Tribes as Indigenous People of India", *Economic and Political Weekly,* December 18. pp. 3589-3595.

6

Dormitories in the Life of the Wanchos of Arunachal Pradesh

SARIT K. CHAUDHURI and NOKKAI WANGSAHAM

Dormitory is a unique traditional institution found among tribes across the world. In the context of India such an institution is found among the tribes of South-Western and Central, Eastern as well North-Eastern India. In fact, four distinct types of bachelor's dormitories are found in India viz. *Dhumkuria* associated with the Oraons of Chota Nagpur, *Ghotul* of the Murias of Bastar, *Morung* of the Nagas and *Moshup* of the Adis (Guha 1964:2). In spite of having some commonalties, such dormitories reflect variations which are culture specific. In the context of North East India, large number of tribes are reported to have dormitories, such as, Nagas, Kukis, Garos, Lalungs etc. and even Gurdon (1914:196) reported that the Lynngam of the Khasi Hills were having male dormitory which is not found among the other sections of Khasis of Meghalaya (Elwin 1991 : 284-289).

Coming to Arunachal Pradesh, such institution played a dominant role in the life of the Adis, Noktes and Wanchos. It is completely faded out among the Tangsas, Sherdukpens, Singphos, Khamptis and Apatanis. Each tribe has its own term for such almost similar institutions. For instance Minyong call it *Dere,* Padam *moshup,* Milan *Hgaptek* and Boris and Ashings call it *Bange* or *Gango,* Noctes call it *Poh,* Wanchos call it *Pa* and *Zipsam,* and Tangsas call it *Looppong*.

In the context of Arunachal Pradesh dormitory can be perceived as a glaring example of vanishing traditional institution remnants of which are still traceable among some tribes.

The present paper concentrates on the dormitories of the Wanchos focusing on the structural and functional implications of those in their life. The study is based on the field work done in Senua, Zedua and Pumao villages and various literature published on the Wanchos.

Locating the Wanchos

The Wanchos are one of the major tribes of Arunachal Pradesh. The community occupied the western the Tisa River in the Tirap district. The main concentration of the Wancho population is in the Longding, Kanubari, Pongchau and Wakka circles of the district. According to the 1981 Census the population of the community was 32,441, spread over nearly 54 villages[1]. The Wancho area is bounded on the north-west by the Sibsagar district of Assam, on the south and the west by the Mon district of Assam, and on the south-east by the Khonsa sub-division of the Tirap district. Almost the entire area is mountainous and is covered with dense forests. It is rich in flora and fauna (Ahmad, 1995 : 400).

The villages are generally thickly populated and are situated on the top of the hills. The boundaries of the villages are well demarcated by the rivers, rivulets and streams. The climate varies considerably from place to place due to the mountainous terrain. The climate is cool in the higher altitudes, but it is moderate and pleasant in the lower altitudes. The rainfall in the region is generally heavy (ibid). They are affiliated to the Tibeto-Burman family of languages though there is a significant variation between the language spoken by the Wanchos in the upper regions and that in the lower ones. Of course, today majority of the people are multilingual and communicate either in Hindi, English or even in Assamese.

The Wancho society is divided into two distinct social divisions: the chiefs and the commoners. The chiefs are called *Wangham* and the commoners are known as *Wangpan*. There are two other groups as well, the *Wangsa* and *Wangsu*, whose social status falls in between the *Wangham* and *Wangpan* groups. *Tangjan*

---

[1] Manlong (2004 : 11) writes that there are about 42000 Wanchos living in more than 50 villages. Whereas Sompha (2004 : 22) mentions that Wanchos constitutes of 50, 128 souls as per 2001 census.

and *Tsangjan* are the two major social divisions of the community based on the places where they migrated from.

The chief of a village generally marries the *wangsa* (the daughter of the chief of another village). The children born of a *Wangham* father (king) and a *wangsa* mother (queen) will have the privilege of becoming a *Wangham* or a *wangsa* because only they carry the sacred and pure royal blood. The children born of a *Wangham* father and a *Wangpan* mother are known as *Wangsa*. The *Wangsus* are the descendants of a *Wangsa* father and *Wangpan* mother. In terms of social hierarchy, the *Wanghams* occupy the first position, the *Wangsas* occupy the second position and the *Wangsus* are next. The *Wangpan* group is considered the lowest. The chief's sons born of a *Wanghpan* mother are entitled to hold certain positions in society. On the occasion of social festivals the *Wangpans* are not allowed to take meals sitting in the same row with the *Wanghams*.

The major resources are land, forests and water. The primary occupation of the people is jhum cultivation though some of them have adopted wet and terrace cultivations also. Rice, millet and maize are the main crops. Weaving, hunting, fishing, making bead necklaces, wood carving, cane work and basketry are their subsidiary occupations. The mode of transaction is cash in the semi-urban areas, while the barter system persists in the villages. These days most of the people are inclined towards government jobs, contract works and business activities.

The traditional village administration is known as *ngowang* (village council), headed by the *wangham* (chief). The post of the *wangham* is hereditary. The council consists of several officials: *wangham, wangsu, wangsa* and *rampo-rampa.* The *wangham* selects the other members of the council. The chief cannot be removed from his office by anyone, but the other members can be removed if they are found guilty. The council is supposed to maintain the law and order in the village. The council members settle all kinds of disputes—those related to land, theft, marriage and divorce. Physical or corporal punishment was given to the offenders earlier, but these days a fine is imposed, either in cash or kind.

Oriya is the main festival and it is celebrated for a good harvest and better health for everyone. The festival continues for five to ten days. Earlier it was celebrated in all the villages on different dates, but now it is celebrated yearly on a community basis in

March or April. Besides *Orya,* the Wanchos have a number of small festivals like *Panjum* or *Pangram, Sacha van,* and *Chaksal:* The last one is celebrated at the different stages of the agricultural operations. Animal sacrifice and dancing by boys and girls are parts of each stage of the festival.

The Wanchos specialize in wood carving and the art of dyeing goat's hair with the help of a local herb. They are skilled in basketry, pottery and weaving. They make bead necklaces with attractive designs. They have oral traditions in the form of folk songs and tales.

The community has traditional trade relations with the people of Burma and Nagaland and also had a close barter trade with the Noctes. They used to get salt in exchange of commodities like bamboo tubes, baskets, mats, opium and many other local products. Now they depend on the market for utensils, clothing, sugar, meat, fish, tea, salt and vegetables. Most of the businessmen in their area are non-tribals who run the markets though some of the Wancho women have started selling some of their hill products at the local markets. Most the school teachers, medical personnel and government officials are non-tribals. Besides trade links, they have matrimonial relations with the Noctes, Tangsas, Adis and Assamese. Earlier they never accepted food items from their neighbouring communities, nor did they have matrimonial relations with outsiders.

Orya is the main festival which is celebrated for a good harvest from the jhum land. It is usually celebrated at the beginning of spring and continue for the whole season in different Wancho inhabited areas along with singing, dancing, eating and drinking. Besides *Onya,* the Wanchos have a number of small festivals and all these collectively reflect a repository of Wancho oral tradition. Wood carving, weaving, bead necklace making can be considered as some of the identity markers of the community.

Structural Aspects

Dormitories of the Wanchos can be classified in to two broad categories; one is made for the males viz. *Paa* and another is made for females viz. *Zipsam Ham.* One of the unique features of Wancho dormitory is that once one Wancho individual becomes its member then he remains as member till death. Naturally traditional notion of bachelor's dormitory does not match with such male dormitory (*Paa*).

Each village has more than one dormitory (both boys and girls); generally at least three are evident. Wancho villages are divided into two main divisions, which may be further sub-divided into smaller divisions, which are called *Jong*. Each such *Jong* has one male's dormitory. But number of girl's dormitory is not always dependent on the number of *Jong*. Number of total girls in a village determines the number of *Zipsam*.

Depending one the number of houses with in a particular *Jong* the number of girl's dormitories varies. Out of these large numbers of male dormitories Chiefs dormitory is known as *Panu*. Dutta (1990; 159) mentioned that the chiefs dormitory is called *Wangham Pa*, which has two *Morungs*, *Panu* and *Pasa* under it.

It is customary for the Wanchos that whenever new villages were established *Panu* (Chiefs dormitory) was constructed first by the village people. Then villagers met together at *Panu* to discuss the various aspects in relation to the establishment of a new village.

Male dormitory, which plays the pivotal role in the Wancho society, has a complete separate structure. Whereas female dormitory does not have any separate establishment as it is located within the house of any Wancho villager. Generally the number of daughters as well as easy accessibility of a particular house and the space available within a house are important criteria to decide the location of a *Zipsam* or girls dormitory.

Almost all male dormitories follow a basic structural similarity though slight variation from one *Paa* to another can be noticed; especially in case of the *Panu*. A rough diagram of a male dormitory (*Paa*) is given in order to have some basic idea about the ground plan of a *Paa* and the distribution of internal space.

Ground plan of a *Paa* is attached herewith to have an idea about the division of space inside the *Paa*.

Description of different segments of *Paa* is given below:

1. *Khokha:* This space is utilized for keeping firewood. It is placed between the *Noi* and the *Kaatuk* (wall).
2. *Paa Saam:* It is the place where the *Kham* (log drum) is kept. It is along the wall but opposite to the *Noi*.

3. *Noi*: It is the room where the members use to sleep. During *Lauden* festival this room is also used for preparing food.
4. *Phong Kha:* This is the fireplace on the ground part of the *Paa*. This place is between the *Waading* and the *Noi*.
5. *Wadding*: *Wadding* is the bamboo-matted floor above the ground level. This is the place where members gather together. Guests are also received here. Youths sleep here by constructing structure like the berth of a train.
6. *Kamtap:* This is also a fireplace on the *Waading*. A frame of wood is placed which is filled up within mud to make it a fireplace. Generally the *Wangham* and the *Wangsas* are seated here during the *Lauden* festival whereas the other members sit usually on the *wadding*.
7. *Waakho:* It is an extension of a *Waading* just like a varandah. This is located just at the reverse side of the entrance. Generally boys sit here to take rest at the end of their works.

DISTRIBUTION OF SPACE WITHIN *PAA*

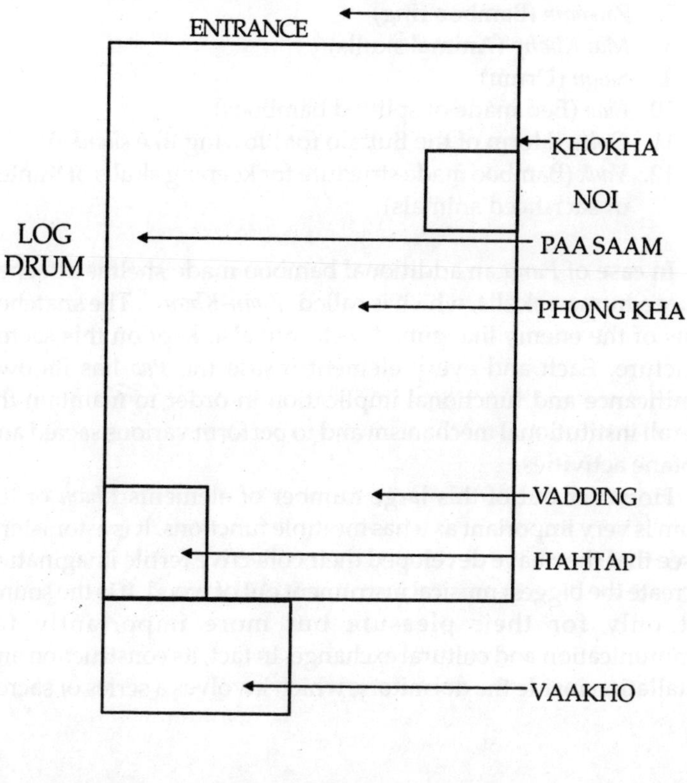

Male dormitories are generally decorated with wood carvings and skulls of different kinds of animals, small as well as big, hunted by the members of a particular *Paa* or scarified during festivals or for other sacred purposes. In this regard *Panu* may have some special attention. During the days of head hunting, skulls were kept inside the *Panu* on bamboo made shelf arranged in rows but sometimes those were just dumped in side the *Panu*.

Items inside the *Paa*

Inside the *Paa* various items are visible which are given below:

1. *Kham* (Log drum)
2. *Kham Thut-Kia* (Beating stick)
3. *Titong* (Wooden seat or stool)
4. *Khokam* (Wooden tray for cutting vegetable and meat etc.)
5. *Sokso* (Bamboo basket)
6. *Sosoh* (Bamboo tube)
7. *Zukaam* (Bamboo ring)
8. *Mai Khang* (Animal skulls)
9. *Saam* (Drum)
10. *Liaa* (Bed made of splitted bamboos)
11. *Oolee* (Horm of the Buffalo for blowing like *shankh*)
12. *Vaak* (Bamboo made structure for keeping skulls of hunted or sacrificed animals)

In case of *Panu* an additional bamboo made shelf is attached to keep human skulls, which is called *'Zaan-Khang'*. The snatched arms of the enemy like gun, *dao* etc. are also kept on this sacred structure. Each and every element inside the *Paa* has its own significance and functional implication in order to maintain the overall institutional mechanism and to perform various sacred and profane activities.

However out of this large number of elements *Kham* or log drum is very important as it has multiple functions. It is astonishing to see that they have developed their collective fertile imagination to create the biggest musical instrument out of wood. It is the source not only for their pleasure but more importantly for communication and cultural exchange. In fact, its construction and installation inside the dormitory, which involves a series of sacred and secular activities, can be perceived as the reflection of their local wisdom. This *Kham* (log drum) is an excellent piece of their traditional craftsmanship, which is gradually fading out. Size of such drum varies from 12 to 30 feet in length made out of a single huge tree (Chaudhuri, 2001).

Unlike the boys, the girls dormitory does not have any separate structure. They make their own arrangements and select a house within the village, preferably of an old widow to pass the night in group. Generally one big room inside such house is used by them. Inside such house they arrange berthlike structure made of bamboos where they sleep at night. In this room they receive boys and exchange gifts. In spite of not having a formal structure like *Paa* the *Zipsam* is a socially sanctioned institution of the unmarried Wancho girls.

Construction of Dormitory

A *Paa* is generally constructed by its members though in some cases members of neighbouring dormitory may be invited to assist. However in case of the construction of Chief's dormitory (*Panu*) all villagers get involved. Such a construction is a big affair for the Wanchos. Naturally, *Jong* members or villagers celebrate such occasion with great feast with dancing and singing. Dutta (1990; 160) has given description about the construction of a *Paa* which he has observed at Longkhaw village in 1958. His observation is given below:

The Pajan morung was constructed on 18th November, 1958. The members of Ngotjong Pa helped in the construction. Generally two morungs participated in the work. All expenditure on fooding was born by Pajan morung. The members of ngotjong morung brought only one bamboo each.

Before the work was started an old member of Pajan morung, who is called Aje pa, performed a ritual called Wanula Jangsa Kole in which he made offering to Bau-jong the supreme God of the Wanchos. The ritual was performed to the east of the plot where the morung was to be constructed. The articles included in the offering consisted of little quantity of rice-beer, few pieces of Sali (a jungle creeper), little quantity of sugar, few seeds of chilli, few pieces of ginger and four numbers of jungle leaf commonly called 'Kau pat'. A container was made with one kau pat where the rice-beer was poured, and on another kaupat, the Sali pieces were kept. The other articles i.e. sugar, chilli seeds and ginger were equally divided and kept on two leaves, one in the name of Bau and the other for Jong. It may be mentioned that according to Wancho belief Bau and Jong are two different identities. The Aje-pa then muttered some incantation. The articles were placed on the ground and no altar or any structure was made for the purpose. After the ritual was over, construction work was taken up. Aje pa then took his share of food after the ritual.

In the morning all people gathered there for construction. The morungs were entertained with tea, banana, orange, sugarcane, biscuits and vegetable curry of banana sucker with blood of pig. The share of each person was one mug of tea, two bananas, three oranges, one small piece of sugarcane, one small packet of biscuit and little quantity of vegetable curry. Sali—consisting of betel nut, betel leaf, lime, tobacco and a piece of jungle creeper was given to all after the tea. Each Sali was carefully tied with a piece of fibre. It was informed that this system of giving tea was a recent adoption. Earlier they used to entertain the people with local drink and cooked rice. The articles were brought from Sapekhati market for which few young boys of Pajen morung went down a week before. Few young boys were in charge of entertainment. The young girls helped the boys in serving the articles. The entertainment was done in batches. After the tea all, except the children become busy in their work.

At 11 O'clock all the people of the morung took their lunch. It was a big feast with rice, rice-beer, meat and vegetable curry. The people of Pajen morung killed one mithun and one big sized pig for mid-day and evening meal. The construction of the morung was completed by 7 O'clock in the evening, and after that evening meal was served. Rice-beer was served to all in plenty. Meal was served by the young girls of the morung and they were helped by six old ladies. Cooking was done entirely by women.

Towards late evening all young boys came to the morung in ceremonial dress—for dancing. The boys of Ngat jongpa morung came in procession to take part in the dance. Merry making and dancing continued till late hours of the night. Rice-beer and Sali was served during the course of dancing also. All members of the village witnessed the dance. Although women are not allowed to enter the morung on other days but on the day of its construction no such restriction is imposed. To drive away the evil spirits a chicken was sacrificed on the next day in the name of Bau-jong. After these sacrifices women are not allowed entry to the morung.

Membership of a Dormitory

As per the social norm each and every male member of a village has to be the member of a *Paa* for which generally they take admission at a very tender age following a ceremony called *Paaden.* However, the Wanghams takes such membership only after attaining the adolescent stage. Similarly *Paaden* of commoners and *Paaden* of the Wanghams differ in terms of items viz. rice-beer, rice, chilly, pork, chicken, bamboo shoot, salt, etc. as well as of the rituals and other processes involved for performing such ceremony. Parents of a *Paa Nawlee* have to share many responsibilities for the ceremony of *Paaden* and it is also linked with their festival called Lauden. After completion of such ceremony a new member of a dormitory *(Paa)* is called *Paa Nawlee.* They need to follow instructions of senior members as well as the rules of *Paa* as per their tradition.

In case of girls in order to take membership of *Zipsam* a ceremony called *Khiatham* is performed. A Wancho girl becomes eligible for membership in a dormitory after the first sign of menstruation. This *Khiatham* is performed in their cultivable field generally at the time of first seed sowing. Generally an aged lady along with the mother of the girl and other members of a particular *Zipsam* accompany the girl for performing such ceremony where she wears a loincloth for the first time which signifies her adulthood. This ceremony follows lot of rituals and then that girl returns to her own house in a village and form that particular day onwards she becomes the members of a *Zipsam.* On the night of *Khiatham* that girl has to go to her *Zipsam* and boys from different *Paas* usually come to sing songs and to cut jokes, etc.

Functions of Dormitories

1. Traditionally the male members of a village gather in the *Panu* to discuss variety of matters related to village life. The price of various items viz, bamboo, *toko* leaf, pig,

chicken and even the *jhum* field are finalised in the *Panu*. In case of the clearing of the village routes people gather inside the *Panu* to decide the responsibilities of different *Jong* members. The decision about community hunting, fishing, construction of *Panu*, construction of chief's house etc. are taken inside the *Panu*. In all these cases after long discussion the Chief gives final verdict in consultation with the *Ngo-Wang* (village council).

2. Every evening after returning from fields the Wancho youths generally gather inside their respective *Paas* and chat by sitting around the fireplace. Besides discussing several matters, they also plan which *Zipsam* to visit at night. They crack jokes and make fun during such gathering.
3. *Paa* is an association where every male member of a village has to be a member following their traditional norms. Each such member needs to abide by the rules and regulation of a *Paa*. Only the eldest members as well as the Wanchams enjoy some special privilege in a *Paa* while dining or drinking.
4. *Paa* also used as the village court. Disputes between members of a same *Paa* are settled in that particular *Paa*. But disputes between members of two different *Paas* are settled at the *Panu* with the intervention of their village council. The *Paa* is a guardhouse for the village and the young members always remain alert. In case of any emergency such as fire or any other exigencies, the log drum inside the dormitory is beaten and immediately people rush to the spot for necessary help. During the days of head hunting dormitory played a very significant role to counter in case of any enemy attack and also in case of any plan for raid to enemy village.
5. *Paa* is also the centre for learning art and craft.[2] Generally older members teach younger member the art of basket making, woodcarving, beating of log drums etc.

[2] In order to understand the linkages between art of woodcarving and dormitory in relation to the Wanchos one can look at the article by Chaudhuri (2005).

6. *Paa* is a sacred place for the Wanchos. After attending a fire accident or even after visiting a dead body one should enter in their respective *Paas* before entering into houses. This act is perceived as an act of purification by the Wanchos.
7. Like *Paa, Zipsam* is also a place where women learn the art of weaving and many other works. *Zipsam* has it own rules and it members have to follow certain functions. The members work together for the houses under a particular *Jong* viz. agricultural land. They also observe a fuel gathering ceremony (Dutta 1990, 164).
8. One of the *most* important aspects of *Zipsam* is that it is the place where folk songs are sung by both boys and girls following a specific pattern. Baruah (1981; i) mentioned that low songs of the Wanchos, specially sung in the dormitory are very melodious, rich in thoughts and beautiful ideas. With the deepening of night, after relaxing in *Paas,* the boys generally visit the *Zipsam* in small groups. In *Zipsam* new lovers present each other with *Chali* (chewing bask) and lime, the girls may comb the hairs of their lovers, and in course of time, courtship is carried on with songs. Usually, the boy first starts singing a song to the girl of his fancy expressing his love and yearning for her and the girl who receives his attention, gives an appropriate reply through her melodious song. It leads to a contest of songs in the form of questions and reply between them and it goes on. On most of such occasion singing is accompanied by dancing where the boys and girls, holding each other form a circle and following the rhythm of songs, move round and round in slow steps.

Norms of Dormitories

Members of the *Paa* and *Zipsam* have to follow large number of norms, which are socially sanctioned. Some of such norms are mentioned below:

1. The boys strictly follow dormitory exogamy and a boy and a girl of the same *Jong* can never marry.

2. Girls are not allowed to enter into the *Paa* at any context except the minor girls.
3. It is compulsory for the *Paa* members (*Paa* youths) to sleep inside the *Paa.* They can only sleep in their house after their marriage.
4. While sleeping inside the *Paa,* a commoner (Wangpan) cannot sleep on the berth, which is placed above the Wangsu, Wangsa, Wangham. Always the Wangsu, Wangsa, Wamgham are given preference to sleep on the top most berths inside the sleeping room.
5. In case of the death of a *Paa* member the other members have to shoulder large number of duties to bury the same.
6. During the days of head hunting, after a successful raid enemy skulls had to be kept inside the male dormitory and those skulls had to be fed ceremonially every year.

Conclusions

From the whole discourse it is evident that both boys and girls dormitories provide lifeline of the Wanchos. These are the institution through which socialization takes place and as a result people became aware of the various norms and values of their society.

In agriculture, religion, traditional polity, sharing of collective responsibilities at the *Jong* at village level, dormitories play a very crucial role.

During the days of head hunting the very question of survival of a village in case of every attack depended on how effectively the villagers organized themselves by using intricate mechanisms to guard house located strategically in any village.

Moreover, it works as a centre of traditional knowledge and transmission of such indigenous knowledge.

However, like many other tribes of Arunachal Pradesh the Wanchos are also passing through the process of transition. And as a result such a vibrant and dominant traditional institution is at the crossroads. Undoubtedly emergence of Christianity remains one of the dominant factors but there are many other factors too, which have cumulatively remained responsible for such an emerging reality. On the issue of relevance of *Paa* and *Zipsam* today,

Wanchos are divided. Does revivalism of dormitory is possible? Whether with certain reforms dormitories can provide a model institution to address many contemporary issues of the Wancho society and culture?

These are some of the dominant questions which will decide the plight of such unique institutions?[3]

REFERENCES

Baruah, T.K.M. (1981). *Wancho Love Songs,* Directorate of Research, Shillong.

Chaudhuri, S.K. (2001). *Beating the Drum and Weaving through the Sodal Spaces.* Paper presented in a Seminar on "Indigenous knowledge system of the Tribes of North East India: Implications and emerging issues held on 15-16 February, 2001 organized by the Department of Tribal Studies, Arunachal University.

Chaudhuri, S.K. (2005). Tribal Art in Contemporary Arunachal Pradesh: A study of Wanchos of Arunachal Pradesh. In T.B. Subba and S. Som (eds), *Between Ethnography and Fiction: Verrier Elwin and the Tribal Question in India.* Orient Longman, New Delhi, pp. 185-200.

Dutta, P. (1990). *The Wanchos,* Directorate of Research, Itanagar.

Dutta, P. and S.I. Ahmed (1995). *People of India: Arunachal Pradesh,* Seagull Books, Calcutta.

Elwin, V. (1991). *The Muria and their Ghotul,* OUP, Calcutta.

Guha, B.S. (1964). *Moshup Abang,* Directorate of Research, Shillong.

Gurdon, P.R.T. (1914). *The Khasis,* London.

Ralongham, M. (2004). Origin and Migration of Wanchos, in *Wanchounu-* Souvenir of 29th Wancho Oriah Festival.

Wangpan, S. (2004). The Wanchos of Arunachal Pradesh, in *Wanchounu-* Souvenir of 29th Wancho Oriah Festival.

[3] This paper is an outcome of a UGC sponsored minor project on the Dormitories of Wanchos sanctioned by the Rajiv Gandhi University authority to S.K. Chaudhuri who likes to acknowledge the help extended by the villagers and specially, Sanwang Wangsa, Sompha Wangsa, Nokkai Wangsaham and Pachoi Wangsa

7

Marriage that was in Manipur

OINAM RANJIT SINGH

The establishment of the institution of marriage is a landmark in the history of mankind. Such institution did not exist among the primitive people. In the early days promiscuity was well founded and sex life was absolutely free.

As civilization advanced, people gave up habit of frequently moving from one place to another in search of food. They started to lead settled life. At this stage food gathering economy turned to food producing economy. In the food producing stage men began to lead some regulated life. In the food gathering stage the sex relationships was promiscuous. Thus motherhood alone could be the ascertainable parenthood without the trace of definite fatherhood. It was only practicable to ascertain fatherhood when sex relationship became exclusive union of male and female. From promiscuity to monogamy there was a long march from pre-agricultural to agricultural economy in which monogamy and monogamous marriage were institutionalised. Thus marriage as an exclusive union of man and woman did not emerge at one stroke.[1] The historical process was a prolonged one as mankind procured the knowledge of cattle breeding, agriculture, art and industry and learnt the use natural resources to the best of its advantage. Agriculture was the threshold of civilization. This was also the threshold of regulated sex life. At different places and at various stages of human development, marriage came into existence in different forms. At the beginning promiscuity was permitted within a tribe, i.e. women in the tribe belonged equally to every man and vice versa,[2] but sexual intercourse outside the tribe was not allowed. The later development was the narrowing down of this circle and gradual weaning of promiscuity. The process was initiated by exclusion of sexual relationship within the tribe of the closer relations such as mothers and sons and then brothers and sisters. This process of exclusion gradually extended to distant relations, till finally a stage was achieved when there remained only a couple, united in marriage. In the beginning this was possibly a union loosely uniting the couple, the dissolution of the union being as simple matter as entering it.[3] They enjoyed freedom of separation and no formalities were required in this regard. The recorded history of early Roman civilization reveals that marriage and divorce were easy matters.

When humanity came to the patriarchal stage, marriage as an exclusive union came to be firmly established through the exclusive union of male and female. Generally in the patriarchal society women came under absolute power of man. In the course of man's ascendancy to power; marriage institution emerged as an exclusive institution for this union. The concept of marriage as sacrosanct also came up with the emergence of the marriage institution that legitimized procreation of children. Marriage is defined by Edward Westermark as the "more or less durable connection between male and female, lasting beyond the mere act of procreation till after the birth of offspring."[4] D.N. Majumdar and T.N. Madan stated that, "Every kind of human grouping comes into being, and is maintained, through a process of recruitment by which various persons become its members. In every human family the majority of its members are recruited into it by being born into it. But before children are born, some women in patrilocal societies; man in matrilocal societies must be recruited into it. A family comes into being through such a communication of spouses. Marriage is the socially recognized form of such recruitment through communication."[5] They further said that "The possibilities of sex-gratification, irregular and institutionalized, outside the family being present in every society, the conclusion becomes compelling that, although regularized and socially sanctioned sex-gratification is a basic reason for the formation of the family and the institution of marriage, yet it is not the only, nor the final cause. Satisfaction of the sexual life is implied in a healthy and normal physical survival, but the exact manner this satisfaction takes place is decided by the cultural traditions of a people. Bio-psychic needs always present themselves to us as culturally reoriented drives. Besides, sex-gratification is not the only purpose of man's existence, and therefore, not the only cultural end to which marriage is directed. .... Marriage ensures a biological satisfaction (that of sex) and a psychological satisfaction (that of having children) on the individual plane; on the wider collective plane, it ensures a twofold survival, *viz.*, that of the group and its culture."[6]

According to L.H. Morgan, in the beginning there was no marriage institution among human beings.[7] From promiscuity, human society evolved group marriages. At that stage all the brothers of a family used to marry all the sister of another family so that every male was equally the husband of every female and vice-versa. Another stage in the evolution of marriage was monogamy with sufficient freedom to establish extra marital relationships particularly with the female members of the bride's family. In the last stage of the evolution of marriage man could marry more than one woman and the stage of monogamy preceded polygamy.[8] But Bachofen says that the early stage was promiscuous.. The progress in agriculture led to the establishment of more prosperous agriculturist males permanently living at one place. They were encouraged to take recourse to polygamy. Condemning the mentioned views Westermark observed that only one type of marriage is available in animal and human societies and that is monogamy. In fact it is not easy to establish any theory in this field. However some sort of evolution must be admitted. The institution of marriage evolved through several stages. It is stated that marriage and family were supposed to have evolved from primitive promiscuity through various forms of plural marriage to monogamy.[9]

The forms of marriage that prevailed among the ancient Manipuris (Meiteis) may be studied under the following heads:

- *Polyandry*: It is a form of marriage wherein a female marries several males at a time. Polyandry is of two kinds: (a) Fraternal polyandry. In this form of polyandry one wife is considered the wife of all brothers who have sexual relation with her and (b) Non-fraternal polyandry. In this form a female has many husbands with whom she cohabits in turn. It is not necessary that husbands be brothers. N. Birchandra Singh states that the system of polyandry existed among the Manipuris (Meiteis) in ancient days before the introduction of the present system.. There was a heritage of matrilineal form of society in Manipur, in which polyandry was a prevailing form of marriage. The system patrilineal has succeeded a matrilineal society.[10] In the early stage of civilization women were totally free in their married life. According to tradition, some of the ancestors (Lairembis) left their husbands without any information or at will and cohabited with another one. Sooner or later they came back to their former husbands either by inducement or by some other means.[11] It is said that Nongthang Leima was the wife of both Sanamahi and Pakhnagba.[12] Laikhurembi was the chief queen of Thongaren but she was handed over to Nongda Lairen Pakhangba by changing her name as Laishna.[13] This woman had elicit connection with Khaba Panthongba and Khuiyoitompok was born out of this. So she had three husbands. They were Thongarel, Nongda Lairen and Khaba Panthongba.[14] Lainaotabi also had three husbands. Thongarel, Poireiton and Nongbal Pombi Luwaoba[15]. The Meitei mythology revealed that there was a system of sharing common wife or taking the wife of elder brother by younger brothers during the life time of the elder brother or after his death. Such system testifies the prevalence of polyandry in some sections of the Meitei society in the early days. It was also a common feature to take forcibly the wife of others by the conquerors in war. But it is also fact that the Meitei kings had established 'Pacha-Loishang' (Women Court) to protect the rights and privileges of the women and immoral traffic right from the time of Nongda Lairen Pakhangba (1st Century AD) in whose time, this Court i.e. Pacha-Loishang was presided over by queen Laisna, wife of Pakhangba.[16] The system of Polyandry was prevalent among the ancient Hindus. Hindu mythology refers to the existence of polyandry. Draupadi was married to five brothers called Pandavas. It is known to be widespread in Tebet. The Marquesens of Polynsia, the Todas of Malbar, the Namib Bushmen, the Yararo of Venezuela, some ancient tribes of Malay Penisula are also supposed to have this institution i.e. polyandary.[17]

From Khagemba Yumbi we are able to assess that "Leinung Yaibirok a Yakkha girl who was polyandrous became the wife of three individuals and in turn gave birth to Nongta Lairen Pakhangba". "Leinung girl, Yakkha girl polyandrous Chakkha—a house wife—became wife of three different kings—in turn-Lei-nung Yabiroka begets Nongta, 'chief of Lai' Pakhangba.[18] Ningthourol Lambuba records, "The Grand-mother or Madam Meitei Queen Lei-nung Chakkha Yabirok, is known as polyandrous, handsome and beautiful, the cream of the Leihou and Leimu, the Chakkha who is polyandrous and who becomes wife of three kings successively, by thy name."[19] It seems that the ancient Meiteis were also not an exception to polyandry. But a deep and critical study as well as investigation in this regard in ancient Manipur is very much needed to know whether such system was actually exited in ancient Manipur or not.

- *Polygamy*: Under this system one man marries many women or a male has more than one wife. The system of polygamy is still found existing to some extent in most countries of the world. Previously it was very popular everywhere. It is more frequent than polyandry. Such system existed in Manipur from very beginning of her history. There are many references to the prevalence of polygamy in ancient Manipur. According to T.C. Hodson, "The Meiteis are polygamous, and the Raja may have three principal wives, with as many as one hundred and eight subsidiary partners.[20] Luwang Punshiba, the fourth descendent of Poireiton had nine wives.[21] Pakhangba (33-154 AD) married Laisa-ra or Laisna and he had also another paramour called Konthing Nurabi.[22] Naophangba (428-518 AD) had two wives namely Kaireima, the daughter of Waklen Tongyai, the younger brother of Yoirangpok Punshiba, the king of Thoubal and Yaoreibi of Luwang clan. Kaireima, the Khuman princess gave birth to Sameirang and Yaoreibi was the mother of Thamanglang.[23] Naothingkhong (663-763 AD) married many girls from the neihbouring clan principalities. Some literary sources stated that he had six wives.[24] Thangjing, the progenitor of Moirang clan had two wives, Wangbarel, the progenitor of Khuman clan had seven wives and so on.[25]

Polygamy was very common among the kings, nobles and rich people. Common people also practiced polygamy under certain condition or other reasons including satisfaction of their sex appetite but polygamous person was treated with hatred and abhorrence in general.

- *Monogamy*: Under this system one man marries one woman at a time. It is the dominating form of marriage. This gives the highest type of affection and sincere devotion. Both father and mother provide earnest attention to the up-bringing of their children. Malinowsky said, "monogamy is, has been, and will remain the only true type of marriage."[26] This system of monogamy was commonly observed or performed by the common people as well as kings, nobles or rich in ancient Manipur. It may be considered as an ideal form of marriage and this system was very common among the ancient Manipuris.

There were eight ways of acquiring wives in ancient India, all of which did not strictly conform to the accepted norms of marriage. Nonetheless they have all been considered as different forms of marriage, clearly defining and describing the way each was performed.[27] The eight forms were (i) Brahma: Marriage to a person of same class by father's choice with full ceremony.[28] (ii) Daiva: In this form of marriage the father gives daughter to the sacrificial priest as part of his fee.[29] (iii) Arsha: In this marriage the father gives his daughter in marriage to the bridegroom, after receiving a cow or a bull.[30] (iv) Prajapatya: A marriage without dowry or bride price.[31] (v) Gandharva: It is a marriage by the consent of the two parties or a love marriage. It has sexual intercourse for its purpose.[32] (vi) Asura: Marriage by purchase.[33] (vii) Raksasa: Marriage by capture.[34] (viii) Paisacha: When a man stealthily seduces a girl who is sleeping, intoxicated, or is made disordered in intellect, or abduction of girl when she is asleep or unconscious.[35] Besides these eight forms of marriage, there existed Anuloma and Pratiloma marriages in ancient Indian society. Marriage of a male in his own Varna or below his Varna is known as Anuloma. And when a girl of higher Varna marries a boy of lower Varna it is called Pratiloma.

Among the ancient Manipuries there were various forms of marriage. These are as below:

1. *Marriage by Capture*: An important method of securing a bride in ancient Meiteis society was marriage by capture.[36] This technique is growing rare with social advancement. However, it continues even then as one of the ways of acquiring a mate among the Meiteis. It is said that Taothingmang (264-364 AD), the son of Khuyoi Tompok (154-264 AD) conquered Lokka-Haokha[37] which is identified with an area of the same name near present Sugunu in southeast valley in the east bank of Imphal river.[38] He married a girl named Hao-nu-khu who belonged to a Hao-khu tribe.[39] B. Kullachandra Sharma stated the marriage of Taothingmang with Hao-nu-khu was marriage by capture.[40] The marriage of Chalamba with Khoiron Tharima also may be described as marriage by capture.[41] Kaokhamba (394-411 AD) was succeeded by his son Naokhamba (411-428 AD). He defeated a Chenglei Chief called Thangji Khongchonba and forcibly married his wife Yaorei Leiyathi Khuman Leinamung, a woman belonging to the descendents of the Yaoreiba family of Luwang clan.[42] W.I. Singh speaks that Naokhomba married the wife Thangyi Khongiromba by force or by forced abduction from the custody of her husband.[43] At the time of marriage she was carrying a five month old child. The marriage of Pakhangba (33-154 AD) with Lainaotabi also came under marriage by capture[44]. Thawanthaba (1195-1231AD) captured Kharoi Mende, the sister of Kaklen Thaniha, the chief of Thawa.[45] W.I. Singh says that the girl, called Kharoi Mende was brought and taken her to wife by Thawanthaba[46] by employing the means of capture or force.
2. *Marriage by mutual consent and elopement or love marriage*: An interesting and most commonly practiced way of securing a bride in Manipuri society right from early period to present day is marriage by mutual consent and elopement or love marriage. This system of marriage is

called as Gandharva in ancient Hindu scriptures. We have ample evidences to show the existence of marriage by mutual consent and elopement or love marriage in ancient Manipur. Naothingkhong Phambal Kaba refers to the practice of marriage by mutual consent and elopement.[47] It is said that Naothingkhong ran away from the Kangla at the age of about 10 or 12 years[48] and went to live along the Shelloi Langmeis in Nongmaijing Hill which is situated to the east of the kingdom. Hongnem Yoi Khunjao Naothingkhong (Naothingkhong) was mad in love with Pitang-nga, a Langmai girl and married her (Pitang-nga).[49] They lived in her parent's house. This is a first reference to the matrilocal residence among the Meiteis in the history of Manipur.[50] Naothingkhong (663-763) was the son of Urakonthouba (568-658 AD). Nungbal Pombee Luwaoba refers to love marriage.[51] The marriage of Nungbal Pombee Luwaoba with Koubrol Namoinu falls under this system of marriage (love marriage) as well as arranged marriage.[52] Thangbi Lanthaba's (1302—1324 AD) marriage with Yoiren Tompokpi, daughter of Moirang king Laijing Khu Telheiba may be regarded as marriage by mutual consent and elopement or love marriage.[53] It is stated that Thangbi Lanthaba, the son of Moiramba of the Poirei (Meitei) king ascended the throne in 1302 AD. His mother gave him the name Yoiren Tompok. Thangbi Lanthaba asked for the hand of Yoiren Tompokpi but her father refused to give his daughter in marriage to the Meitei king. Yoiren Tompokpi secretly sent message to the Yoiren Tompokpa through messengers that she was ready to accept the proposal for marriage. On the appointed day Thangbi Lanthaba invaded Moirang and subdued it. Yoiren Tompok or Thangbi Lanthaba got married to Yoiren Tompokpi.[54] From Khongjomnubi Nogarol we come to know that 'six Luwang girls went to purchase fish to a lake. They met six boys who used to catch fish in the lake and sell them to fishwives. The six boys said to them we have not caught any fish and let us stay this night here together. The girls replied "we cannot because our fathers and brothers will beat us if we do that. Still the boys insisted. The girls yielded at last and spent the night with

their lovers in the hut on the shore of the lake'. "Their lovers said in the morning" if your fathers and brothers chastise you, let us ascend heaven together to the feet of Soraren, the King of gods. As anticipated, the girls' fathers and brothers turned them out of their homes for their improper conduct and for having love affairs with a class of people regarded as untouchable in those days ....
The six Luwang women or girls could not find their lovers on the way. They started to climb the hills on the north-western fringe of the Manipur valley. One after another, on their way to heaven—their eyes were anxiously searching for signs of their lover's coming.'[55]Their co-habitation was the system of marriage by mutual consent or love marriage'.[56] The marriage of king Paikhomba (1666—1697 AD) with Maram Chanu Ingalei (girl of Maram) was love marriage.[57]

Thus in the case of marriage by mutual consent and elopement or love marriage the consent of the boy and the girl is very essential. This marriage is done through mutual decision of the boy and the girl. Neither the father nor the kinsmen need have a hand in bringing about the marriage.

3. *Arranged marriage or marriage by engagement*: The most approved form of marriage in Manipur right from ancient days to present day is of course the marriage by engagement or arranged marriage. Among the other types of marriage this marriage is the best and the highest form of marriage. Marriage by engagement is done through parents of the parties with or without the consent of the boy and the girl. Here the consent of both the parents is extremely important. Such marriage was very unexceptional and popular among the Manipuris in ancient period. It is evident from Panthoibi Khongul that when Panthoibi attained marriageable age, Khaba Shokchrongba, the chief of Chenglei and his wife desired to get her (Panthoibi) married to their son Tarang Khoinuch. They sent presents of sweetmeats, fruits etc. to her parents and requested for the hand of Panthoibi for their son.[58] This marriage was a typical example of arranged marriage.[59] Khuyoi Tompok (154-264 AD), the son of Nongda Lairen

> Pakhangba (33-154 AD) married a girl named Langmainu Ahongbi belonging to the Selloy-Langmai tribe who settled on the Langmai-ching. Their marriage was performed through arranged marriage or marriage by engagement.[60] A marriage was arranged between Nungpan Pompi Luwapa and Koubrol Namoinu.[61] It was carried out in accordance with the tradition of arranged marriage or marriage by engagement. Marriages of Naothingkhong (663-763AD) with Ewanglon Namun Chaobee, Meidingu Kainou Irengba (984-1074AD) with Khyoirol Haoreima Tamheib, Taningaowe, the king of Awa (Burma) with Chakpa Makhao Ngambee, the daughter of king Charairongba (1697-1709 AD) of Manipur and so on were included in the group of arranged marriage or marriage by engagement.[62]

In ancient Manipur both payment and non-payment of bride price were followed. We find that the chief of Chenglei and his wife wanted to get Panthoibi married to their son Tarang Khoinucha. They offered her bride price in nice untarnished coins and a pair of nice bullocks.[63] It is equivalent to Arsa of Hindu scriptures. When a Manipuri princess was given in marriage to a Shan ruler of Kabaw valley, the bride price of this princess was seven elephants. She was known as Kabaw Leima Sana Hekpi.[64] During the reign of Paikhomba (1666-1697 AD) a girl from Manipur was married to a chief of Kacharis. A palanquine was given as bride price but her mother refused the bride price and an elephant was given instead.[65] Thus the system of offering or taking bride price was a fashion in the Manipuri society from early period.[66] A marriage without bride price is also mentioned in Hindu scriptures as Prajapatya marriage which is also practised in Manipur.

In ancient time there were major ethnic groups or castes in Manipur. They were Lai, Mee, and Teen.[67] Lai caste claimed themselves as the higher caste. Marriage with low cast people also seems to have prevailed in early days under certain restriction. For example, Konthoujam Lairembi who belonged to a lower caste was taken as wife by Sorarel (Tari) who belonged to a higher castes.[68] This type of marriage may be indentical to the Anuloma of ancient Hindus. Khongchomnubee Nongarol stated that six Luwang girls were turned out by their fathers and brothers for their improper conduct, having love affair and cohabiting with six Haoku Pakhang, a class of people considered as untouchable in those days.[69] The wedlock of six Haoku Pakhang, low caste with six Luwang girls of a higher caste stands in comparison to the Partiloma form of marriage of the ancient Hindus.

At different places and various stages of human development marriage came into existence in different forms. In the Meiteis society, a boy and a girl could become husband and wife through one of the rituals: (a) Luhongba (b) Keinya Katpa and (c) Loukhatpa. It was the custom of the Meiteis that a marriage should not take place within the same Yek (clan) or same Sagei (clan) as it is exogamous. Yek is an exogamous group within which marriage is not allowed. Gangmumei Kabui states that now Yek and Salai are used almost in the same sense. Hence Yek-Salai is within the degree of prohibited relation[70]. It is believed that the marriage rules viz. Yek Salai, Mungnaba, Shairuk Tinnaba, Pee Tinnaba and Pen Tinnaba were adopted during the reign of Pakhangba (33-154 AD). Yek Salai means the kinship relation of the clan and lineages and sub-lineages having a common ancestor. Marriage within the clan was not approved and such restriction was known as Yekthoknaba (having consanguineous kinship). Thus, marriage in early Manipur was a union of the male and female not only to satisfy biological need. Most probably in early days, the rites of Laitin thaba/Apokashathaba (offering of oblation to the ancestors), worshipping of the Almighty, ancestral gods, Lainingthou Sanamahi, local and guardian gods etc, were performed to seek their blessings. The rites of 'Meetam Nga Thaba' (sending away of fish or set free the two fishes in the pond) etc. were dominant features. So, marriage among the Meiteis became an institution having a religious character attached there to.

REFERENCES

1. Dr. Paras Diwan and Peeyushi Diwan (1990). *Modern Hindu Law*, Allahabad, p. 62.
2. *Ibid.*
3. *Ibid.* p. 63.
4. Edward Westermark, *A Short History of Marriage*, London, 1926.
5. D.N. Majumdar and T.N. Madan, *An Introduction to Social Anthropology*, Noida, p. 61.

6. *Ibid*, pp. 67-68.
7. L.H. Morgan (1877). *Ancient Society*, New York.
8. *Ibid*.
9. T.B. Bottomore (1986). *Sociology*, Bombay, p. 180.
10. N. Birchandra Singh (2006). *The Meitei Society*, Delhi, pp. 40-41.
11. *Ibid*. p. 42.
12. *Ibid*.
13. *Ibid*. p. 37.
14. *Ibid*.
15. *Ibid*.
16. Gangmumei Kabui (1991). *History of Manipur*, Vol. I, Delhi, p. 86.
17. Vidya Bhushan and D.R. Sachdeva (1989). *An Introduction to Sociology*, Allahabad, p. 263.
18. *Khagemba Yumbi*, MS; W.I. Singh (1986). *The History of Manipur (An Early Period)*, Imphal, p. 263.
19. *Ningthourol Lambuba*, MS.; *Ibid*. 264.
20. T.C. Hodson (1989). *The Meitheis*, Delhi, p. 76.
21. W.I. Singh, *Op cit*. pp. 330, 535.
22. *Ibid*. p. 537.
23. Oinam Bhogeswar Singh(Ed) (1967). *Ningthourol Lambuba*, Imphal, 1966, p. 16; N. Ibungohal Singh and N. Khelchandra Singh (Ed), *Cheitharol Kumbaba*, Imphal, pp. 2-3.
24. W.I. Singh, *Op cit*. , p. 546.
25. N. Birchandra Singh, *Op cit*. p. 43.
26. B. Malinowski (1944). *A Scientific Theory of Culture and other Essays*, Chapel Hill, univ. of N. Carolina Press.
27. Prabhati Mukherjee (1994). *Hindu Women Normative Models*, Calcutta, p. 52.
28. *Arthasatra* of Kautilya (hereinafter *AS*). 111.2.12; *Manusmrti* of Manu (hereinafter *MS*). p. 111, 27.
29. *Ibid*. *MS*. 111.29.
30. *Ibid*. *MS*. 11.30.
31. *Ibid*. *MS*. 111.27.
32. *AS*. 111.2.13; *MS*.111.32.
33. *Ibid*. *MS*. 111.31.
34. *Ibid*. *MS*. 111.33.
35. *Ibid*. *MS*.111.34.
36. B. Kullachandra Sharma (1998). *Meiteigi Luhongba Amasung Louna Leinabagi Wayel Wakhun*, Imphal, pp. 9, 13 and 15.
37. Gangmumei Kabui. *Op cit*. p. 99.
38. *Ibid*.
39. W.I. Singh, *Op cit*. p. 540.
40. B. Kullachandra Sharma, *Op cit*. pp. 9-10.

41. Ng. Manijao, *Cheengda Shapta Ingalei*, Impahl, (1970); B. Kullachandra Sharma, *Op cit*. p. 10.
42. N. Angou Luwang (Ed) (1983). *Pakhangba Nongkarol*, Imphal, p. 29; O. Bhogeswar Singh (Ed) (1966). *Ningthourol Lambuba*, Imphal, p. 10; *Chengleirol Puya*, MS.
43. W.I. Singh, *Op cit*. p. 541.
44. *Thirel Nanamba Puya*, MS; B. Kullachandra Sharma, *Op cit*. p. 15.
45. Gangmumei Kabui, *Op cit*. p. 133.
46. W.I. Singh, *Op cit*. p. 561.
47. *Naothingkhong Phambal Kaba*, MS.
48. W.I. Singh, *Op cit*. p. 545; Gangmumei Kabui, *Op cit*. p. 107.
49. *Naothingkhong Phambal Kaba* MS.
50. Gangmumei Kabui, *Op cit*. p. 107.
51. *Nongbal Pombi Luwaoba*, MS.
52. B. Kullachandra Sharma, *Op cit*. p. 8.
53. *Ibid*.
54. W.I. Singh, *Op cit*. , p. 352; Gangmumei Kabui, *Op cit*. , p. 136-137.
55. *Khongjomnupee Nongarol*, MS; R.K. Jhaljit Singh. *A History of Manipuri Literature*, vol I. Imphal, 1987. p. 5.
56. B. Kullachandra Sharma, *Op cit*, p. 9.
57. *Ibid*.
58. *Panthoibi Khongul* MS; R.K. Jhaljit Singh, *Op cit*. p. 146.
59. B. Kullachandra Sharma, *Op cit*. p. 11.
60. *Ibid*.
61. *Ibid*, K. Yaima Singh (Ed), *Pakhangba Phambal*, Imphal, 1967, p. 35.
62. *Ibid*, p. 13; O. Bhogeswor (Ed), *Op cit*; B. Kullachandra (Ed), *Thangmoirol*, Imphal, 1989; L. Ibungohal Singh and N. Khelchandra Singh (Ed), *Op cit*, Imphal, 1989, p. 67.
63. *Panthoibi Khongul*, MS; R.K. Jhalajit Singh, *Op cit*. p. 146.
64. Gangmumei Kabui, *Op cit*, p. 207.
65. *Ibid*. p. 229.
66. N. Birchandra Singh, *Op cit*, p. 63.
67. Kh. Chandrasekhar (Ed), *Loiyumba Shilyen*, Imphal, 1975, p. 48; N. Birchandra Singh, *Op cit*. p. 49.
68. *Kongthoujam Nongarol*, MS; N. Birchandra Singh, *Op cit*. p. 48.
69. *Khongchomnupee Nongkarol*, MS; R.K. Jhalajit Singh, *Op cit*. , p. 51.
70. B. Kullachandra Sharma, *Op cit*. p. 69.

8

Student/Youth Movement with Special Reference to North-East India*

S.B. CHAKRABARTI

The presentation starts with a personal context, which takes the author a little down the memory lane. My effective and active student life can be bracketed between 1959-1966 (starting from the Xth standard to post graduation). In the lower classes in school our extra-curricular activities and attention were confined to sports and cultural activities and specially observing the birth anniversaries of the very eminent personalities of the country. These functions gave us different types of stimulations, for example, if it was Netaji Subhas Chandra Bose's martyr or Kshudiram's birthday we usually got a thrill about freedom movement, which we did not personally experience in our own life but a message always used to charge us in that direction; if it was Rabindranath Tagore's birthday we were emotionally engaged in the performance of recitation or songs of Tagore for a few days. In all such cases our minds were released from the usual routine syllabus for sometime and this created lot of impact on our imagination in various directions. But the one example that lifted our thinking on an unusual height was the food movement of 1959. Students of schools, colleges and universities participated in huge number protesting against the police firing, which resulted in the death of a few students on the spot. The background of this movement and the consequent political developments provided a

* A version of this paper was presented at a seminar in the Department of Anthropology, Gauhati University, March, 2007.

political space to a young mind like me and many others to incline towards political activism. This tempo gained momentum with the unimaginable American onslaught perpetrated against the freedom fighters of Vietnam during the sixties. In between these two instances there were occasional communal disturbances apart from the Indo-Chinese and Indo-Pak wars, all during the time span as I have already mentioned. One more important development, by accident, molded my intellectual orientation and that is choosing anthropology course in the post-graduate class with apprenticeship in conducting fieldwork among the disadvantaged tribal groups in the interior rural areas of West Bengal. To be very brief, my active engagement in various political programmes gave me a firm footing to enable me to analyze the macro politico-economic factors behind the national and international events. Simultaneously my exposure to a micro situation with the training in anthropological field investigation gave me an altogether different objective approach in getting into the truth of diverse human inter-relations and interactions by direct observations. Unknowingly, perhaps, this exposure also created a passion of love for various sections of human groups with varied socio-cultural background. Automatically, a sense of appreciation and tolerance for the so-called 'they' induced in me to consider all human/cultural groups specially the weaker sections of populations as part of 'we'. Years passed by. Left political ideology got variously divided. I entered into academic profession at that juncture. Lots of unusual vicissitudes in national and international political arena had taken place since then. Anxiety and agony still accompanied me every now and then, because the dialectics of human nature, the most difficult academic postulate on the earth, kept my interest aloft to know me, us and the innumerable neighbours-near and distant.

II

Perhaps I have left by default a few hints in the big preamble regarding students/youth movements. Let me now take up the subject directly. Some scholars have already discussed that student or youth movements sometimes cannot be separated out for obvious reasons. Going by the consideration of age grouping, Nandy (1977) estimated that about 0.8 per cent of the youth are in educational institutions and the politically effective youth is naturally high in urban centres. Another estimate of 1961 census was that taking the 15-24 age-group rural India has more than 15 per cent youth, whereas it is more than 31 per cent if the age-group is taken between 15-34 (Chakrabarti, 1977). Some scholars have shown that percentage of aged between 15-24 years rose to 19.5 per cent in 1990 compared to 18.2 per cent in 1960. However, one thing is certain that the formidable section, which is roughly considered to be placed between childhood and maturity, or adolescence and maturity, forms about one fifth of the total population. They may be identified as rural and urban or tribal and non-tribal. They may be located in primary production or professional and bureaucratic persuasions. They are visible in ethnic, political and religious mobilizations. They bear the heritage of caste or class affiliations. They may be spearheading the domain of informative technology or may be pursuing the creative excellence in the field of art, literature, performing arts and so on and so forth. The nature of their presence makes a difference when contextualized in pre-colonial, colonial or post-colonial time frames. They may be looked upon in the backdrop of the hills and the plains dichotomous terrains. Last but not the least, there might be studies specially in the context of the twentieth century world youth movements, which were known largely for assertion of democratic rights, rightful place in political governance, revolt against racial prejudice and indiscriminate ethnic violence, reaction to imperialist domination and nuclear war and the like in the countries such as Spain, Portugal, Poland, France, Brazil, Canada, Belgium, USA and many others. Penetration of capital and market in various forms, spread of formal education and emergence of middle class intellectuals were the key factors in understanding the problems of the youth and their movements.

III

In studying youth movement, the scholars across the boundary of social sciences have emphasized on the social formations in North-East India. They have observed certain commonalities as well as distinct socio-cultural variations among the numerous ethnic groups living in North-East India. To put it in brief, Baruah writes, "The region, today known as North-East India, is not a historical one. It is a politico-administrative construct initiated by the British administration and strengthened by the independent India" (2005 : 28). He further observes, "Our experience in North-East India suggests that emerging middle classes or educated elites, who do not have the resources like big land holdings, capital and numerical strength find it convenient to use ethnicity for the purposes of mobilization (*Ibid.* 30). His idea has been that in the absence of feudal or capitalist class representative, the educated elites or the educated middle class comes to occupy hegemonic positions in their respective communities. Bhagabati in his Presidential Address at the Annual Conference of Eighteenth session of North-East India History Association (NEIHA) drew our attention to the fact that "While the pre-colonial setting was fluid and flexible, the colonial and post-colonial settings have been less so and societal boundaries became more rigid, adding in the process distinct cultural orientation—the phenomena we call ethnicity. In addition, the post-colonial period is also characterized by revivalist trends, so that various social formations look to their primordial cultural assets to define and consolidate their boundaries" (1998 : 13). He further observed, "The phenomenon of immigration in the colonial and post-colonial periods, which led to the hardening of the boundaries of social formations in Assam into 'Sons of Soil' (*thalua*) and 'outsiders' vying for the limited jobs, assets an resources of the respective territories" (*Ibid.* 14). Sinha and Aeir also brought in the question of generality and specificity in the social formations of North-East India (1994). They hold the view that extension of political networking and expansion of market in North-East region were caused due to the direct intervention of the British administration for their own purpose. This exposure acted as a backdrop to what has happened subsequently. So far, by and large, Assam was the general point of reference. But after independence, with the rise of tribal elite, the demand of autonomy in some form or the other got tremendous support base and the result of later history is so well known.

The impetus of the rising middle class intellectual consciousness in Assam was initially influenced by the tradition of 'Bengal renaissance'. In this connection one may refer to Chatterjee when he says, "There did exist a rather unique socio-economic situation in Bengal. The very size of the middle class was, by the early decades of the twentieth century, much larger than anywhere else in India. Culturally, it was fairly homogeneous, being predominantly upper-caste Hindu, until there occurred in the twentieth century the emergence of a significant Muslim middle class" (Chatterjee, 1985 : 84). The university and college education including professional courses being established much earlier in Calcutta, catered to the need of many students/youths of other states primarily of Eastern and later North-Eastern states. As a result the message of students/youths movements, specially the left oriented movements, reached these areas during pre and early post independence period.

IV

The development of student/youth movement in Assam has been a major subject to some scholars of this region. For example, Meeta Deka's Ph.D. thesis entitled "A Historical Perspective of the Years of Students Protest in Assam 1905-1972: An Exploration of its Roots" (NEHU, 1991) may be mentioned in this regard. She traced historical roots through the literary movement prior to Independence and ultimately emphasized on the turning point during 1979-84 when Asom Gana Sangram Parishad (AGSP) was formed on 25.09.1979 at Kanoi College in Dibrugarh by the executive body of AASU. These six-year-long students' movements turned to 'Gana Andolan' (mass movement) where the main issue became the infiltration of foreign nationals among other things like problems of industrialization, food crisis, introduction of state language, medium of instruction in the university, linguistic and regional identity of the Assamese people etc. (1996). The role of Assamese students in the freedom movement was studied by Borah (1994). He pointed out the formation of Assam Students' Conference in 1916 under the Chairmanship of Laxminath Bezbaruah. Other eminent names like Chandranath Sarma, Omio Kumar Das etc. were also mentioned in this connection. Among other issues boycott of foreign goods in Tejpur Conference in 1919 under the Presidentship of Prafulla Chandra Roy figured very much in his analysis. He also mentioned about Assam Students Federation in 1939-40 under the Chairmanship of Humayun Kabir. The involvement of the students in Assam during 1942 Quit India Movement was also mentioned, though during those days the numerical strength of the students were not much because the literacy rate was only about 10 per cent . He further pointed out that Cotton College was at the centre of such movements.

The travel route of the ideological import could be a subject of study for interested scholars. It is apparent that during pre-independence days the hub of activities of the students/youths was Calcutta (now Kolkata) which then got precipitated in some parts of Assam. The wide range of issues varied from broad national political goal to state level economic initiative including the question of ethnic identity, inter-state migrations, infiltrations and the like. After the independence with the gradual emergence of number of tribal Autonomous Hill Councils, Union Territories and finally curving out of some states specially bifurcating the regions from Assam, the character of student/youth movements in North East India was perhaps changed more towards ethnic mobilization, cultural autonomy and exclusive possession over local resource base. The students/youths movements in all the states of North East India are to be understood in this changed perspective. Let us very briefly touch upon some examples from the remaining states in the aggregate of seven sisters. In Arunachal Pradesh, following the patterns of AASU, the students have formed a body known as All Arunachal Pradesh Students Union (AAPSU). Among the major issues, refugee problem, border dispute with Assam, suspension of trade license to non-Arunachalese, infiltration of foreign nationals etc. were highlighted. The youth here also were facing an inner struggle of cultural or religious identity. The increasing trend of Christianity is being resisted by the indigenous faith known 'Donyi-Polo' (Dhar, 1998; Mibong, 2002). In Meghalaya the Khasi Students Union (KSU), which became very strong at one point of time, was established in 1978 as a constituent of Meghalaya Students' Union (MSU), which was formed on 25.01.1976. Before that there was Meghalaya Students' Association (MSA), which was formed on 23.05.1970. The KSU, which was initially a bit away from direct involvement in politics and religion, became active in larger socio-political issues since 1987 (Nongkynrih, 1998). In Nagaland the major concern of the students/youths has been against the atrocities of army against the civilian population (Mao, 1998). The same holds true in case of Manipur. A distinct development has been extra-ordinary in nature here. The participation of women of Manipur valley in agitation during pre-independence days has established a tradition. Way back in 1904 and 1939, Manipur was known for two great *nupilans* (female's warfare) against the oppression of the

British Political Agent and Marwari traders, respectively (Zohol, 1998). Again since 1980, Manipur has witnessed so many agitations and movements of the women. In addition to this the history of the Manipur Students' movements were largely influenced by the ongoing freedom struggle of the country as well as by the democratic political ideals like liberty, equality and fraternity. The All Manipur Students Federation was established in 1946, with the demand for free primary school education on the one hand and for establishing human rights on the other. The All Manipur Students Union was established in 1965 and became a strong political body for state politics (Urmila, 1998). In case of Mizoram, Mizo Students' Union played important role in the affairs of Mizo National Front (MNF). The Students Joint Action Committee came into being in May 1985 to mobilize public opinion in favour of the conclusion of peace talks. The Mizoram accord was signed on 30th June 1986 (Deb, 1998). Sangkima reported that with the rising trend of Christianity and also devolution of power of the traditional chief the institution of '*Zawlbuk*' (bachelor's dormitory), which was the main agency in molding the social life of the Mizos, lost its importance. Formal education also played its part in this change. The Young Lushai Association was formed in 1935 and Young Mizo Association (YMA) was formed in 1948. The YMA played an important role in the transformation of the Mizo society (1986). In case of Tripura a social movement known as Janasikhsa Andolan (mass literacy movement) by the Tripura Janasikhsa Samiti (1945) became instrumental in mobilizing the students/youths in extending education to the backward rural masses, specially the tribals. Some of the present day senior political leaders like Dasarath Deb were in the leadership of this movement. Two things happened in 1951-71. The percentage of tribal population to the total population decreased substantially and sizeable landed properties were passed on to the non-tribal population. The students/youth sections were also divided into various political camps. The students under the stronghold of the left parties had a number of demands divided into political, economic and educational issues (Pal, 1986). Roy noted that a section of tribal youth organized a social movement under the banner of Gana Mukti Parishad. Their main objective was to eradicate superstition, to fight illiteracy and to drive away the alien culture. In 1967 the progressive youths initiated a new move to form the Upajati Juba Samiti. This Samiti later became a regional political party (1998).

V

In view of the brief presentation of some empirical facts as well as general discussions let us now make an attempt to summarize the whole thing. While studying social movements in a generalized way, Rao suggested looking at it as a collective mobilization through either informal or formal organization. These movements, according to him, are generally oriented towards bringing about change in the existing system of relationships. A sense of deprivation formed the core of such movements (1984). Karna in an attempt to understand the perspectives of social movements in the context of North East India brought in four aspects, namely meaning, source, ideology and organization (1998). We have observed in the light of preceding narrations that the students and youth movements could hardly be delinked. There are two broad trends of understanding the students/youth movement—(1) to consider them as a necessary part of the general political movements and (2) to assess them in terms of specific situation originating out of the demands primarily concerned with education and related opportunities. In the process, especially during the recent times, we perhaps tend to overlook two other emerging areas of student/youth movement, namely—(1) the creative production in the field of art, literature, performing arts etc. and (2) the negative forces unleashed through extremely organized agencies to divert the creative faculties of the students/youths. The latter is the sensitive area of introducing the serious abuse of drug and sex. In this connection it may be incidentally mentioned that perhaps we have given scant attention to the negative impact being focused by the print and electronic media in this regard.

The students/youths throughout the globe in general and those in India and North East India in particular have gone through the ordeal of socializing themselves in different ideological climates, viz. liberalism, conservatism, nationalism, socialism, catholicism, fascism etc. (Watkins 1964). Simultaneously, the students/youth of North East India have also experienced the trauma of a threat perception rendering towards demographic imbalance, relative deprivation and loss of cultural identity. This has happened especially after the independence with the rise of middle class intelligentsia and tribal elites who participated in local to national political activities. Side by side, another trend is also marked, specially among some tribal groups like the Khasi, the Adi where a revivalism is set against the rising Christianity gripping the students / youths by and large. Seng Khasi and Donyi-Poloism are cases in point.

In the modern age of globalization, the free movement of capital and market networks along with the ideological sub-servience to over all technological command have created a climate of increasing lust for material comfort of life leading to erosion of community life and moral values. The students/youth movements in this country, which inherited a good tradition of vibrant intellectual consciousness and commitment to the cause of nation building, got very many interruptions at different junctures of social transformation. This is mainly due to the over-ambition for gaining immediate and shortcut social, economic and political gains. The analysis of students / youth movements in North East India has to see all the major global, national and regional forces for a meaningful and useful understanding of the problems in future.

REFERENCES

Baruah, Apurba K. (2005). "Conceptualising Regionalism in India: A North Eastern Perspective" *Proceedings of North East India History Association (NEIHA)*, Twenty Fifth Session, Shillong.

Bhagabati, A.C. (1998). Presidential Address, *NEIHA, Eighteenth Session*, Tripra.

Borah, Jagat (1994) "Assam Students and Their Activities in the Freedom Movement", in *NEIHA, Fourteenth Session*, Jorhat.

Chakrabarti, Satyabrata (1977). "Changing Life of the Rural Youth: Some Perspectives" in *Youth: Change and Challenge*, Ed. Dhurjati Mukherjee, Calcutta: Firma KLM Pvt. Ltd.

Chattrejee, Partha (1985). "The Fruits of Macaulay's Poison Tree", in *The Truth Unites*, Ed. Ashok Mitra, Kolkata: Subarnarekha.

Deb, B.J. (1998). "Youth Movement in Mizoram: A Study of Student Politics", in *Social Movements in North East India*, Ed. M.N. Karna, New Delhi, Indus Publishing Co.

Deka, Meeta (1991). A Historical Perspective of the Years of Students Protest in Assam 1905-1972: An Exploration of Its Roots, Ph.D. Thesis, NEHU, Shillong.

——,———— (1996). Students Movements in Assam, New Delhi, Vikas Pub. House.

Dhar, Bibhas (1998). "Youth Movement: A Symbol of Modernization in Arunachal Pradesh", in M.N. Karna Ed. (Ibid).

Karna, M.N. (1998). "Introduction", in M.N. Karna Ed. (Ibid).

Mao, X.P. (1998). "Youth Movement in Nagaland", in M.N. Karna Ed. (Ibid).

Mibong, T. (2002). "The Donyi-Polo Faith and the Process of Homogenization Among the Tribes of Arunachal Pradesh", in *Culture, Religion and Philosophy: A Critical Studies in Syncretism and Inter-Faith Harmony, Ed. N.K. Das,* New Delhi, Rawat Publication.

Nandy, Ashis (1977). "Students and Politics in India" in Dhurjati Mukherjee Ed. (*Ibid*).

Nongkynrih, A.K. (1998). "Youth Movement in Meghalaya", in M.N. Karna Ed. (*Ibid*).

Pal, Himansu (1986). "Students Movements in Tripura 1950-1970", *NEIHA, Sixth Session,* Agartala.

Rao, MSA (Ed) (1984). Social Movements in India, Delhi, Manohar Publications.

Roy, Jagat Jyoti (1998). "Youth Movement for Social Reformation in Tripura", in M.N. Karna Ed. (*Ibid*).

Sangkima, (1986). "Young Mizo Association: Its History, Features, Some Aspects and Its Role in Transforming Mizo Society", *NEIHA, Sixth Session,* Agartala.

Sinha, A.C. and L.T. Aeir (1994). "A Note on Social Formations in North-Eastern Frontier Region" in *Tribal Situation in North East India,* Ed. Sarthak Sengupta, New Delhi, Inter-India Publications.

Urmila, Ningthoukhongjam (1998). "Students in Manipur Politics", *NEIHA, Seventeenth Session,* Aizwal.

Watkins, Frederick M. (1964). The Age of Ideology-Political Thought, 1750 to the Present, New Delhi, Prentice Hall.

Zehol, Lucy T.V. (1998). "Women's Movement in Manipur: Some Observations", M.N. Karna Ed. (*Ibid*).

9

Society and Politics in Manipur

KSH. BIMOLA DEVI

Every ethnic group or community has its own social norms, beliefs, practices and customary laws. An ethnic group or a community can have a stable society only when the social norms, beliefs, customary laws etc. are adhered to firmly by the members. A society consisting of many ethnic groups or communities can also have stability if the members of the group comply with their own social norms, belief etc. as prescribed by their own religions or customary laws. A given society can be more stable if the members belonging to different groups or communities respect each other's social beliefs and religions.

No ethnic group or community can be free from politics. Politics as a way of life and political culture always exists in every society, big or small. The political system may be chieftainship, autocratic or democratic, monarchical, Presidential or Parliamentary etc. There is close connection between the social component and the nature of the political system in any given society.

Social Composition

There are many ethnic groups in Manipur inhabiting both in the hills and in plain districts of Manipur. The tribes may broadly be divided into two, namely the Nagas and the Kukis. Both of them may be further divided into many tribes and sub-tribes. In addition, there are also Muslims communities known as Meitei Pangals in the Valley of Manipur. The Meiteis, who inhabit in the valley of

Manipur, are the major community, numbering about 14 lakhs. There are also Bengalis, Assamese, Rajasthanis, Biharis, Oriyas and other people in the urban areas of Imphal. Most of these people belong to the business groups and the working class (labourers) groups in the state of Manipur. The non-Manipuris coming from different parts of India live in the urban area of Khwairamband bazaar, especially in the Thangal bazaar of Imphal city. Thus the society in Manipur may be described as a heterogeneous society.

Society and Politics in the Pre-British Period

In the early period of the history of Manipur, the society mainly consisted of the people belonging to seven clans i.e. the Ningthouja, the Angom, the Khuman, the Luwang, the Khaba-Nganba, the Sarang-Leishangthem and the Moirang. Though each clan had its own social norms and beliefs based on customary laws, the people belonging to the seven clans had accepted and followed common norms acceptable to all of them. The people were mainly agriculturists, though not possessed their own Patta lands. The surnames were given by the king based on the nature of occupation of the people. The social norms, beliefs and practices of the people of seven clans were amalgamated into one under the political authority of the Meitei rulers. The society of Manipur since 33 A.D. had consisted of different groups and classes. The society was based on feudal character. At the top of the social political hierarchy, there was the king enjoying supreme authority in the administration of the state. Below him were the nobilities who enjoyed higher social status because of their political position as ministers, assisting the king in the discharge of his functions. Most of these nobilities possessed cultivable land which were given as gifts by the king. The Brahmins, who came from outside the state in the 15th and 16th centuries also enjoyed higher social status. They were Hindus whose main function was to perform religious rites and rituals in the Manipuri society. In all social festivals and religious ceremonies the Brahmins were accorded the highest social respect and honour by the non-Brahmins. They also enjoyed the possession of cultivable land given as gifts by the king of Manipur. The other social groups having lower social position were the common people and farmers who did not own cultivable lands. They may be classified as tenants in the society being controlled by the higher class of people who possessed land. The lowest social strata were occupied by groups who acted as slaves to the nobilities and the king of Manipur.

Society and Politics During the British Period

The Society of Manipur during the British Period was characterized by Hindu Vaisnavite culture inherited by the people of Manipur right from the 18th century. There was one religious organization called Brahma Sabha as the apex body of the Manipur society regulating the do's and don't's of the religious norms and practices of Hindu Vaisnavism among the people of Manipur. Any person who had violated or had acted against the prescribed religious norms and practices were severely dealt with and was given, in some cases, even capital punishment. There were many cases of families or villages declared as outcastes by the Brahma Sabha for a period of time. These individuals, families and the members of the outcaste villages were not allowed to perform religious rites and rituals of the Brahma Sabha. Even when a person died, the family or the outcaste villagers was not allowed to burn the dead body according to Vaisnavite Hindu culture. The members of other families or villagers were also not allowed to join or attend any event or occasion performed in the outcaste family. These individuals, families or villagers were allowed to return back to the mainstream of the Vaisnavite Hindu Manipuri society only after paying the fines fixed by the Brahma Sabha. Many families and villages were declared outcaste by the Brahma Sabha during the British period. The Maharaja as the head of the Brahma Sabha exercised their powers indiscriminately thereby resulting in suppression of the grievances of the people of Manipur mainly in the valley of Manipur. Different types of taxes, even including tax for putting chandan (sacred mark) in the forehead of a Vaisnavite, were levied. The Manipuri society looked like a stable society having regular social and religious order but it was in fact an imposed stable society with a strict religious discipline exercised by the Brahma Sabha.

The economic condition of the Manipur society was also in a deteriorating situation. The British authority headed by the Political Agent controlled four major subjects i.e. Defence, Foreign Affairs, Coinage and Communications. This resulted in the drainage of the economic resources of Manipur. Manipur, though a Princely state, was more or less under the control of the British authority not only in the four major subjects but also in the economic and internal affairs of the state. Clear examples of this trend were the first women's movement of 1904, the Agitation against water tax, 1923, the second women's movement, 1939 etc. The effect of this social and economic instability was felt by some educated persons like Hijam Irawat. Though employed in the government service and married with a Princess, Hijam Irawat was more concerned with the exploitative policies of both the British authority and the Maharaja of Manipur. He started to take up social activism promoting the interest of the people who were declared outcaste by the Brahma Sabha. He formed different organizations for the farmers, women, youths and students by mobilising people and making them aware of the socio-economic and political situation of Manipur. He worked heart and soul for the upliftment of the people of Manipur in different areas like literature, sports, Drama etc. As a result of his different activities, the people belonging to all walks of life became aware of the oppressive and exploitative rule of the British authority and the Maharaja of Manipur. It was under his influence and leadership that the demand for a democratic form of government emerged for the first time in Manipur in the late 1930s.

Social and Political Change 1947 to 1950

The society of Manipur was deeply affected by the outbreak of the Second World War, 1939, Imphal being one of the battlefields in the war between the Allied forces and the Axis power. For about 5 years i.e. 1939 to 1944 there was no normal life in Imphal and its adjacent areas. It was only in the later part of 1944 that normalcy returned slowly through opening educational institutions, offices and other establishments. When stability appeared in the society of Manipur, the demand for the introduction of democratic government was started with new spirit and vigour. Hijam Irawat was the unquestioned leader for the social and political changes in Manipur. The opposition leaders branded him as a communist in order to curb his popularity. In a meeting of all political parties convened at Aryan Theatre in July, 1946, Irawat was charged as a communist and insisted him on declaring himself as a communist.

Irawat with his followers walked out from the meeting and with the rest of the members he formed a political Party named Manipur Congress.

In the meantime, there were changes in the political scenario of the state due to the change in the political power in U.K. after general election, 1945. The Labour Party with Clement Attlee as Prime Minister took up steps, by sending Cabinet Mission to India, for granting of Independence within a short period of time. This new change had also indirectly affected the ongoing politics in Manipur. The political parties had demanded the introduction of democratic government in Manipur. This movement was a strong political force in the changing political process of Manipur. The Maharaja of Manipur felt the need for introducing democratic elements in the administration of Manipur. After getting independence on 15 August, 1947, the Manipur State Constitution Act, 1947 was enacted and elections were held in 1948 under the said Act. A Unicameral State Assembly was constituted with the elected members. The members of the Council of Ministers were elected by the members of the State Assembly. The Chief Minister who was appointed in Consultation with the Ministers had acted as a link between the Maharaja a Constitutional head and the elected members. This marked a stage of political transition from the rule of the Maharaja to that of a democratic government. But this democratic government could not last long as Manipur got merged with the Indian Union on 15 October, 1949. With the enforcement of the Constitution of India on 26 January, 1950, Manipur was placed in the category of Part C State.

The society in Manipur during the period 1947 to 1949 remained stable. The social order was mainly based on Hinduism. The section of the educated class got enlarged. Most of them got employment in government jobs enjoying higher status in the society.

Society and Politics, 1950 to 1972

The nature of the functioning of the political authority exercised by the Chief Commissioner had given a negative impact on the peaceful and stable social order of Manipur The concentration of the political power in the hands of the Chief Commissioner who acted on behalf of the President of India had created dissatisfaction in the minds of the people of Manipur. The members of the Advisory Council, as the name indicates, were only advisors to the Chief Commissioner. The latter was not bound to accept the advice given by the advisors. The people of Manipur had started movement demanding higher political status for Manipur. It took time for Manipur to have a legislature of the own. Only in July 1963, the then Territorial Council consisting 30 elected and 2 nominated members was converted into a Territorial Assembly. Following another strong political movement, it was only 21 January, 1972 that Manipur had achieved the status of a full fledged Statehood within the Indian Union.

Social and Political Changes 1972 to 1979

With the attainment of full fledged state, Manipur as a unit of Indian federation came to enjoy legislative, executive and financial powers as given in the Constitution of India. The people of Manipur were quite happy and satisfied with the upgradation of the political status of the Manipur. But the political instability during this period had resulted in the emergence of new class in the society who believed in unfair means and corruption. Political defections among the MLAs became rampant during this period. Engineers and Contractors were given higher social status in the society, encouraged by the ruling class. There were as many as seven Ministries formed by different political parties during a period of seven years. Corruption emerged as an important factor for getting government jobs and services. The number of educated youths had also increased. The emergence of many underground organizations in the late 1970s had led to another political dimension in the political instability of Manipur. The movement for reviving the indigenous religion of the Meiteis called Sanamahi was another social movement since middle of 1970s.

Society and Politics 1980 to 1992

The year 1980 marked an important phase in the social and political life of Manipur. The imposition of the Armed Forces Special Power Act, 1958 in the whole area of Manipur in 1980 had resulted in the instability of the social life of the people. The security personnel exercising their powers under the Act in order to control the insurgents and killed many innocent persons including women and children. There were also many cases of rape, molestation, forced disappearances etc. in the early part of the 1980s. These happenings had indirectly led to the formation of women groups called 'Meira Paibis' in every locality, mainly in the Imphal valley first and then slowly in the rural areas of Manipur. The main objective of these Meira Paibis was to protect the youths and the men folks from the arrest and torture by the security personnel.

The imposition of Section 144 of the Indian Penal Code and Curfew by the government became the normal means to control the rallies and demonstrations organized by the womenfolk of Manipur. There were always tussles between the security personnel and the womenfolk of Manipur on the issue of arrest of persons under the Armed Forces Special Power Act, 1958.

Manipur Since 1992

Manipur entered another new phase of social and political crisis since the beginning of 1990s. The conflict between two major ethnic groups namely the Nagas and the Kukis broke out in 1992 having its root in Moreh—a border town between India and Myanmar. The killings of Kukis by the Nagas in the hill areas of Manipur and vice-versa continued for four years, from 1992 to 1996. There was no normal life in the 4 hill districts of Manipur namely Senapati, Tamenglong, Chandel and Ukhrul. The Churachandpur district was the only undisturbed district during the said period. The clashes between the Nagas and the Kukis had resulted not only in killing of many innocent persons and burning of houses but also in internal displacement of many persons and families. The issue of ethnicity became very serious giving rise to the question of ethnic identities, ethnic interest etc. The ill feelings and the enmity among the different tribes in Manipur became deeply rooted. The Naga-Kuki conflict during 1992 to 1996 had again led to another ethnic conflict in Churachandpur district between the Kukis and the Zoumis in 1997-1998. The large migration of the Kukis in Churachandpur district as a result of the Naga-Kuki conflict had created an imbalance between the original settlers and the new migrants. On the whole we may conclude that the hill areas of Manipur were in the hot turmoil for about six years. On the other hand, the valley of Manipur having four districts namely the Imphal East, the Imphal West, the Thoubal and the Bishnupur districts was greatly disturbed by the armed conflict situation between the State forces and the non-State forces. The social life of Manipur was so disturbed that no person could predict what would happen in the next moment.

Manipur witnessed growth of many militant armed groups based on ethnicity since late 1990s, particularly among the Kukis and the Muslims of Manipur. In the name of sovereignty or homeland, these ethnic armed groups were mainly guided by the protection or promotion of their people belonging to their ethnic groups. Perhaps the youths belonging to different ethnic groups in Manipur felt the need of having armed wings to protect and defend themselves from the armed aggression of other ethnic group, larger and stronger.

The changing socio-political culture in the mindset of the people belonging to different communities and ethnic groups took a negative turn towards hatred, ill feelings, misunderstandings, suspicions etc. The polarization of the people along the ethnic lines became the main feature of the social life of Manipur since the late 1990s. The political agenda of the NSCN (IM) to create Nagalim consisting the Naga inhabited areas of Manipur, Assam and Arunachal Pradesh again added on another important social and political issue in Manipur. The extension of the Ceasefire Agreement between the Government of India and the NSCN(IM) in June 2001 by adding 'without territorial limit' had led to a mass uprising on 18th June, 2001 resulting in the death of 18 persons. The conflict between the Nagas and the Meiteis was mainly on the territorial integrity of Manipur. The Meiteis felt that the geographical boundary of Manipur would greatly be affected if the Naga inhabited areas are taken out to create Nagalim as proposed by the NSCN(IM). The emergence of many revolutionary armed groups among the Kukis like the Kuki National Army (KNA), the Kuki National Organisation (KNO), the United Kuki Liberation Front (UKLF), the Kuki National Front (KNF), the Kuki Revolutionary Army (KRA), Kuki Liberation Army (KLA) etc. have created conflicts and misunderstandings among the tribes belonging to the larger Kuki fold. The revolutionary armed groups largely dominated by the Meiteis were the Revolutionary Peoples Front (RPF), the United National Liberation Front (UNLF), the Peoples Revolutionary Party of Kangleipak (PREPAK), the

Kangleipak Communist Party (KCP), the Kanglei Yayol Kanba Lup (KYKL) etc. They are already pursuing their political agendas and activities. The Peoples United Liberation Front (PULF), an underground organization of the Muslims of Manipur, also started its activities since the middle of 1990s. In addition, many anti-social elements and groups are taking advantage of the already disturbed social atmosphere of Manipur. The common people are suffering from the underground organizations, the State and Para-military forces and the anti-social groups. The existence of many organizations, both underground and voluntary organizations, in a small state of Manipur having a population of only 24 lakhs has given a negative impact on the mindset as well as on the developmental process of the state. Lack of co-ordination and understandings among the different organizations has added to the sufferings of the people. Corruption and mal-administration have become the order of the day resulting in the widening of the gap between the rich and the poor. A new middle class playing an authoritative role is emerging as a strong social and political force in the state of Manipur.

10

Women's Movements in Conflict Situation in Manipur

TH. BINARANI DEVI

A society is regarded as a developed society when there is social justice, equality and freedom from exploitation. The absence of these leads to exploitation, poverty and powerlessness. In the absence of distributive justice conflicts take place in the society. The structural constraints let loose by an inequalitarian society make any conflict resolution initiative inadequate. To initiate a change towards just society, it requires organised movement and development action. Peoples' organization, community solidarity and network can bring about change in the exploitative social and economic order towards betterment of the human kind. Economic growth alone can not lead social development and human betterment. Greater emphasis needs to be given on social opportunities and services.

The process of organised movement and development action for a just society demands participation and involvement of the women community. The roles of organised movements and the commitments of the well-informed and enlightened citizenry in transforming the society are well recognized in history. Participation of women in the development decision and in the development process has now got policy support. In the developing country like India and in the remote, under-developed, border states thereof such role of women is highly significant.

Women Social Movement

Historically the women community in the remote state of Manipur has assumed great role in the process of development and conflict resolution. The women community in Manipur enjoys higher freedom and the society puts less restriction on their movements, food habits, attire and allows widow remarriage. On the other hand in Manipur the role of the women is higher but their status is not. The customary laws and social norms put the women community in subjugation. The dilemma of the women community in Manipur is whereas their public role is historically significant, they are captives in the private spaces of households and kinships.

With such limitations, social development of the women community faces greater challenge. Whereas the central purpose of social development is gender equality, many forms of discriminations and subordinations hinder gender just development. In its wider meaning development is not just about material development, it embraces recognition of cultural heritage, ecology & environment, spiritual development and regeneration of the traditional authorities. Despite all limitations the women of Manipur go hand in hand with the male counterparts in many development activities. The women community provides moral, emotional and physical support to the male community. In the past the great queens of Manipur provided valuable advice to the kings on public issues and when necessary assumed administrative roles and often impelled the kings to reverse the royal decisions. The state of Manipur is perpetually conflict-ridden. The women community came forward not only for the development of the state but provided an important agency for conflict resolution.

From the early 20th century, the women movements became well organised and ideology based. Their roles in political reforms and social transformation have been historically registered in the *Nupi Lan* (women rebellion) of 1904. This was the beginning of their organised movement against the *Lallup* system (compulsory forced labour) introduced by the British. Under this system, on the order of the Political Agent, at least one able-bodied male member of household was forced to extract teak wood from Kabow valley for construction of house of the Assistant Superintendent of Police. The Meitei women took the lead role in the organised movement against the *Lallup* system. The colonial government let loose all sorts of coercive measures to curb this movement. Oppressive laws were proclaimed and people were debarred from assembling in a group in one place. The women community faced the wrath of the British government but did not retreat from their movement. They did not obey the proclamations of the British government and entered into the residence of the Political Agent and the Superintendent. They received injuries but the British officers were not able to control their protest movement. The British government was compelled to stop the *Lallup* system in order to restore peace in the state.

The women movements did not stop there. With the accession of Manipur to the Indian Union in 1949, the earlier hopes of the people of Manipur were shuttered. In the name if protection of law and order many democratic rights of the people of Manipur were violated and draconian laws were imposed in the state. This oppressive situation was largely responsible for the rise of extremism in the state. From the late 1970s and 1980s the entire Imphal valley was brought under heavy combing operation by the army in order to flush out the extremists. During combing operation a large number of innocent people including the women suffered loss including life loss. The women organizations in Manipur took a serious note of the state violence let loose by police and para-military forces. These organizations with other local women started to guard the households and other family members. It was made compulsory that every household should join in case of serious problem that could affect the peaceful atmosphere of the locality. Since then the women in different localities organised themselves against combing operations and other types of violence. In different occasions, the women community from different sections gathered in front of the Chief Minister's or Governor's residence and shouted anti-combing operation slogans, staged hartals, demonstrations and bund etc. The protest movement of the women agencies of Manipur against police and military access, bad governance and against shortage of basic needs yielded some results.

Though the state is yet to fully respond to the demands of the women organizations and to ensure dignity of them, the women organizations relentlessly struggled for the common cause of the society. In the armed conflict situation in Manipur many people are killed and kidnapped. Many newly married women are forced to commit suicide to save themselves against rape and social abuse by the security forces. With the increase of state violence in the state particularly against the youth and the women, the women community in Manipur staged unrobed protest March against custody rape and killing of Ms. Manorama by the Assam Rifles personnel on 11th July 2004. The demonstrators carried the honour of their community on their bodies and demonstrated that by raping them the army would defile the entire community.

Manipur created a new history of women's movement when Irom Chanu Sharmila launched hunger strike since November 3, 2000 in protest against killing of ten civilians at Malom by the Assam Rifles personnel following a bomb attack by the underground outfits on the armed personnel on 2nd November 2000. Even she shifted her hunger strike base to New Delhi for six months (October 2006 to March 2007). The national leaders did not pay heed to her demand for removal of AFSPA-1958. Sharmila was frustrated and came back to Imphal on 4th March, 2007. Another reason for her return to Imphal was the promises made by almost all the political parties in Manipur during the assembly poll (2007) campaign to lobby for repeal of the Act. Shri O Ibobi Singh, the Chief Minister of Manipur commented in front of the AICC leaders in New Delhi during March in connection with Sharmila's protest move that, the Act had already been lifted from seven assembly segments of Imphal municipal area and that the law and order permitting, the Act could be repealed from the entire state. But Sharmila is still continuing her hunger strike because the people of Imphal East and West are not only the worst sufferers of the Act, the remaining population are also sufferers. In the name of maintenance of law and order in the state and for bringing welfare to the society, a number of draconian laws have been enforced in the state causing untold suffering of the masses.

Fifty-eight years after the UN Declaration of Human Rights, the society of Manipur is suffers from violation of these rights. Both men and women have become victims of violence. Many innocent people have lost their lives due to state violence. Many voluntary organizations of Manipur including the All Manipur Nupi Marup, the Kuki Women Human Rights Network etc. are up against the draconian acts and rules. They are trying to protect minimum right to the people, that is right to life. There were many incidences of state violence that resulted in rape of the innocent women, series of killing, custody death, looting of property by CRPF and in innumerable sufferings of the mass. Unfortunately, the government remained conspicuously silent.

Economic Role of the Women

Though Manipuri society is strictly patriarchal, the women take the whole responsibility of the family. They also take financial responsibility for the households. The second *Nupi Lan* (women movement) of 1939 was launched against export of rice from Manipur in a domestic food scarcity situation. The Marwari traders exclusively controlled rice export trade. They used to export rice to other parts of the British India. These traders who settled permanently in Manipur were the top trade leaders. They established monopoly in purchase of rice and procured paddy from the cultivators and local petty traders. They used to offer higher price than the local traders. As a result the local people suffered a lot. The women community came forward to stop export of rice from Manipur. In this movement they has to encounter the state force.

At present there is no large-scale industry in Manipur to provide job opportunities to the unemployed youth. The major occupation of the people is agriculture. The valley of Manipur that constitutes less than one-fourth of the total land area of the state is the main supplier of all the agricultural products to the other parts of the state. At the same time the valley area is the targeted place for construction of buildings for business and living purposes. This expansion of infrastructure reduced agricultural lands and the state is impelled to import foodgrains from outside the state to make up foodgrain shortage. The state also suffers foodgrains shortage when the two National Highways—the NH 39 and NH 53 are blockaded for any reason. Under this situation the women community work hard for economic sustenance of the households. They do petty business and sale food items, clothes and other things in the local markets. Some women both in the valley and in the hills of Manipur work as professionals in different white-collar jobs. However, the condition is worse in the remote hilly and poor tribal areas of the state.

Rural poverty in the state and particularly in the remote hill areas is very acute. Against the 27 per cent rural poverty in India, Manipur has 40 per cent rural poverty. Two factors are responsible for high percentage of poverty in Manipur. (i) Rural families who have abandoned farming or are alienated from land do not produce food. They buy food; (ii) the rural poor migrate and work as low paid casual workers in the urban service sector. Most of them work in the unorganized sector.

Livelihood crisis resulting from failed agriculture perhaps could be addressed through the long tradition of thrift and credit in Manipur. Policy promotion of Self-Help-Groups (SHG) might open new avenues of self-employment and income in the high poverty-concentrated rural areas. But it is not only credit supply that can help them addressing the livelihood problems. The women community needs entrepreneurship and production training, training on rules of business, organizational capacity-building training and above all a clear marketing policy of the state for the goods and products of the SHGs. Rural finance is another significant issue to lead the SHGs ahead. Modernization has to a large extent impacted the traditional economic activities in the state. Traditional occupations in handloom and handicrafts are not expanding. This caused rise in unemployed women labour force and marginalization of the women labour in the villages. Such unemployed women labour army finds their place in the dingy lanes of Imphal, Churachandpur, Ukhrul and Moreh towns; in the pavements of market towns; in the kitchens of the middle class; in sand and stone quarries and construction work sites; pan dukans, clinics and parlours; in hotels and even in brothels. Such state of womanhood in the state of Manipur goes against the history of self-esteem, pride and self-dignity.

Against the Indian claim as the biggest democracy and as the land of non-violence, the women movements in Manipur has been treated with derision and hence considered irrelevant. To countervail this, many women movements became aggressive, crude and more violent. The question here is whether their role is making a negative impression in the minds of the common people? I think not. I am of the view that the women community needs to re-affirm solidarity and to uphold the historic torch of liberation movement in order to make the society just and developed.

REFERENCES

Laldena, History of Modern Manipur, Orbit Publishers & Distributors, New Delhi.

Bimal J. Dev, (ed) Manipur—Culture and Politics, Mittal Publication, New Delhi.

B.K. Gokhale, A Study of Political Theory, Himalayan Publishing House, New Delhi.

M.N. Karna, (Ed), Social Movements in North East India, Indus Publishing Co. New Delhi.

K. Saradamani (ed) Women, Work and Society, Indian Statistical Institute.

K. Manimohan Singh, Nupilal, K. Premlata Devi, Imphal,

L. Yaima Singh & R.K. Maipaksana Singh, Nikhil Hindu Manipur Mahasabha, Manipuri Pradarshini, Imphal.

Naoriya Phullo and Eigi Wareng, Friends Industrial Press, Imphal.

Panchani Chandrasekhar, Manipur Religion, Culture and Society. Konark Publishers Pvt. Ltd. New Delhi.

Bela Rani Sharma, Women, Marriage, Family, Violence and Divorce, Mangal Deep Publication, Jaipur.

Th. Binarani, Social and Political Changes in Manipur 1947-87, Unpublished Ph. D. Thesis, Manipur University.

Amnesty International Report, 2007.

The Times of India, (*English Daily*) Guwahati.

11

Impact of North East Indian Tribal Values and Culture on the Hill Region's Socio-Economic Development in the Pre-plan Period

J. B. GANGULI

Human values play a crucial role in motivating people to perform activities in different spheres of life. Max Weber in his famous work; "The Protest Ethic and the Spirit of Capitalism" noted the different economic performances of Protestant and Catholic communities.... "Protestants eat well while Catholics sleep well." The former are more active and enterprising who value material gain while the latter prefer leisure to income-earning. Francis Fukuyama in his famous paper titled "The End of History and the Last Man" observed "One needs look no further than the recent performance of Vietnamese immigrants in the U.S. school system when compared to their black or Hispanic classmates to realize that culture and consciousness are absolutely crucial to explain not only economic behaviour but virtually every other important aspect of life as well."[1]

Being keenly interested in understanding the continued stagnation in the field of productive activities of the people, particularly the tribal people of North-East India, I have noted the basic values of their life and culture that account for the vicious circle of low production, saving and accumulation, lack of capital formation and no growth.

In the hilly sub-region of North-East India consisting of the North-

East frontier tracts (now Arunachal Pradesh) the Naga Hills District (now Nagaland) the Lushai Hills District (now Mizoram), the North-Cachar Hills, the Mikir Hills, the Khasi Jaintia Hills (now Meghalaya) and the Hills of Tripura and Manipur most of the producers practised *jhum chash* (shifting cultivation). Such a system of production was a typical case of stationary economy where production was predominantly for self-consumption only and the system of exchange was almost non-existent. There was no production and accumulation of effective surplus and as such no development and growth. The prevailing means and methods of production held the producer, as it were. "in iron fetters fast in his tracks."

This stationary circular flow of life is accountable by the fact that people were by and large contented with producing that much which was enough to meet the subsistence needs. Many of them had no urge for producing more for saving and accumulation.

The tribal people's world view was narrow and was circumscribed by what may be called Village Centric. They were unable to think beyond the boundary of their inhabited area and their close neighbours. Moreover they were contented with whatever they could produce today without bothering about what would happen tomorrow. Thus it is evident that both the space and time concepts in their psyche were extremely narrow and limited.

Ideology plays a crucial role in motivating people to produce more and accumulate saving for capital formation and development. The tribal society and culture were shaped by egalitarian values. Theirs was a casteless one without any sharp class distinction. And there was no middle class that is generally ambitious and forward-looking. Such cultural traits were absent among these communities.

Division of labour on the basis of caste, for specialization in productive activities was not there as their's was a casteless society. Of course division of labour on the basis of sex was there. Some productive activities, such as hunting, cutting of trees for shifting cultivation and fighting battles with enemy tribes were the exclusive domain of men. But in the agrarian activities the women community predominated. They sowed seeds, did weeding and harvesting though not exclusively. Women even handled selling and buying of production and consumption goods respectively. There was no *purdah* system. Therefore women enjoyed the freedom of movement. The activities connected with weaving, knitting, sewing, cooking, tending, poultry, piggery etc. were the tasks mainly performed by women. It is obvious that when division of labour is based on sex and not professional skill, efficiency of production remains at a low level.

Another bane of tribal culture was the system of slavery. And any slavery-linked economy can hardly achieve progress in directing human enterprise to produce enough surplus for accumulation.

Their marriage system was free from the pernicious dowry system. It was, however, linked with the active participation in work by the groom in the father-in-law's house. This helped to overcome shortage of male labour for the pursuit of *jhuming* activities.

Their system of inheritance of property was not favourable for generating sharp skew in the ownership of property among the scions of parents after their death. Acquiring of wealth, however , was not universally absent. Some of the tribal people did posses wealth and power in the society. One form of valuable wealth was their domesticated animals, mainly, *mithun*. And among some tribes such as the Apatanis of Apatani Vally (Arunachal Pradesh) who developed scientific irrigation and sustainable cultivation practice the system of ownership of property and sales and purchases of land existed. The Apatani Valley was a prosperous one. Similarly the Angamis of Nagaland practiced highly effective permanent system of terrace cultivation where also ownership of land as a productive asset obtained. They valued land as an important property to own like the Apatanis.

These sketchy descriptions of value systems of some tribes help us to understand existence of inter-tribal and inter-village socio-economic inequalities.

REFERENCES

1. Francis Fukuyama, The End of History? The National Interest Summer 1989, Washington DC 20036 (202).
2. J. A. Schumpeter, The Theory of Economic Development, Chapter 1, p. 6, contains an elaborate discussion on the circular flow of economic life.
3. J. B. Ganguly (1986). The Economic Conditions and change in North-East India, Changing North-East India, ed. A. P. Sinha, Gagan Publishers, Ludhiana, pp.13-14.

12

Society, Culture and Development

XAVIER PFOKREHE MAO

I wish to argue out a thesis that society primarily and basically consists of ideas that give rise to what is known as culture & development. Before I put forth my views I wish to critically examine some of the prevalent views about man and society.

One of the most influential views of man and society is that man is a lump of flesh and blood. The so-called mind, spirit and higher values of life are just figments of imagination; they are impositions from outside. This view of man gives rise to a particular view of society. This is, society consists of individual human beings. Historically speaking, this view of society goes in the name of contractual theory of society and state. Though the contractual theory of state and society was advocated against divine theory, yet it played a very important role. It gave impetus to the socio-political movement that tried to justify absolute freedom for man. But a little reflection will show that the contractual theory does not have any historical base. It is an ideology advocated in order to eliminate the divine theory of state and society. The theory had its hey days and moulded the attitude of the people as well. This clearly shows that the primary components of society are not the physical entities of human beings. This view leads us to conclude that ideas, ideologies and value systems primarily constitute the society.

The organismic view discards so called social contract as absolutely unhistorical. There is no historical record to show that a contract was ever entered into at any point of time by any body. Society and state are built into the very nature of man as it were.

This led the great Greek philosopher Aristotle to argue that man by nature is a social animal. So much so that he cannot live without society. That is why some philosophers conclude that society and individual are two sides of the same coin. In short, they are the obverse and reverse of the same coin. Organismic biology and the organic theory of society thus go hand in hand. German philosopher Hegel was the chief protagonist of such a theory. All types of culture and all forms of development are integral & innate to human society. In other words, the so-called external forces and causative factors of any culture and development are really insignificant. This appears to be deterministic and fatalistic interpretation of development and culture but in reality this is not so. This theory simply draws our attention to the fact that development and culture cannot be conceived without reference to a society. In fact, the externalist view of development and culture is to be accepted only with a pinch of salt. If culture and development are intrinsic to society then freedom and effort of man to change his/her lot is uncalled for. This view makes the freedom lovers to suspect the efficacy of this theory. Are the growth of culture and the so called development spontaneous phenomena or they stand in need of external agencies? This question needs to be answered but the organicists have evaded the question. In reply to this question various answers have been mooted. One such answer is that culture and development are internally connected. In short, a particular culture gives rise to a particular development or even hinders it. Max Weber the German philosopher and sociologist is the chief advocate of such a view. According to Weber it is the Protestant brand of ethics that gave rise to capitalistic growth and development. Further, Weber argues that capitalism did not grow in India because of strong belief of Indians in law of Karma and renunciation. Industrial growth and capitalistic development took place in Western Europe because of Protestant ethics and culture.

Let us examine the Weberian thesis. In a very important sense the Weberian thesis speaks the obvious. It is this: If culture is the totality of what man has created then development whether economic or non-economic is bound to be part of culture. Further this thesis does not have any scope for interference of man with the process of culture. As a matter of fact, there is constant interaction between culture & development.

Let us explain this point a little bit. To begin with, culture is not something that is visible and tangible. As we have hinted earlier culture consist of a set of ideas, attitudes and ideologies and value systems. Development theories in this sense constitute and integral part of culture. If this is so then cultures are made, created and are subject to change at any time. This is what we wish to characterize as transcending culture and this transcendence is possible only through constant reflection, analysis and examination of what we call culture.

With this background in mind let us discuss society, culture & development in India in general and North-East in particular. The multiethnic, multilinguistic, multi religious & multicultural nature of Indian society is both a boon and a bane to it. Cultural pluralism adds colour to Indian society but at the same time it puts stumbling block to economic & cultural progress and development. Sheer physical vastness of the country stands as a natural barrier to communication. This is so much so that people from one part of the country can find it difficult to understand their counterparts belonging to other part of the country. For instance, when many educated people in Orisa, Bengal and even Tamil Nadu meet the Naga students, they ask them if they are from China. Twenty five years back when the writer of the paper was travelling by ship from Mumbai to Goa on an excursion, was asked by the ticket collector to show his passport and visa thinking that I was from China or Japan. In this sense the huge size of the country creates hindrance in way of communication and interaction.

Thus multi culturalism has been creating hindrance on way to economic, social and educational development in the country. There are cultural and ethnic communities in the country who oppose all types of socio-economic changes. To cite some instances: years back the Central Government proposed to extend Railway line from Gauhati to Shillong, The Khasi Students Union (KSU) alongwith some political parties raised hue and cry and opposed the proposal. Their argument was that extension of Railway line to Shillong would encourage the outsiders (Dakhar) to enter into Meghalaya. Consequently the proposal was dropped. Further, in the eighties North-Eastern Hill University Shillong (NEHU) gave a proposal to the Central Government to allow them to open Engineering and Medical Faculties. The proposal was okayed but as usual it did not see light of the day because of similar opposition.

At a time, there was also opposition in Meghalaya to take away all Central Government offices and not to open any new one. All these clearly show how ethnic, cultural and religious pluralism stand on way to development.

Now the question is: how to overcome and get rid of these impediments? The founding fathers of Indian Constitution including some conscientious politicians and statesmen devised and introduced the concept of secularism to fight against the cancer of divisive forces. But this did not succeed. In due course of time all the political parties without any exception tried to rake up and mobilize communal forces for power game.

This is true that there is no substitute to democracy but the fact remains that democracy appears to be the worst form of government for the simple reason that political power holds the key to economic power and in a democratic set up individuals and political parties struggle hard somehow to capture and if possible to share political power. This strange and rapacious instinct in politicians brings about grinding halt to all types of development, whether economic, political, social or educational.

What is to be done now? How to improve the situation? In answer to this it can be said that there is no single method to cure this malaise. It is the duty of all enlightened citizens, politicians, teachers and student leaders to come forward and save the situation. But this is the most difficult task. Either we have to turn pessimistic and keep on brooding that nothing could be done or we pick up courage, look within and accumulate strength to change the prevailing situation. Such efforts should be made by all concerned to create a new culture free of all sorts of complexes and inhibiting forces. Success of development depends on culture and culture is created by man and it is not a given concept. It is created, made, unmade, modified and altered by men in the society in order to bring about appropriate and desired development.

13

Family as the Primary Agency of Education: Among the Poor Khasis of Shillong City

GITA PYAL

Introduction

Shillong is Meghalaya's capital and is also the headquarters of the East Khasi Hills District of Shillong. It is situated at an altitude of 1,496 metre above sea-level. The total area of the state is 22,429 Sq.Km with a population of 2306069. The density of population per square kilometer is 103. The percentage of Literacy in the state is 63.31 per cent. Male literacy rate is 66.10 per cent and female literacy rate is 60.41 per cent (2001 Census). The state is now divided into seven administrative districts. The Khasis, the Jaintias and the Garos predominantly inhabit in these districts.

The city of Shillong which was the summer capital of Assam during colonial rule, gradually became thickly populated by the traders, professionals and the missionaries over time. The importance of Shillong city not only as an administrative center, but also as trading center increased. After the birth of Meghalaya, the importance of this city further increased. The pull factor of the city brought many people from outside the region who got the social opportunities that a city like this could offer. In course of time the skewed development process in the state made a clearly visible rural-urban divide in which there was prosperity in the urban areas and poverty in the rural areas. The rural areas became supply areas for sustaining the Shillong city. Subsequently the rural areas started to be impoverished. The natural resource endowments in the rural areas became restricted due to timber operation and infrastructure building. The livelihood option of the rural poor became very restricted. This led to the rise of rural unemployment. A large section of the rural people started to migrate to the city in search of good hope. Some families migrated permanently and started to live in the down towns of the Shillong city. Most of these families because of their poor economic background could not find suitable occupation in the organized sector. They started to work in the unorganized sector. These people constituted the poor Khasis in Shillong city.

The families in the Khasi families play the most significant role in education of children and are the primary agencies for education and socialization of the children. The infants can develop as human beings in a family environment. The family lays stress on the kinship patterns. The mother-child relationship is typical in such kinship patterns. There is a strong bond of love and affection between mother and child and the position of the father is less definite. However, among all other people in the family his status has a clear recognition. The family initiates the process of education and teaches the typified ways of living, roles and of collective behaviour to the children. In the infant stage the role of the mother in educating the children is more significant. The early socialization process and early education of the children including the girl children start with the mothers. The mothers are primary teachers of the reproductive roles of the girl children. They are the primary teachers to the girls about menstruation and its rituals, health care and chastity. Apart from educating the children in different social norms, reproductive role and sex education, the Khasi mothers also give training to their girl children to undertake and run small business and manage petty shops in the urban setting.

In the urban setting the role of the secondary institutions is more significant in early childhood education and socialization. Nevertheless there are certain serious limitations of secondary agencies that often denies equal opportunities to all sections of the children. The richer class in the Shillong city does not depend on the family as the primary agency of education. With the growth of secondary institutions in the urban setting, the role of family as educator has largely diminished. The well-to-do families send their children to the formal schools. With the spread of missionary education particularly in Shillong city, the richer class people send their children to the pre-primary school and the children continue to learn from the formal schools throughout their childhood and adulthood. Some very rich people send their children to the metropolitan cities for education. But on the other hand there has been tremendous increase in under-privileged population whose children are deprived of formal education. Though education is the key to development and plays its role in bringing prosperity, welfare, security and qualitative improvement of the society, exclusion of the disadvantaged children from formal education is a cause of great concern. The children of the poor urban Khasi families often fail to provide uninterrupted educational opportunities to their children. They are to engage their children in income earning activities and formal education is less attended concern in these families. This inequality is generally maintained in many ways that restrain admission of certain categories of children to formal institution run by private owners. This includes higher fee structure, higher work burden, unfriendly selection procedure etc. Though the Christian Missionaries had laid the foundation of formal education in Meghalaya in the 19th century and subsequently the state government had helped the efforts of the missionaries through according recognition and even grant-in aid, the children of the poor communities were largely excluded from formal education.

In the urban setting therefore family as the primary agency of education of the Khasi children has survived as parallel institution of education and socialization. Mostly, the mothers of the poor Khasis have assumed the traditional roles in educating the children. They set the role models for the children. Though most of the poor families work in the unorganized sector, for all practical purposes, there is traditional division of work between the mother and the father, the wife and the husband, the woman and the man in the families. The father understands his dual role as father of the children and as uncle to his nieces and nephews. Accordingly he has the double role as educator in his own house and in the house of the sister. Similarly the mother has to retain her traditional role in educating the children. Through this family-based education, the children use to learn different coping strategies and survival education in the city like Shillong. Greater responsibility for children's education therefore lies with the family rather than with the secondary agencies in this matter. Such children as first learners receive education on their duties and responsibilities as individuals and as social beings, learn norms, rituals and taboos from the family. In most of the Khasi families in the Shillong city, the parents give religious education to their children. Even today in a large number of Khasi families, the children are taught to say their daily prayers, worship in the religious shrines, pay respects to the elders and show devotion to God. The family also helps in the intellectual development of the children. Many of the rural styles of life are inherited from the families and from informal teaching and learning process. In many poor Khasi households in this city, we therefore find strong prevalence of rural features. In other words The Khasis of Shillong city have retained even today many important element of their tradition. Under this situation coordination between the parents and formal education does not take place.

Major socio-economic change demands a system of education conducive to that. The family-based education in this sense does not substantively contribute to major socio-economic changes. A formal and high cost formal education on the other hand contributes to promote socio-economic changes. Family-based education of the poor children in the Khasi society therefore fails to promote real social change.

Khasi today are in transition under the influence of global economic order and new social forces. The city of Shillong is already exposed to the outer world. This gives opportunity to the educated elites to derive major benefits of socio-economic change. English education, Christianity, spread of communication and connectivity of the region contributed to the changing process of the Khasi life in Shillong. The focus of education on human resource development is not only to evince change in the socio-economic order but also to bring about transformation in thought, behaviour, motivation and skill. The traditional family-based education does not suit to this emerging need for human resource development. No amount of family-based education of the poor children can actively participate in evincing major socio-economic change in the city of Shillong. Informalisation of education of the poor children always would keep them excluded and marginalized in this process of socio-economic changes.

If education is considered a key factor of development, discrimination and neglect to the poor children have to be removed and the right to equal education has to be guaranteed. This calls for wider responsibility of the state to address these problems through not only more investment in formal education but also in motivating the poor children to come to the formal education system.

Female child education impacts maternal and child health and enhances knowledge and skill of the mothers. It is true that the incidence of infant and child mortality rates is higher among the poorly educated mothers. The family-based traditional health care and pre and post-natal care are not sufficiently safe. But the poor town dwellers lack knowledge, availability and accessibility of secondary health care and awareness. This also calls for wider responsibility of the state to address these problems through more investment in health but also in spreading awareness about mother and child health and clinical service.

The state's role in female education and health is more important for economic growth and physical well-being. In the family-based education the reproductive roles of women remain unchallenged. Many a time there are mishaps during the birth of a child due to untrained and unhygienic traditional birth attendants. But once formally educated, the women often become career conscious and marriage conscious. In today's world, the Khasi society is witnessing a lot of changes in family relationship, attitudes and values. Education, new work culture and urban living have given women new options. In the family, husband and wife equally share decision-making power. Indeed there is sharing of responsibilities and decision-making at household levels. They became more aware of societal problems and are more knowledgeable about their rights and entitlements. This in turn affects fertility behaviour.

But all these are happening in the affluent Khasi families of Shillong town. The poor children and the women are still captive of ignorance and are deprived of secondary education and health care systems. More and more poor women and girl children therefore should be brought under formal education and secondary health care systems.

REFERENCES

Bhattacharya, S., Sociological Foundation of Education, Atlantic Publishers, New Delhi, 2003.

Chacko, P.M., Matriliny in Meghalaya Tradition and Change, Regency Publications, New Delhi, 1998.

14

Gender Dimension of Social Sector Development in Manipur

ASHA THOKCHOM

Introduction

Development has invited a constantly provoking debates among the economists. Development encompasses multi-dimensional phenomena as embodied in the various jargons viz. economic growth, employment creation, jobs and justice, redistribution with growth, basic needs, bottom up development, participatory development, human development and sustainable development. In recent years the focus is laid on human development which is concerned with the improvement in various aspects of people's lives, i.e. social, political and economic. Changes in society of which people are the members, may be economic, social, political or cultural in nature. In fact incorporating economic growth more fully within the ambit of the human development strategy is a theme addressed in the HDR, 1996. In focusing on human development we go beyond a vision of development based on just its material aspects, though these are important for the elimination of poverty and the attainment of acceptable living standards for all countries and social groups. The normative framework for human development is today reflected in the broad vision set out in the Millennium Development Goals, the internationally agreed set of time-bound goals for reducing extreme poverty, gender equality and advancing opportunities for health education.

Social Sector

Some basic indicators of social sector refer to the activities which contribute to human capital formation and human development through education, health and medical care, sanitation, water supply, equality of economic opportunities, housing conditions etc. Again, social sector may also refer to the value system of the economy, such as values of freedom, gender equality, nationalism, habit of saving and control on consumption, long-term perspective instead of immediate gains etc. The components of the social sectors are supposed to contribute to the promotion of such values both at the micro individual level and at macro societal level.

Education, health and medical care are closely interlinked. It may also contribute to taking a longer term perspective with regard to each of the socio-economic activities of the individual rather than the short or medium term perspective. Similarly, the value of the preservation of national identity may influence the type of education that should be developed in an economy. The value of prudence and avoidance of consumerism while being consistent with the Indian ethos, may also contribute to the value components of the social sector. The restraint on consumption and promotion of savings may directly influence the environment, posing limits to growth. Environment cost may cause limit to industrialization.

Social sector is a complex framework consisting of several inter-dependent sub-sectors or components. Hence, when we are analyzing the effect of any policy measure on the social sector, the analysis cannot be limited only to a given component. It may also have to consider the inter-dependencies of the sub-sectors of the social sector.

Tables 14.1 Indicators of Progress of Social Sectors in Manipur

Indicators	*Units*	*Ref. Year*	*Level*
Per Capita	1993-1994 Prices	2004-2005	14901
Incidence of Poverty	Percent of Population (Lakhs)	2004-2005	17.3
Male Literacy Rate	Percent	2001	77.87
Female Literacy Rate	Percent	2001	59.70
Sex Ratio (Female/Male)	Per 1,000 Males	2001	978
Infant Mortality Rate	Per 1,000 life births	2002	13

Sources: 1. Economic Survey 2006-07. (S-12, S-115).
2. Census of India 2001. 3. NSSO Report No. 508 (61/10/1).

Viewed from the perspective of progress achieved over time, there has been a steady progress in Manipur on several indicators of social development. There is reduction in the incidence of poverty, rise in the proportion of literates in the population, greater life expectancy at birth, lower rate of infant mortality and maternal mortality and so on. Table No. 1 provides review of this progress.

Table 14.2 Trends of Social Sector Expenditure by Central Government (Centre and State Government Combined)

Item	*2001-02 Actual*	*2002-03 Actual*	*2003-04 Actual*	*2004-05 Actual*	*2005-06 RE*	*2006-07 BE*
Total Expenditure	644,746	704,904	796,384	869,757	1,009,668	114,929
Expenditure on Social Sector	137,843	145,226	156,893	177,016	222,210	247,572
Education	68,071	72,535	76,878	85,793	102,628	117,812
Health	28,578	31,457	45,193	39,078	50,164	56,932
Others	41,194	41,243	45,193	52,146	69,418	72,828
			(In Percent)			
As Percentage of GDP :						
Total Expenditure	28.26	28.77	28.85	27.82	28.30	27.19
Expenditure on Social Sector	6.04	5.93	5.68	5.66	6.23	6.04
Education	2.98	2.96	2.79	2.74	2.88	2.87
Health	1.25	1.28	1.26	1.25	1.41	1.39
Others	1.51	1.68	1.64	1.67	1.95	1.78
			(In Percent)			
As Percentage of Total						
Expenditure :	21.4	20.6	19.7	20.4	22.0	22.2
Expenditure on Social Sector	10.6	10.3	9.7	9.9	10.2	10.6
Education	4.4	4.5	4.4	4.5	5.0	5.1
Health	6.4	5.8	5.7	6.0	6.9	6.5
Others						
			(In Percent)			
As Percentage of Social Sector						
Expenditure:	49.4	49.9	49.0	48.5	46.2	47.8
Education	20.7	21.7	22.2	22.1	22.6	23.0
Health	29.9	28.4	28.8	29.5	31.2	29.4
Others						

Source: Economic Survey 2006-2007.

Trends of Social Sector expenditure by Central Government in 2001-02 is 137,843 which increased by 247,572 in 2006-07 in absolute term. But in terms of GDP it declines, which is shown in Table 14.2.

Table 14.3 Trends in Annual Plan (Manipur)

Sector	*2001-02*	*2002-03*	*2003-04*	*2004-05*	*2005-06*	*2006-07*
Social Services	171.72	166.78	208.48	362.52	393.82	432.66

Source: Manipur Budget at a Glance, 2006-2007.

Social Sector services in Manipur increases but still it require further improvement.

Gender

Gender Development emphasizes the most important aspects of the Quality of Life in Development and indicates the specifics of gender planning methodology to address structural and institutional constraints of gender equalities. Most of the plan proposals submitted by the local government to the central authorities are based on the enhancement of sectoral allocations for every plan period when major policies are already laid down from the center, and the state governments are mandated to implement the policies. The plan proposals need to be based on the structural realities and investigate into the local context, characterized by complex inter-actions of tradition, orthodoxy, and gender discrimination. Thus the women of Manipur, though play an extremely active role in socio-economic processes, are still insufficiency empowered to make visible impact in the society. In the background of the Millennium Development Goals, their need for improving the quality of life needs careful analysis and strategy. In the local or regional context recognition of gender equity and justice is yet to be properly conceptualised for inclusion of women in public actions. The Gender Development Index (GDI) brings the additional dimension of equitable development of the society into greater focus.

The HDI and GDI for India have continued to lag behind. It is ranked 96th for GDI.

Gender and Planning Policy for Manipur—A Theoretical Perspective

Overall improvement of the quality of life of the entire population on the basis of their full participation in the development process is being increasingly recognized as an important development strategy. Women, who comprise half of humanity, play a major role in the development of a society, and hence it is important to make special efforts to empower women especially through the planning process. In fact, gender issues occupied the central stage of development process in most countries including India. Empowering women to reduce gender inequalities in the society is presently a major concern of policy-makers and planners all over the world.

Scheme-wise Break Up of Women and Child Development Division (WCD), Dept. of Social Welfare, Manipur (Draft Eleventh Five Year Plan 2007–2012).

(Rs. In lakhs)

Total Child Welfare	7457.36	
Total Women's Welfare	177305.00	
Grant in Aid to Manipur State Social Welfare Board (50% State Matching Share)	90.00	18.00
Total: State Plan WCD	9974.41	2111.98
Total: Nutrition	16350.00	3270.00
Total: Central Sponsored Scheme	27501.17	5443.83

Source: Planning Department, Government of Manipur.

We see a variety of schemes and packages for women and children. But most of the schemes are still permitted with a welfarist approach to women.

Table 14.4 Human Development Index

State	*1981*		*1991*		*2001*
	Value	*Rank*	*Value*	*Rank*	*Value Rank*
Manipur	0.461	4	0.536	9	n.e.

Source: Human Development Report 2001, Planning Commission; Quoted from Tenth Plan documents.

Manipur ranked 4th in 1981 in human development, which declined to 9th position in 1991, so human development, as indicated by the human developmental index has not happened in Manipur over the years.

Literacy

There was a greater percentage increase in female literacy but this might indicate only the fact that the initial percentage was very low. The percentage of literate female is very low in both India and Manipur, but Manipur has a higher percentage of literate females than India as a whole.

Table 14.5 Literacy Rate

State	*Year*	*Literacy Rate*	*Male*	*Female*
Manipur	1991	59.89	71.63	47.60
	2001	68.87	77.87	59.70

Source: Census of India, 2001.

In 2001, 77.9 percent of men were literate, while only 59.7 percent of female were literate. Basic need like education is still beyond the reach of majority of females. Even basic education is still beyond the reach of majority of females of Manipur. The commitment and seriousness of the women learner are higher. The girls are topping at examinations from high school level onwards, but the literacy level for females is still very low compared to men. The awareness of women education is not high, and many young girls are prematurely absorbed in marital life before completing education. Women's education is yet to be harnessed with appropriate strategies.

Employment

Work Participation Rate

From the table 14.6, we note that male participation rates are consistently higher than female participation rates. The male participation rate fell from 47.31 in (1961) to 45.61 in (1971) in Manipur. Female rate fell from 44.48 to 24.66. This sharp decline might be due to conceptual changes in the definition. The totals of main and secondary workers still remain grossly under-estimated.

From 1971 onwards, the male participation rates have

consistently declined, while female participation rates have increased in Manipur.

Table 14.6 Proportion of Workers as percentage to population (Work Participation Rates)

Year	*1961*	*1971 (Main Workers Only)*	*1971 (Main Workers of Secondary Workers)*	*1981*	*1991*	*2001 (Main Plus Marginal Workers)*
(1)	(2)	(3)	(4)	(5)	(6)	(7)
Manipur Person	45.88	34.57	35.23	43.20	42.18	43.6*
Male	47.31	45.31	45.61	46.80	45.27	48.1*
Female	44.48	23.62	24.66	39.48	38.96	39.0*

Sources: 1. Calculated from raw data of workers obtained from various census reports.
2. *PCA-CD5; Census of India 2001.

Table 14.7 Unemployment Rates for Manipur and India by Sex and Sector

State	*Year*	*Rural*		*Urban*	
		Female	*Male*	*Female*	*Male*
Manipur	1999-2000	2.5	2.4	10.3	7.4
	2004-2005	1.2	2.0	8.2	5.3
Indian	1991-2000	1.5	2.1	7.1	4.8
	2004-2005	2.1	3.1	9.1	4.4

Source: National Sample Survey Organization, 55th round (July 1999-June 2000) and 61th round (July 2004-2005).

Note: Figures relate to usual states of individual. The employment rate is defined here as the number of persons unemployed per 100 persons in the labour force.

The unemployment rates of female workers are higher than that of male workers in both rural and urban areas for Manipur in 1999-2000, but in 2000, in rural areas, male unemployment rate became higher. For India as a whole female unemployment rate was higher than that of males for India as a whole in urban areas in both the years.

Health

One of the major aspects of social sector relates to health. According to the National Family Health Survey (NFHS-3) 2005-06, the prevalence of anemia and malnutrition in women in the reproductive age group results in inter-generational cycle of malnutrition and anemia. Therefore, this issue needs to be addressed on priority basis.

Table 14.8 Health Status of Manipur

	Expectation of Life Birth, 1991		*Infant Mortality Rate*
	Male	*Female*	
Manipur	68.64	72.42	36

Source: Directorate of Economic & Statistics, Govt. of Manipur.

Life expectancy at birth is the most reliable indicator of health status of a society. The intensity of health problems in life expectancy at birth and falling in infant mortality rate indicate that the health conditions in Manipur have considerably improved. As seen in Table No. 14.8 and 14. 9.

Table 14.9 Infant Mortality Rate 2002

State	*Male*	*Female*	*Persons*
Manipur	12	21	13
India	69	40	63

Source: Economic Survey 2006-2007 (S-115).

AIDS

AIDS has been become a major public health problem in the state since 1986. It is affecting a number of youths in Manipur.

According to MACS, the number of people living with HIV positive touches the figure 26,983 till June 2007. Number of HIV Positive reported to be 21,031 (sero-surveillance) and 5,908 (sentinel surveillance).

Table 14.10 Epidemiological Analysis of HIV/AIDS in Manipur

State	*No. of HIV Positive since 1986–2007 (June)*	*No. of AIDS Case*	*No. of Male*	*No. of Female*
Manipur	26,983	4131	3042	1089
Death due to AIDS	—	604	491	113

* 604 is the total death cases due to AIDS.

Source: Data from Manipur AIDS Control Society (MACS)

The HIV/AIDS is one of the responsible factors for pulling down the quality of life of the people of the state. If due attention is not given it might affect the entire generation.

Access to Safe Drinking Water & Sanitation

Another important aspect of development of human resource and the quality of life is the provision of safe drinking water and sanitation.

Table 14.11 Depicts the Access to Safe Drinking Water in Households in Manipur

Table 14.11 Access to Safe Drinking Water in Households in Manipur vis-a-vis India

	Tap/Hand Pump/Tubewell		
	Rural	*Urban*	*Total*
Manipur	29.3	59.4	37.0
India	73.2	90.0	77.9

Poverty

The eradication of poverty has been an integral component of the strategy for economic development. Poverty is a curse. It degrades human life. In fact, it is the root cause of all other problems. It is synonymous to poor quality of life, deprivation, malnutrition, illiteracy and loss human resources.

Table 14.12 Number and Percentage of Population below poverty line by states 2004-05

Sl. No.	*States/UTs*	*Rural*		*Urban*		*Combined*	
		% age person	*No. of Persons (Lakhs)*	*% age person*	*No. of Persons (Lakhs)*	*% age person*	*No. of Persons (Lakhs)*
1.	Arunachal Pradesh	22.3	1.94	3.3	0.09	17.6	2.03
2.	Assam	22.3	54.5	3.3	1.28	19.7	55.77
3.	Manipur	22.3	3.76	3.3	0.20	17.3	3.95
4.	Meghalaya	22.3	4.36	3.3	0.16	18.5	4.52
5.	Mizoram	22.3	1.02	3.3	0.16	12.6	1.18
6.	Nagaland	22.3	3.87	3.3	0.12	19.0	3.99
7.	Sikkim	22.3	1.12	3.3	0.02	20.1	1.14
8.	Tripura	22.3	6.18	3.3	0.20	18.9	6.38
9.	All India	28.3	2209.24	25.7	807.96	27.5	3017.2

URP Consumption: Uniform Recall Period consumption in which the consumer expenditure data for all the items are collected from 30 days recall period.

Notes: Poverty Ratio of Assam is used for Sikkim, Arunachal Pradesh, Meghalaya, Mizoram, Manipur, Nagaland and Tripura.

Source: Kurukshetra A Journal on Rural Development Vol. 55. No. 7. May 2007.

The number of people living Below Poverty Line category is 3.95, which is shown in Table 14.12; many of them are women and children.

Conclusion

Regulatory framework for social sector is to specify standards for the quality of services as well as standards for the processes.

Manipur still has inadequate access to basic living facilities. Scarcity of water affects women more, who have to go further and further in search of water for household purposes. In fact, fetching water also consumes considerable time and energy of women.

Economic policy should be guided by philosophy of redistribution of assets in order to ensure growth with social justice. Higher social spending is needed to improve the quality of life of its citizen and to achieve the goal of becoming super power by

2020. Increased spending should be accompanied by good governance in centre and state.

REFERENCES

Asha, Thokchom (2007). Population Growth and Quality of Life: Issues and Challenge (A Case of Manipur) Seminar Paper (4-5 June, North East India Council for Social Science Research, Shillong)

Data available from Manipur AIDS Control Society (MACS), period September, 1986 to June, 2007.

Data available from Manipur Budget at a Glance. 2006-07.

Data available from the Office of Employment Exchange, Govt. of Manipur (2007).

GOI, (2001). Economic Survey 2006-07, Ministry of Finance GOI.

Kurukshetra, A Journal on Rural Development. Vol. 55. No. 7, May 2007.

Maishnam, C. (2007). The eleven plan, Union Budget 2007-08 and the Higher Education Seminar Paper (8-9 April, Manipur University).

Nagesh, Kumar (2000). Indian Economy under Reforms, An Assessment of Economic and Social Impact. Bookwell.

Sophia, Arambam (2007). The eleven plan, Union Budget 2007-08 and the Higher Education Seminar Paper (8-9, April, Manipur University).

Souvenir, One Day State Level Seminar on Women for the Women, 18th July, 2006. Organised by, *The Pioneering Ladies Association of Manipur*, Imphal.

Yojana, A Development Monthly. May 2007.

15

Bio-Social Diversity among Caste Populations of Assam

DEBASHIS BASU

Introduction

Indian population ranging from North to South, and East to West comprises of different communities, largely tribal and non-tribal. Again this non-tribal proportion includes castes, Muslim, Christian communities, etc. These populations vary from each other in terms of language, religion, culture, habitat, and geographical locations. In the north-east India the populations mostly dominated by tribal communities have a small proportion of caste population which practice marriage strictly within their community and provides a unique opportunity to describe genetic variation. In such populations gene differentiation is generally studied after Wright's (1951) F_{ST}. Wright's F_{ST} is the correlation between two gametes drawn at random from each sub-population and measures the genetic differentiation of sub-populations. Afterwards Nei (1973) also proposed a method regarding genetic differentiation which makes partitions of the total gene diversities within and between sub-populations. In this paper an attempt has been made to estimate the gene differentiation and genetic distance at ABO locus among eight caste populations of Assam.

Materials and Method

The data on gene frequencies of *p*, *q*, and *r* alleles of ABO system among eight caste populations of Northeast India representing their respective positions in the traditional social hierarchy were collected from the published literatures so far available.

The gene diversity (heterozygosity) within and between the sub-populations has been estimated after Nei (1973). The gene diversity of the total population (H_T) can be expressed as:

$$H_T = H_S + D_{ST}$$

Where H_S is the average gene diversity (heterozygosity) within sub-populations and D_{ST} is the average gene diversity between sub-populations. The gene diversity between sub-populations (D_{ST}) is relative to that of the total population (D_{ST}/H_T is G_{ST}) which is called the coefficient of gene differentiation with a variance calculated as suggested by Chakraborty (1974). The genetic distance between the populations, among all eight caste populations has been computed by the method after Nei (1972). From the distance matrix thus obtained the dendrogram for eight caste populations has been constructed by the Unweighted Pair Group Method (UPGM) after Sokal and Sneath (1963).

Results and Discussion

Distribution of Alleles' Frequencies

Table 15.1 ABO Allele Frequencies (*p*, *q*, & *r*) among Caste Populations of Assam

Sl. No.	*Population*	*No*	*p*	*q*	*r*	*Source*
1.	Brahmin	536	0.1720	0.2420	0.5860	Das *et al*, 1986
2.	Kalita	895	0.1730	0.2140	0.6130	—do—
3.	Hira	266	0.1490	0.1740	0.6770	—do—
4.	Jogi	411	0.1640	0.1680	0.6680	—do—
5.	Kaibarta	532	0.2050	0.2220	0.5730	—do—
6.	Kumar	236	0.1750	0.2050	0.6200	Das & Ghosh, 1970
7.	Baishya	145	0.1460	0.1580	0.6960	Das *et al*, 1973
8.	Koch	102	0.1731	0.1266	0.7003	Sengupta, 1992

Table 15.1 provides the distribution of gene frequencies of *p*, *q*, and *r* alleles of ABO system, respectively. The same Table shows

that O allele is found to be proportionately higher over other alleles among these caste populations. The same observation is also reported by Chakraborty *et al*, (1986) and Rajkumari and Srikumari (1987).

Gene Diversity

Table 15.2 provides the values for gene diversities of *p, q,* and *r* alleles and heterogeneity chi-square in the caste populations. The inter-caste differences in gene frequencies are highly significant for the three alleles and the degree of variation is higher in B allele in the caste of populations. The G_{ST} value, coefficient of gene differentiation ranges between 0.83 per cent and 5.72 per cent (Basu, 1998). The higher value of G_{ST} is observed in the B allele which is followed by A and O alleles.

The estimate of G_{ST} has been calculated for eight caste populations. The results obtained are given in Table 15.2. The total and average gene diversities, intra and inter-populations are 52.38 percent , 52.01 percent and 0.37 percent respectively. The average gene diversity between populations is only 0.71 percent of the total genic variation in the caste populations of Northeast India.

Table 15.2 Analysis of Heterozygosity in the ABO Allele Frequencies Among the Caste Populations of Assam

Allele	H_s	D_{ST}	D_{ST}	G_{ST}	X^2
A	0.140861	0.143425	0.002564	0.018205	113.71
B	0.153092	0.161850	0.008758	0.057207	357.32
O	0.229932	0.231840	0.001908	0.008300	51.84
Gene Diversity	0.523885	0.520127	0.003758	0.007173	—

The magnitude of Inter-populations gene diversity thus obtained, indicates that only a small fraction of gene differentiation is attributable to variation between populations and since these populations are endogamous ones, it indicates also that no gene flow has taken place to that extent among them; therefore, it can be assumed that these populations are at an early stage of gene differentiation. In other words, about 99 per cent of variation exists within the castes.

Genetic Distance

For the analysis of genetic distances between the populations several methods (Sanghvi, 1953; Cavalli-Sforza and Edwards, 1967; Balakrishnan and Sanghvi, 1968, Nei, 1972 & 1973) are also followed. In the present paper the method after Nei (1972) has been followed to estimate the genetic distances between the populations. The minimum genetic distance between two populations X and Y is given by the following formula:

$D_m = D_{xy} - (D_x+D_y)/2$, where D_{xy} is a measure of gene differences between two randomly chosen individuals, one from X and other from Y, while D_x and D_y are measures of gene differences between two randomly chosen individuals one from X and other from Y, respectively.

One may notice that the populations furnished in the dendrogram show that Brahmin occupying higher strata in the Indian social hierarchy, is followed by Kaibarta, Kalita and Kumar in one cluster. Generally Kalita find themselves among these populations next to Brahmin. But the matrix is hardly structured in the same fashion. According to Hindu Varnasram system the Brahmin occupies the higher tier of the social hierarchy, which is followed by Kalita, Baishya, Kumar, Jogi, Koch, Hira, and Kaibarta. As in the present situation based on the dendrogram (Fig. 15.1) Kalita and Kumar together show minimum genetic distance measure (0.00013) making a cluster next to Brahmin and Kaibarta (0.00185), which together make a large cluster of four populations. A study (Kumar *et al*, 2004) of genetic analysis based on 11 genetic markers describes that (along with Brahmins and Chetris of Sikkim) Brahmins, Kaibartas, Kalitas (and Muslim) of Assam form a loose cluster, who do not only share the same linguistic family but also have the same ethnic affiliation. Basu *et al*, (2005) has reported the same genetical trend among these populations. In another two clusters i.e., Hira (scheduled caste population) and Baishya (general) are genetically close to each other (0.00042), and Jogi and Koch (0.00217) together form second cluster. The maximum genetic distance measure between Brahmin and Hira is observed to be 0.06757 which confirms their respective positions in the traditional social hierarchy ranking. The smallest value of genetic distance between Kalita and Kumar observed in this analysis may be the result of migration. It is reported to have opined by Nei and Feldman (1972) that the identity of genes in two populations is very high unless the migration rate between them is very small. Still, it is suggested that to get the reliable estimates of the average heterozygosity and genetic distance a considerable number of Loci rather than number of individuals per locus should be studied (Nei & Roychoudhury, 1974). However, it is reported by Majumder and Roy (1982) that study of locus-by-locus analysis and correlate the individual similarity or dissimilarity matrices with incidences of different diseases, has to be carried out to find out the patterns of selective pressures at different loci. Therefore, locus-by-locus analysis is also of interest in isolating a subset within a set of loci and can be considered more useful for the biological classification of populations (Rajkumari and Srikumari, 1987).

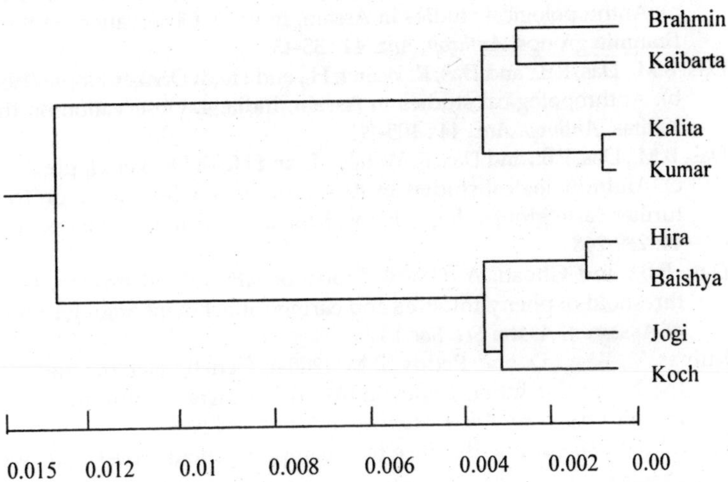

Fig. 15.1 UPGM Tree for the Caste Populations of Assam

REFERENCES

Balakrishnan, V. and Sanghvi, LD. (1968). Distance between populations on the basis of attribute data. *Biometrics*, 24 : 859-65.

Basu, D. (1998). Gene differentiation at the ABO locus among the tribes, castes and Muslim populations of Northeast India. *North-East India Council for Social Science Research*, 22 : 56-60.

Basu, D., Kumar, V. and Reddy, B.M. (2005). Genetic Heterogeneity and Population Structure: A study of North East India with reference to neighbouring populations. In: Das, R.K. and D. Basu (ed.) *North East India in Perspective: Biology, Social Formation and Contemporary Problems*. Akansha Publishing House, New Delhi, pp. 38-59.

Cavalli-Sforza, L. and Edwards, AWF (1967). Phylogenetic analysis; models and estimation procedures. *Am. J. Hum. Genet.* 19: 233-257.

Chakraborty, R. (1974). A note on Nei's measure of gene diversity in a structured population. *Humangenetic*, 21 : 85-88.

Chakraborty, R., Walter., H, Mukherjee, B.N., Malhotra, K.C., Sauber, P, Banerjee, S, and Roy, M. (1986). Gene differentiation among ten endogamous groups of West Bengal, India. *Am. J. Phys. Anthropol.* 71 : 295-309.

Das, B.M., Das, P.B., and Das, R. (1973). Genetic distances in respect of ABO blood groups among the four castes of Assam (India). *Humangenetic*. 20 : 179-181.

Das, B.M., Das, P.B., and Das, R. Walter, H., and Heidi Danker-Hopfe (1986 a). Anthropological studies in Assam, India, 3. Observation on three Brahmin groups. *Anthrop. Anz.* 44 : 35-43.

Das, B.M., Das, P.B., and Das, R. Walter, H., and Heidi Danker-Hopfe (1986 b). Anthropological studies in Assam, India, 4. Observation on the Kalitas. *Anthrop. Anz.* 44 : 105-115.

Das, B.M., Das, P.B., and Das, R. Walter, H., and Heidi Danker-Hopfe (1986 c). Anthropological studies in Assam, India 4. Observation on four further caste groups (Jogis, Hiras, Kumars, Kaibartas). *Anthrop. Anz.* 44: 239-248.

Das, P.B., and Ghosh, A. (1970). Study of ABO blood groups, taste threshold of phenylthiourea and earlobe attachment among Kumar of Assam. *J. Assam Sci. Soc.*13.

Kumar, V., Basu, D. and Reddy, B.M. (2004). Genetic Heterogeneity in the Northeast India: Reflection of Tribe-Caste continuum in the genetic structure. *Am. J. Hum. Biol.* 16(3) : 344-355.

Nei, M. (1972). Genetic distance between populations. *Amer. Nat.* 106: 283-292.

Nei, M. (1973). The theory and estimation of genetic distance: In Morton, *Genetics of Population Structure* (University of Hawaii, Honolulu).

Nei, M. and Feldman, M.W. (1972). Identity of genes by descent within and between populations under mutation and migration pressures. *Theor. Populat. Biol.* 3 : 460-465.

Nei, M. and Roychoudhury, A.K. (1974). Sampling variances of heterozygosity and genetic distance. *Genetics* 76: 379-390.

Rajkumari, J. and Srikumari, C.R. (1987). Gene differentiation at ABO locus in twenty castes and twenty-two tribes of Andhra Pradesh, India. *Am. J. Phys. Anthropol.* 72 : 95-99.

Ramana, G.V. and Narahari, S. (1995). Gene differentiation at ABO, MN, Rh (D) loci among tribes of Andhra Pradesh. *South Asian Anthropologist* 16:1-8.

Sanghvi, L. D. (1953). Comparison of genetical and morphological methods for a study of biological differences. *Am. J. Phys. Anthropol* 11 : 385-404.

Sengupta, S. (1992). A morpho-genetical study among the Koch population of Dibrugarh, Assam. *Bull. Deptt. Anthrop. Dib. Univ.*18-19 : 39-50.

Sokal, R.R. and Sneath, F.H.A. (1963). *Principles of Numerical Taxonomy*. San Francisco: Freeman.

Wright, S. (1951). The genetical structure of populations. *Ann. Eugenics*. 15 : 323-354.

Das, P.B., and Ghosh, A. (1970). Study of ABO blood groups, taste threshold of phenylthiourea and earlobe attachment among Kumar of Assam. *J. Assam Sci. Soc.* 13.

Kumar, V., D. Basu and B.M. Reddy (2004). Genetic Heterogeneity in the Northeast India: Reflection of Tribe-Caste continuum in the genetic structure. *Am. J. Hum. Biol.* 16(3):344-355.

Nei, M. (1972). Genetic distance between populations. *Amer. Nat.* 106 : 283-292.

Nei, M. and Feldman, M.W. (1972). Identity of genes by descent within and between populations under mutation and migration pressures. *Theor. Populat. Biol.* 3 : 460-465.

Nei, M. (1973). The theory and estimation of genetic distance: In Morton, *Genetics of Population Structure* (University of Hawaii, Honolulu).

Nei, M. and Roychoudhury, A.K. (1974). Sampling variances of heterozygosity and genetic distance. *Genetics* 76: 379-390.

Rajkumari, J. and Srikumari, C.R. (1987). Gene differentiation at ABO locus in twenty castes and twenty-two tribes of Andhra Pradesh, India. *Am. J. Phys. Anthropol.* 72 : 95-99.

Ramana, G.V. and Narahari, S. (1995). Gene differentiation at ABO, MN, Rh (D) loci among tribes of Andhra Pradesh. *South Asian Anthropologist* 16 : 1-8.

Sanghvi, L.D. (1953). Comparison of genetical and morphological methods for a study of biological differences. *Am. J. Phys. Anthropol* 11 : 385-404.

Sengupta, S. (1992). A morpho-genetical study among the Koch population of Dibrugarh, Assam. *Bull. Deptt. Anthrop. Dib. Univ.* 18-19 : 39-50.

Sokal, R.R. and Sneath, F.H.A. (1963). *Principles of Numerical Taxonomy*. San Francisco: Freeman.

Wright, S. (1951). The genetical structure of populations. *Ann. Eugenics*. 15 : 323-354.

Part II
Development

16

Between South and Southeast Asia: Recasting India's Northeast in the Age of Globalization

SAMIR KUMAR DAS

Development of the Northeast has always been one of Professor B. Datta Ray's abiding concerns as a socially committed intellectual. He is certainly not one of those who pursue their academic concerns from the ivory towers. With his feet firmly on the ground, for him the ground realities are never the end of the world. He is also seriously committed to changing the ground realities. His ethical concerns and social commitments constantly push him beyond the given order of things. Development—as I see it—comes as only a part of his larger ethical pursuits. To speak of development as the state's responsibility as much as the people's right at a time when development was considered as an act of charity by the state was indeed a courageous and audacious act. But then, to educate as the Greek philosophers tell us, has always been an audacious act. Doesn't it take too much of a courage and audacity to educate others? Development by contrast has become the new buzzword today. One can only oppose it only at the risk of becoming obsolescent. He has been instrumental in transforming the terms of development discourse. Now we talk about development of the Northeast by way of hitching her into the newly emerged economies of China, her immediate neighbour and South East Asia. This paper takes a cautiously optimistic view of the newly adopted economic policy. While India may develop, India's Northeast as I argue in this paper may not. We need to take certain specific steps so that the region may develop from India's 'Look East' policy. In a world where development has set up the terms of a politically correct speech act, it takes another kind of audacity to express one's trepidations about it. Time is always difficult for us if we decide to tide against it. As I write this paper I draw immense inspiration from Dr Basudeb Datta Ray's life and works. I dedicate this paper to his honour.

India's Northeast—as we know, is the cusp where South Asia gradually converges with Southeast Asia or vice versa and an otherwise vast and culturally contiguous space with the history of almost incessant immigration from both sides gradually reorganized into a number of heavily territorialized nation-states with rigid and nearly impenetrable international borders around them.[1] We also know that the region is yet to come to terms with this newly emergent reality and much of what is called, 'India's Look East Policy' is supposed to address this problem without disturbing whatsoever the given order of nation-states. The paper makes a critique of the Look East Policy as it is enunciated in its present form on the ground that it views historical and cultural contiguities primarily as a foreign policy asset to be tapped and exploited in order to facilitate the trade flow of goods and services across the concerned countries. The paper argues that if India's Northeast were to benefit from her much-touted Look East Policy, the region needs to be thoroughly recast in a way that will have its obvious implications for the nature and character of our nation-state. In simple terms, there is more to the Northeast than what India's look East policy would have us believe.

While many of Northeast's present conflicts have been as old as the formation of the region particularly in the wake of India's Independence and the reorganization of international borders around it, rethinking in terms of policy alternatives to get out of the impasse is only a recent development that took off in a significant way only since the early 1990s. Of course there were notable exceptions to this broad trend. But in general we have to acknowledge that there was an acute policy void which may be explained in part by the Northeast's emergence as a completely landlocked and therefore a 'lost' region and the attendant realization that there is very little that we can do in order to bring it at par with the rest of India and in part by New Delhi's persistent dismissal of these conflicts as simple law and order problems calling for equally simple law and order solutions. It is indeed unfortunate that New Delhi took over four decades to recognize what is commonly described as the 'uniqueness' of the Naga issue and accordingly the issue begun to be viewed as a 'political' problem only very recently. Whatever significance India's Look East Policy holds out for the Northeast will therefore have to be appreciated in the light of the sudden policy impulsion concerning the region.

Yet, the Northeast is widely expected to be a potential beneficiary of her Look East Policy primarily in two significant ways: One, the region could expect to gain enormously if trade is conducted over land across the region.[2] The region is likely to benefit directly from it by way of enhancing its share in the commodity composition and finding a vast market in a presently recovering Southeast Asia, besides enjoying its indirect spillover effects. This assumption itself is somewhat extravagant, given that a substantial part of India's trade with Southeast Asia continues to be of maritime nature and is routed outside the Northeastern region primarily through the port city of Vishakhapatnam (popularly known as Vizag) in Andhra Pradesh. Unless trade is carried out through surface or wherever necessary, intermodal communication (which according to a stream of policy analysts writing on the region is not only perfectly possible but makes good economic sense), the policy will have very little—if at all, to do with the region. Much of the literature on Northeast's claim to have a share in the advantages and benefits accruing from India's Look East policy is devoted to an analysis of the economic rationality implicit in the case being made for such unhindered trade flow between India and Southeast Asia across the Northeastern region standing on the strategically important cusp between several nation-states. The paper proposes to follow a different track—not simply because this has already been widely travelled but because viewing the region through the prism of economic rationality underlying the Look East policy is bound to offer a very limited albeit, an utterly blinkered perspective to us.

Two, the Look East policy can benefit the region, provided it is designed to invoke and emphasize geographical and cultural continuities between such evidently unhistorical and absurd, Washington-centred categories as, South and Southeast Asia by way of facilitating human movements across the international borders. Even as late as in November 2004, the Joint Declaration on ASEAN-India Partnership for Peace, Progress and Shared Prosperity set forth 'development of regional infrastructure and road, rail, sea and air transportation links to increase connectivity that would facilitate greater movement of goods and people' as one of its valued objectives (reproduced in Gupta et al 2005 : 21).

While much of India's Look East Policy according to this Declaration is inspired by the need for facilitating human movements between South and Southeast Asia, the commonalities and continuities of 'cultural heritage' are being invoked and emphasized almost as a clichéd ritual in all the relevant documents—primarily as part of the expansion of trade, tourism and the otherwise usual cultural exchange activities. As Prime Minister Dr. Manmohan Singh in his 'North East 2020' puts it:

> Full advantage may be taken of the Look East Policy of the Government of India. ASEAN markets provide big opportunities for NER, particularly in areas such as promotion of horticulture, floriculture and medicinal herbs. *Affinity in the cultural background will make our products acceptable and saleable* once the connectivity is improved. Air connectivity could also be considered when the need arises. Potential sectors in this regard are IT, tourism, mine and minerals, gas, oil, downstream industries, education, health services etc. The collective wisdom of NEC is in the best position to take a holistic view at the regional level and catalyze the implementation of government policies in liaison with the concerned Ministries (Singh 2005 : 3-4, emphasis added).

Northeast, according to the Prime Minister's 'Vision 2020', is thus called upon to develop in a way that it produces commodities easily marketable in ASEAN markets and build infrastructural support appropriate for the purpose. Northeast's development is envisaged in terms of its ability to cater to the seemingly expanding foreign markets in these countries. Cultural affinities are seen only as a means to an end and add to the 'acceptability' and 'salability' of Northeast's products. In simple terms, as is evident from the relevant documents, human movements that are supposed to take place in future as part of trade, tourism and cultural exchange activities require no special legal and political regime that might mark a departure from the established rules and norms characteristic of our nation-state. Human movements are not envisaged as a means of addressing some of the tangled ethnic and identity problems that the Northeastern region has been facing in the wake of Independence and reorganization of India's borders with the neighbouring countries. These movements are seen as only secondary to trade, tourism and usual cultural exchange activities. Look East policy is never seen as offering any opportunity to the region for solving its complex problems generated from alarming immigration from across the borders. Much of it occurs independently of so-called trade, tourism and cultural exchange activities. Many of the ethnic groups and communities living particularly in the bordering areas have their ethnic cousins left across the international borders consolidated as a result of the formation of nation-states around the region. Many of these divided groups and communities want to reunite with their counterparts across the borders. If various reports are to be believed, the region continues to be one of the most favourite destinations of ethnically contiguous population groups coming from the neighbouring states of Bangladesh, Nepal, Myanmar and other countries. While borders of a modern state are supposed to be surgically precise separating the nation from the outsiders, those around the Northeast have been exceptionally messy and by the admission of a section of our leaders, statesmen and security analysts, indefensible.

But, Look East Policy as Ayoob argued in 1990 was designed as an extension of India's overall 'framework' of economic and strategic concerns (Ayoob 1990 : 95) and unless the policy is backed by a separate legal, institutional and political regime geared to address the specific problems of the region, there is a possibility that the Northeast will fall prey once again to India's so-called overall framework of economic and strategic interests and concerns.

In a paper published not quite long ago (Das 2005) on the possible impact of Look East Policy on the region's emerging ethnoscape, I expressed a note of cautious optimism and argued that unless suitably designed, this might in fact spell a disaster for the region. It dealt more with how ethnic considerations are likely to blur the imperatives of economic rationality and less with the appropriate design of a possible policy. This paper is complementary to it in the sense that it dwells precisely on how this can be appropriately designed in order to address some of the concerns specific to the region. These relate to the three critical and largely overlapping issues of borders, citizenship and labour migration respectively. The rest of the paper is developed in three sections centring on these three issues. All this will have its implications for the state of our nation-state in the age of globalisation.

Softening Borders

First, the plea for softening borders particularly with Myanmar, China and Bangladesh springs basically from the recognition of the imperative necessity of facilitating rapid transportation of tradable goods and services and exploiting the 'opportunities' that remain beyond them. Borders are seen in the existing policy literature not as boundaries but as gateways to opportunities and of international trade and commerce (Verghese 2004 : 15-23). It is interesting to note that almost nobody speaks of human movements that may take place and are continuously taking place independently of and albeit outside the ambit of trade relations. We have to recognize that borders of the region also serve as the first point of entry or exit of people who cross them in order to be with those whom they consider as their cousins with the same perceived ethnic descent. The strong ethnic affinities that continue to exist across the borders even after several decades of reorganization of international borders in the region are evident whenever ethnic cousins cross the borders face problems in their part of the territory in order to be with those whom they consider as part of the same ethnic descent.

Robbins Burling's study for example points out that the Garos of Madhupur, now in Mymensingh, Bangladesh, despite many of their visible differences with their brethren living in the Garo Hills of Meghalaya in India feel that the place across the international borders is the land of their ultimate refuge. Thus, when they were attacked by the Pakistan army during the Indo-Pakistani war of 1971, about 15,000 Garos crossed over to India. In other words, that ethnicities and identities cut across well-drawn international borders is responsible for almost incessant migrations and cross-migrations. Not many Garos as Burling informs us were left in East Pakistan at that time (Burling in Raha & Ghosh eds. 1998 : 360). Any prolonged repression of these fraternal sentiments often generates strong irredentist reactions across the international borders. The Mizo National Front (MNF) for example demanded at one stage of insurgency the merger of all Mizo-inhabited areas of India with the neighbouring Myanmar where there is already a substantial body of people of Kuki-Chin descent—same as that of the Mizos.

Much of the insurgency in the region is predicated on the recognition of the region's geographical and cultural continuities with the neighbouring countries. Most of the insurgent organizations look upon the region as part of the greater 'Indo-Burma' region and once came together under one Indo-Burma Revolutionary Front. Although some works have been done—albeit sporadically by a few sociologists and social anthropologists of the region (see for example, Barbora 2005), we still await a sensitive historian to recover for us the imaginative history of the Indo-Burma region and its political implications. The region has been a standing witness to a series of acute xenophobic and anti-immigrant movements in almost all parts particularly since the early 1980s. However, the United Liberation Front of Assam (ULFA) notwithstanding its initial reservations decided to swim against the current and in a document released in 1992 described the 'people of Assam' as 'a collection of immigrants'. Yet as late as in 1991 in its letter to the UN Secretary-General, it maintained:

> The people of Assam, being determinate population as on 26th January 1950 i.e., on the point of the birth of the Republic constituting the Political Sovereign is *being allowed to be overrun by illegal migration* from Bangladesh, the erstwhile East Pakistan. Indian Laws have been separately framed for Assam seeking to legalise illegal migration (emphasis mine).

ULFA's anti-immigrant stance underwent a complete turn around by the middle of 1992 when it released the otherwise controversial pamphlet mentioned above. The pamphlet gratefully remembers the contributions made by the immigrants to different sectors of social life in Assam. It was for instance mentioned that the immigrants have been responsible for rendering the embankments and shifting river islands (popularly known as 'chars') cultivable. It is also unfortunate that they became 'pawns' in the hands of 'wicked' politicians and were used as 'vote banks'. The document 'considers the people of East Bengali ethnic group migrating from East Bengal to Assam as one of the main constituents of the public life of the people of Assam' and redefines 'the Assamese' not merely as the 'Assamese-speaking people' but as 'the veritable mixture of all ethnic groups living in Assam' (ULFA 1992:5, 6). The immigrants of the East Bengali origin so far held as potential candidates for expulsion were rechristened as, *Asombasi Purbabangeeya Jangoshthi* (East Bengali ethnic community living in Assam). Much of ULFA's subsequent political practice, as we know, harped on the historical and demographic continuities between Assam on the one hand and East Bengal/East Pakistan/Bangladesh on the other. If there is history of nation-states and international borders separating them, there is also the contra-history that always opens before us alternative possibilities of reenacting it. The contra-history interrupts the history of nation-states at every moment and imposes on them the onerous obligation of negotiating and coming to terms with it. All histories of nation-states in the region are closely shadowed by contra-histories of what could have happened but never had happened.

If ULFA's plea for recognizing the people of East Bengali origin as an inseparable part of the 'the people of Assam', a section of Naga rebels currently involved in the peace negotiations with the Government of India calls for the 'unification' of all Naga-inhabited areas—in some cases even falling outside the present territory of India under a single administrative dispensation that they prefer to designate as 'Nagalim'. In a sense therefore it represents the opposite of what ULFA demands. The Naga rebel literature is marked by an unmistakable yearning for reunification of 'Naga-inhabited' areas of the present Indian states of Nagaland, Manipur, Assam, Arunachal Pradesh and of course Myanmar. The Nagas of Myanmar are referred in the rebel literature as 'Eastern Nagas' and it is true that in the current debate on 'unification' of Naga-inhabited areas, the question of 'Eastern Nagas' is not being brought in, but as the Naga negotiators themselves acknowledge, the unification of Naga-inhabited areas within the present Indian

Union is being seen as the essential first step towards larger integration. The way states and administrative units have been created and reorganized in the region has been responsible for the fragmentation and 'dissection' of the 'Naga nation'. As Kaka Iralu, a Naga ideologue, argues:

> Rather than attempting to dissect other people's lands for a greater Nagaland, we had instead been victims of territorial dissections by foreigners for two centuries. Presently we have been dissected into Burma and the Indian states of Manipur, Assam, Arunachal Pradesh and Nagaland. The actual fact is one where some of our neighbours have become geographically bigger at our expense (Iralu 2001 : 30).

The Naga negotiators involved in the ongoing peace negotiations with the Government of India since 1997 are fond of emphasizing "the desire of all Nagas to live together under one administrative arrangement". The demand for 'unification' of Nagalim is reflective of their desire of mitigating the 'arbitrariness' involved in the creation and reorganization of states and administrative units in the region. It is widely believed that the creation of 'Nagalim' consisting of all Naga-inhabited areas of India stretching across such states as, Nagaland, Assam, Manipur and Arunachal Pradesh will be the essential 'first step' towards its further integration with the Naga-inhabited areas of the present state of Myanmar. The Naga case aptly reminds us of what Edward Said argued about the Palestinians, who according to him, fight not just for a piece of territory but against the 'territorial fetish' hitherto imposed on them insofar as they are subjected to live under administratively defined spaces and not the homeland of their desire (Said 2000 : 186). The way states and administrative units are reorganized since the colonial times itself creates a problem and displaces communities that get scattered between distinct and at times sovereign political units.[3]

Sanjib Baruah in one of his policy papers written evidently with the grand objective of making the Northeast benefit from India's Look East Policy, calls for 'transnational politics of recognition' (Baruah 2004 : 18) of identities of this nature that cut across the given borders of nation-states. Elsewhere, he stretches the point further and makes a case for conferring citizenship on the immigrants and outsiders who have already become an integral part of the political economy of the region. The transnationality that he speaks of, as we will have occasion to see a little later, looks one-sided insofar as it is confined to the project of citizenizing the outsiders. It also presupposes a certain softening of borders that facilitate easy identification and movement of people across borders without the impediments that stringency of border control by any modern nation-state otherwise implies, in a way acceptable to both the parties. While all theories of recognition have been centred on a notion of the other whose recognition serves as the precondition of defining selfhood, they seldom take into account the possibility that the production and reproduction of borders that separate modern nation-states from each other ironically contribute to the *othering* and dismembering of the self and makes it imperative on its part to recover it by way of piecing the fragments together and creating a new collective self in future. Much of the politics of recognition therefore secretes not so much from the other but from the dismemberment of the self that has been transformed into other.

In this connection, it will be instructive to point out that we need to experiment with institutions that will make such exchanges and transaction between people across two or more sovereign states possible without destabilizing the relevant countries or jeopardizing their security and territorial integrity. Never before in the political history of India since independence, has there been such an intense debate on institutional alternatives particularly with reference to India's Northeast. One, reform-minded scholars and activists like B. K. Roy Burman (quoted in Routray 2001) recommend a Scandinavian SAMI-like multi-layered parliamentary system in which ethnic communities scattered over different nation-states will have the right to represent themselves instead of being bound by the territorial limits of the existing nation-state. Two, Verghese recommends the formation of what he calls, a Naga Regional Council where the Nagas from outside the present state of Nagaland will have a say in the cultural matters of the Nagas. He proposes to revise the concept of Naga nationhood that is historically seen to be embedded in territoriality by that of non-territorial peoplehood.[4] It implies that people drawn from various territorial spaces can represent themselves in appropriately devised political institutions. Three, Sanjib Baruah (2005) in a recently published paper pleads for constitution of a bicameral legislature in which the upper house will consist of the representatives drawn from outside Nagaland. I have always argued that the initiation of this debate suggests that our polity has come of age. But this also requires that a space is created within the society for alternative institutional imagination and the institutional debate comes as the second step—next only to the formation of a civil society space in the Northeastern region.

Doubled Citizenship

Secondly and as a corollary to the first, such softening of borders also presupposes recognition of the double if not the multiple nature of people's identities. Insofar as one's ethnic identity is perched between two or more nation-states, probably the instrumentality of double citizenship could be a tribute to one's ethnic and community identity.

While appreciating the critical role the outsiders have been playing whether by rendering land cultivable and initiating the local people into the art of settled cultivation or by contributing to the region's prosperity or even otherwise, Sanjib Baruah makes a strong case for conferring citizenship on them.[5] This, he feels, will reduce their vulnerability to a highly discriminatory citizenship regime (he calls it, two-tiered citizenship regime) that has already been put in place in the region since the colonial times:

> The choice in northeast India today is not between a set of restrictions that dual citizenship would introduce for the first time and a uniform national citizenship where all Indian citizens have unrestricted rights to movement, residency and property ownership. What exists on the ground is a set of rule that distinguishes between citizens and denizens, rules that have fuelled an increasingly exclusionary politics of homelands and have been prone to generating ethnic violence and recurrent episodes of displacement. Dual citizenship in such situations would be able to introduce for the first time a regime of civic citizenship that will be in line with the actually existing political economy of the region (Baruah 2003 : 64).

One wonders why Baruah takes it for granted that in a region like India's northeast that is otherwise marked by acute xenophobia and frequent nativist outbursts, the regime of dual citizenship—once introduced, will be acceptable to one and all and the local people will automatically shed off their hitherto held ethnic prejudices and predilections and will allow themselves to be driven by the considerations of economic rationality implicit in his advocacy. It is one thing to rethink our policies hard but completely another to make them work in the region. It will be difficult—if not impossible, to implement the policies that promise to swim against the dominant popular sentiment. In the absence of any social audit of the policies that we seem to prescribe for the region and pre-assessment of their impact, we might end up by heightening the alienation that already exists between the rulers and the ruled and exacerbating the given asymmetries. Besides, the alternative of dual citizenship is of partial and one-sided nature. While it seeks to citizenize the outsiders migrating to and settled in the region, it does not factor in the possibility of people who may be willing to migrate from out of the region and be at one with their kith and kin residing in the neighbouring countries. These aspirations as we have pointed out are no less real and unless we are able to address them now, the crisis that the region has been facing might get deepened in future.

Our suggestion of double citizenship is meant for redressing this lacuna. Let us cite an example. Naga Mothers' Association felt alarmed at the rising incidence of fraternal killings by the members of two rival factions of National Socialist Council of Nagaland/Nagalim (NSCN) particularly since the mid-1990s. The two factions, although have concluded separate ceasefire agreements with the Government of India, could not arrive at any sustainable ceasefire agreement between them till today. There have of course been ceasefire agreements signed between them valid only for certain localities. As part of its 'Shed no more blood' campaign, a delegation of Naga Mothers' Association visited Myanmar in order to initiate talks with the Khaplang faction of NSCN with the objective of stopping fratricidal warfare between the two factions of NSCN. The visit was not only confidential but apparently 'illegal' for none in the delegation crossed over with valid official papers. This emanates from the belief that a durable solution to the Naga question cannot be solved if it is addressed solely from the Indian side. What the Naga Mothers have done is no doubt exemplary but should not be construed as a solitary example in the entire region. As we have said, the reorganization of international borders in the region has made it imperative for the communities to keep the links and liaise with their ethnic cousins, brothers and sisters in apparently 'illegal' ways. International borders have not prevented them from keeping up such kinships and linkages; they have only made them 'illegal'.

We suggest that double citizenship that is not anchored in the territorial limits of any particular country could offer a way-out of the problem being mentioned here. The double that we are talking about is not so much to make them citizens of two (or more) countries across which their ethnic identities are spread. The double is what interrupts and ruptures one's identity as Indian citizen and makes it perpetually ambivalent. The double hence should be taken as a strategy. The case is analogous to the present state of European citizenship that also incorporates within itself certain duality and ambivalence that philosophers like, Etienne Balibar have been gesturing to. Mezzadra has aptly summed up this discourse in the following terms:

> ...we have the space for the development of a set of social and political practices through which others of citizenship *claim and affirm their own autonomy*. ... We can frame these practices using the concept of subjectivation: while they challenge the distribution of parts—and the *borders*—that make a concrete social order possible, they point at different ways of being political, compelling the institutional shape of citizenship itself to come to terms with the claims that have literally no part within it (Mezzadra 2005 mimeo)[6].

In an age when people's identities refuse to be subsumed by their given identities as citizens of particular states, it is important that states come to realize this phenomenon. Liberal states everywhere find it difficult to disentangle the citizen's doubled existence for there is no reason why a liberal agenda of rights could always be subsumed within the compass of nation-state. There is always an 'inelegant upbraiding' of rights with nation-state that claims to be liberal. We need to experiment with institutions that will recognize their doubled existence without destroying the given order of nation-states.

Labour Migration

Thirdly, we have also to recognize that in the era of globalisation there will remain different groups and grades of people other than the commonplace binary categories of citizens and foreigners. The so-called 'illegal migrants' largely employed in low-paying, extremely uncertain and absolutely unorganised sectors of the economy constitute such a lot and it will be simply impossible for us to detect, disenfranchise and deport them. Assam since the movement of 1979—1985 serves as an illustration. While all the estimates based on politically motivated guesses made during the movement ranged between 8 to 45 lakhs (one lakh = 100,000) of illegal settlers, the Asom Gana Parishad government that came to power in 1985 could only detect a few hundreds of them during its tenure (1985-1990). The 'work permit' regime proposed by Sanjoy Hazarika and others (Hazarika 2000) is meant to address and alleviate the problems that spring from the supposedly huge number of immigrants in the region. Many policy analysts would argue that labour mobility particularly in the age of globalization looks nearly unstoppable, notwithstanding the national borders and restrictions imposed on international migration. Under these conditions, it would be difficult to put in place a legal regime that continues to take impenetrability of borders for granted. Rather a work permit regime advocated by some scholars would go a long way in solving the problem. The work permit regime entitles the immigrant worker to work in another country in a group where cheap labour is in great demand, but not to stay and settle or be regularized as citizens. The group collectively serves as a guarantee against the possibility of their 'melting' into the vast sea of citizens. While it is possible to keep a tab on the group of workers it is not so in the case of a single individual. The demand for cheap labour is met by the steady supply of immigrants from across the borders. The economic rationale is bound to work in favour of immigration. It is necessary that it does not create any political problem for us and elicit xenophobic reactions from the natives and the locals. The work permit according to Hazarika is going to be issued for a fixed period and unless renewed the group as a whole, will have to quit once the period is expired. This is the only alternative that, to their mind, is capable of solving the dilemma of separating the citizens from the workers. It is also important to note that a work permit regime cannot operate without any substantial improvement of India's bilateral relations with Bangladesh. It is necessary to enhance that country's stake in resolving the issue and making it realize that an Alice-in-Wonderland policy of maintaining that not a single Bangladeshi migrates to and is settled in India, will not do. A work permit regime can function only with Dhaka's approval.

Globalization in other words makes it impossible for us to continue with the same old border control regime and the sooner we realise its anachronistic character, the more the Northeast as a region can benefit from our Look East Policy most importantly, not at India's expense. Otherwise, the region might lose out yet again to 'the overall framework' of Indian foreign policy. The real challenge is to make them meet. This is certainly not going to happen in the short run. In our tearing hurry to reap the benefits of globalization, let us not give the region another miss.

NOTES

1. For an understanding of the notion of space implicit in India's Look East Policy see, Chatterjee (2006) in this volume.
2. It will be instructive to keep in mind that there is more to India's Look East Policy than simply trading across the borders, although international trade seems to be the key component of the policy. Thus it is for instance argued that 'since the acceptance of globalization by Indian and South-East Asian countries in the 1980s, India's trade has been taking a diametrically opposite direction from West to east' (Goswami & Gogoi in Barua ed. 2005:462). Thus, maritime security has become one of the components of Look East Policy (*see*, Rao 2006 in this volume).
3. Thus, in a recently held dialogue on 'Internally Displaced Persons (IDPs) in India's Northeast' held in Kohima on 24-26 August 2006, some of our colleagues from Naga People's Movement for Human Rights (NPMHR) pointed out that the reorganization of states and administrative units *per se* has been responsible for the 'displacement' of Nagas as a people. The prefix 'internal' in the phrase 'Internally Displaced Persons', according to them, is seriously flawed insofar as it accepts the given reorganization of states and administrative units as given and unalterable.

4. He makes this point in his note submitted to the first workshop on 'State building challenges in Asia' organized by East West Center Washington at Washington DC from 30 October to 4 December 2005.
5. We define citizenship not so much in legal terms but in the sense of its capability of investing us with rights.
6. I thank Prof. Sandro Mezzadra for having made his report on the larger project on European citizenship available to me.

REFERENCES

[*All translations from original non-English sources are mine. SKD*]

Ayoob, Mohammed (1990). *India and Southeast Asia: Indian Perceptions and Policies*. London: Routledge, under the auspices of the Institute of South East Asian Studies, Singapore.

Barbora, Sanjay (2005). 'Autonomies in the north and the northeast: More freedom or the politics of frontier management?', Policies and Practices 7, Kolkata: Calcutta Research Group.

Baruah, Sanjb (2004). 'Between south and southeast Asia: Northeast India and the Look East Policy', CENEAS Papers 4. Guwahati: Centre for Northeast India and Southeast Asia Studies (CENEAS), Omeo Kumar Das Institute of Social Change and Development, Guwahati, Assam, India.

Baruah, Sanjib (2003). 'Citizens and Denizens: Ethnicity, homelands and the crisis of displacement in northeast India' in *Journal of Refugee Studies*, 16(1).

Baruah, Sanjib (2005). 'Nations within nation-states', *The Hindustan Times*, 13 October.

Burling, Robbins (1998). 'The border that divides the Garos' in M. K. Raha & Aloke Kumar Ghosh (eds.), *North-East India: The Human Interface*. New Delhi: Gyan.

Chatterjee, Shibashis (2006). 'Space and India's Look East Policy' in this volume.

Das, Samir Kumar (2005). 'The ethnic dimension', *Seminar*, 550, June.

Goswami, Homeswar & Jayanta Gogoi (2005). 'Trading across China, Myanmar, Bangladesh and India:

Impact on north-east India' in Alokesh Barua (ed.), *India's North-East; Developmental Issues in a Historical Perspective*. New Delhi: Manohar/ Centre De Sciences Humaines.

Gupta, Arvind, Mukul Chaturvedi & Akshay Joshi (2005). *Important Documents in Security and Diplomacy*. New Delhi: Manas.

Hazarika, Sanjoy (2000). Rites of Passage: Border Crossings, Imagined Homelands, India's East and Bangladesh. New Delhi: Penguin Books.

Iralu, Kaka (2001). *How Then Shall We Live? Reflections on the Political, Economic and Religious Implications of Naga Nationhood*. Kohima: Kaka Iralu.

Mezzadra, Sandro (2005). 'The concept of the property of the self, individual autonomy and the modern European discourse of citizenship' (mimeo).

Rao, P. V. (2006). 'Maritime dimension of India's Look East Policy' in this volume.

Routray, Bibhu Prasad (2001). 'Analysing an Insurgency: On the trail of negation' in *Bharat Rakshak Monitor*, 49(2), September-October.

Said, Edward (2000). 'Invention, Memory, Place', *Critical Inquiry*, Winter.

Singh, Manmohan (2005). 'Northeast 2020', *Yojana*, December 2005.

ULFA (1997). 'Asombasi purbabangeeya jangoshthiloi ULFA rahvan' (in Assamese), [Call to the East Bengali ethnic group living in Assam] in *Budhbar*, 24 June.

Verghese, B. G. (2004). 'Borders matter more than boundaries from the northeast looking out' in *Man and Society: A Journal of North East Studies*, 1(1), Spring.

17

Institutional Reforms, Governance and Growth: A Case Study of North-East India

ASOK KUMAR RAY

Incorporating institutions in macroeconomic growth and in growth management is a recent phenomenon. The assumption that 'poor institutions retard growth' led the political economists of globalisation to incorporate the concept of institutions in the growth theory under globslization. These institutions included restructuring the institutions of good governance in the recipient countries in order to ensure rule of law, property rights and personal security of the investors; to improve capability of the domestic political institutions and to address political instability and investment risks. Good governance included a wide range of indicators and became conditional to foreign aid and investment in these countries. Under globalization free economies demand removal of pervasive restraints on economic freedom. One of the major focii of institutional reforms is therefore to seek and establish liberating institutions in the countries of investment and aid. A society's institutional foundation consists of:

(i) Formal laws, enforcement institutions and legitimated use of force as rational choice. It includes in other words legislative, executive and judicial reforms.
(ii) On the other hand, informal and spontaneous institutions are built by social interactions, networks, and community

based organisations etc. that are based within a community.

These include ethics, values, norms, customs, conventions, work practices, and professional standards. These rules are enforced in informal ways. Such informal institutions are also important in the reform process and these came to be considered significant in the growth theory. The whole range of institutional reforms also includes supranational institutions under globalisation that often act beyond the state institutions of governance in order to ensure safety, efficiency, effectiveness and Pareto Optimal growth. In the growth-oriented institutional reforms, the major institutional reform in terms of redistribution of land and other rural assets as the keystone to growth was, however, grossly undermined. The growth-centric institutional reforms virtually became a growth management reforms package to the denial of distrutive justice to the people.

In India institutional and governance reforms were initiated in the larger context of macro-economic growth. Reforms took place at macro, meso and micro levels. At the macro level institutional reforms included international agreements on trade and market liberalization, bilateral treaty rules and bilateral investment treaties, regional cooperation and supranational adjudicative bodies to deal with investment-related disputes. These became the potential weapons for multinational companies against developing country government and society. Such agreements are entered into between two countries for reciprocal encouragement, promotion and protection of investment on one another's territory by companies based in either country. At the meso level it included pro-liberalization policies of the state in all sectors of economy, policy regulations on cross border trade, foreign capital flows and fiscal reforms, executive reforms and governance reforms. Strategic partnership of GO, NGO and CBO was also promoted for smoothening efficient and market-led growth. Partnership was also sought for building synergy between GO, NGO, CBO and corporate sector. At the micro level it included decentralization of political power, promotion of civil society organisations and community-based organisations and networks of partnership and social capital. These institutional reforms are expected to address market imperfections in the less developed and the developing countries and to promote market-led, efficient and socially acceptable growth. At the same time these reforms at all the levels could help establish and strengthen the investment regime under globalisation. The meso and micro-level reforms fall largely within the state and the society spheres whereas macro level reforms fall within the international spheres that are dominated by global capital. In the final analysis therefore the meso and micro institutional reforms stood as domestic pillars for global capital and macro institutional reforms stood as supra national pillars. Eventually these domestic pillars so constructed remained subordinate to macro level (supra-national level) institutional reforms. The macro level (supra-national level) institutional reforms put heavy pressure on the developing countries as the resolution of any trade-related conflict between the investor and the recipient is not subject to standard judicial systems of the recipient countries. Rather these conflicts are governed by tribunals and similar bodies specified in the treaty. This amounts to privatization of commercial justice, with no accountability of the decision-makers in this regard. The two important such bodies of the World Bank's private arbitration body for investment disputes are the International Centre for Settlement of Investment Disputes (ICSID) and the United Nations's Commission for International Trade Law (UNCITRAL).[1]

The North-Eastern India

In the northeastern region of India institutional and governance reforms were initiated in the global context of the reforms of which India became a part. Terrorism in the region was found to be the major threat and concern for the foreign direct investors. Terrorism in the region itself got the major focus in the institutional reforms process. It needed an adequate policy option to ensure security of FDI, infrastructure and private investment and to strengthen regional trade cooperation. Terrorism, though a legacy of the past, assumed a different dimension in the contemporary growth economy in the northeast India. In the pre-globalization era, terrorism in the northeast targeted the internal colonization of the Indian state whereas in the post-globalization era terrorism arose largely out of growing unemployment, social insecurity and exclusion of the regional youth from the growth process. This posed governance threat and discouraged outside investment in the region. In order to win investors' confidence and to create congenial social environment for foreign direct investment the state governments of northeastern India anchored series of institutional reforms programmes. At the meso level, it included market-focused industrial and agricultural policy reforms in almost all the states of the region. The states in the northeastern India adopted FDI friendly industrial policies even to the detriment of the regional interest and the natural resource endowments of the region. Such policy reforms were expected to turn the tide of investment towards the region. A Draft Vision Document on "Peace, Progress and Prosperity in the North Eastern Region: Vision 2020" prepared by the National Institute of Public Finance and Policy was commissioned by the North Eastern Council (NEC) under the DoNER Ministry.[2]

At the meso level major reform was done in the North Eastern Council (NEC). Reform of the North Eastern Council (NEC) was made by entrusting to it the multiple tasks of development, promotion of border trade and security in the region. It was instrumentalised in privatizing the 'loss making public sector units, helping northeastern states prepare project reports for international financing of major infrastructure projects and integrating the northeast region to the South Asian Regional Economic Zone. The NEC was also expected to act as the lobbying agency for the northeast both at national and international levels. It was thought that the NEC should be equipped with technical and private sector experience. Other institutional measures included creation of regional finance institutions called NEDFi, a DoNER Ministry with a non-lapsable fund.

Secondly at the macro level, the Look East Plolicy, that almost went under carpet over the decades, was revived in the institutional reforms programme. This policy implicated the northeast in many ways. The major contours of the policy were to use the trade, market infrastructure and communication routes of northeast India for market entry into southeast Asia. Apart from the market focus of the Look East Policy, the policy was made instrumental in containing insurgency in south Asia. The policy was made instrumental also for evincing regional efforts of the SAARC countries for trade promotion and for containing felony in the region. The SAARC Summit made commitments for mutual cooperation among the South Asian countries for containing regional insurgency. Regional cooperation as per the Look East Policy invigorated in the reform process of the 1990s. Such cooperation had major mandates of regional trade, infrastructure building and peace and had synergised development goals with regional security needs. Institutional reforms also made the state of India assume the role of power state and the power image of the Indian state was sharpened with the imposition of draconian acts like Unlawful Activities (Prevention) Act, 1967, Armed Forces Special Powers Act, 1958 and National Security Act in this region. Imposition of these opopressive acts in this region may be viewed in the larger policy context of governance security.

At macro level the institutional reforms included a large number of Regional Trade Agreements (RTA) and Regional Cooperations. These as many people thought, could be able to overtake the multilateral trade negotiations under WTO and to lead the fate of the people towards progress and prosperity. But in fact such regional cooperations and regional agreements could not slow down the progress at WTO. On the other hand these did build blocks for the multilateral agreements. The major purpose of these regional coopeartions and regional groupings were to facilitate the process of globalisation of market, ensure peace and security and to serve the purpose of global trade growth. The whole scenario of the regional cooperations and regional groupings may be understood through what we call the "Domino Policy".[3] The northeast India is implicated in many such regional cooperations and agreements. The different regional groupings implicating the northeastern India include, SAARC, BIMSTEK, ASEAN, GMC, SAGQ, BCIM, South Asia Business Forum etc. Integration of the regional economy with the global economy demanded corresponding integration of the national economy with the global economy. Such integration would facilitate free flow of capital, goods, services and trade facilities in this region. Vital institutional restructuring for political stability, uniform rule-based system and governmental efficiency to strengthen its enforcement mechanism were required to be the pre-conditions for such intervention. Such regional cooperation did not necessarily go by the regime argument of one section of political economists of structural adjustment. Thus regime difference between Myanmer and India did not disable them to agree on common programmes for trade, infrastructure building and for curbing cross-border insurgency. Lack of adequate infrastructure, investment and business supporting institutions, perpetual restlessness in this region were found supply bottlenecks in this region. The conditionality requirements diverted the public expenditure towards ensuring security in this region. The macro level policy reforms have gone to the extreme of taking the task of internal governance by bilateral agreements.

The US Counsul, General Henry V. Jardine visited Manipur University on August 24, 2006. He remarked that "as a sign of our strategic cooperation here in East India, in September last year our two Armies conducted joint jungle warfare training in Mizoram. We also saw last November, the successful completion of a joint air force exercise: COPE-India at Kalaikunda Air Field. The exercise was the largest exercises between our two air forces and involved an extensive array of the latest air force technology. Both air forces shared information, gained excellent experience, and created an environment of mutual respect and understanding. It was also remarked that "These developments do not compromise India's sovereignty or independence. These are agreements between two equal, important partners, who look to the future and understand what some of their shared values and objectives must be"[4].

Although this remark pointed that it did not compromise India's sovereignty, it in fact did. Defence as one of the most sensitive sector should not be shared with any others for the sake of sovereignty. This itself is therefore against sovereignty. But bilateral agreements like this have been the parts of institutional reforms in the era of globalisation. The Defence Partnership between America and Mizoram is a unique example of how power state can operate with transnational support as per Defence Framework Agreement of June 2005. In fact South Asia as a region has become more vital to America's long-term military, economic and political interests.

But the trade-off between institution and growth on the one hand and denial of redistribution subsistence on the other hand could not be ignored. Although S.P. Shukla Commission found basic need, resource and infrastructure deficits and deficits of understanding, the 10th Plan became ambitious to open new opportunities under the new trade regime in this region. But things did not happen as expected. FDI flow in this region became vertical.

The new institutional economics brought in SEZ to displace the common property regime in the northeast. Highly subsidized industrial, agricultural and trade policies caused resource slipping. No major industry came up while many industries were declared sick. This created educated unemployment and caused jobless growth in this region. The 'movement of natural persons' became far restrictive in the era of globalisation. Looking from the wide angle of the WTO Rules on Trade and Services that are embedded in the General Agreement of Trade and Services (GATS), the services that are traded can be classified in four modes:

- *Mode 1*: services supplied from one country to another known as 'Cross-Border Service' (eg. Services provided across countries through telecom network);
- *Mode 2*: consumers or farms availing of a service in another country called 'Consumption Abroad' (eg, tourism);
- *Mode 3*: foreign companies setting up subsidiaries or branches to provide service to another country known as 'Commercial Presence' (eg, foreign banks setting up operation in a country);
- *Mode 4*: temporary movement of service providers either in an individual capacity or as a part of an establishment to provide service overseas, called 'Movement of Natural Persons' in GATS jargon (eg, consultants providing services abroad in individual capacity). Inspite of India's initiative for operationalisation of Mode 4 services and liberalization of market access for 'movement of natural persons' in the categories of semi-skilled workers, the developed countries including the American Congress have made Mode 4 non-negotiable as it is politically sensitive and displacing qualified American workers. This has disabled the developing countries to achieve Mode 4 services.[5]

These developments at the global level provided a renewed framework of conflict in this region. While insurgency reduced productivity of capital and discouraged private investors, increasing unemployment and loss of social security arising out of such growth model in turn led to new lease of unrest. At the governance front, in the absence of any institutionalized mechanism for conflict resolution, promotion of community-based organizations and micro-institutions and eventual promotion of social capital instrumentalised the archaic communities to act as bulwark again the potent unrest and discontentment. In the context of northeastern India such micro institutions included a wide range of institutions including SHG, Joint-Forest Management Community, Community Forest Management Committee[6] and the whole package of communitisation of public services (as in Nagaland). On the other hand capital inflow justified force as a 'Rational Choice' in the growth process and intensified militarism in the region. This trivialized political analysis of the regional insurgency and criminalized the entire community.

At the micro-level promotion of Self-Help Groups and Joint Forest Management Committees, community forest management (in Assam, Arunachal Pradesh, Manipur, Mizoram, Nagaland, Tripura);[1] Communalization of public Institutions like Village Development Board, Village Education and Health Committees, Village Electricity Management Board (Nagaland); self-help groups in Manipur, Tripura etc. tended to build social capital for smooth growth. From the strict angle of political economy the micro institutional reforms of such nature not only made the community institutions instrumental to global mandate of market economy but also opportuned the traditional money-lenders to re-appear in the garb of micro-finance institutions.

This in turn gave rise to subaltern globalization through trans-border insurgency, drug peddling, gold and arms smuggling. This region therefore produced more conflicts and deprivation. The growth model of the early 1990s on the other hand denied distribution, to avoid rent-seeking activities of the people and to avoid higher taxation on the rich. The advocates of the market-led growth model were of the view that high rent-seeking behaviour and redistribution would discourage investment and therefore would discourage growth. Moreover the finance capital regime under globalisation gave focus largely on speculative capital, not on productive capital. This practice downplayed the growth theory. The institutional reforms process in this region had to subscribe to this standpoints of global finance capital regime and had to adopt security-linked development strategy and gave highly subsidized packages to FDI. This scenario invalidated the hypothesis of institution-growth binary in the region.

REFERENCES

1. For details, see Asok Kumar Ray, Revisiting North East India in the Era of Globalisation, Om Publication, New Delhi, 2007.
2. The Assam Tribune, September 27, 2007.
3. Asok Ray, *Op cit.*
4. Remarks of US Consul General Henry V. Jardine to The Manipur University on "EMERGING TRENDS IN U.S.-INDIA RELATIONS" August 24, 2006.
5. Developing Countries and Trade in Services, CENTAD, New Delhi, Jan-March 2007.
6. CFI Supports Indigenous Communities in Northeast India.
7. Phase I of CFI's project conducted research to produce 15 community forestry case studies throughout the seven states of NE India and profiles of each states: Arunachal Pradesh, Assam, Manipur, Meghalaya, Mizoram, Nagaland, and Tripura. In addition, a documentary video, "Sacred Forests of Meghalaya" was also produced. In Phase II, CFI has focused its efforts on four pilot project sites in Meghalaya and Manipur. The proposed goals and strategy involve a multi-faceted set of activities including: protection and conservation of high biodiversity areas through indigenous institutions, facilitating Swidden transitions to more sustainable management of forest lands for livelihood requirements, and the formulation of policy and programme environments that are supportive of community forest management systems that are appropriate for northeastern cultural contexts.

18

The Coming of Tea in the Brahmaputra Valley

KEYA DASGUPTA

A growing interest in the study of plantation systems has been noticed in social science literature since the last few decades. One explanation has been the continuity in form in plantation regions. From being almost coterminus with colonization, much should have changed over the long period since colonization formally ended, from the political ties that have defined the metropolis-colony relationship, the scale of enterprise to technology, the boundaries and definitions of the market, and especially the institutional arrangements that have defined the relationships revolving around the question of labour. Yet significant features of present-day plantation organization have been found to be 'startingly similar' to those preceding it.

Even though plantation enterprises as dominant units of production have spread globally since the seventeenth century, almost coterminus with imperial expansion and colonisation, they have differed in the form in which they were developed and in their relative positions vis-à-vis the regional economy and society. In many countries 'the influence can be traced to virtually all aspects of human life because plantations are fully integrated in the economic and social order'.[1] In others, the plantation sector has been almost cut off from the regional economy and society, with very weak or no linkages with the latter. The particular elements in the social, economic and spatial structure inherent in the plantation system have given rise to distinct regional enclaves in the background of the traditional economy. In the valley of the

Brahmaputra in Assam, the northeastern state of the Indian sub-continent, a region where tea plantations were initiated as a commercial venture for the first time in the sub-continent, we find close similarities with the latter, though strands of the former are also seen to exist. One of the arguments that is aimed to be put forward in the present article is that irrespective of the region in question, the period of its ascent, the sources of capital and power, plantation systems the world over have markedly left their imprints on entire societies, economies, polities, manifested in the spatial organization of the regions in question. Such imprints over space still remain the broader context within which such regions have moved forward in time.

II

'Those of a generalizing turn of mind', wrote Sidney Mintz, 'find the plantation system of interest because it has been so effective a mode of colonial "development", for so long, in so many places, and for so many European powers.'[2] Distinctive patterns of spatial development at different levels, at different scales, in different contexts, in different regions, are reflective of some of the impacts of colonialism. Space in colonised territories has been organised and constantly reorganised within a global matrix of 'modernising' forces. The impact of such impulses has varied. At each phase, new points and areas are known to have joined the operational space, to get reflected in a sequence of stages of spatial organisation. These stages can be characterised by certain spatial concepts. These are movements: migration, trade; networks: river, road and railways; nodes: indigenous, service, market, administrative and others. The hierarchies created thus would tend to be concomitant with the specific needs of power and capital in the specific phases of development.

Through the evolution of a colonial economy and society based primarily on mines and plantations, several elements were introduced in the region's spatial structure not prevalent in the pre-colonial spatial matrix. There is need to probe, for such analysis, not only within the confines of the region, but also beyond, to areas that fell within the orbit of the interrelationships. The products of plantations catered to the needs of metropolitan centers of power located in the west. The processes through which this was achieved necessitated movements of capital, goods and people at different levels: both national and international. Thus even though our focus is on the plantation system in the Brahmaputra Valley, our context is much wider.

III

One must not assume however that pre-colonial Brahmaputra Valley was a spatially undifferentiated territory. The economy and society based primarily on agriculture and artisanal production were in the main self-sustaining. Yet, one cannot ignore the development of regional trading networks, even though these were insignificant in volume, and at a very preliminary stage of development.

The inception and consolidation of the export-oriented plantation economy of tea had significant effects on the wider spatial structure. Plantations brought along with them a completely new notion of economy, society and polity, accompanied by several appendages hitherto unknown in the region.

The background in which tea plantations were established in the Brahmaputra Valley was marked by a system of land tenures that set off vast tracts of wastelands as a distinct category from the land under traditional cultivation. There thus emerged two distinct sets of land tenures in the region: one for traditional and the other commercial agriculture, i.e. tea. Wastelands in the Brahmaputra Valley basically comprised of the different types of forests and grasslands, spread over the length and breadth of the region. Information relating to the extent of such land is fragmentary in nature, but an account of the province in 1841 estimated it at 'considerably more that one-half the extent of its area'.[3]

From the very beginning of the promulgation of the wasteland tenures, a marked distinction between wastelands and land meant for traditional cultivation had been maintained. This was particularly so in respect of the rates of land revenue. Wastelands were meant to be leased for 'special cultivation', exclusively, and were barred from the cultivation of the traditional staples of the region. Land meant for traditional cultivation could, on the other hand, be leased for 'special' cultivation. In other words, while the tea planters had access to both types of land, the wastelands were barred for traditional agriculture. Consequently, the planters could exercise their option freely and encroach upon land under traditional crops, if suitable tracts of wastelands had already been exhausted, or there were exceptional advantages in this course. That they made the best of both worlds is borne out by contemporary evidences relating to the extent of land taken up for tea under tenures other than wasteland grants. And the conclusion is inescapable that even if wastelands, which were the special preserves of the tea plantations were kept out of consideration, a marked discrimination was being practiced in favour of 'special', i.e. commercial crops as against traditional cultivation in the ordinary tenures of the region.[4]

The institutional factors governing the grant of wasteland for the purpose of tea cultivation thus laid the foundation of a system that was kept aloof from the subsistence economy of the region in which it developed. This duality exercised a tremendous impact on the economy, and the ensuing repercussions manifested themselves in many ways.

The conditions that gave rise to the establishment of plantations, and the institutional factors that determined the pattern of its development in the initial stages have thus left a deep imprint on land settlement in the Brahmaputra Valley. The changeover from a land use of a basically subsistence nature to one where the export-oriented commercial sector occupied commanding heights, was not gradual. Within fifty years of its inception, the rate of expansion of plantation acreage far out-stripped that of the area under traditional crops. Such transformations in the use and organization of space were clearly reflected in some of the cartographic sources, produced under the aegis of both official and planting interests, although most often than not the interests between the two overlapped. In the broad spectrum that characterized these spatial changes, from the level of the region, the district, to the individual plantations, one could clearly see a region being gradually taken over by powers that subserved interests not of the region, its people, its economy, but those of a world beyond.

The process through which plantations came to be super-imposed on the structure of the indigenous economy thus left along its trail a series of repercussions. These could be summed up, in the words of Clifford Geertz, writing on Indonesia, as representing an 'effort to superimpose commercial economy upon subsistence economy in such a way as to stimulate the first and tranquilise the second'.[5]

IV

'At various times and places the plantation has existed as an institutional isolate, or as part of a social system dominated by other institutions, but normally it survives only by generating and controlling a system of institutions around itself'. As evident from studies undertaken in several plantation societies the world over, 'this institution has systematized entire social orders.'[6]

Plantations were representative of a system that was significantly labour intensive. Work in the tea plantations brought about significant changes in the pattern of employment of a basically subsistence agrarian economy. The very nature of the economic and social organization of the enterprise was such that it necessitated the employment of a year-round labour-crew of numerous unskilled workers kept under economic if not political servitude, along with a highly centralized decision-making apparatus, where the management organisation was authoritarian, and the workers and decision-makers were separated by social and economic differences. 'As a source of labour supply for the plantations, slavery and then indenture resulted in the legacy of societies that consist totally of transplanted peoples'.[7] The plantation system has always been recognized to be one of the main settings for multi-cultural demographies the world over. The scenario in the Assam plantations since the mid-nineteenth century was representative. As compared to other tropical plantations in sugar, tea or coffee, the sources of labour were most often the same, the only difference being that for Assam, the migration streams were inter-regional, whereas for the Caribbean or Mauritius or other parts of Southeast Asia, they were international. It would be interesting to map these diverse, though often overlapping contours of labour migration for plantations in varied geographical spaces, a common denominator being the sources of labour. 'The creation of a new social order from elements drawn from different societies and cultures could be achieved', it was observed, 'only if there was sufficient authority and control to bring these diverse elements into line, for a common purpose'.[8]

In the Brahmaputra Valley of Assam, in the third quarter of the nineteenth century, the plantation entrepreneurs, faced with a shortage of cheap and servile local workforce, took recourse to the immigration of thousands of labourers from economically depressed areas of the sub-continent. Through a system of legal compulsions initiated by the colonial state, starting with the Workman's Breach of Contract Act in 1859, they initiated the 'indenture system' of labour recruitment in the Brahmaputra Valley. This system initiated for overseas migration of labour to the West Indies in the 1830s was almost akin to slavery that preceded it, except that the workers were paid wages.

The marginal representation of local inhabitants in plantation employment cannot merely be explained by employment potentialities in the other sectors of the economy. In the light of the increasing pressure on agriculture, the facile explanation offered by the planters and administrators that there was a 'want of industry' in the Assamese, resulting in their 'apathy' to hire themselves for plantation work is definitely unacceptable. The sub-human working conditions in the plantation enterprise acted as the major disincentive for the indigenous population to accept employment therein.

But a people uprooted from their own habitat, without any links with the surrounding community, would provide the ideal workforce for the exploitative mechanism of the plantation enterprise. In the relative incapacity of the migrant labourer to resist the inequities of the system lay the advantages of the indenture system. The system had already proved successful in other colonies.

Recruitment of a migrant workforce for tea was initiated in the 1840s. Initially, this was neither systematically regulated, nor properly organised. But the felt need of planters with the support of the government gradually shaped the pattern that crystallised during the years to come.

The processes of immigration of hundreds and thousands of indentured labour into a low-density region, to their settlement in the tea plantations have offered an interesting field of enquiry in social science research. Yet, the overall spatial context within which these took place: from the districts of emigration, through the depots in Calcutta and other centers, the accompanying changes in the routes and modes from a wholly river-dependant one to one where the railways played a dominant role, is an area, that I feel, needs more in-depth analysis.

V

The characteristics of the economy and society that preceded this period being basically subsistence in nature, did not call for interactions of any significance with areas outside its orbit. The insignificant volume of trade that was carried on was either with the neighbouring hill tribes or with the province of Bengal, where imports far exceeded exports in value. Exports consisted primarily of products from the agricultural sector of the region, and was representative of an agricultural economy where traditional cottage industries also had a significance. Such local and regional trading circuits, though not substantial, were almost taken over by long distance trading networks that called for far more efficient and speedier modes of communications.

With the introduction of tea, distinct trading networks evolved in a region that had so far kept itself outside an institutionalized trading orbit. These networks catered to the demands of a metropolitan economy and society, was export-oriented and depended significantly on imports. The outward moving trade consisted almost wholly of tea, whereas the incoming trade consisted of provisions including grain and pulse for the labouring population, manufactured goods, cotton piece-goods, both of European and Indian origin, and other items of conspicuous consumption to cater to the needs of an alien population—the tea planters, mainly of British origin, and the labouring population from other states of the sub-continent. An interesting fact in this context is that a considerable magnitude of indentured labourers from distant economically depressed districts of the Indian sub-continent comprised a bulk of the traffic moving into the region. The overwhelming volume of trade emanated from the 'modern' sector, the plantations, to destinations beyond the confines of the region. The traditional sector was left largely to itself, trading little either with the modern sector, or with the world outside. The enclavised pattern of transport development, characterized by the emergence of a distinct 'market space' is reflective of this scenario.

VI

The superimposition of an export-oriented plantation enterprise on a subsistence economic base thus brought about a qualitative change in the pattern and processes of movement of goods and people that necessitated the development of a transport network that could meet the demand of the emerging system of commodity flows. The pattern of this network, the processes through which it emerged, and the objects behind its development form the subject of our present analysis. It offers us certain insights into the ways in which the spatial structure of a colonial economic system evolved over time.

The transport network that existed in the pre-tea Brahmaputra Valley comprised basically of roads and railways. The roads linked primarily the administrative centers, and other nodes of local importance to other parts of the region. The numerous mountain-passes that connected the surrounding hills served the purposes of barter trade with the hill tribes. The condition of roads, as noted by Robinson,[9] was quite unsatisfactory even in 1841. The overland routes to Bengal remained impassable during rains. Communication with that province was still maintained through the River Brahmaputra.

The network in existence in the 1840s was incapable of fulfilling the requirements of the newly emerging commercial sector, which, for its very survival needed an improved and extensive transport system. Policies were formulated by the planting community, backed by state patronage. The government took an all-out initiative to serve such interests. As the outcome, a new system of transport network emerged, which was a combination of three modes: roads, rivers and railways. The first two were already in existence although the network of roads was later extended. The third, a new entrant constituted the modernised element in the system of communication in the region, in the last two decades of the nineteenth century.

Penetration of modern forms of transport was the special feature of the process of opening up. The region was gradually brought within the orbit of a wider trading area—national as well as international. A number of measures were taken up for the improvement of the road network. The government on its part took certain institutional measures of far-reaching significance.

That such initiatives were clearly to serve planting interests were clear from the alignments finally approved, evidence of which exists in the volumes of deliberations in the Annual Reports of the Indian Tea Association, the histories of the tea companies, as well as in other archival sources.

In the geography of a region like the Brahmaputra Valley, the river played a very significant role in the transportation system—both before and after the introduction of tea. The River Brahmaputra, flowing along the length of the region also formed the only natural transport link between the Valley and the adjacent province of Bengal. Its several tributaries and distributaries linked the interior of the valley with the main river way. This mode of transport, in the second half of the nineteenth century was primarily intended to facilitate the immigration of labourers, the export of tea, and the import into the region of products such as rice. The river did constitute the main backbone in the transport network till a long time, except that this network was strengthened further with other modes.

The railways became the paramount factor that determined the economic geography of the region since its introduction in 1882, to cater to commercial interests in oil, coal and tea. They extended and strengthened the already existing route network. They brought in a breakthrough in the system of communication in the sense that they provided speed and regularity on the one hand, and offered the added advantage of through traffic and certainty of operations at all seasons, on the other.

The phases of railway development in the Brahmaputra Valley are marked by certain significant features. Linking the plantations to the steamer ghats and roadways was the earliest endeavour. On the other hand, the rising demand for a more efficient and speedier mode of communication with the seaport led to the construction of the two trunk routes connecting the valley with the ports of Calcutta and Chittagong. Such developments were to markedly alter spatial matrix of the region in the coming years. The accompanying map illustrates the development of the railway network in the region in the initial decades, from a river and road-based network to one where the railways gained paramount significance.

Such developments have been known to be characteristic of colonial economies where the desire to reach areas of potential

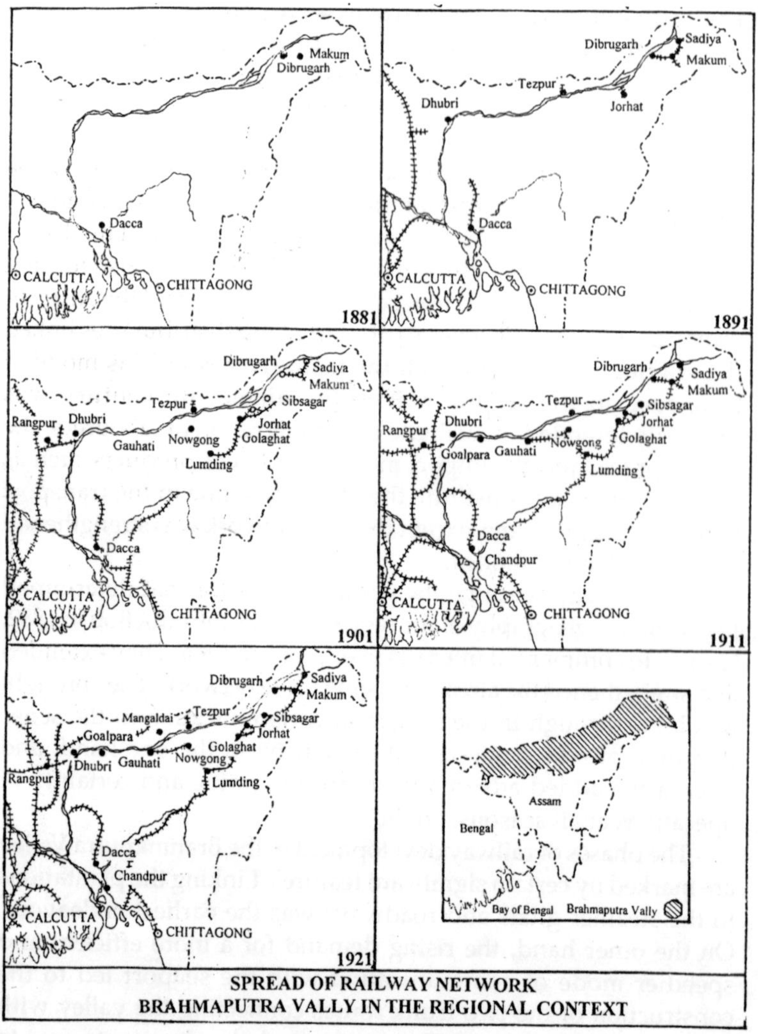

SPREAD OF RAILWAY NETWORK
BRAHMAPUTRA VALLY IN THE REGIONAL CONTEXT

agricultural production, areas of mineral exploitation, or to connect an administrative centre on the sea coast with an interior area of political and military importance, existed. Experiences in Africa, Asia, and the West Indies overlap. The difference lies perhaps in the crop, the mineral, or the source of European power. Taaffe, Morril and Gould have conceptualized the spatial manifestation of transport expansion in underdeveloped countries, with special reference to West Africa.[10]

VII

A hierarchy of urban centres and nodes emerged in the spatial structure of the region, and also beyond to cater to the needs of the system that was emerging. These centres were intended primarily for organising services geared towards the exploitation of the produce of the hinterlands. They seldom had any productive function of their own, and were very seldom conducive to the development of the region or its people. Towns that were the focal points of administrative control as well as nodes—located at transport junctions, to subserve the export-oriented, import-based plantation and mining economies, had their presence clearly marked. Centres that served other tertiary functions survived on their intermediary position between the internal and external economies. Depending on their relative positions vis-à-vis the plantations, transport links and trade channels, these urban centres continued to form distinct units in the spatial frame of the Brahmaputra Valley under colonialism. Noteworthy among these were Dibrugarh, Tinsukia, Doomdooma in Lakhimpur district; Sibsagar, Jorhat, Golaghat, Nazira in Sibsagar district; Tezpur in Darrang district and Nowgong in the Nowgong district. The internal structure of most of these urban centres were reflective of their role in the economy and society.[11] Most of these centers, surrounded by plantations, had shops to cater to the migrant population, clubs for the Europeans, repairing shops for tea machineries, financial centers, etc. The morphology of these growing urban centers, with distinct commonalities, as available in accounts, represented in maps, substantiates the above.

The Brahmaputra Valley was brought within the orbit of the metropolitan economy through a network of port towns along with centers at different levels of hierarchy. Calcutta, followed by

Chittagong were the ports that mediated in the system of economic interaction between the export economy and the metropolis. A spatial model incorporating the basic elements and characteristics of the regional structure under colonialism provided the framework within the dynamic relationship between the 'port enclaves of dysfunctional development', the mines and plantations, and the hinterland of primary production, were related through a network of satellite centers that subserved market, transport and administrative functions.[12] Beyond the confines of the region thus, other urban centres functioned within the dictates of the colonial economy. In the hierarchy of settlement units under colonialism, these were known to have been placed at levels higher than the regional centers.

Several elements got introduced into the morphology of the cities, especially Calcutta, as a consequence. Agency houses, Auction houses, Depots for the handling of both overseas and inland emigration, traffic of plantation labourers brought in from the surrounding rural areas to be again transported to the distant tea plantations in northeast India, were elements introduced into the city's land-use gradually. Hugh Tinker gives a brief account of some of these Depots in Calcutta, mainly catering to the traffic of indentured plantation labourers for overseas plantations, and named after these countries.[13]

VIII

Moving down the hierarchy of the spatial units observable in the present context, we come to the level of the plantations. One could probably consider individual plantations to conform to the definitions of a settlement system. The plantation was normally a self-contained production unit, which also housed its members and provided for their daily needs. But it was also a space, with well-established boundaries. Spatial divisions were clearly marked within the plantation. These were dependant mainly on considerations such as land use and hierarchy in the employment scenario. Only a part of the land taken up was given over to tea, and a portion of the estate was devoted to food and fodder crops and even to the pasturage of cattle. A major part was kept away for speculation. 'Although it is extremely difficult to generalize about plantation layout for the whole of the period of its ascendancy', it has been observed, 'it is nevertheless clear that the planters paid detailed attention to the subject. Their aim was not only to fit the component elements of the field and factory together in a way that best facilitated production.'[14]

To cater efficiently to the administrative, technical, and social functions within the plantation therefore, the built forms were very consciously ordered. The same sort of principal guided the layout of the workers' accommodation, the 'coolie lines', the most important function of which, after housing, was to facilitate control and discipline. Labour barracks were normally found together in one section of the plantation. The overseer's accommodation was generally placed near this area. Clustered thus, the workers were more observable and manageable. Barracks were built often in straight lines following in all possibility, the style of military barracks. Housing reinforced the control mechanism of the plantation, reflecting in its distribution and quality, the stratification and rigid hierarchies of plantation society.

IX

Space is both political as well as ideological. Moulded and shaped from historical and natural events, the transformation of space has been a political process and though apparently objective in its pure form, it is a social product. It is necessary therefore to make a distinction between space *per se*, that is space as a contextual given and the created space of social organization and production.

The specificities of space are products of interrelations, and their combined effects. These constitute the sphere of the 'existence of multiplicity', and thus the sphere of 'coexisting heterogeneity', which could perhaps be formulated 'as a simultaneity of stories-so-far.'[15] Space in developing countries such as India, countries that have lived through a considerably long phase of colonialism, is a conjuncture of diverse and heterogeneous smaller spaces. With almost no assimilation of the 'modern' sector with existing indigenous forms, the vestiges of the colonial era still remain in the post-colonial, bearing almost the same relationships.

The inception and growth of tea plantations in the Brahmaputra Valley under colonial aegis since the middle of the nineteenth century, and the transformations that were brought about in the organization of space gradually, are clearly reflective of the above. We have observed in the region a general sequence of stages in the evolution of the spatial structure under colonialism, manifested through the development experience of the plantation system vis-à-vis the rest of the region.

Although our questions have been posed within a historical setting in this study, the answers do have a contemporary relevance, since the remnants of a colonial heritage manifested in its spatial structure continue to thwart healthy coordinated development in the Brahmaputra Valley, even today.

NOTES AND REFERENCES

1. Beckford, G.L. (1972). Persistent Poverty-underdevelopment in Plantation Economies of the Third World, Oxford University Press, London.
2. Sidney W. Mintz (1974). Caribbean Transformations, The Johns Hopkins University Press, Baltimore and London, p. 54.
3. W. Robinson (1841). A Descriptive Account of Assam, London, p. 217.
4. This has been discussed at length in my article, 'Plantation Economy and the Land Tenure System in the Brahmaputra Valley: 1839-1914', Economic and Political Weekly, July 16, 1983.
5. Clifford Geertz, Agricultural Involution: The Process of Ecological Change in Indonesia, University of California Press, Berkeley and Los Angeles, 1968, 84
6. E. Thompson, 'The Plantation as a Social System', in Plantation Systems in the New World, Washington D.C., 1959.
7. Beckford, *Op cit*, 37
8. *Ibid.*, p. 38
9. W. Robinson, (1841). A Descriptive Account of Assam, London, Imprint, Sanskaran Prakashak, Delhi, 1975, p. 245
10. E.J. Taaffee, R.L. Morrill and P.R. Gould (1963). 'Transport Expansion in Underdeveloped Countries: A Comparative Analysis', Geographical Review, Volume 53.
11. This has been discussed in my article, (1995). 'Urban Centres in the Spatial Structure of the Brahmaputra Valley under Colonialism', Proceedings of the North East India History Association, Fifteenth Session, Shillong.
12. The model is analysed in detail in Boudhayan Chattopadhyay and Moonis Raza, (1976). The Indian Journal of Regional Science, Volume VII, No.1. This has been discussed in Moonis Raza and Atiya Habeeb, 'Characteristics of Colonial Urbanization: A Case Study of the

Satellitic "Primacy" of Calcutta', Occasional Paper No.1, Centre for the Study of Regional Development, School of Social Sciences, New Delhi, p. 7.

13. See for details, Hugh Tinker, (1974). A New System of Slavery: The Export of Indian Labour Overseas: 1830-1920, Oxford University Press, London, p. 136-137.
14. Adrian, A. Graves (1986). 'The Structure and Organisation of the Wage Labour Plantation in Queensland, 1862-1900, in Sue Eakin and John Tarver (Eds), Plantations Around the World, Louisiana State University Agricultural Center, Louisiana.
15. For a detailed discussion on this see Doreen Massey, (2005). For Space, Sage Publications, London, Thouand Oaks, New Delhi.

19

Land Administration in the Char Areas of Assam: The Task Ahead

GORKY CHAKRABORTY

Introduction

For any considerable group of people, land is basic to life. Socio-culturally, however, the importance, interpretation and value judgment associated with the term 'land' vary widely among various population groups differentiated by their socio-economic organizations and occupational patterns. A population group practicing hunting seems to differ in their interpretations of the term 'land' compared to the other group in the food-gathering stage. Similarly, the values attached to 'land' by the fisher folks and pastoralists are different. But the social organizations of all these occupational groups are weaved around land (although differently in terms of access, management and control of land and land-based resources) in such a way that the meaning of 'land' for all of them comes to the twilight zone of political, economic and historico-axiological categories[1].

On the other hand, in feudal or post feudal societies, land provided a major foundation for social prestige. Land ownership became hereditary in nature and provided social prestige. In feudalism people who owned land only mattered and others were thrown to an inferior position. Land became the basis of economic security and wealth. Similarly, land also became the basis of political power. This happened in history of mankind where citizenship and franchise were the prerogatives of the landowning class to the exclusion of others. Simultaneously, land also came to relate with sentiment, family prestige, religious, historical and other related values and connotations[2].

Therefore one of the sources of perceptual hiatus on land between traditional and non-traditional societies lies in history and epistemology. Experts are of the opinion that broadly, there are two concepts related to land. According to one group, land is simply a form of property that one trade at will; according to the other group, a sense of stewardship is always attached to land and the community has an interest in it. According to the later concept, the real value of land can never be expressed in terms of market and this inability constitutes a fundamental difference between traditional and market economies in assigning importance to land. Moreover, traditional societies are more concerned with the products of land and not with land itself. To them, land is rarely valued for its accessibility to a market or production of marginal yield or rent. But these aspects are inseparably linked with land among the non-traditional societies practicing market economy[3].

In the light of this broad based framework concerning land, in this paper, we seek to analyze the various connotations related to land in the *char* (mid-channel bars found in the river or the river islands) areas of Assam, both in terms of its historical continuity and in term of its emerging reality. In our discussion in the next section, we try to understand the colonial rationale of declaring uncultivated and/or uninhabited land as 'wasteland'. The paper then deals with the actual process of transformation of the natural habitats, such as *chars,* into areas of human habitations in the name of wasteland development by encouraging the immigrant farm-settlers from erstwhile East Bengal to settle in Assam. Simultaneously, the paper takes a stock of their contribution towards the agricultural development of the state. In the process, we also elaborate upon the legal and revenue settlement status of land in the *char* areas.

Wasteland: The Colonial Rationale

It seems that to colonial Britain, any uninhabited and unused land in its colonies was deemed as wastelands. Such lands were to be transformed into revenue yielding fields through the pursuance of various economic activities. In terms of the colonial policies, these wastelands in its peripheries were the *built-in-depressors* that hampered the process of development in the colonies, which ultimately restricted the inflow of income and revenue to the colonial-centre. But other than the 'revenue-generation' aspect, we believe that there were certain 'conceptual differences' also in terms of interpreting the term 'land' (including ownership, proprietorship and utilization of land) and land based resources between the colonial administrators and the natives, which generated the concept of wastelands. The colonizers, groomed in the *milieu* of industrial capitalism and the locales, entrapped in the tribal-feudal continuum, were destined to have divided opinion regarding the issue of land. This division of opinion of the British at the conceptual level was manifested in the process of land administration in the colonies in general and in its colonial peripheries in particular. In this section, we deal with the colonial rationale of wasteland in a nutshell.

To the colonial administrators, wastelands in their colonies were those, which were out of the purview of cultivation and settlement of population. It included highlands, forest, marshes, *chars*, land covered with grass and reeds and/or any other uninhabited area. Since they were outside the purview of taxation, they were nothing but wastes for the colonial state. The administrators therefore wished to bring these so-called wastelands under the purview of the sovereign authority. So the British administrators, in line with Weber's empirico-positivistic notion of rational choice found nothing illegitimate about the use of physical force by the colonial state for the use and appropriation of resources, including land. Similarly, the colonial administrators with the jurisprudential terminologies such as *res nullius* (meaning, that which is not assigned by the sovereign belong to the sovereign) and *terra nullius* (meaning no-man's land)[4] found nothing unusual in prefixing 'waste' to any uninhabited and/or unused land and its eventual appropriation for revenue generation.

But the native's interpretation based more or less on the historico-comparative view associated with Ehrlich was totally different. To the natives, it is social behaviour rather than state, which is the source of legitimisation of law and use of resources in a particular area. Their tradition steeped in ethno-history was based in the legal terminology of *lex loci rei sitae* (meaning law of the people where the asset exists)[5] which due to their usufruct nature did not treat any land as waste since all land belonged to the user or the community at large and on the other, all unused land (whenever necessary) had the scope of utilization in the emerging future.

This hiatus generated due to difference in interpretation of resource (land) and its use between the colonizers and the natives and the ultimate implementation of the colonial interpretation of law, led to the declaration of no man's land as wastelands by the colonial administrators. This as subsequent history proved, resulted in transformation of natural habitats into areas of human habitation in Assam. The highly fertile *char* areas of the state were no exception to this phenomenon. In the next section, we discuss about the human habitation in the wastelands, including the *char* areas by the immigrants from the densely populated districts of erstwhile East Bengal and their contribution towards the development of agriculture in the state.

Human Habitation in the Wastelands for the Development of Agriculture

Depending upon the colonial interest, the geographical boundaries of British India kept changing till the last days of the *raj*. The British administrators were mainly guided by the motive of revenue maximization and cost minimization of the administration along with securing the safeguard of the frontiers of the British Empire. In order to achieve these objectives they never hesitated to initiate geographical reorganization (without showing any respect to the notions of social and/or ethnic boundaries of the people residing in a region) of the north eastern region nor did they bother about the socio-cultural effects of settling large number of immigrants from far-off places into this region under different pretexts.

The large-scale settlement of immigrants into Assam for bringing about a change in its economy started in 1858-59 with the importation of 400 labourers from Banaras, Ghazipore, Chota Nagpur and Bihar to serve the labour requirements of the emerging plantation sector in the state[6]. Once the process started in plantation, there was no looking back. It continued unabatedly over a long stretch of time. The advent of the *char* dwellers from the densely populated districts of erstwhile East Bengal into Assam in the name of wasteland settlement and development of agriculture in the state was also an attempt in that direction.

The economy of Assam during the last quarter of the 19th century exhibited dual characteristics. On the one hand, there was a near stagnation in the agriculture sector (due to various reasons) managed by the local inhabitants and on the other there was rapid expansion in the emerging modern sector (such as tea, railways, transport and communication, oil, plywood etc), which was developed largely by people from outside the state under the patronage of the colonial administration. The expansion of these emerging sectors required large-scale influx of working people from outside the state. This increased rapidly the demand for food-grains (along with various other things) within the state, which the stagnating agricultural sector was unable to meet. The higher demand for foodgrains was therefore met through imports from outside the state. It is estimated that the annual import of food-grains into Brahmaputra valley, increased from 0.3 million *maunds* around 1872 to 0.7 million *maunds* during the last five years of the 19th century[7].

The indigenous peasants in Assam showed little inclination to increase the area under cultivation and reap the benefit of the rising demand of foodgrains within the state[8]. Above all, the colonial policy of *'robbing the peasants to pay the planter'* also acted as one of the important deterrents (among various others) in the process of agricultural growth in the state. In fact, the British administration used the land revenue policy in such a manner that the main burden of enhanced revenue could be borne by the indigenous peasants while the European planters would contribute little. The peasants overburdened with steep rates of land revenue showed little interest in increasing the area under cultivation. It is reported that during 1869 to 1905, land revenue increased by 80 per cent while the area under cultivation increased by 17 per cent only[9]. Similarly, there are estimates that while the index number of total tea acreage in Assam Proper steadily increased to 192 (taking 1884-85 as the base year) during 1900-01, the comparable index of total gross cropped area rose to 113 only during the same period[10]. Thus, the preferential treatment towards to the European planters and overburdening of the indigenous peasants with higher rates of land revenue proved to be one of the major retrograde steps towards expanding the base of agriculture in the state.

The colonial administrators wanted to change the stagnant agricultural situation in Assam by encouraging farm labourers from various densely populated districts of East Bengal (presently Bangladesh) to migrate, settle and cultivate in the sparsely populated areas of land abundant Assam. They were encouraged to bring the uncultured wastes and fallow lands including the *char* areas in Assam under cultivation, which could not only raise the foodgrain production but also could generate additional revenue through the cultivation of cash crops, particularly jute. But this colonial scheme did not materialize in the short run since the peasants from East Bengal showed little inclination to migrate and settle in the wastelands of Assam. It was only during the first Partition of Bengal in 1905 (when Assam and East Bengal became one province under one administration), when for the first time, the process of large-scale migration of population (from East Bengal) started into the wastelands of Assam.

The Census Report of 1911 for the first time mentioned about the movement of these people from various densely populated districts of East Bengal to Assam (mainly Goalpara district). During 1904-11, there were 54000 migrants from East Bengal to Assam Proper. After 1911, fresh batch followed them and they moved into various districts of the Brahmaputra Valley as well. By 1921, altogether 141 thousand East Bengal immigrants had settled in Goalpara and 117 thousand in Assam Proper[11]. In other words, during the period 1900-01 to 1920-21, the population of Assam increased by 41 per cent mainly due to immigration[12]. The number of immigrants increased to 575,000 during 1931 and in between 1931 to 1951, the total number of immigrants was about 430,000. Thus, it is estimated that in 1957, the total number of farm-settlers from East Bengal must have been around one to one and a half million, which was between one-tenth to one-sixth of the total population of the state[13].

These farm-settlers from East Bengal brought in huge tracts of waste and fallow lands under cultivation in Assam, particularly in the Brahmaputra Valley. It was during this period that the *char* areas of the Brahmaputra and its tributaries were transformed from natural habitats into areas of human habitation. It is estimated that in the Brahmaputra Valley, a total of 737,367 acres of land was settled with the immigrants from Mymensingh during 1920-21 to 1929-30. This increased to 5,967,000 during 1930-31 to 1939-40 and during 1940-41 to 1947-48 another 6,213,000 acres of wastelands was settled with the immigrants from East Bengal[14]. In the over all analysis, out of the 1.1 million acres of wastelands settled with all the immigrants in Assam, East Bengal farm-settlers accounted for nearly half a million acres. In fact, due to the immigration and their settlement (along with tea cultivation), wasteland in Assam was reduced from 9.93 million acres to 6.83 million acres during 1947-48. The cropped area under cultivation increased from 2.40 million acres to 4.79 million acres during the period 1901-02 to 1947-48 and the area sown more than once increased from 0.21 million acres to 0.71 million acres during the same period[15].

Along with bringing large areas of waste and fallow lands under cultivation, the skilled and hard working East Bengal farm-settlers introduced new crop varieties and also provided a commercial touch to agricultural operations in the state. Crops such as jute, buckwheat, sesame, linseed, mustard, onion, garlic, tobacco, sugarcane and number of spices, condiment and vegetable were commercially cultivated by these immigrants. Their biggest contribution was made towards large-scale cultivation of jute. Earlier to their advent, jute cultivation was very limited in Assam. From a meagre of 5 thousand acres during 1901-02, it increased to 277 thousand acres by 1941-42[16]. This was the single biggest contribution of these farm-settlers towards cash crop production in Assam. It is observed that in all the crops cultivated by the immigrants, the increase in area sown was substantially higher compared to those crops where their involvement was marginal, e.g. acreage of crops such tobacco, sugarcane, rapeseed and mustard etc. showed a substantial rise whereas cotton, a crop where their involvement was nominal, showed a stationary trend.

Similarly, average rise in production of crops cultivated in the four immigrant prone districts (Goalpara, Kamrup, Nowgong and Darrang) of the Brahmaputra Valley was far higher than the state average. It is estimated that during 1924-25 to 1947-48, the production per acre of autumn paddy increased by 11.27 per cent in these four immigrant prone districts compared to 5.3 per cent only for the province as a whole. For winter paddy, it was 12.05 per cent and 5.20 per cent respectively. For rapeseed & mustard, it was 6.30 per cent and 4.4 percent. For sugarcane it was 19.95 per cent and 7.7 per cent and for jute; it was 18.85 per cent and 8.80 per cent respectively[17].

Therefore, the huge transfer of population from East Bengal into Assam and subsequent grant, sale and occupation of waste, fallow and uncultivable lands changed the agricultural scenario of the state dramatically. There was not only a rise in the area under cultivation but also greater availability of foodgrains in the state. The state also gained revenue by exporting jute[18] and other commercial crops grown by these immigrant cultivators. Thus, it is evident that the colonial government gained considerably due to the advent of the farm-settlers from East Bengal to Assam. However, the moot question remains as to what legislative safeguard was provided by the government to the land of these settlers, particularly in the *char* areas of Assam? In the next sections, we discuss about the land legislative and revenue settlement policies related with these areas of the state during the colonial period.

Land Legislation Concerning the *Char* Areas

Due to the temporary life span of land in *char* areas[19], enactment of legislation concerning its possession and other related aspects, is difficult. However, history seems to reveal that there have been attempts to frame rules and legislations for administering these areas from very early days of civilization.

It is believed that the Romans[20] were one of the first people to develop laws of alluvion and dilluvion, a process, which they regarded as natural phenomenon. They not only dealt with these processes in their jurisprudence but also mentioned in details regarding the riparian rights (both, in sea and river) of such formations and de-formations. Similarly, in the Halsbury's Law of England[21], one comes across discussion about the doctrine of accretion and the fundamental rights accruing from such accretions.

The earliest legal enactment regarding land legislation in *char* areas was The Bengal Alluvion and Dilluvion Regulation, 1825. Section 4(3) of this Regulation states that when "a *char* or island is thrown up in a large navigable river (the bed of which is not the property of an individual), or in the sea, and the channel of the river or sea, between such island and the shore may not be fordable, it shall according to established usage, be at the disposal of the government"[22]. But if the "channel between such island and the shore is fordable at any season of the year, it shall be considered an accession to the land tenure or tenures of the person or persons may be most contiguous to it, subject to several provisions" [23].

Nevertheless, problem arose in implementing this Regulation since various regions of Eastern and Northeastern India came under the British domain at different points of time and had different types of land revenue administration. As a result, it was decided that this Regulation would be a statutory law in some areas (i.e. in those places, which were parts of British India during 1825) while in others, the spirit of this Regulation will be followed and disputes will be resolved according to the principle of justice, equity, customs and good conscience. Therefore, in Assam, the spirit of this Regulation was followed since the state came under British tutelage in 1826.

Following the spirit of the Regulation, in Assam, during 1897, under Section 3 and 5 of the Scheduled Districts Act, 1874, a notification was issued in the Assam Gazette (1242J) through which The Bengal Alluvion and Dilluvion Regulation of 1825 came into force in Assam. This legal enactment was valid in the state for the next 32 years. But suddenly, during 1929, through a notification (2402R) under Section 3(c) of The Scheduled District Act, 1874 it was stated that the areas concerning the districts of Cachar, Kamrup, Darrang, Nowgong, Sibsagar, Lakhimpur and Eastern Duars of Goalpara District shall be excluded from the purview of the Regulation. Incidentally, all these areas excluded were under Temporary Revenue Settlement. Another notification (713-L) was issued during 1937, which restricted the application of this Regulation to the districts of Sylhet, Goalpara (except Eastern Duars), Garo Hills, Khasi & Jaintia Hills and Naga Hills only[24]. Here, it should be mentioned that while the continuation of this Regulation in Sylhet and Goalpara districts (both permanently settled areas) were understood yet inclusion of other hilly areas under its purview, were somewhat confusing. Therefore, it seems that although a sketchy legislative provision concerning land in *char* areas existed during the colonial era, yet its interpretation and implementation was ambiguous and whimsical.

On the other hand, there were various contentious aspects related to land in *char* areas, which remained outside the purview of legislation e.g. in any river basin re-emergence of *char* is a common phenomenon but neither The Bengal Alluvion and

Dilluvion Regulation of 1825 nor Assam Land and Revenue Regulation, 1886 deals with this issue directly. Due to its contentious nature, there have been several court cases, related to the aspect of re-emergence of *char* and their ownership. Based on these legal disputes, certain outstanding judicial decisions[25] was promulgated, which paved the way for certain broad guidelines to deal with this issue in the absence of legislative provisions. Accordingly, it was stated that eroded land reformed on the old site continues to be the property of the owner provided it has not been completely abandoned meanwhile. Abatement of revenue is said to be an indication of complete abandonment. Although, under Section 34(c) of the Assam Land and Revenue Regulation, 1886, there is a provision for reduction of revenue by the Deputy Commissioner, for land, which has been washed away, yet due to the attachment of large number of complicated explanations with this section, it is believed that if an owner appeals for abatement of revenue for the part of his eroded land then there is maximum likelihood that he will loose the ownership of the eroded land[26].

Moreover, problems also arise when a part of the *char* or the whole is eroded and a part of it re-emerges these are attached to a nearby landowner. Under these circumstances, both according to Roman, English and Bengal Alluvion and Dilluvion Regulation (1825) as well as principles of equity and justice, the land acceded belong to the person to whom it has been acceded. But in reality, the person whose land gets eroded seldom agrees to accept the ownership of the new owner. Therefore, this natural process often becomes the major source of quarrel and conflict among the *char* dwellers.

Again, there are provision that if the tenant continues to pay revenue for the eroded land, then after its re-appearance, the land will belong to the original owner. Nevertheless, there are conflicting references of time-period (for which revenue has to be paid for an eroded land) in various legislations. While the Assam Land and Revenue Regulation, 1886 refrains from mentioning any time-period in this direction, the Goalpara Tenancy Act, 1929 under Section 83(2)(a) states that the tenants interest in the diluviated land subsist till 20 years or till 3 years after the re-appearance, whichever is less[27].

Thus, it seems that although there was some attempt to formulate legislation concerning land in the *char* areas in the colonial period yet its interpretation and implementation often lacked clarity, which led to undue complication. Moreover, there were various aspects related with land in the *char* areas, which remained outside the purview of these legislations that generated considerable ambiguity among the *char* dwellers.

Land Revenue Administration of the *Char* Areas

During the pre-British era, the *faringati* land remained outside the purview of taxation, as settled cultivation was not practiced in these lands. Similarly, in *chapori*, marshy and *char* lands, wherever cultivation took place, it was revenue free. But the British administrators in their effort to bring in more land under cultivation wanted to utilize these lands and placed them under annual revenue settlements. Therefore, it was only during the British era that these lands came under the purview of revenue administration.

Mills was one of the first British officials to mention about the aspect of revenue settlement in these areas. According to him, since the *chapories* are not permanently inhabited, there should not be heritable rights in them. He suggested that not more than one *chaporie* should be settled with one *Mouzadar* at a time. The *Mouzadar* can then settle *ryots* temporarily in these areas, who can initiate cultivation[28]. Similarly, Captain Gordon advocated for the classification of the *chaporie* lands in Darrang district into several divisions, which could be settled with the *ryots* in annual terms. He also pleaded to the revenue officials for revenue remission of eroded *chapories*, since it brought untold misery to the *ryots* in these areas[29].

In Goalpara district, the small island formed by the Brahmaputra was used as pastures for herds of cattle, brought from various parts of Bengal annually. Since the district was under *Zamindari*, these lands belonged to the *Zamindars*. They levied an annual tax upon the cattle herd owners, known as *kahacharai*. Gradually, these *chars* were encouraged for cultivation by offering favourable terms to the *ryots*. The *ryots* were provided with remession of rent for the initial years, locally known as *pali* and the *patta* so allotted was called as *pali patta* [30].

In Sylhet, another permanently settled area in Assam, *chars* was known as *charbharat*, which was initially included under temporary revenue settlement. The *charbharat* therefore belonged to the state and not to the landowner. However, in 1894, *charbharat* was settled with the owner of the property to whose land it was attached. But the mode of revenue settlement however, remained temporary or annual in nature[31].

Therefore, it seems from the discussion that during the colonial period, revenue settlement pattern in the *char* areas (whereever applicable) has been annual or temporary, both in permanently settled and in *rayatwari* areas of Assam.

Present Reality Concerning Land Legislation and Revenue Administration of the *Char* Areas

It is an established fact that the *char* dwellers have contributed a lot to the development of agriculture in the state but the colonial state on their part provided little legislative safeguards for these lands. However, the irony is that although there were some legislative provisions concerning land in these areas during the colonial period, the post-colonial land legislations in Assam refrained from mentioning anything about the *char* areas of the state. As a result, land in these areas remained a source of conflict and discord for its dwellers even in the post-colonial period.

The Assam Temporarily Settled Areas Tenancy Act—1971 is an important legislation, concerning land in the state. This legislation was enacted by replacing The Goalpara Tenancy Act, 1929, Sylhet Tenancy Act (for Karimganj sub-division), 1936 and the Tenancy Act of 1935 applicable to all other temporarily settled areas of Assam. But the irony is that although the earlier legislations had some enactments about land in the *char* areas, this new legislation of 1971 is completely silent about these areas. As a result, these areas remain outside the purview of land legislation in Assam. In the absence of proper legislation, when a new *char* emerges on the Brahmaputra, it becomes the property of the state government, which either keeps it as grazing reserve or settles it with the cultivators as per the Land Settlement Policy Resolution in force. However, in reality, people in the densely populated *char* areas do not wait until the Government undertakes the systematic settlement. They immediately occupy the newly formed *char.* As it happens without the sanction of state authorities, the *char* dwellers become encroachers and remain so until their land is settled under the provisions of land settlement or the *char* is eroded by the river [32]. Emergence of *char* and its ownership has therefore remained a source of conflict and insecurity among the *char* dwellers due to the absence of proper legislative provisions.

In terms of land revenue settlement, the *char* areas can be divided into two categories namely—*chars* where there has been cadastral survey or K-category *char* and those where cadastral survey has not been initiated or Non-K category *chars*. The reality is that the vast majority of the *chars* in Brahmaputra and its tributaries belong to the Non-K category. Among the *chars* where cadastral survey is completed, one will come across three different patterns of land revenue settlements namely, *touzi*, *ek chonnia* and rarely *meadi* settlements (other than encroached government land known as *khas*). In case of *touzi* land, the user does not enjoy ownership right but has the right to use it by paying the required land revenue (payment of which is again a rare occasion in the *char* areas), either as *touzi khazana* (in case of allotted government land) or as *bedakhali jarimana* (in case of unallotted occupied government land). The state may by virtue of law, can order to vacate *touzi* land at any point of time. After a long possession, these lands may convert into *ek chonia* or annual leases. The annual lease, issued for one year does not confer the owner with any right of transfer or sub-letting, and the right of inheritance is limited to the year of issue only[33]. Periodic leases or *meadi patta* are rare in *char* areas of Assam and those where it exists, largely belong to those *chars* which were once a part of the mainland but has been detached due to flood and accompanying erosion[34]. A periodic lease confers right of both transfer and inheritance at least up to the period of next settlement [35].

Here, it should be mentioned that although there has been three attempts during the post-independence period related to revenue settlement of land in the *char* areas of Assam yet it could not yield any concrete results due to lack of 'political will' on the part of the state government. The first attempt undertaken during 1979, in the erstwhile permanently settled areas of Goalpara district was stopped half way due to the launch of Assam Agitation, which surcharged the political environment in Assam in such lines that were not conducive for the continuation of the project. Again, the process started during 1983 but then it was discontinued due to lack of revenue staff. The process was re-initiated during 1994, when it was decided that in few selected districts of the state, where the *char* land has been in existence and occupied for more than 15 years, settlement measures would be undertaken. It was also decided that in the process, six *bigha* of land would be settled per household [36]. However, this time the process met premature death as the 'ghost' of illegal migrants occupying the *char* land haunted the political establishment and various organizations of mainland Assam and therefore they opposed the programme.

Thus, the absence of proper land revenue settlement in the *char* areas adversely affects the life of the cultivator in these areas. They not only remain outside the purview of several state sponsored welfare and credit schemes but also suffer from insecurity due to the lack of proper land revenue settlement measures.

The Task Ahead

To any population group practicing agriculture, land holds the key to their survival. But for the *char* dwellers, land has a politico-economic connotation too since other than being source of livelihood, land provides an identity to their existence, which due to geo-political reasons is always under the scanner. Again, considering their socio-cultural roots, land is their most prized possession and history bears testimony to the fact that it is for the sake of land that the forefathers of the present day *char* dwellers sacrificed everything—from motherland to mother tongue. Simultaneously, considering the environment in which they inhabit, land provides insurance to them against the unforeseen uncertainties of nature. Similarly, in their densely populated social milieu, land holds the key to their upward mobility along the social ladder and prestige within the community.

However, the land for which the *char* dwellers stake their life and livelihood is under continuous flux. Ironically, it has neither natural stability nor the legislative protection of the state. Under such a situation of apathy and inaction on the part of the state apparatus, the toil and sacrifice of the *char* dwellers in transforming the landscape of these areas to reap gold from these otherwise wretched lands, go without recognition. On the contrary, they remain as 'suspicious' citizens both in the *char* areas as well as in the mainland (where they migrate either due to land erosion and/ or due to economic compulsions).

In order to provide due recognition to their toil and hard work and to usher in an era of development, we propose certain broad policy suggestions related to land in the *char* areas of Assam.

1. There should be a proper study of all the land legislation related with land in *char* areas both in the colonial and post-colonial period in India and abroad for preparing a proper set of special legislations to administer these areas.
2. The state government should attempt for making a meaningful set of land revenue policies for the *char* areas. It is pertinent to have proper cadastral survey in these areas (both in the river Brahmaputra and its tributaries) and according to the nature of existence and quality of land, revenue settlements should be undertaken. Permanent deeds can be issued for *char* land, which has become comparatively stable over the years.
3. While undertaking land revenue settlements for the *char* areas in Assam, it should be noted that the *chars* in the northern fringe of the river Brahmaputra are more stable compared to those in the southern side and therefore a proper study of the nature concerning the location and geomorphology of the *char* is imperative for proper revenue administration.
4. The state should consider flexible provisions for payment of land revenue by the *char* dwellers at the nearest possible revenue office. As the locations of the *chars* are under flux, payment of land revenue at the district headquarters, in which the *char* was originally located, is more than often difficult. Decentralization of land revenue collection at the *char* village level can also be a meaningful option.
5. Motivated land revenue administrative staffs are necessary for administering these areas. They should not only visit and survey these areas but also have the acumen and authority to deliver justice to disputes concerning erosion of old *chars* and emergence of new *chars*.
6. There should be a proper rehabilitation package for the victims of land erosion in the *char* areas, else, the *char* dwellers affected by erosion will always be the victims of

'suspicious' identity in the eye of the fellow citizens of the region.

7. Above all, the state government should have the adequate 'political will' to deal with the issue of land administration in the *char* areas. There should also be a proper dissemination of information regarding the *char* areas so that there is a change in the mindset of the people and organizations in the mainland areas of Assam, who are more than often, haunted by the belief that the *char* areas are the abodes of illegal immigrants from across the international border.

NOTES AND REFERENCES

1. For detailed analysis concerning the interpretation of 'land' in tribal and non-tribal societies see the paper presented by Roy Burman, B.K., "Society, Ecology and Land Reforms in Tribal India" in a seminar on *Agrarian Structure, Land Reforms and Agricultural Growth* organized by G.B. Pant Institute, November 1987.
2. Experts vary widely regarding the 'values' and 'use' attached with land e.g. according to Ely and Wehrwein, well-known experts on issue related with land includes nature, space and property only. Ely, Richard, T., and Wehrwein, George, S., *Land Economics* (Madison: University of Wisconsin Press, 1940). On the other, scholar like Barlowe, mention at least seven major meaning attached with the term land. (i) It is a space, or room or/and surface, (ii) it is nature or natural environment, (iii) it is a factor of production, (iv) it is a consumption good, (v) it is a situation or location, (vi) it is a property with legal connotations, and (vii) it is capital. Barlowe, Raleigh, *Land Resource Economics: The Political Economy of Rural and Urban Land Use* (New Jersey: Prentice Hall, 1958). For further details on land and its various meaning, see Sillis, David, L., *International Encyclopedia of the Social Sciences, Vol.8* (The MacMillan Company & The Free Press, 1968).
3. An elaborate analysis on this issue is presented in Herskovits, Melville, J., *Economic Anthropology: The Economic Life of Primitive Peoples* (New Delhi: Eurasia Publishing House, 1964), particularly in the chapter titled Land Tenure
4. Roy Burman, B.K., "Issues in Land Reforms in N-E Tribal Area", *Mainstream*, August 1 and 8, 1987
5. This has also been elaborated in Recommendations and Policy Options of Workshop on *Land Reforms: Agenda For The North East*

held on 3-5 April, 1995 organized by Institute of Social Change & Development, Guwahati for Land Reforms Unit, Lal Bahadur Shastri National Acdemy of Administration, Mussoorie.

6. Goswami, P.C., *The Economic Development of Assam* (Ludhiana: Kalyani Publishers, 1994).
7. Guha, Amalendu, *Planter-Raj to Swaraj : Freedom Struggle and Electoral Politics in Assam, 1826-1947* (New Delhi: ICHR,1977).
8. It is stated that although the deficit of supply over demand for rice in Assam was met through imports yet the price of rice increased steadily in the state. As per estimates, the price of rice increased from 19 *seers* a rupee in 1873 to 10 *seers* a rupee in 1901. But the Assamese *ryots* benefited little from this price rise as they could not generate enough surplus for the market during the same period. Sharma, Manoroma, *Social And Economic Change In Assam Middle Class Hegemony* (Delhi: Ajanta Publications, 1990).
9. Mali, D. D., *Revenue Administration in Assam* (Gauhati: Omsons Publications, 1985).
10. *Op cit.* No. 7.
11. *Census of India, 1951, Vol. III, Assam, Part I.*
12. *Op cit.* No. 7.
13. *Op cit.* No. 6.
14. *Census of India, 1951, Vol. XII, Assam, Part IA.*
15. *Op cit.* No. 7.
16. *Op cit.* No. 6.
17. Doullah, Sujaud, M., *Immigration of East Bengal Farm Settlers and Agriculture Department of the Assam Valley: 1901-1947* (New Delhi: Institute of Objective Studies, 2003).
18. It is estimated that during 1947, out of the total quantity of exports from Assam, 62.5 percent, in case of railways and 37.5 percent, in case of waterways comprised of jute and overwhelming quantity of these jute exported were produced in the immigrant prone areas, including the *char* areas. Medhi, S.B., *Transport System and Economic Development in Assam* (Guwahati: Publication Board, Assam, 1978).
19. The geomorphology of the *chars* are affected by various factors such as the flow pattern, amount of discharge, bed load and sediment load of the river along with the topography of the river basin, which influences the process of *char* formation. Among them four major factors which influence the process of *char* formation are:
   (i) the existence of braided channels in the Brahmaputra;
   (ii) the gradient of the river;
   (iii) generation of the large quantities of suspended particles along with bed load; and
   (iv) the geology of the region particularly the presence of friable and shallow, as well as sand mixed with cobbles, boulders and

rocks along with the seismic instability of the area works together, which help in the process of *char* formation.

The extremely braided channels of the river along with its suspended particles and bed load combine during floods giving rise to 'almond' shaped alluvial formations, locally known as *chars.* These *chars* thereafter become an integral part of the fluvial system of the Brahmaputra. They are extremely unstable and can be wiped out by erosion during the next flood. For further discussion on geomorphology of the *char* areas see, Bhagabati, Abani, Kumar, "Biodiversity and Associated Problems in the Islands of the Brahmaputra, Assam", *Geographical Review of India*, Vol. 63, No. 4, 2001.

20. *The Institutes of Gaius* under Roman law mentions alluvion as another natural mode of acquisition. It also states that an island that arises in the middle of the river is the common property of the proprietors on both banks of the river and if it is not in the middle of the stream, it belongs to the proprietors of the nearest bank. Moreover according to them, accession caused by natural action of a river can be divided into four categories namely, (i) which is imperceptibly added to land by a river is termed as *alluvio* or *alluvion*; (ii) which is being detached from the land of one person by the open violence of a river and becomes united with the land of another is known as *avulsion* or *avulsion;* (iii) which spring up in the middle of a river is called as *Insula Nata*; and (iv) bed abandoned by a river is known as *alneus relictus.* Where as land that is gained from shrinking back of a river or a sea is mentioned as dereliction. For details, see Saikia, K.N., *The Assam Land And Revenue Regulation, 1886* (Guwahati: Lawyer's Book Stall, 2003).
21. The Halsbury's Laws of England mentions that where a tidal water recedes gradually and imperceptibly from the land, or land by alluvion or dereliction is added to the dry land or foreshore, so that it becomes situated above the high-water mark of ordinary tides, or above the low-water mark, it belongs, if above the high-water mark, to the owner of the dry land to which it is added, and if above the low-water mark to the owner of the foreshore. For details, see *Ibid.*
22. Ganguly, Kalayanmoy, Justice (ed.), *The West Bengal Laws (Annotated), Vol. I* (Calcutta: Hindustan Law Book Company, 1999).
23. *Ibid.*
24. *A Study Of The Land Systems of North Eastern Region, Vol. I, Assam* (Gauhati: Law Research Institute, 1982).
25. There are few instances of legal disputes and promulgation of justice by the courts on issues related to land in *char* areas. Some of the cases include Lopez vs Madan Mohan (13 MIA 467), Ramnath Tagore vs Chandra Narayan Chowdhury (1 March 136), Imam Bandi vs Hargobinda (4MIA 403), Radha Prasad Singh vs Ram Coomar Singh

(3 Cal. 796) etc. Details are available for some of the cases. In the Boroji Manipurini (Appellant) vs. The State of Assam and Others (Respondent), 1958 (AIR, 1958, 34) it was held that a land which has gradually and imperceptibly come out of the river-bed and added to the land of a riparian owner becomes part of the land belonged to him and is considered as his property...if it is considered an increment to the tenure of the land to which it has accreted...
Similarly, in another legal dispute between Sudhangshu Ranjan Dasgupta (Appellant) vs. Manindra Kumar Paul and Others (Respondent), 1972 (AIR, 1972, 3 & 34) it was pronounced that... any land accreted to plaintiff's periodic *patta* land by recession of river contiguous to such land automatically becomes part of the plaintiffs' land and cannot be allotted to any other person on the ground that the plaintiff had land in excess of ceiling fixed by The Assam Fixation of Ceiling on Land Holdings Act, 1957. For further details see, *Ibid*, (Appendices).

26. In Section 83 of the Goalpara Tenancy Act 1929 there are references about abatement of rent for the land lost due to diluvion. The Act states that "If the entire land of a tenure or holding or a portion of such lands are lost by diluvion, the rent of the tenure or the holding shall be abated by an amount which bears the same proportion to the rent of the whole tenancy, as the area lost bears to that of the whole tenancy". It also states that "when the entire tenure or holding has been lost by diluvion, the rent of the portion thereof which appears shall be calculated in like manner on the basis of the rent existing when the entire tenancy was lost". *Report of the Land Reform Commission, 1981*, Government of Assam.
27. Similar reference is also there in a postcolonial land legislation of Tripura. Under Section 18(2) of The Tripura Land Revenue and Land Reforms Act, 1960 the time-period mentioned is 12 years or until 1 year after the re-appearance. *Op cit.* no. 22.
28. Mills, Moffatt, A.J., *Report On The Province of Assam* (Gauhati: Publication Board, 1984).
29. *Ibid.*
30. Hunter, W.W., *A Statistical Account of Assam* (Delhi: Low Price Publication, 1990)
31. *Op cit.* No. 9.
32. *Op cit.* No. 22.
33. Sarma, Ramani (2000). *"Farm Production Decisions in the Char Areas of Central and Lower Brahmaputra Valley Zone of Assam—A Comparative Study"*, an unpublished Ph.D. Thesis, Dibrugarh University.
34. In those *chars*, where revenue settlement has been accomplished, there are certain practical problems, in the event of land erosion, which results in discontinuation of revenue payment. It is observed

that when a landowner suffers due to erosion, he is compelled to move to other areas (usually to various mainland areas of the state and the northeastern region) to earn his livelihood, where it is almost impossible for him either to collect the details of the eroded land or to pay revenue for the same. For details on related aspect see Jana, Jyotirmoy, "Brahmaputror *Char* Anchol Aru Khetiyokor Somosya" in Hussain, Ismail (Sr.) & Hussain, Anowar (eds.), *Char-Chaporir Jiban Charyya* (Guwahati: Natun Sahitya Parishad, 2000).

35. According to the estimates of the *Char* Areas Development Authority, in the *char* villages of the Barpeta district, where revenue settlement has been done, only 17.76 per cent of the land is under *meadi* or permanent settlement, whereas 38.76 per cent under *touzi* and 43.48 per cent under *ek chonia* settlements. As quoted by Goswami, Atul, Chandra, " Char Anchalor Eti Arthonaitik Samikhya" in Hussain, Ismail (Sr.) & Hussain, Anowar (eds.), *Char-Chaporir Jiban Charyya* (Guwahati: Natun Sahitya Parishad, 2000).

36. Seikh, Ahizuddin, "*Char* Ancholot Bhumi Sottwo Aru Mati Pattanor Samasya" in Hussain, Ismail (Sr.) & Hussain, Anowar (eds.), *Char-Chaporir Jiban Charyya* (Guwahati: Natun Sahitya Parishad, 2000).

20

Some Aspects of Sustainable Socio-Economic Development in North Eastern Region of India

P. C. DUTTA

The North East of India (NER) constitutes the states of Arunachal Pradesh, Assam, Manipur, Meghalaya, Mizoram, Nagaland, Sikkim and Tripura. Flanked by hills and with the mighty Brahmaputra River slashing a central path between its north and south, the NER is bounded by the States of Manipur, Meghalaya, Mizoram, Nagaland, Tripura with Assam at the heart. Arunachal Pradesh lies to its north and Sikkim a little away in the North West bordering China and Bhutan. Bangladesh and Myanmar lie to its southwest and east. The torrential Brahmaputra deposits its rich alluvial silt along the banks of the plains of Assam. Tropical rain forest, rich in flora and fauna, spread their arms across Arunachal Pradesh into Assam. Assam is a land where tea is the most powerful industry, handicrafts is a major occupation and martial arts is a favoured sport. The western side of the North East is connected to the eastern part of the Indian sub-continent by a narrow land corridor, sometimes referred to as the Siliguri Neck or "Chicken's Neck". The eight states that comprise the region reflect ecological and cultural contrasts between the hills and the plains; there are also significant elements of continuity. The economy of NER has got its definite identity due to its peculiar physical, economic and socio-cultural characteristics. At the time of independence, the states of NER lagged behind the other parts of the country in terms of development indices. The economy of the region was mono-crop based with traditional slash-

and-burn method of agriculture and few small and cottage industries. But since independence, economic development and government sponsored urbanization programme have brought about significant changes in the structure of the economy.

The very pattern of economic development in the third world countries resulted in increasing imbalance in distribution of income and in throwing a large number of people below poverty line. Development is a complex process with multi-dimensional structure depending upon its resources in general and infrastructural facilities in particular. Poverty is the worst form of environmental degradation because it forces an extremely sub-standard quality of life upon a large segment of society and causes deprivation from such basic needs of human existence as shelter, nutrition, hygiene and health service, education, safe drinking water, sanitation and other physical infrastructure. (Dutta, 1996).

Development scholars and third world analysts have effectively argued with economic data and statistics that high rates of population growth are economically unsustainable. The resources in Third World countries are limited and are barely able to keep up with rising population figure. When population figures expand beyond the ability of the resources to expand, it increases poverty and creates more demand than supply in terms of welfare service, healthcare, education and food subsidy. The point here is that accelerated population growth cannot match with accelerated expansion of services and food production, eventually leading to greater poverty and unemployment. At the national level, it reduces capacity to attain sustainable economic development. Thus *"population growth is a major impediment to sustainable development,"* and high rates of population growth are an obstacles to development in general.

Sustainable development, that is, *'meeting the present needs without compromising those of the future'* (WCED 1987)[1], involves important inter-generational equity considerations, including those related to the environment. Environment is of importance not only because of its effects on the psychic and non-economic welfare, but also because of its impact on production over the long-term (World Bank 2000)[2].

At the Millennium Summit in September 2000 the world leaders agreed on a set of goals to guide global development in the 21st century. This came to be known as The United Nations'

Millennium Development Goals (MDGs). MDG includes among other things, halving extreme poverty and hunger, achieving universal primary education and gender equity, reducing under-five mortality and maternal mortality by two-thirds and three-quarters respectively, reversing the spread of HIV/AIDS, halving the proportion of people without access to safe drinking water and ensuring environmental sustainability. They also include the goal of developing a global partnership for development, with targets for aid, trade and debt relief [3].

When Indian economy was grappling with more serious problem of the eighties the earlier mixed economy approach was evaluated and it was realized that Indian economy must acquire improvement in productivity, absorption of modern technology and full utilization of resources. At the same time it was supposed that the private sector would play an important role in shaping the country's economy. As a result in 1991, New Economic Policy (NEP) was introduced by the Government of India for structural adjustment and Liberalisation, Privatisation and Globalisation (LPG). Under such policy profit motive was the guiding principle for investment. Domination of profit motive paved the way for development of those regions where the developed infrastructural facilities were quite high.

Further, Economic welfare does not merely depend upon the level of development but also on distributive justice. In the plural nature of the country, differences in natural resources, climate, topography, vegetation and density of population can be identified easily and the North Eastern Region of India (NER) is no exception to it. Unequal distribution of wealth and resources caused regional disparity in the country. Explosive increase in Indian population thinned down the quality of life of the masses and made them victims of skewed distribution of resources. Additional problems are rapid urbanization, growth of large cities without adequate infrastructural robustness, migration of the poor into already overcrowded cities and higher pressure on existing the facilities and infrastructure available in urban areas. One of the major areas of concern in the region is the vulnerability of the rural and urban poor to higher mortality and poor health care.

In the recent projection, Dyson (2004) estimated that the population of India is likely to be 1.4 million by 2026 and 1.6 billion by the year 2051. These projections were done by taking optimistic assumptions, such as the TFR will fall to around 2.1 births per woman by 2026-21, life expectancy will be approximately 67 years for males and 70 for females. The working age population will be approximately 1.5 times as large in 2026 as it was in 2001. If woman's participation increases, there will be an average annual addition of 8 million people to the labour force annually between 2001 and 2026. If recent trend in economic growth and employment intensity continues until 2026, there will be a significant increase in the level of unemployment. Even an annual economic growth rate of 8 per cent up to 2026 will not avoid future increase in unemployment level.

Almost all the countries in the world have imbalances at regional and sub-regional levels in equitable share in the national assets. In order to reduce such imbalances, the planners and policy makers make efforts and evolve strategies.

Dutta (2003) brought out the facts about the regional disparity in NER and found that the states of NER are suffering from paucity of funds to improve their socio-economic backwardness. It was further observed that the states of NER are far behind other states of the Indian Union in terms of basic amenities such as health, education, safe drinking water, banking facility, food security, communication etc. Economic development of a country may not be possible without regional development and equitable distribution of resources of the nation. Iniquitous distribution gives rise to various types of socio-economic problems.

"This optimism about India's growth prospect is shared by most international observers who now believe that India has the potential to achieve sustained growth at 9 to 10 p.c. for the next 20 years. By 2040 India is expected to be the third largest economy in the world after the US and China. Population growth has showed down to around 1.5 p.c. and is continuing to decline. This means that if the GDP grows between 9 and 10 per cent per year then per capita income growth in the next 20 years could be somewhere around 8.5 p.c. or so"., the Deputy Chairman, Planning Commission of India expressed.[4]

From the above review of literature on economic development, it is clear that with the introduction of New Economic Policy (NEP) and Structural Adjustment Programme (SAP) at national and international level, the states of NER are lagging behind. As development is a complex process, the present study will discuss the population explosion of the region and some of the indicators of socio-economic development such as education, per capita income, agriculture, irrigation, power, industries, tea industry, banking, health, nutrition and food supply, housing, safe drinking water etc. The analysis is being made on the basis of published and unpublished secondary sources and statistical data. The study gives valuable recommendations for the planners and policy-makers of the region.

Demographic Profile and Population Explosion

The NER covers an area of 2.63 lakh sq. km. which accounts for 7.9 per cent of total geographical area of the country. With a total population of 38.86 million, as per 2001 census (Table 20.1), it accounts for 3.8 p.c. of total population of India. According to India's Health Ministry, India's population which was 238 million in 1947 touched 1.012 billion in March 2001 and is expected to be 1.263 billion by 2016. The share of population of NER, in comparison to all India, increased from 2.89 p.c. in 1951 to 3.78 p.c. in 2001. Among the various states of NER of India, the geographical area of Arunachal Pradesh is the highest that covers 83,743 sq. km. In terms of population, Mizoram is the smallest state in the NER. The decadal growth rate of population (1991-2001) is the lowest in the state of Tripura 16.03 p.c. followed by Assam (18.92 p.c.) and highest in the state of Nagaland (64.53 p.c.) followed by Sikkim (33.06 p.c.). The region's growth rate of population (21.61 p.c.) is higher than the national average of 21.35 p.c. during 1991-2001. The density of population varies from 13 in Arunachal Pradesh to 340 in Assam followed by 305 in Tripura. The density of population of the region is 147.65 which is almost half of the national density (324) in 2001 while it was only 34.29 in 1951. It is remarkable to note that the sex ratio in NER has consistently shown excess of males over females as noted for India. In India, there are only 933 females per 1000 males in the total population. Amongst the states of NER, it is highest in Manipur (978) followed by Meghalaya (975), Tripura (950) and Mizoram (938). The other states are lying below the national level. It seems that there is more male migrants in the region and lowering the sex ratio of general population.

support. It is striking to note that Sikkim has to focus on "product differentiation" as Sikkim faces competition from other north-eastern States.

Table 20.4 Trend of SSI Growth in North-Eastern Region

State	*1997-98*	*1998-99*	*1999-00*	*2000-01*	*2001-02*	*2002-03*
ANP	4,456	4,546	4,694	4,750	4,797	5,022
	(7.00)	(2.01)	(3.26)	(1.19)	(1.00)	(4.70)
ASM	34,258	36,482	38,303	40,419	42,947	45,193
	(6.84)	(6.49)	(4.49)	(5.52)	(6.52)	(5.23)
MNP	5,322	5,447	5,587	5,778	5,868	5,974
	(3.08)	(2.35)	(2.57)	(3.42)	(1.54)	(1.81)
MGH	2,982	3,247	3,505	3,778	4,044	4,213
	(8.87)	(8.87)	(7.94)	(7.79)	(7.04)	(4.18)
MZM	3,907	4,313	4,490	4,610	4,970	5,293
	(6.40)	(10.39)	(4.10)	(2.67)	(7.94)	(6.49)
NGN	712	982	1276	1,600	1,969	2,513
	(15.78)	(37.92)	(29.93)	(25.39)	(23.06)	(27.63)
SKM	294	306	322	333	341	351
	(4.60)	(4.06)	(5.53)	(3.08)	(2.39)	(2.92)
TRP	1,798	1,867	1,931	1,967	2,000	2,020
	(3.90)	(3.83)	(3.31)	(1.86)	(1.67)	(1.00)

Note: Figures in brackets are the percentage increase over the previous year figure.

Source: Basic Statistics of NER 2006.

Results of the third census of SSI unit reveal that while 3.11 p.c. of the total number of persons are employed in the SSI sector in the country (24932763), that in the NER is not in tune with the census figure. As per Draft Report of the Task Force on Development Initiatives for the NER, Sept. 2005, Gross out put of NER is estimated at Rs. 5024.41 crores while for all India the figure is 2,82,269.98 crores.

The state economy of Tripura is characterized by low capital formation, inadequate infrastructure facilities, geographical isolation and communication bottlenecks, inadequate exploitation and use of forest resources, low industrial field and high unemployment. Financial performance of Assam during the Tenth Plan period under different sector heads i.e., Agriculture and Allied Activities, Rural Employment, Irrigation and Flood Control, Energy, Industry and Minerals, Social Services and other sectors has shown progress and the State Government has been in a position to utilize 86.4 p.c. of the agreed outlay. Although a late starter in the planning and development process due to sustained efforts and investment in development activities since 3rd Five Year Plan, the State of Nagaland achieved significant progress particularly in the sectors of Road, Transport, Water Supply, Power, Education and Health. During the 40 years, almost all the villages in the state are covered by public transport. Total length of roads in the state has reached to 10255 Kms. while the state covers an area of 16579 Sq. Km. and there are 4 National Highways passing through the state. (NE News Letter, February 2007).

Tea Industry

Tea is indigenous to India of which the country can take a lot of pride. This is mainly because of its pre-eminence in foreign exchange earning and in contributing to the country's GNP. In all aspects of tea production, consumption and export, India has emerged as the world leader. Tea accounts for 31 per cent of global production. It is perhaps the only industry where India has retained its leadership over the last 150 years. Since independence tea production has grown over 250 per cent , while land area has just grown by 40 p.c. There has been a considerable increase in export in the past few years. Total net foreign exchange earned per annum is around Rs. 1847 crores. The labour intensive tea industry directly employs over 1.1 million workers and generates income for another 10 million people approximately. Women constitute 50 p.c. of the workforce.

The Tea Industry of NER is the world's largest tea growing region having 16 p.c. shares, and is the largest producer and exporter of tea in India (share 55 p.c.). The production of tea in the state of Assam was of the tune of 438.9 thousand tones during the period 2002-03 which increased to 454.1 thousand tones in 2003-04 but decreased to 443.3 thousand tones in 2004-05. In case of tea production in Manipur, it has increased from 76000 kgs. in 1998 to 97 thousand kgs. in 1999 but it decreased slightly to 96 thousand kgs. in 2000. However, Indian tea producers suffered the most in terms of drop in average tea auction price compared with other auction centres around the world between January to October 2002 (*Business Standard*—Saturday, January 11, 2003).

The *Table 20.5* shows the picture of Tea Industry in NER

(Annual Export) during the 5-year period (2000-04). The Assam Government has decided to offload a majority stake, and, along with it, Management Control of Assam Tea Corporation (ATC). It has already invited expression of interest for the move. The divestment of ATC could be either through outright sale of a 74 per cent stake in the company, or through long-term lease of individual gardens. The State Government, however, is believed to prefer the option of leasing out its gardens on a long-term basis, to selling off a controlling stake in the company. The corporation, created by taking over sick tea gardens in the '70s, has, by now acquired a total of 14 tea gardens scattered over the six districts of the Brahmaputra and Barrak Valleys. The combined capacity of the 14 gardens is around 8 million kgs. The corporation also has about 10 factories to process tea leaves to produce black tea. According to the ATC Annual Report, average production over the past five years was between 6 to 6.5 million kgs. (*The Telegraph*—Monday, November 05, 2001).

Table 20.5 Production, Export and Import of Tea

	2000	*2001*	*2002*	*2003*	*2004*
Production	846	854	826	857	830
Imports	14	17	22	7	25
Exports	207	183	201	173	190
Consumption	653	673	685	697	710

Source: Report of the Meeting of the Committee on Financial Sector Plan for NER, March 2006.

The figure in table 20.3 shows the annual production of tea in Assam (ASM), Tripura (TRP), West Bengal (WB), other states of North India (OST), Tamil Nadu (TND), Karnataka (KRNT), Kerala (KER) and India (IND) during the period 1995-2000. The graph shows that Assam's share is the highest (53 p.c.) in country's total production (754 million kg.) in 1995 which decreased to 52 p.c. in 2000. However, during the period the production increased by 7.28 p.c. in the state while for the country, the production increased by 9.21 p.c. In this regard Karnataka stands at the top with 20.81 p.c. followed by West Bengal (12.74 p.c.) and Tamil Nadu (11.34 p.c.).

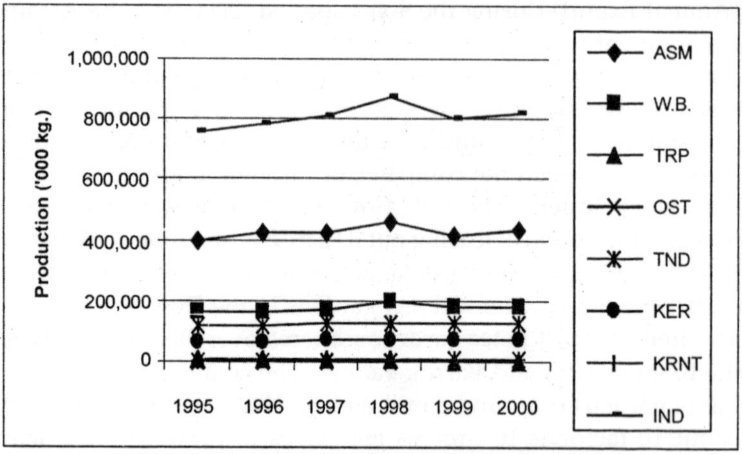

Fig. 20.3 Annual State-wise Tea Production

Banking

Financial infrastructure is essential for economic development. Banks have expanded their network extensively particularly during the last two decades in different states of NER. The number of branches of Scheduled Commercial Banks (SCBs) in NER was 1935 in 1996 that gradually increased to 1941 in 2001 but then it decreased to 1915 in 2003. After 2003 it started to increase again and stood at 1952 as on March 31, 2005. The figure was 1920 as on March 31, 2004. With respect to NER (1952), the percentage of number of branches in Assam is 63.27 and with respect to India (28958) it is only 1.81 p.c. However with respect to India (66970 nos.), there were only 2.87 p.c. branches in NER as on March, 2004 which increased by 1.67 p.c. as on March, 2005. The number of scheduled commercial bank branches operating in the State of Arunachal Pradesh was 68. The credit deposit ratio was 24.40 p.c. as compared to the national average of 66 p.c. as on March, 2005. During the financial year 2004-05, there were 228 bank branches of all type of commercial banks. Out of these 138 branches in rural areas, 44 branches in semi-urban areas and rest 46 branches in urban area are functioning in the state. In all Scheduled Commercial Banks, total deposit was Rs. 232100 lakhs in March 2004, which rose to Rs. 265100 lakhs in March 2005. On the other hand, total credit was 59100 lakhs till March 2004 which rose to

Rs. 78600 lakhs in March 2005. The credit deposit ratio stood at 29.65 per cent as compared to the national credit-deposit ratios of 66.04 per cent as on March 31, 2005. As on March 31, 2004 the number of scheduled commercial bank branches in Mizoram was 78. The number came down from 79 as on March 31, 2000. The CDR was 38.37 p.c. as on March 31, 2004. Commercial Banks located in Meghalaya have an important role to play in its development particularly in the rural areas. As on March 31, 2003, the number of scheduled commercial bank branches in Meghalaya was 180. The deposit stood at Rs. 2164 crore and credit stood at Rs. 623 crore. The credit deposit ratio was a low 23.79 p.c. as compared to the All India average of 59.37 p.c. as on March 31, 2003. Financial assistance in the form of short or medium term loans etc. should be more liberal for Meghalaya where the economy is underdeveloped. As on March 31, 2004 the number of scheduled commercial bank branches in Nagaland was 69 that came down from 70 as on March 31, 2000. As compared to the national average of 58.72 p.c., the CDR in Nagaland was as low as 16.84 p.c. as on March 31, 2004.

The Credit-Deposit Ratio (CDR) of banks in NER has fallen from 47 p.c. as on end of March 1991 to 26 p.c. as on end March 2003. But after that it has increased to 35 (as against the national average of 66) as on the end of March 2005. The CDR of banks of all the states of NER including NER and India as a whole for the periods 1997-98 to 2004-05 is shown in Fig. 20.4. It is important to note that during the period (1997-98 to 2004-05) the CD ratio decreased in case of Manipur (25.42 p.c.) and Tripura (14.70 p.c.). The highest percentage increase was observed in Meghalaya (200 p.c.) followed by Mizoram (121.74 p.c.) and Arunachal Pradesh (84.62 p.c.). The state of Assam has the lowest (3.03 p.c.) followed by Nagaland (27.78 p.c). However, percentage increase in the CD ratio in NER (16.67 p.c.) is low as compared to the All India.

Corruption and its Impact

In India, corruption attacks the fundamental values of human dignity and political equality of the people and hence there is a pressing need to formulate a fundamental human right to corruption-free service. Corruption affects India at all levels of governmental decision-making and in the distribution of state largesse. India is ranked 72nd out of 91 countries in the Corruption Perception Index, 2001, prepared by Transparency International (TI). Corruption in India not only poses a significant danger to the quality of governance, but also threatens in an accelerated manner the very foundations of its democracy and statehood. Corruption and indiscipline survive on each other's willingness to accommodate, tolerate and provide encouragement. Corruption is anti-poor.

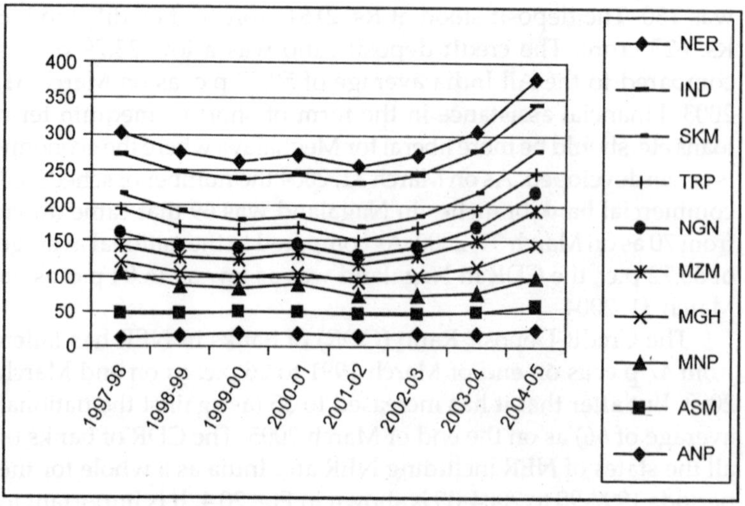

Fig. 20.4 Credit Deposit Ratio of SCBs in the NER

Note: Figures are as on end of March of respective year. (*Source*: RBI)

For instance, a substantial portion of foodgrains, sugar and kerosene meant for the public distribution system (PDS) and for welfare schemes for the poor, including the Scheduled Castes (S.Cs.) and the Scheduled Tribes (S.Ts.), goes into the black market. Hardly 16 per cent of the funds meant for the S.Ts. and the S.Cs. reach them (Consultation Paper on Probity in Governance, National Commission to Review the Working of the Constitution, 2001). Members of the political and official classes, unscrupulous dealers and businessmen misappropriate the rest. No development process will have any meaning and relevance if corruption is institutionalised and interferes with people's struggles for right to development. C. Rajkumar (2002) has stressed that if there is no discipline in society, no real or meaningful development or progress is possible.

India's experience with corruption has shown that laws, rules, regulations, procedures and methods of transaction of government business, however sound and excellent they are, cannot by themselves ensure effective and transparent administration if the political and administrative leadership abuses powers for personal gain (Sunil Sondhi, 2000). The states of NER are badly affected by corruption in all spheres of life. Perhaps the corruption at all levels is the main cause of the region's backwardness.

Conclusion and Suggestion

Under the above circumstances, the states of NER have drawn attention of the social scientists, scholars, policy-makers and planners of the region. The region is unable to cope up with the NEP and SAP imposed by the Government of India. However, we cannot do away with the changes introduced by the Government of India. Considering the geographical features and special characteristics of the NER, Central Government has formulated different strategies and floated Schemes for socio-economic infrastructure, creation of job opportunities, upgradation of culture, education and creation of economic base for bringing people to the main stream. Despite abundant natural resources, the state of Assam in particular and the NER in general have remained backward because of pressure on limited resources, perpetual floods, over dependence on agricultural, poor irrigation, poor road and rail links, inadequate telecommunication connectivity and ethnic disturbances. Lack of transparency of the political leaders is the main obstacles in attaining the actual development of the region. The natural resource endowments and education levels of the population notwithstanding, the NER represents one of the least developed regions of the country. The State Government of Sikkim has already identified areas for setting up of growth centres. The New Industrial Policy, provides a list of locations for setting up of the new industrial units. The Government has already declared Rangpo-Gangtok, Melli-Jorethang and Jorethang-Rishi and Ranipool-Gangtok as industrial corridors for giving land to the investors on a lease basis. However, despite several preventive measures taken by the Government and NGOs the region is still backward in socio-economic spheres. The rapid development in groundwater-based irrigation in many states led to ground water depletion, because of which the life of drinking water supply source becomes short. Hence, following suggestions may be made for the sustainable development of the region.

To control the population growth, emphasis should be on successful implementation of family planning programme. The success of family planning programms in the 21st century depends on various factors. Elimination of social disapproval of family planning is necessary. Such disapproval impedes adoption of contraception. The scope of coverage needs to be broadened to encompass not only women or men who are interested in limiting their births but also those who are interested in achieving other ends. Family planning should also be a joint responsibility of both men and women. It is evident that men do influence the use of contraception and so educating men to appreciate family planning might lead to increased use of contraception. (Letamo and Bainame, 2000). Thus, IEC (Information, Education, Communication) component of family planning programmes needs to be strengthened in order to increase the use of contraceptives.

The Government should give priority to set up various technical and professional institutions to enhance the capacity and improve the quality of education and training for the people of NER along with the projects for the development of transport and communication system for linking the whole of NER with the main stream of the country.

One of the main challenges before India is to reduce the problem of unemployment. Thus, creation of sufficient employment for skilled personnel should be the targets. Efforts should be made to provide sufficient and proper inputs and to utilize the available human resources to accelerate economic growth and overall development. In the coming years there will be an increase in the elderly population in India for which the government should have to bear proper responsibility and care to meeting the needs of those elderly population.

The Government must devise a system which ensures equal opportunities to the poor in obtaining higher education and training or in getting a start in trade and industry or secured employment. Another important measure is the introduction of a comprehensive Social Security Scheme (SSS) guaranteeing to each individual a minimum standard of living. The family welfare programme is also an indirect nutrition programme since by reducing family size, it will not only increase the per capita availability of food but also will result in all round facilities including health care.

It is important to note that poverty is one of the serious problems in India. About 82 p.c. of the total poor lives in the countryside. As a consequence, little attention has been given on the urban poor since independence. Urban Poverty is a complex and multidimensional problem. If serious attention is not paid to this underprivileged section, it is likely to pose a severe threat to the urban system of our economy.

There is need to develop a broad economic base to secure social welfare and to provide equal opportunities and access for the advancement for all the citizens of the region. The governments should prepare proper plan and policy to eliminate poverty in the village and urban areas and for this small scale home based industries need be encouraged. The Government should develop an economic system not overly dependent on foreign loans. While NER should not be isolated economically, it should maintain the integrity of the national economy. It is most important to develop a balanced economic system that is open and transparent and free of corruption, collusion and nepotism. Protection and privilege only to a small political and economic elite at the cost of the poor need be eliminated.

The Government should develop an economic system to address regional economic development in tune with political, cultural and social life. It should strive to eliminate structural poverty as well as the culture of poverty. It should be based on economic development on the principles of sustainability and efficient use of natural resources. During planning exercise, the authority should take into account Region's ethnic and religious diversity, demographic conditions, the vertical and horizontal arrangement that divide society and should try to minimize the social and economic disparities within and between every group in society.

Proper institutional support should be extended to the

agricultural sector and small to middle-scale industries to ensure sustainability. The emphasis should be on fostering self-reliance.

The Government has a role in setting standards in the use and management of natural resources and the environment. It is difficult to recruit employees with high competence and to ensure that they remain honest. In addition, the non-transparent recruitment system prevails in public employment. Nepotism and bribery have vitiated the recruitment system. Care should be taken to cleanse the system.

The importance of using safe water, using water as a socio-economic good and the problems related to water quality in any specific area should be highlighted. In order to guarantee a balanced and sustainable growth, the scarce natural resources need to be conserved and utilised in a prudent manner.

Discrimination on grounds of gender continues to characterize labour relations and wage system in the region as well as in the country. The most common form of gender discrimination is found in wage disparity. The women are still considered as secondary earners. Hence it is suggested that wages should be based on equity and the quality of work.

However, no policy in the region will be successful unless the people of the region are involved in the policy-making process. Hence, people's participation, particularly women's participation is urgently needed in any development programme of the government.

NOTES

1. WCED (World Commission on Environment and Development), (1987). *Our Common Future* (The Brundtland Commission Report), Oxford University Press. Oxford, UK.
2. World Bank, (2000). Entering the 21st Century: World Development Report 1999/2000, OUP New York:
3. Millennium Development Goals:
   Goal 1: Eradicate extreme poverty and hunger,
   Goal 2: Achieve universal primary education,
   Goal 3: Promote gender equality and empower women,
   Goal 4: Reduce child mortality,
   Goal 5: Improve maternal health,
   Goal 6: Combat HIV/AIDS, malaria and other diseases,

Goal 7: Ensure environmental sustainability, and
Goal 8: Develop a Global Partnership for Development.

4. Montek Singh Ahluwalia, Deputy Chairman, Planning Commission of India delivered the Convocation Address at the 8th Convocation of Bharati Vidyapeeth University, Pune on Saturday, 31st March, 2007.

REFERENCES

Balk, D. (1994). *"Individual and Community Aspects of Fertility and Women's Status in Rural Bangladesh"*, POPULATION STUDIES, 38, 21-45.

Dutta P.C. (1996). *" Quality Variation of Some Food Items of Consumption in North Eastern Region (NER)"*, Indian Journal of Regional Science, Vol. 28 (1).

Dutta P.C. (2002)." *Population Growth and Environmental Crisis in North East India : Problems* and *Remedies"* in Development Priorities in North East India(ed), B. J. Deb, Concept Publishing Company, New Delhi.

Dutta P.C. (2003). *"Regional Disparity and its Consequences in North Eastern Region of India"*, in 'Economic Liberalization and Regional Disparities in India—'Special Focus on the North Eastern Region'(ed.) A. C. Mahapatra & C.R. Pathak, Star Publishing House, Shillong.

Dyson, T. (2004). "India's Population—The Future" in Dyson et al (eds.) TWENTY FIRST CENTURY INDIA, Oxford University Press, New Delhi.

Elo. I. T. (1992). "Utilization of Maternal Health Care Services in Peru—The Role of Women's Education", HEALTH TRANSITION REVIEW, 2(1), 29-51

Jeffery, Roger and Basu Alaka M(ed) (1996): "Girls' Schooling—Women's Autonomy and Fertilitry Change in South Asia", Sage Publication, New Delhi.

Le Vine, R.A., Le Vine, S.E., Richman, A., Uribe, F. M.Tapia, Cottea, C.S.and Miller P.M. (1991). "Women's Schooling and Child Care in Demographic Transition—A Maxican Case Study", POPULATION AND DEVELOPMENT REVIEW, 17(3), 459-496.

Letamo, G. and Bainame, K. (2000). "Reproductive Decision-making : Do men really matter?", A Paper presented at Fourth International Conference on Social Science in Health entitled Africa Health at Crossroads: Challenges for the next Millennium, organized by the Department of Demography and SOMANet and held at the University of Botswana, Gaborone, 7th-11th August.

Mandelbaum, D.G. (1988). "Women's Seclusion and Men's Honor—Sex Roles in North India, Bangladesh and Pakistan", University of Arizona Press, Tuson, Arizona.

Okafor, C.B. (1991). "Availability and Use of Services for Maternal Child Health Care in Rural Nigeria", INTERNATIONAL JOURNAL OF GYNEACOLOGY AND OBSTESTRICS, 34(331), 331-46

Rosso, Joy Miller Del and Marek Tonia (1996): "Class Action—Improving School Performance in the Developing World through Better Health and Nutrition", The World Bank, Washington D.C.

Singh D.P. (2005). "Migration in India—Evidence Based National Sample Survey Data", DEMOGRAPGY INDIA, Vol. 34, No. 2, pp. 271-298.

United Nations (1993). "Women's Education and Fertility Behaviour—Recent Evidence from the Demographic and Health Surveys", U.N. New York.

Visaria, L. (1993). " Females Autonomy and Fertility Behaviour—An Exploration of Gujrat Data" in International Union for the Scientific Study of Population (IUSSP), Proceedings of the International Population Conference, Montreal, Vol. IV, IUSSP, Liege.

21

Tourism in North East India: Exploring the Paradise

ELANGBAM NIXON SINGH

Introduction

Constant dwelling at one place makes its inhabitants weary and peevish. All human beings naturally want a change either for a long duration or for a temporary period. It is a natural desire to move from one place to another for social, natural, political, cultural, religious, physical or commercial purposes. Thus, travelling is an ancient phenomenon of mankind. It dates back to the time immemorial. Most of the ancient travels were unplanned having not much significance. But as civilization grew and moved further conscious travels began to invade the world. As such, tourism today signifies the movement of a large number of people from one place to another, from different strata of society from their hometowns for more than a day and for purposes other than business, a phenomenon which grew in Europe during the post-Industrial Revolution in the 19th century (Gupta, S.P. and L. Krishna 1974 : 1).

By and large, it is widely admitted that tourism is one of the few sectors that can bring about a real growth in the economy without creating significant regional or economic disparity. Tourism is also globally recognized as the most promising industry having tremendous growth potential. It is highly revenue yielding sector. This industry has of late made inroad into the mainstream of the economy quietly but firmly. Over the last few decades tourism has been generating receipts, larger than the world trade. About four million foreign tourists visited India in 2006 and brought in foreign exchange worth more than $6.5 billion. According to World Travel and Tourism Council, the Indian Tourism Industry is set to grow at the rate of 10 per cent annually over the next decade (Times of India, July 19, 2007). According to projections, by the end of the first quarter of this century tourism will grow at a faster rate than the world's collective wealth!

Objective of the Paper

The objectives of the paper are as follows:

- To study the present scenario of tourism in the North East India,
- To study the present scenario and the larger problems and prospects of the development of tourism in North East India, and
- To suggest ways and means for development of tourism in North East India.

North East India—An Outlook Ahead

North East India, popularly known as NE, comprises of the eight states of Arunachal Pradesh, Assam, Manipur, Meghalaya, Mizoram, Nagaland, Tripura and Sikkim, is geographically situated in the North East corner of India, at Latitude 21.57°N-29.30°N and Longitude 88°E-97.30°E with an area of 25.5 million Sq. Km. (7.8 per cent of the land mass of the country). NE shares the international boundaries of India with China to the North, Bangladesh to the South West, Bhutan and Nepal to the North West and Myanmar to the East. This region is connected with the rest of India only through a narrow corridor in North Bengal, known as Chicken Neck, having an approximate width of 33 km. on the eastern side and 21 km. on the western side. About 70 per cent of NE is hilly region and the topography varies within each state. Mountains and hills cover most of the land mass of Arunachal Pradesh, Mizoram, Nagaland, Meghalaya; about half of Tripura, 20 per cent of Assam, 90 per cent of Manipur and almost entire land mass of Sikkim. The plains of the region are mainly made up of separate landmasses—the Brahmaputra Valley and the Barak Valley in Assam and the Tripura plains in the South. In Manipur, the valley is small, comprising only about 10 per cent of the total area of the State. The Brahmaputra Valley stretches longitudinally for about 730 km, from North Lakhimpur to Dhubri districts in Assam. The Barak Valley, formed by the River Barak and its tributaries covers the districts of Cachar, Karimganj and Hailakandi of South Assam. The Tripura plain is an extension of the Ganga-Brahmaputra plain. The topography of the hills is generally rugged and vast areas are still inaccessible. The flora and fauna of this region are numerous and varied. NE is regarded as one of the 7 most bio-diverse regions of the world (hottest hotspots) (Myers 2000). Hill ranges forming part of the Himalayas guard the northern side of the region. The area is made up of mountains above the snow line and plains just a little higher than the sea level. Cherrapunjee and Mawsynram, places having the highest rainfall in the world, are in Meghalaya. Many endangered species of fauna like the one-horned-Asiatic rhino, white winged-wood duck and Golden Langur can be spotted in the reserved forests and National Parks of NE. These unique and varied natures of the region make it one of the most beautiful geographical regions of the country—ready to be explored by the tourists of different tastes and habits. This land is also very rich from the angle of heritage and culture. The Vaishnavite culture, which bloomed in the 15th century in Assam and in Manipur, is regarded as one of the most revolutionary modifications of hitherto untouched Hinduism. The *Satras* of Majuli (the largest River Island in the world) still bears the testimonies of the bygone era. The famous *Pung Cholam* (drum dance from Manipur) reminds the world of its rich tradition and culture. The Krishna Leela Dance of Manipur and the Satriya of Assam are recognised as classical dance forms of India with Kathakali and Odissi. The region is rich also in folk culture and literature. The Nagas are easily recognised in almost all parts of the world for their unique tribal culture. Naga villages offer the examples of the most disciplined traditional village councils known as Naga Ho Ho. Arunachal too is a pleasant mixture of different tribes. It is often overlooked that North East India is a *Craft Heaven*, and craftsmanship is jealously guarded as a part of the heritage by almost all tribes in the region. The plains and the hills are equally bloomed with the culture of crafts for personal use. It is needless to emphasis that such a variety of exquisite crafts is normally not seen in a small geographical area like the NE. Concerned organizations should be committed to bring the crafts and craftsmen out of the backyard of their traditional homes and open them up to the world market. As a step towards fulfilling this, *Craft Tours* can be organized for the visitors. *TexTourism* has been a success in many South East Asian countries including Thailand, Laos and Vietnam. Drawing inspiration from these success stories we can start showcasing this huge textile-producing region. It is well known, however, that NE possesses more than 550 varieties of orchids, which is said to be almost 70 per cent of the total orchid species identified so far. This can comfortably be marketed to the tourists from all over the world who love to have exotic flowers. It may be mentioned here that Singapore has taken up this opportunity is a big way to become one of the most successful destinations for the orchid lovers. NE has more species endemic to the region. In order to boost this sector *Orchid Tours* can also be arranged.

Salient Features of North East India

- It is virgin.
- A unique stifling paradise, having more than 150 tribes.
- A wholesome climate throughout the year.
- Polite and hospitable people.
- A heritage that is maintained religiously and lived.
- A diverse eco-system—as diverse as only the seven regions throughout the globe.
- Satellite and other electronic communication including that of air and surface connectivity improving progressively.
- Abundance of Natural endowments—pristine and unexplored tourism resources—forest, rivers, rich bio-diversity, Himalayan Mountains and so on.
- Rich Cultural Heritage—multi ethnic communities, colourful festivals.
- Reasonably efficient air connectivity with Delhi and Kolkata and within the region.
- Tourism reorganized as a key industry by all neighbouring states.

Table 20.1 Population Trend in North East Region (in '000)

States	Year					
	1951	*1961*	*1971*	*1981*	*1991*	*2001*
Arunachal Pradesh	—	337	468	632	865	1091
Assam	8029	10837	14625	18041	22414	26638
Manipur	578	780	1073	1421	1837	2389
Meghalaya	606	769	1012	1336	1775	2306
Mizoram	196	266	332	494	690	891
Nagaland	213	369	516	775	1210	1989
Sikkim	138	162	210	316	406	540
Tripura	639	1142	1556	2053	2757	3191
N E R	10260	14501	19582	24752	31547	38495

Table 20.1 shows the per cent decadal variation of total population for different states of NER for the period 1951-2001. It is remarkable to note that highest variation occurred in the state of Tripura (78.7 p.c.) during the period 1951-61.In Nagaland, it is 64.41 p.c. during the period 1991-2001 which increased from 14.41 p.c. during 1951-61. Decadal percentage variation for the country (21.34) is less than any states of NER except Tripura (15.74 p. c.) and Arunachal Pradesh (13.86 p.c.).

The growth of population of an area is determined by three factors, namely fertility, mortality and migration. Internal migration is caused by movement of population within the country. The movement of people within a country indirectly reflects the level of development and regional imbalances in economic terms. The decision to move out is influenced by a host of social, economic, political, cultural and developmental factors. Economic opportunity largely causes movement of people from place to place in search of better employment, transfer of job etc.

Further, the housing situation and housing shortage in the region have become a matter of grave concern for the decision makers as well as common people for quite some time. The problem of housing shortage is aggravated by the population explosion. The constant migration of people from rural areas to cities in search of jobs also puts housing and basic services in the urban areas under strain. A well-balanced housing policy, it is felt, has to be designed to conserve our increasingly depleted natural resource reserves to the extent possible while at the same time cater to the growing need for shelter. However, affordability is critical for housing and infrastructure services. The State Governments of the region have to come forward in liberalizing the legal and regulatory regime to give a boost to housing and supporting infrastructure and promote participation of private sector and cooperatives in housing activities.

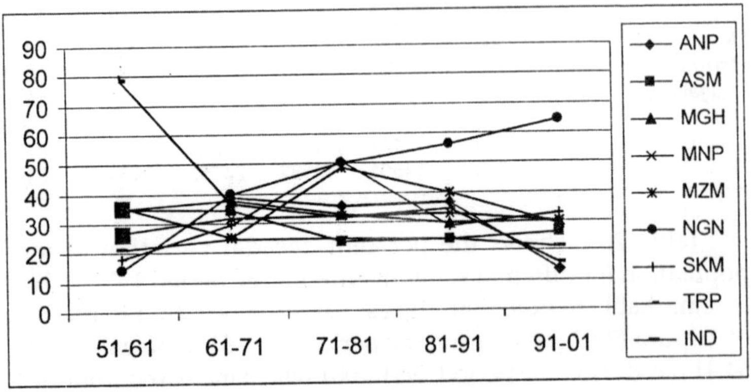

Fig. 20.1 Per cent Decadal Variation of Total Population in NER

Education

Literacy and education are important criteria to gauge the progress of individuals. Education can affect lives of people in several ways. It enables women to assume more autonomy or power in traditional gender stratified society and give them greater control over their own lives and stronger voice in matters affecting themselves and their families (Mason, 1984, 1992). Education can lead to changes in many aspects of women that impinge on their reproductive behaviour, provide information, autonomy, or knowledge and exposure to modern practices and information; decision-making autonomy, physical autonomy and physical mobility and confidence in dealing with the outside world in extracting the benefit from available sources, social autonomy, or access to and control over economic resources and increased self reliance in terms of social status and acceptance (Levine *et al.*,1991; Balk, 1994; Elo, 1992; Visaria, 1993; Mandelbaum, 1988; Okafor, 1991; United Nations, 1993).

In the recent years, female education has come to the forefront of development planning for tackling the problem of high fertility in developing countries. Social and Demographic Research has shown that education of women resulted in marriage at later age, fewer children per family, less infant and child mortality and healthier, better-reared and educated children. Female education is an important factor not only in imparting new knowledge and information, skills and values for improving participation in the labour force, but also in enhancing their status within and outside their immediate family. Thus, schooling is envisaged to have a long-term effect on women's position in family and society (Jeffery and Basu, 1996).

There are some notable features in regard to literacy rate in the states of NER. Except Arunachal Pradesh (41.59 p.c.) and Meghalaya (49.1 p.c.), the literacy level of the region's population is above the national level (52.21 p.c.) according to 1991 census while in 2001, percentage of literacy in Arunachal Pradesh (54.74 p.c.), Meghalaya (63.31 p.c.) and Assam (64.28 p.c.) are below the national percentage of 65.38 p.c. Education occupies an important place in the planned programmes of the Meghalaya Government. The North Eastern Hill University (NEHU) is the only central university in the state. According to the census report of the Government of India, percentage of literate persons of Meghalaya was 49.1 in 1991 and in 2001, it went up to 63.31. But its All India rank dropped down from 22nd position in 1991 census to 27th position in 2001 census. However, the female literacy rate is highest in Mizoram (86.13 p.c.) followed by Tripura (65.41 p.c.) and lowest in Arunachal Pradesh (44.24 p.c.), the only state in NER below the national level.

The percentage of population of age 6 and above who are literate varies from 52 p.c. in Arunachal Pradesh to 91 p.c. in Mizoram. It is to mention that in every states of the Indian union there is a big gender gap in literacy that inhibits attainment of total literacy. Enrolment in various stages of education is growing at a faster rate, but the proportion of girls is low and it declines sharply at higher stages of education. The highest gender gap is found in the states of Manipur (24.03 p.c. points), Arunachal Pradesh (21.76), Tripura (20.93) and the lowest is found in Mizoram (7.01) followed by Meghalaya (8.27). However all the states of NER are below the all-India (24.84 p.c. points) level. Low female literacy has strong repercussions on enrolment of children, population growth, child care and acceptance of family welfare measures.

Health and Nutrition

Health is a social goal and is considered as an integral component of social and economic development. Most of the health problems come from illiteracy, poverty, ignorance, over crowding, poor environmental conditions and uneven distribution of institutional health care. India is today facing a double problem of child nutrition and nutrition related degenerative diseases among the adult population. The fact sheets of the third round of the National Family Health Survey (NFHS-III), conducted in 29 States in 2005-2006, indicate that health and nutrition status of India's women and children is poor and suffers from systemic crisis. At the all-India level, 45.9 per cent of children below 3 years that is, about 45 million little girls and boys, are underweight or malnourished by standard weight-for-age criterion. Not enough attention has been paid to the factors affecting bone health. It is observed that there are only 4.32 p.c. of public health centres in the states of NER and only Assam has 64 p.c. public health centres among the states of NER. Less than 10 p.c. are there in each of the other states of the region. The same patterns are also observed in case of sub centres and community health centres. Thus, it is necessary to increase the number of health centres in these backward states of NER so that health problems of this region can be minimized. This is a grim warning to the policy-makers that high rates of economic growth alone will not bring about improvements in public health and nutrition. Many countries that are lower than India in terms of GDP have taken better care of their children. The Central and State Governments must make a comprehensive policy effort, backed by full financial commitments with a view to provide adequate nutrition and health care to every citizen and basic school education for every child in India.

Drinking Water

Water resources of a country constitute one of its vital common assets. Although India occupies only 3.29 million sq. km. geographical area, which forms 2.4 p.c. of the world's land area, it supports over 15 p.c. of the world's population Thus, India supports about one-sixth of world population, 1/50th of world's land and 1/25th of world's water resources. It is observed that the maximum amount of water is required in the state of Assam, which is approximately 2.33 p.c. as compared to India's requirement in 1991, which has later risen to 2.63 p.c. in 2001. Thus, there is an increasing trend of water requirement in 2001 over 1991. Regarding the safe drinking water facilities, all the states of NER, except Arunachal Pradesh (70.02 p.c.) have lesser facilities than the national average of (62.3 p.c.). It is striking to note that only 16.21 p.c. of total households of Mizoram can drink safe water. Thus, conservation of water is important and the people of NER should take active step for management of drinking water quality.

Per Capita Income

NER is amongst the poorest regions in the country. The per capita income of the region is Rs. 12407 which is less than the national average of Rs.17978 (2001-02). The pattern of agricultural growth has however remained uneven across regions and crops. The per capita income of Arunachal Pradesh at current prices was higher than the nation's average by Rs. 1043 in 1993-94. However, since 1996-97, the per capita income of the state has been lagging behind the national average. The per capita income at current prices during the year 2004-05 was estimated at Rs. 19566 and Rs. 10266 at constant prices (1993-94). The respective figures for the year 2000-01 were estimated at Rs. 10931 and Rs. 6813 while for the country the respective figures were estimated at Rs. 16564 and Rs. 10313 in 2000-01. The NSDP of Arunachal Pradesh at current prices for the year 2004-05 was Rs. 224612 lakh and at constant prices (1993-94) it was Rs. 117853 lakh. The per capita income of the State of Meghalaya also constantly lagged behind the national average. The economy of Mizoram is mainly agrarian with agriculture and allied activities contributing 29 p.c. to the NSDP of the state. Jhum or shifting cultivation is the usual practice and nearly 60 p.c. of the population is engaged in agriculture in this state.

The Net State Domestic Product (NSDP) of Assam in real terms i.e., at constant prices (1993-1994) has been estimated at Rs. 1783.78 crore in 2003-04 as against Rs. 16788.37 crore in 2002-03 and Rs. 16172.81 crore in 2001-02. Thus, NSDP registered a growth of 6.24 p.c. in 2003-04 over 2002-03 as against a growth of 3.81 p.c. in 2002-03 over 2001-2002. The NSDP at constant (1993-94) prices during the year 2001-02 was Rs. 193461 lakh. During the period

1993-94 to 2001-02 the NSDP at constant prices grew at a compound annual growth rate of 6.28 p.c. as compared to the Net National Product (NNP) growth of 6.29 p.c. The per capita State Domestic Product (NSDP) i.e., per capita income of Assam at constant prices (1993-94) has been worked out at Rs. 6520 in 2003-04 as against Rs. 6221 in 2002-03 and Rs.6066 in 2001-02. Per capita income of Assam gradually increased from Rs. 5544 in 1990-91 to Rs. 5796 in 1997-98 which decreased to Rs. 5664 in the next year (1998-99) and then increased to Rs. 6756 in 2004-05. The growth of gross state domestic product (GSDP) of Assam at constant prices (1993-94) increased from 4.5 p.c. in 2001 to 5.5 p.c. in 2003-04 but then it decreased to 5.3 p.c. in 2004-05. The percentage of urban population in Assam was 11.10 p.c. according to 1991 census which increased further by 1.8 p.c. according to 2001 census (12.90 p.c.). Thus more than 87 p.c. of total population live in rural areas and the economy of the state largely depends on the development of rural areas.

The NSDP of Manipur at current prices for the year 2001-02 was Rs. 320478 lakh. As compared to the previous year, it registered a growth of 8.82 p.c. compared to all India NNP growth of 10.27 p.c. During the period 1993-94 to 2001-02, the NSDP at current prices grew at a compound annual growth rate of 6.82 p.c. as compared to the NNP growth of 6.29 p.c. As in other states of the NER, the per capita income of the state of Manipur has constantly lagged behind the national average. The disparity has been rising gradually. The per capita income at the current prices in 2001-02 was Rs. 13213 as compared to that of the all India figure of Rs. 17947. The per capita income at constant (1993-94) prices in 2001-02 was Rs. 7976 as compared to all India figure of Rs. 10754. The per capita income at constant (1993-94) prices was Rs.6813 in 2000-01 as compared to the all India figure of Rs10313 in 2000-01.The per capita income at current prices in 2000-01 was Rs.10931 as compared to all India figure of Rs. 16564.

The NSDP of Tripura at current prices for the year 2000-01 was Rs.418350 lakh registering a growth of 9.72 p.c. over the previous year's figure of Rs. 381272 lakh. During 1993-94 to 2000-01, the NSDP at current prices grew at a compound annual growth rate of 14.52 p.c. compared to the NNP growth of 13.73 p.c. NSDP at constant (1993-1994) prices in 2000-01 was Rs. 260739 lakh. During 1993-94 to 2000-01, the compound annual rate of growth of NSDP at constant prices was 7.04 p.c. while the NNP growth was 6.28 p.c.

The NER continues to be a net importer of foodgrains even for its own consumption. In spite of covering 7.8 p.c. of the country's total geographical area, NER produces only 4.0 p.c. of the country's total foodgrain while agriculture provides livelihood support to 70 p.c. of the population of NER.

Agriculture

As in the other states of the Northeast, Arunachal Pradesh's economy is mainly agrarian. Foodgrain production of Arunachal Pradesh was 2.05 lakh MT in 1999-2000 registering a growth of 13.25 p.c. over the previous year's production. The foodgrain yield was 1126 kg./ha. in 1999-2000. There is great potential of fishery sector in Arunachal Pradesh. But the problems of flood, under utilization of aquatic resources, unscientific method of production in the state hinder this potential. Agriculture is the mainstay of a large majority of the population of Assam. As per 2001 census, 53 p.c. of total work force are engaged in agricultural activities. The contribution of agriculture to Net State Domestic Product of the state is 31.19 p.c. in 2003-04. The agriculture in the state mostly depends on rainfall. One of the most serious problems adversely affecting the state's agriculture is the recurrence of devastating floods.

Assam is rich in natural resources like oil and natural gas, coal, rubber, tea and some minerals like granite, limestone and kaolin. The present state is much smaller than what it was forty years ago. It is still the largest economy in the North East. Although it is more industrially developed than other North Eastern states, it is primarily an agrarian economy with 74 p.c. population engaged in agricultural and allied activities. As per 2001 census, 53 p.c. of total work force are engaged in agricultural activities. But during the period 2000-05, the overall scenario of agriculture was not praiseworthy. The contribution of agriculture to Net State Domestic Product of the state was only 31.19 p.c. in 2003-04. The production of winter rice steadily decreased from 2713 thousand tones in 2001-02 to 1800 thousand tones in 2004-05. Same trends were observed in case of Autumn rice, Summer rice, cotton, Jute etc. (Fig. 20.2). As per the report of livestock census 2003, the total livestock population in Assam was 140.23 lakh as against 134.67 lakh in 1997. The livestock products such as milk, egg and meat play a vital role in the economy of Assam. As per the State Directorate of Fisheries, present level of annual fish production is 1.86 lakh metric tones (2004-05) which increased by 15.41 p.c. in comparison to 2001-02.

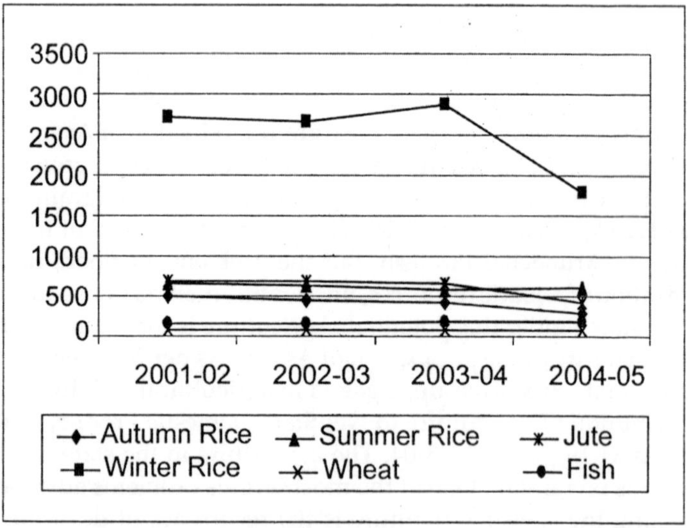

Fig. 20.2 Agricultural Production in Assam (*in thousand tones*)

The economy of Manipur as that of the other northeastern states of India, is mainly dependent on agriculture. The majority of the population of the state get there means of livelihood from the agricultural sector as they have accepted agriculture as the primary occupation. Total foodgrains production in Manipur was of the tune of 4 lakh tones as in 2001-02 out of which total production of Rice was 387 thousand tones. As per 2000-01 statistics, agriculture and its allied activities contributed 33 per cent to Manipur's NSDP at current prices. The economy of the state of Mizoram is mainly agrarian with agriculture and allied activities contributing 29 p.c. to the NSDP of the state. Jhum or shifting cultivation is the usual practice. Nearly 60 p.c. of the population is engaged in agriculture in this state. Total production of paddy in Mizoram was 109.2 thousand MT in 2002-03 which increased to 114.6 thousand MT in 2003-04 but then decreased to

99.02 thousand MT in 2005-06. Similarly, the production of pulses decreased to 2737 MT in 2005-06 from 4986 MT in 2002-03. However, the production of Maize increased over the said period by almost 53 p.c.

Agriculture plays an important role in the state's economy. Agriculture employs more than fifty per cent of the total workforce of the state of Meghalaya. It contributes nearly 30 p.c. to the State's NSDP in 1999-00. Agriculture not only supplies raw materials such as cotton, jute, ginger etc. for industries outside the state but also provides inputs to small agro-based industries in the state such as turmeric, paddy, cereals and pulses maize etc.

Almost three–fourth of the working population in Nagaland is engaged in the primary sector. Like the other states of the north east, Nagaland is predominantly an agrarian economy. Rice is the staple food. Agriculture occupies about 70 p.c. of the total cultivated areas, Nagaland has been identified as a potential area for promoting food processing industries. The agriculture and allied sectors in Nagaland offer good inputs for development of a host of industries including floriculture, horticulture, rubber plantation and allied industries, sericulture, tea cultivation and processing, bamboo shot preservation, mushroom cultivation and processing, piggery, poultry etc.

Sikkim's economy is largely agrarian, based on traditional farming methods on terraced slopes. The state is gifted with abundant natural resources. The resources can be grouped into biotic or a-biotic, both of which can be renewable. Biotic resources include agriculture crops, fodder and forests. The rural populace grows crops such as *cardamom*, *oranges*, *apples*, *tea* and *orchids*. Rice is grown on terraced hillsides in the southern reaches. Sikkim has the highest production and largest cultivated area of cardamom in India. Because of the hilly terrain and lack of reliable transportation infrastructure, there are no large-scale industries. *Breweries*, distilleries, tanning and *watch*-making are the main industries. These are located in the southern reaches of the state, primarily in the towns of *Melli* and *Jorethang*. The state has an impressive growth rate of 8.3 p.c., which is the second highest in the country after *Delhi*. The economy of Sikkim is mainly based on agricultural and animal husbandry. Approx. 11 p.c. of the total geographical area is under agriculture. Agriculture is of the mixed type and is still at the subsistence level rather than at commercial level. The work force participation rate as per 1991 census is 40.44 p.c. The female work participation rate in Sikkim is also much higher than the national average. Cultivators account for the greater majority of the people in the state and their percentage is 57.84 p.c. Agricultural labourers as a whole constitute only 7.81 p.c. of the workers in the state. The household and other industries are negligible, but other workers (Tertiary Sector) at the state level represent a good percentage of population. The decreasing ratio of worker at the state level indicates the low level of economic diversification. The importance of agriculture can be judged by the high percentage of population (Approx. 65 p.c.) engaged in it. Animal husbandry is an integral part of the household economy of the region. There are certain household industries which substantially add to household incomes. The past one and half decade has witnessed a tremendous upward swing in various development programs giving a new thrust to the Sikkim economy. This process has increased wage employment opportunities. Though most of the inhabitants are basically agriculturists, they have diversified into tertiary jobs and Government services.

Tripura's economy is primarily agrarian. Agriculture and its allied activities contributes nearly 34 p.c. to the state's NSDP. Agriculture in Tripura includes traditional Jhum (shifting) cultivation. After Kerala, Tripura is the largest producer of natural rubber and the rubber produced is of superior quality. The state also has the distinction of being the highest producer of True Potato Seeds in the country.

It is observed that NER produces rice to the tune of 5350 thousand tones which is only 7.36 p.c. as compared to all India level. The respective percentages of production in case of maize and wheat are 2.52 p.c. and 0.20 p.c. The total foodgrain production in NER with respect to the country is only 4 p.c. (Table 20.2)

Irrigation

The NER has considerable unexploited irrigation potential, especially in states like Manipur and Tripura. So far, about 19 p.c. of the total potential of 5.7 lakh hact. could be exploited in Assam, against the national achievement of 40 p.c. So far, Manipur could attain the level of about 10 p.c. of the total potential to cover 65000 hact. The potential in Tripura for irrigation has been assessed at

2.81 lakh hact. The topographical conditions in Mizoram, Meghalaya, Nagaland, and Sikkim are not congenial to groundwater irrigation schemes and therefore the development of surface irrigation has better prospects. (*Source:* Draft Report of the Task force on Development Initiatives for the NER, Sept. 2005.).

Table 20.2 Foodgrain Production in NER as on 2002-03
(in '000 tonnes)

	Rice	*Maize*	*Wheat*	*Total Foodgrain*
NER	5350.00	260.00	127.00	5927.00
All India	72653.00	10303.00	65096.00	174188.00
NER as percentage of All India	7.36	2.52	0.20	4.00

Source: Draft Report of the Task force on Development Initiatives for the NER, September 2005.

Power

The degree of economic growth is correlated with the generation and consumption of electricity. As per Power Ministry data, 2004, share of Arunachal Pradesh in Central Sector stations was 117 MW and the installed capacity in the State Sector was 45.43 MW. The total installed capacity was 162.43 MW. As on 31st March, 2005, 60.46 p.c. villages were electrified in the state while the percentage of rural household having electricity was 44.53 p.c. as on March 31, 2004. Per capita consumption of electricity was only 68.61 KWh in 2000-01. Although Mizoram has a vast hydel potential, the progress in this sector is still very slow. In Mizoram, power is generated by only two types—Hydel and diesel. As per Ministry of Power data, Mizoram's share in Central Sector stations in 2004 was 49.10 MW. Manipur's share in the Central Sector stations was 105.50 MW as on 30th September, 2004, while the installed capacity in the state sector was 48.61 MW. The total installed capacity in the state was 154.11 MW.

Power is the basic infrastructure requirement for the growth of industries as well as economy of any state. In spite of having immense potential of power generation in the state, the performance of this sector is not encouraging. Assam accounts for only 0.12 p.c. of total power generation in the country during

2003-04. The average per capita consumption of electricity in the State was 104 Kwh. in 2003-05 as per Economic Survey Assam, 2005-06, which is far below the national average of 359 Kwh in the same year. Since the past several years, the overall power supply position in the state has not been much satisfactory. It is important to note that there is no hydel power generation in the state. Thermal power generated 46 million units in the year 2001-02 but after that it went into the dark. Total power generation scenario in the state is not at all sufficient for healthy economic development. The generation has shown declining trend from 840.406 Million unit in 2001-02 to 756.435 Million unit in 2004-05. At the peak hours, power shortage gradually increased from 10.20 p.c. to 24.50 p.c. during 2001-05. It showed maximum shortage during 2003-04. During the same period, the estimated requirement of power in the state was 3788.525 MW, while the availability was 3376.284 MW. The overall power supply position in the state during 2005-2006 was not much encouraging and the state had to witness erratic power supply during the year.

The rivers in Meghalaya present an ideal scope for generation of hydel power. The projects in Meghalaya are Sunapani Hydel Project, Umtru Hydel Project, Umium Hydel Project, Tura Diesel and Nangal Bibra. Meghalaya consists of towns and thousands of villages situated in rural areas. Some of these villages are located in inaccessible parts of the state. Despite the vast potential, the power generated within the state of Nagaland is quite insignificant. According to the Annual Administrative Report of the Department of Power, the total power generation was 3.21 (MW) and the total purchase was 230 (MW) in 2000-01. Thus the State could generate only 1.39 p.c. of the total power requirements. The State mainly purchases power from NEEPCO, NHPC and PGCI. As per Ministry of Power data, Nagaland's share in Central Sector stations as on September 30, 2004 was 71.10 MW, while the installed capacity was 101.46 MW. It is important to note that, as on August 31, 2004, the percentage of electrified was 100 p.c. As compared to the national average of 355 kwh., the per capita consumption of electricity in Nagaland was 84.74 kwh. and the percentage of rural households having electricity in the state was 47.16 p.c. The state of Sikkim has also huge potential for hydel power. As per 2001 data, the per capita consumption of electricity in the state of Sikkim was 182 Kwh.

Tripura has two sources of power generation—Hydel and Thermal. The state also has natural gas, which can be used for thermal power generation. Out of the two major sources of power generation, thermal power accounts for more than 77 p.c. while the remaining is generated from Gomati Power Project (hydro). Due to the increase in the demand for electricity, the state is experiencing persistent power shortage and hence frequent power cuts are scheduled. During 2000-01 the total installed capacity was 85.35 MW, total power generated was 318.38 MW, total purchase of power was 268.00 MW in 2000-01 which is 8.85 MW higher than that purchase in 1999-2000. The total units sold to ultimate consumers in 2000-01 were 388 MU. Despite commendable successes, the position in relation to needs remains highly unsatisfactory. It is observed that a large expansion of this source of energy is required. As such about 79.80 per cent of the villages and 100 per cent towns are electrified which raises both the income and expenditure of the department. But it is found that expenditures far exceeds the income. Kutir Jyoti, a centrally sponsored scheme to give assistance to the people living below poverty line is providing electricity free of cost. Till 1997-98 there were 6217 connections under this scheme that went up to 15688 in 1998-99 and to 37979 in 2000-01. As on 30th September, 2004, Tripura's share in the central sector stations was 93.10 MW, while the installed capacity in the state sector was 127.36 MW. The percentage of rural households having electricity was 28.50 p.c.

Industries

Industrially, the NER continues to be the most backward region in the country, and the states in the region hardly have any industrial base, except perhaps Assam, because of its traditional tea, oil and wood based industries. Meghalaya has made some headway in setting up of small and medium industries. There are a number of factors responsible for lack of industrial growth in the region like poor infrastructure, inadequate supply of electricity, violence and extortion etc. The growth of all industries; large, medium and small has been uneven. The number of functioning large and medium industries in the NER has been negligible. The status of industries in the NER is shown in the Table 20.3. It is important to note that in the state of Assam, the number of large and medium industrial units decreased from 129 in 1999 to 120 in 2003. This declining trend has been observed in the states of Arunachal Prtadesh (As on 31-03-05, there are only 14 industrial estates in Arunachal Pradesh) and Nagaland while in the states of Meghalaya and Tripura the number of units increased. Most of the states of this region have failed to gear up industrialization.

Table 20.3 Large and Medium Industries in NER (as on March 2003).

State	*No. of units in 1999*	*Percentage*	*No. of units in 1999*	*Percentage*
ANP	17	9.55	15	7.04
ASM	129	72.48	120	56.34
MNP	12	6.74	12	5.63
MGH	10	5.62	49	23.00
MZM	1	0.56	1	0.47
NGN	7	3.93	5	2.35
SKM	N.A.	N.A.	3	1.41
TRP	2	1.12	8	3.76
NER	178	100.00	213	100.00

Source: Draft Report of the Task force on Development Initiatives for the NER, Sept. 2005 & IIE, Guwahati.

The overall performance of Manufacturing and Processing Sector in Assam has not been much encouraging during 2004-2005. Provisional data available for the year shows a positive growth in the production of industrial items like Petroleum (Crude), Wheat, Flour, Cement, Jute Textiles, etc. over the level of production of the previous year. On the other hand a decrease in production has been noticed in respect of items like Tea, Fertilizer, etc. during the said year. Other industrial items maintained more or less same level of production during 2004-2005. The Mining Sector of the state has shown a mixed performance in production during 2004-2005. During the year, production of Petroleum (Crude) registered a growth of 2.9 per cent and that of Natural Gas (Utilized) increased by about 0.39 per cent whereas the production of Coal and Limestone recorded decrease by 14 per cent and 10 per cent respectively.

Industrialization has long been recognized in the strategy of development. It is unfortunate that the state of Tripura is yet to come out of industrial backwardness. The Central Government has declared the entire state as 'A' category backward area for the purpose of giving central investment subsidy. It is to be noted that the state of Mizoram is a notified backward area and is categorized under " No Industry State". As on March 2000, number of large and medium industries in the state was only one. This shows very sick position in industrial sector of Mizoram. In Meghalaya, industries have been classified into two groups, viz., registered manufacturing industries and unregistered manufacturing industries. In both ways, Meghalaya can be identified as one of the industrially backward states in the country. Due to inadequate industrial infrastructure, lack of mineral resources and transportation, the industrial growth is limited in Nagaland. Despite vast natural resources endowment Nagaland is considered as one of the most industrially backward states of the country. The industrial structure of Nagaland may be classified, based on resource uses into agro-based industries, mineral-based industries, forest-based industries and other industries. In case of medium scale industries in Nagaland, there were virtually no industries during the 60's.Handicraft and Handloom production only met domestic needs. From 1970 onwards a few medium scale local resource-based industries have come into existence. The Small Scale Industries began to emerge since 1970s based on local resources.

Small Scale Industries

The Handloom Industry plays a vital role in providing employment to a huge number of population. The NER has the highest concentration of household units in the Handloom Sector in the country and more than 50 per cent of weavers belong to the NER states.

Table 20.4 shows the trend of growth of Small Scale Industries (SSI) in the states of NER during the period 1997-98 to 2002-03. Over the period (1997-2003) highest percentage of growth rate occurred in the state of Nagaland (252.95 p.c) followed by Meghalaya (41.28 p.c.) and Mizoram (35.47 p.c.) while it is the lowest in both the states of Arunachal Pradesh and Manipur (12.25 p.c.). By observing the percentage increase over the previous year, it can be noted that for different states it ranged from 1.00 p.c. to 37.92 p.c. Highest variation is observed in the state of Nagaland that ranged from 15.78 p.c. (1997-98) to 37.92 p.c. (1998-99). In case of Tripura, it ranged from 1.00 p.c. (2002-03) to 3.90 p.c. (1997-98). The process of setting up large and medium scale industries in the State of Tripura is not satisfactory due to several constraints like limited size of market, lack of skilled and semi-skilled manpower, inadequate infrastructure, insurgency and extremist problems.

Development of small-scale industrial sector (SSI), therefore, is the only alternative to the economic backwardness. In spite of the vast scope, the development of SSI in Tripura still remains at a very nascent stage, although as a result of a few policy measures to provide financial and technical support, the SSI sector has grown in the recent years. Yet it is not satisfactory in the context of regional or national growth rate. For providing employment opportunities in the rural areas and thereby strengthening the rural economy, Khadi and Village Industries plays an important role. The Mizoram Khadi and Village Industries Board was formed in March 1986 as a non-profit making body. The board provides financial assistance to the registered individuals, institutions, co-operatives and departmental units. The total number. of units registered upto 31-03-2001 reached 5772. It also provides technical guidance and training. However, the topography and varied climate conditions in Mizoram facilitated the successful introduction of Mulberry, Eri, Muga and Tasar. The total number of farmers engaged in sericulture activities during 2000-01 was 3332 and the production of raw silk during 2000-01 was reported to be 2064.88 kg.. The major crafts of Meghalaya are cane and bamboo, carpets, musical instruments, jewellery, fibre-crafts, textiles etc. The Nagas have a rich tradition of art and craft. The major crafts of Nagaland are artistic textiles, cane and bamboo straw etc. woodware, metalware, bangals and beeds, gems and jewellery. The art of weaving is still popular among the Naga women, especially in the rural areas. Handicrafts and handloom industry has the potential to generate income and employment in a big way. The traditional crafts like carpet weaving, cane and bamboo crafts, spinning wool, handmade paper and Thanka paintings are famous and enjoy government support so far as training is concerned. The high quality traditional handicrafts and handloom products may have a good market, both nationally and internationally. However, marketing of the product depends on tourism promotion outside the state by the Government and adequate supply of input and infrastructure

- Availability of trained and trainable manpower.
- English and Hindi are easily understood and spoken throughout.

World Tourism Organization's Vision 2020

The World Tourism Organization, the apex body of tourism few years back, predicted that US$ 2000 billion will be generated by the industry within the year 2020 (Bezbarua 1999). It has analyzed the emerging trends and factors, which will influence the future growth pattern of the industry. Some of the important observations of World Tourism Organization are summarized below:

- By 2020, there will be 1.6 billion international tourist arrivals and tourism receipts will rise to a staggering US$2000 billion globally.
- There will be sustained average annual growth rate of 4.3 per cent (for arrivals) and 6.7 per cent (for receipts) throughout the world till 2020.
- In spite of this growth only 7 per cent of the world's population will become potential tourists. Thus according to World Tourism Organization the industry would be still in infancy even in the year 2020.
- The top 10 tourist receiving countries would undergo major changes and *China* would be receiving maximum number of tourists (estimated to be 137.1 million with a market share of 8.6 per cent) by 2020. France the traditional market leader, would come down to the third position. China will have an average growth rate of 8.0 per cent in tourist arrivals during the period 1995-2020.
- There will be changes in the top tourist originating countries. Japan, China and Russian Federation will emerge as the new major outbound tourist countries.
- Though Europe will remain the largest tourist-receiving region, its share will come down to 45 per cent from the present 59 per cent.
- South Asia will grow at a rate of 6.1 per cent per annum during the period but its share will grow only up to 1.2 per cent from the present 0.7 per cent.

Recent Trends and Emerging Issues

New research has shown that the impact of economic activity in tourism and travel is much wider than that currently captured in national income accounting. Presently, tourism industry in India is estimated to support 5.3 million jobs directly, but the trickle down effects of this industry are such that its share is 6.8 per cent of total employment and 8.2 per cent of G.D.P. Tourism and travel goes beyond providing products services directly for tourists' consumption such as lodging, food, etc. but there is also the corresponding effect on a number of enormous and diverse ranges of activities like security service, food and beverages supplies, furnishing and furniture products, glass-iron and steel products etc., (World Travel Council 2001).

India, though larger in size and richer in tourist offerings than many of the leading tourist destinations, is responsible for only less than 1 per cent of the total tourist receipt (Sarma 2003) generated in the world. India received only around 3.54 million tourists in the year 2004-2005 (FHRAI 2005). India, till the recently, has been considered a *serious* and *spiritual* destination rather than a destination where one can relax and have fun (Sarma 2000). However, this concept is gradually changing with aggressive promotional campaigns taken up by the National Tourism Organizations (NTOs). As in the case of all developing nations the communication network used by the average traveller in India had been limited to the traditional information sources till the other day. The Internet connectivity was also minimal till the recent times. Hence, the marketers heavily relied upon PR in print and electronic media, printed brochures, fliers, post cards and formal and informal referrals. Apart from these, the newest trend in the country has been the extensive use of the distribution channel, i.e., the tour and travel operators and agents. Ironically enough, the Indian tourism industry traditionally has not been accustomed to using advertisements unlike their counterparts elsewhere in the globe. Therefore, the visitors are not used to receive messages through advertisements. Even with modernization the country's share of the total tourism receipt has been predicted as low as 1.2 per cent , even though the growth in the Indian industry will be much higher than the global one (while predicting the country's share it is safely assumed that all tourists visiting south Asia will be visiting India too.). Whatever small the percentage looks like this is translated to be a whopping US$ 24 billion. In the present exchange rate regime this is Rs.1, 08,000 crore in just a single given year (2020).

Sustainability of the industry should be the prime consideration when we think of tourism in NE India around 2020. We must realize and understand what we have to offer to a visitor and package the same in a "non-destructive" and "non consumptive" way to the tourist, who is willing to enjoy the resultant experience. While doing so, we must think about the generations of future and make sure that they also equally (if not more) benefit from the industry. This is a great constraint in developing the regional tourist potentials. At the same time the industry must benefit the stakeholders so that they realize the importance of preservation and conservation of the tourist assets we have inherited. It must also contribute to a great extent towards marketing the regional domestic products so as to improve the quality of life of the local inhabitants. This is possible only when there is huge number of visitors. However, as indicated earlier we must avoid the destructive mass tourists and for this we need a sensible and well-planned promotion-cum-education campaign. Tourism industry has been instrumental in shaping the economy in many nations and regions throughout the globe. For example, Fiji achieved almost 14 per cent of GDP from the tourism industry (Narayan, 2005). We are all aware of the economic success stories of tourism industries in the countries like Mauritius, Thailand, Spain, Greece, Indonesia, Singapore, Hawaii etc. In a society like ours, which is dominated by agriculture only, tourism can offer one of the few viable options for achieving economic development and prosperity. It is widely argued that in order to pass on the good effects of economic development to the population at large we must have labour intensive techniques of development, especially in the NE region. It is observed that sericulture including craft works; pisciculture and tourism have got tremendous potential in helping in this direction. We are aware of the multiplier effects of tourism spending. This effect may be still widened with good insight and strategic interventions by the policy-makers. This could reduce leakage out of the local economy. These strategies have got direct relationship with the constraints mentioned above. Apart from contributing to a healthy percentage towards economic development of the region, the industry within a span of 15 years from now should be able to help society fostering universal brotherhood. Reaction of the society towards tourism and the tourists is difficult to predict because at different points of evolvement of the industry the society's reaction differs. In many cases local population become unfriendly towards the tourist industry and the tourists.

An Approach

NE can host tourists with diverse needs and wants. It has been a topic of constant discussion and debate as to which type of tourists could be attracted to a destination, particularly the NE. The ill effects of unplanned tourism and visitor non-sense are in front of us. We can very well learn a lesson from the neighbouring Thailand, and also from other third world countries promoting mass tourism. Up market tourists in Mediterranean, for instance, use over six times as much water per capita as rural residents in the same area. On the contrary five thousand nuns at a five-day religious meeting are likely to cause much less environmental impact than 100 teenage bikers visiting for a few hours (Middleton and Hawkins, 1998). In popular Indian destinations also, one can see the environmental and cultural tensions originating from tourism industry. But then, the optimists would always insist on the steady flow of number of tourist. According to them differentiation between mass tourism and alternative tourism can be taken up afterwards too!

A Peep into the Future

It is apparent that Northeast India as a whole needs a big push or a kick-start to put the economy on the path of development. Looking 'east' provides an opportunity to overcome problems of distance from markets. Tourism provides a marketable product which does not depend on raw materials from outside. In a comparable situation of economic doldrums in the '80s, Mexico could step out of the traditional models of economic growth to depend on tourism as an important input. This strategy showed remarkable results. Outlining the experience, Mexico's planning Minister summed up[1] that tourism was relevant because—

- Agriculture and manufacturing are location specific, but tourism can be promoted and developed almost anywhere. It is therefore an ideal tool for decentralized regional development.
- It provides infinite product possibilities—anything under the sun if properly packaged and marketed—such as culture, heritage, nature, sun and beaches, cruises, business, conventions, spirituality, adventure, sports, ethnicity and so forth yield dividend. The benefits are more spread out and not centred on urban areas as in the case of most industries.
- Being a personal service it is hard to automate and is therefore labour intensive.
- The foreign import component of investment in tourism is very low. In Mexico as a whole it was estimated to be 6-8 per cent as against 35-45 per cent for the automobile industry. In the case of the Northeast the component would be even more negligible. The tourist expenditure within the country is almost always equivalent to cash. It therefore has an advantage over traditional exports in respect of immediate cash flows.
- The multiplier effect of tourism is very high. The ripple effects are widespread and the benefits are shared by an incredibly large number of service providers, like lodgings, food and beverages, handicraft, local transportation, guides, shopping, entertainment, photography. In the total range of services, many of the service providers are not visible at all.

These are only some illustrative examples and all the observations are relevant to the Northeast. The employment intensity of tourism in the Indian context was demonstrated by an oft-quoted sample survey of the Ministry of Tourism.[2] According to this survey, for every million rupees invested, at 1985-86 prices, the comparative employment generation in some of the sectors were as follows—agriculture 44.7, manufacturing 12.6, mining and quarrying 2.6, railways 0.9, other transport 13.8, tourism 47.5, and hotels and restaurants 89.0.

Another recent survey by the Ministry[3] shows the impact of tourism on local level employment. About 96 per cent of the total income of artisan households in Kerala and 90 per cent in Rajasthan come from tourism related income. The study also indicates that 'tourism plays a vital role in enhancing the standard of living of the artisan families... As regards folk artists, their average per capita income during the peak season is nearly four times that in the lean season. ...Share of female employment is the highest in the lower income segment of the artisan households.'

The tourism potential of the Northeast has not been fully exploited. The Ministry of Tourism calls the region a 'paradise unexplored'. Global tourism has been booming and future projections show that this trend will continue. The new generations of travellers who are 'money rich and time poor' are increasingly looking for unique experiences. More and more people are looking at tourism as less of a journey and more of an experience—a phenomenon that is called the emergence of the 'experience economy'.

For this new and growing breed of tourists the Northeast with its variety and uniqueness has immense attraction. The rich natural beauty and its diversity, exotic cultural and ethnic mosaic, flora and fauna and the serenity of the virgin, unexplored ecosystems provide possibilities of a totally different experience for the tourists.

The rationale for a trade led growth strategy for the Northeast as integrated to the 'Look East' policy has been well explained. The landlocked Northeast, it is explained, is ideally placed to link India with ASEAN both in geographical and commercial senses. The Northeast also has strong cultural and historical linkages with the East, which could be exploited to forge economic cooperation.

So far as tourism is concerned, such an approach comes out of India's tourism experience of the last decade. This was a decade of good growth thwarted by continuous crisis—the Gulf war, the nuclear tests and subsequent economic sanctions, the Kargil War, terrorist attack on Parliament, the Gujarat earthquake, the Afghan War and the Iraq War, just to mention a few. The infamous 'advisories' issued by the national governments in Europe and USA—the countries from where most of the tourists come—adversely affected the tourism flow to India. Globally, in the first three years of the new millennium, tourism saw many ups and downs. The wars, the 9/11 incidents and the SARS, adversely affected tourism growth. Nevertheless, in almost 50 years since the World Tourism Organization started keeping statistics, tourism growth has shown negative results only three times and two of them came during the first three years of the new millennium.

One key lesson learnt during this time was that in periods of crisis, regional tourism and domestic tourism become the mainstay of the industry. Unfortunately, Indian tourism depends heavily on the long haul tourists from the West. Whereas globally the ratio of interregional to regional tourism is 20:80, in case of India it is almost exactly the other way round. The marketing strategy of the Ministry of Tourism is now identifying new markets for tourism and this search is aligned with the 'Look East' trade policy.

Such a policy shift is particularly relevant and important for the Northeast. Because it is situated far away from the main entry points of tourists, the Northeast is at disadvantage in attracting foreign tourists from the West. This is reflected in the negligible tourist flow to this region. In 2002, out of about 5.8 million visits to the states (by 2.75 m. tourists), the Northeast received only about 22000. If the figures of Sikkim are excluded, all the other seven states of the Northeast accounted for only 12000 visits.

Looking to the East is fortunately a natural marketing option for the Northeast. By 2020 the Asia Pacific Region will be the second largest tourist generating market in the world. The world tourism projection shows that by 2020 this region will generate 405 m of the total 1561 m tourists. These countries have continuous geographical land links with the Northeast. China is already vigorously developing tourism in its southern provinces to take advantage of this outbound tourist market of the region. These areas have cultural, historical and ethnic links with the Northeast. The tourism marketing strategy of the Northeast should focus on these links to establish a natural flow of people within the region, including the Northeast.

In such a strategy it will be of crucial importance to develop access to this region. Presently in the western tourist dominated scenario, access to the Northeast is seen as a constraint. While air access will have to be developed as a *sine qua non* for tourism development strategy, fortunately, the Asian Highway Project is looming in the horizon as a great opportunity for the region. The Asian Highway, if properly planned and integrated, can completely change the tourism scenario of the region. It proposes to cover 90,000 km. in 25 countries, of which 40,000 km. will be international routes and 50,000 km. will be regional routes. ESCAP, which is spearheading the project, recognizes the excellent tourism potential of the Asian Highway. It has already undertaken a survey to identify the potential and possible bottlenecks so that timely action can be taken to remove them.

Here is a golden opportunity for the Northeast to exploit. The plan of action for the Northeast with the objective of using the Asian Highway as its link to the East, could be, among others –

- The international route touches only a part of the Northeast. Therefore, integrated feeder communication links should be developed through the national and state planning processes, in consultation with ESCAP. This will require quick coordination among the states and identification of suitable implementing agencies.
- A comprehensive tourism potential survey should precede the planning of routes to form the feeder to the Asian Highway. Among other things, the routes planned should be able to serve and promote the most important tourism destinations.
- Tourism cannot be developed in a vacuum. It requires social and economic infrastructure for proper growth. As a first step to planning, a survey of the infrastructure gaps should be undertaken. Thereafter, the projects should be prioritized on the basis of their overall importance to the trade led growth strategy. A major component for tourism should be the development of wayside amenities along the Asian Highway and feeder routes. In Japan a concept of community based tourism and wayside facilities called 'Michi-no-eki' has proved immensely successful. Under this scheme, the facilities are community run in partnership with the private sector. The centres not only provide facilities but also work as outlets for local handicraft and handloom products and showcase local culture, cuisine etc. Such involvement not only provides better economic benefits for the people, but also ensures better visitor experience.

If the very high expectation of the 'Look East' Policy for economic opportunities through tourism is to become a reality, the Northeast must first make an assessment of its own competitive advantage and then plan strategy based on such assessment. The South Asian Growth Quadrangle of Bangladesh, Bhutan, India and Nepal (BBIN) will also directly touch the Northeast. The Asian Development Bank (ADB) has explored these growth possibilities with its South Asia Sub-regional Economic Cooperation (SASEC) initiative. Under this initiative, the main tourism strengths of the region have been identified as (*i*) sustainable eco-tourism and (*ii*) the Buddhist circuit.

In both areas the advantage of the Northeast is apparent. The SASEC concept of the Buddhist circuit is in fact very comprehensive. It goes beyond the traditional circuit of places where Lord Buddha lived, meditated, attained enlightenment and *parinirvana*. It covers places of living Buddhism like Ladakh, Sikkim and Arunachal (Tawang). Art, culture and archaeology of Buddhism are also integrated into the total Buddhist circuit concept. A significantly large number of tourists from the Asia Pacific Region are Buddhists and, therefore, these attractions may open up new interest in the Northeast.

Unfortunately, despite its comparative advantage in this area, tourism is not perceived as an important economic activity. The first task in the socio-economic planning of the region should be to create awareness about the place of tourism in general and of sustainable tourism in particular. But such awareness creation efforts can start only when the governments give importance to tourism and provide priority of this industry in the planning process.

Most of tourism planning in the region are of *ad hoc* nature. It is essential to move away from such an *ad hoc* nature to draw up realistic plans of action and chart out the future directions clearly. Every state must bring out a pragmatic tourism policy, not couched in general terms but clearly defining an actionable plan. It should indicate the Government's commitment to sustainable tourism, assign a place to tourism in development planning and to the roles Government and other stakeholders play. The policy should identify the organizational pattern to implement the policy and a system of monitoring and accountability.

A tourism policy would remain on the wish list of the tourism department alone unless it draws total Government commitment. Tourism being a multi-dimensional activity depends on the involvement of many other agencies for its success. Other departments like roads, culture, forest and so on, can play an important role in the development of the total tourism product. For achieving maximum coordination, institutional arrangements should be put in place.

Domestic tourism plays a key role in Indian tourism. Against the average ratio of about seven domestic tourists for every foreign tourist in the total picture internationally, the ratio for India is about 100:1. In absolute terms the figure of total domestic tourists is about 300 million against three million foreign tourists. The Northeast has a insignificant share of this huge number of tourists who contribute to employment and income generation in other states. Movement of domestic tourists will gradually improve the image of the place and the demand created will lead to development of essential infrastructure. This process will then facilitate movement of foreign tourists.

Tourism planning for the Northeast states, whether to cater the domestic or the foreign tourist would be most attractive and cost effective if based on an integrated NE perspective. The attractions of the different states should complement each other and enhance the total attraction towards the region. Unfortunately the concept of totality of NE tourism suffers from two fundamental inadequacies: First, poor internal communication between the states. The road communication is arduous and time consuming. Air communication has of late improved, but is not yet tuned to tourism requirements. Coordinated planning of tourism for the NE is possible only when internal communication by air becomes efficient and reliable.

Second, there is lack of an organizational setup. There is no organizational setup that can harmonize action for projecting NE tourism as a whole. Prospective tourists who wish to visit and sympathetic entrepreneurs who want to market the NE find it exasperating to draw up an integrated schedule for the whole region. There is too much of dependence on the Government and too little incentive for the private sector to enable them to play an effective role. If tourism in the NE has to grow, a common platform of all the states, involving the Government and non-governmental agencies, should be immediately formulated.

These are only a few illustrative areas where action has to start on a priority basis. The action agenda is long because the Northeast has a lot to catch up with. Human resource development, institutional arrangements for people's participation, greater resources mobilization for tourism, public-private partnership building are some of the issues that demand attention for tourism to grow.

Problems of Tourism in North East India

- The lack of infrastructure and the vexed issue of the Protected and Restricted Areas Permit System are the main factors hampering the development of tourism in North East India. As such, the flow of foreign tourists is not upto the mark.
- The deteriorating law and order situation in North East India is also another important factor affecting the flow of both domestic and foreign tourists. Tourism and insurgency do not go hand in hand in any region. This has been proved beyond doubt in Punjab and Kashmir. The same is true in North East India where tourism has been 'ill-fated' in the thickness of insurgency and counter insurgency. Though the State Governments have declared tourism as an industry these factors adversely affect the industry to grow. The State Governments have to effectively address the problems of insurgency through prospective solutions by means of political dialogue with various insurgent groups in this region.
- The frequent administrative changes in the states of the region, unstable Governments and transfer of staffs in the Directorate of Tourism of the States, also hamper the natural growth of this industry. A stable Government with regular staff and line agencies, and a long-term action planning will enhance the growth of tourism sector. It will also help remove disparities of growth in this sector.
- Lack of investment by private sector, non-governmental organizations and lack of professionalism in tourism in North East India also hamper its growth. There is need for a development strategy for the tourism industry through awareness campaign, heavy promotional strategies, organise tourism fairs and festivals and encourage participation of travel associations and tour operators.

- One problem peculiar to North East India is allotment of land for this sector. In Meghalaya and some other states, land ownership lies with the community and not with the state. Customary laws on land holdings and transfers differ from area to area. So, special arrangements will have to be worked out for allocation of land for hotel and resorts, etc.
- To promote tourism, the State Governments have already declared tourism as an industry. However, real boom is expected only after the lifting of the Protected Area Permit and Restricted Area Permit Systems from all states of North East India. Moreover the State Governments have to provide certain facilities such as reduced tariff rates for electricity and water supply, tax relief, subsidies in loans from industrial and financial institutions, etc. to those involved in the business of tourism. Unemployed youths could benefit by involving themselves in this sector.

Prospects of Tourism in North East India

- Government of India has accorded special attention for North East.
- DONER and NEC are active and are taking active interest in tourism and have accorded top priority to this sector.
- Asian Highway from Malaysia via Thailand and Bangladesh to India will be passing through North East while going to Delhi and beyond.
- Asian Development Bank is preparing a Sub-Regional Plan for development of tourism covering Bhutan, Bangladesh, India and Nepal. North East Region figures prominently in this Plan because of the Asian Highway.
- Besides the intra-regional tours there are opportunities for promoting cross-border tours to neighbouring countries like Bhutan, Bangladesh, Thailand, Malaysia, Nepal etc.
- Potential for private sector's investment in tourism projects.

Tourism Planning

In the field of tourism, the need for planning is of paramount importance. Any region, whether it already has an active flourishing tourist industry or is contemplating it, has to cautiously address many crucial issues before launching tourism development before this industry is developed on long-term basis. Any short term arrangement only to overcome trade deficit would make the industry instrumental and unsustainable. The United Nations Conference on International Trade and Tourism convened in Rome (1963), and the International Union of Official Travel Organization (IUOTO) Seminar held in Prague (1964), strongly emphasized the need for planning in tourism and also made several recommendations for planning at national, regional or at local levels.

Tourism planning is therefore not only concerned with the physical planning of tourist facilities but also with the natural and cultural resources presented to the tourists. Thus, a major function of the tourism planning is to protect, preserve and develop both natural and man-made environment. It is an integrated and inter-disciplinary approach requiring experts from diverse fields such as geography, history, sociology, anthropology, economics, commerce, cultural, engineering, architectural, ecology and management. It also requires the pro-active role of the state and the judiciary. The aim of tourism planning is a balanced growth of demand and supply and optimum harmonization environmentally and socially useful resources. Hence, tourism planning, after all, is about demand and supply in which the planning process involves an assessment of supply of resources and potential demand upon it (Robinson 1976).

The Central Government laid down the policy programmes in co-ordination with various line Ministries. Apart from various activities of the Ministry of Tourism and Civil Aviation and the Ministry of Finance prescribe the total outlay of the tourism sector and determine the taxation for the industry. The visa policy for the foreign tourists is decided by the Ministry of External Affairs. The ecological and environmental guidelines for tourism purposes are provided by the Ministry of Environment and Forests. The Ministry of Home Affairs finally determines access to sensitive areas and deals directly with the security needs.

The State Governments play the developmental and promotional roles. Development of infrastructure facilities and providing basic necessities such as water supply, electricity, accessibility, accommodation, recreation and maintaining the law and order, etc. are in the hands of the State Governments.

The investors in the private sector play the role in selling the tourism products to the tourists. The private sector comprises mostly the tour operators. The public private partnership in this industry is very much essential for the development of proper planning of tourism.

In short, an all out effort has to be made to make the regulated tourism for regional development. The local population should come in direct contact with each other. The government is to see that the benefits derived from tourism reach the grassroot level and that there is no adverse impact on culture and environment in Northeast India. It is needless to emphasize that the development of tourism in Northeast India needs be integrated with the regional socio-economic development. Such a multipurpose integrated model needs to be formulated so that the local population is involved in the development process. In such a process, the maintenance of the recreational features of the landscapes also needs be interlinked with patterns of socio-economic development. The State as well as Central Governments and voluntary organizations have to make co-ordinated efforts in this direction. In short, planning strategies should be initiated for integrated tourism development in Northeast India.

Recommendations

- To meet the requirements of the tourists, Northeast India should promote itself as single package that could be developed with the joint venture of the State Governments under the proposed Northeast India Tourism Development Corporation. Similarly, a preparation of common pool budget is necessary for improving transport and travel facilities in such a package.
- Highly potential sites and centers should be declared as Tourism District or Special Tourism Area by the Government and to develop such areas as a tourist attraction, steps should be taken up to extend package of incentives and tax benefits for a period of 10 years or so to attract foreign investors.
- Steps should be taken for special international packages in consultation with the travel and tour operators in neighbouring countries like Bangladesh, Nepal, Bhutan,

Myanmar, Thailand, Japan etc. as soon as Guwahati Airport becomes a full fledged international airport.

- Restricted and Protected Area Permit Systems should be abolished as soon as possible from the region. All necessary projects for infrastructure should be taken up quickly. The Inner Line Permit should be readily issued at all major tourists offices, railheads, airports, and state entry gates along the national highways.
- The railways should offer special holiday tours and travel concessions during holiday seasons or festivals for all those visiting Northeast India. Chartered flights should be permitted for National packaged tours. Low budget tours should also be encouraged for trekkers, campers, young people, and even for the domestic tourists.
- To increase the involvement of investors in the private sector, there is an urgent need to have a development strategy for the tourism industry with heavy promotional advertisements through organizing fairs, awareness campaigns and participation of travel associations and tour operators and non-governmental organizations, etc. It is a well-known fact that festivals are the surest methods of attracting tourists and creating awareness about one's heritage.
- To promote tourism, we need aggressive marketing approach to reach out to high-spending foreign tourists. Therefore, Destination Northeast India has to be well advertised through travel agencies, tour operators and promoters in the country as well as abroad.
- The Government should initiate programmes to expand tourist facilities to attract at least a part of foreign tourists from neighbouring countries through liberalization of the visa regime.
- While planning to boost tourism industry, State Governments should augment the supply of enough of electricity and water to tourism related activities with necessary incentives at least for a period of ten years at industrial rates instead of commercial rates, and the tariff must be frozen at least for a similar period.
- Both the Central and State Governments should have an optimistic approach at the Ministerial level with the

coordination of NEC for a well-defined policy to channelize their efforts towards building up the tourism industry.

- Tourism courses particularly for guides, hotel staff and other interested personnel should be arranged in collaboration with the different universities and training institutions of the region.

However, no development plan would succeed unless the people are involved in the planning process. For this purpose, the need and desire of the people should be ascertained and with their participation, appropriate planning measures can be undertaken. 'Even a five thousand mile journey must start with the first step,' goes an old Chinese proverb. There is a long journey ahead for the Northeast as it tries to look eastward. A beginning has to be made soon for exploring the paradise called 'Northeast India'.

FOOTNOTES & REFERENCES

1. Antonio Savignac, quoted in Indian Tourism Beyond the Millennium by M.P. Bezbaruah, (1999). Gyan Publishing House, New Delhi, p. 125.
2. M.P. Bezbaruah, *Op cit.* p. 123.
3. Ministry of Tourism, *Tourism Statistics*, 2002, p. 117.
4. Bezbaruah, M.K. (1999). *Tourism: the Global Scenario,* Indian Tourism: Beyond the 5. Millennium, New Delhi: Gyan Publishing House.
5. Middleton T.C. and Hawkins R. (1998). *Sustainable Tourism: A Marketing Perspective*: Oxford
6. Sarma, M. K. (2000). Destination positioning of Northeast India based on preferences and perceptions tourists. Unpublished doctoral dissertation, Tezpur University, Tezpur.
7. Sarma, M. K. (2003). Towards positioning a tourist destination: A study of Northeast India. *Asean Journal of Hospitality and Tourism, 2(2),* 104-117.
8. Raj, Anita (2004). Tourist Behaviour: An introduction. In Aparna Raj (Ed.) *Tourist Behaviour: A Psychological Perspective*. pp. 3-23. New Delhi: Kaniska
9. Narayan, Paresh Kumar (2005). The structure of tourist expenditure in Fiji: evidence from unit root structural break test. *Applied Economics, 37(10),* p. 1157-1161.
10. Narayan, Paresh Kumar (2004). Economic impact of tourism in Fiji's

economy: empirical evidence from the computable general equilibrium model, *Tourism Economics, 10*, pp. 419-434.

11. ———, (2005). Tourism Statistics for India in www.fhrai.com/mag-News/magTourismStatisticsIndia.htm browsed on 19/12/2005.
12. Seth, P. (1997). *Successful Tourism Management*. p. 91 New Delhi: Sterling Publishers Pvt. Limited.
13. Gupta, S.P. and L. Krishna (1974) *Tourism, Museum and Monuments in India*, Oriental Publications Delhi, p. 1.
14. Kunwar, R.R. 2002); *Anthropology of Tourism: A Case Study of Sauraha*, Adroit Publishers, India
15. Lowry, L.L, 1994: *What is Travel and Tourism and is There a Difference Between Them; A Continuing Discussion*, New England Journal of Travel and Tourism, England p. 28-29.
16. Modi, S. (2000). *Tourism and Society: Cross Cultural Perspective*, Rawat Publications, India Oḳada, FE 1969.
17. Price MF/Harrison D. (1996). *Fragile Environments, Fragile Communities? An Introduction: People and Tourism in Fragile Environments*, John Wiley and Sons Ltd.
18. Robinson (1976). *A Geography of Tourism* McDonald and Evans, London, p. 14.
19. Singh, Wilson W. (2004). *A Historical Study of Tourism in North-East India*, Unpublished doctoral dissertation, Manipur University, Imphal.
20. Kaoba, Yumnam (1999). *Tourism in North East India—A Geographical Study*, Unpublished doctoral dissertation, Manipur University, Imphal.

22

Urbanization in Meghalaya

SUROJIT SEN GUPTA

"Urbanization may be defined as a process of concentration of non-agricultural occupations and land uses around a single nucleus or multiple nuclei" (Prakasha Rao. V.L. and Tiwari, V.K., 1986). The settlements thus emerge create a distinctive physical and social environment, different from the adjoining regions. It provides contrasts in terms of occupations, socio-economic awakening and levels of social and economic interaction (Chandna and Sidhu-1980). The urban centers are characterized by the concentration of power and tend to influence the 'whole socio-economic milieu of the area'. Urbanization is essentially associated with the economic development and diversification of occupation caused by the 'movement of people from agricultural communities into other and generally larger non-agricultural communities.' (Carter-1982).

Processes and Determinants of Urbanization

Processes

While dealing with the basic concept of urbanization, it is difficult to escape a reference to such concepts as suburbs, rural-urban fringes, urbanism etc. The prototypes of suburbs are believed to have existed during the medieval times. Suburbs are those urbanized residential communities that lie outside the corporate limits of a large city but are culturally and economically dependent upon the central city (Dobriner-1958). The concept of rural-urban fringe is essentially a sociological concept similar to the 'semi-urban' concept prevalent in the U.S. and Western Countries. The rural-urban fringe is that area in which the countryside is in the process of transformation from rural to urban mode of settlement (Duncan, and Reiss-1956). Sociologists have also used the concept of urbanism. It normally refers to the process by which a section of population adopts an urban way of life even while residing in the countryside (Wirth-1938). The social institutions that are commonly associated with urban living, penetrate into the countryside. It thus brings about a revolutionary change in the pattern of social life. It exercises its pervasive influence on the rural hinterland.

Geographers use the term urbanization more commonly to refer to a process of transformation. Lampard (1965) suggests that a distinction should be made between the three aspects of urbanization, that is, behavioural, structural and demographic aspects. The behavioural aspects of urbanization refer to the experience of elders and the changes in the pattern of their behaviour over time. The structural aspect of the process of urbanization refers to the changes in the economic structure and economic activities of the whole population. The demographic aspect is the process of population concentration. (Lampard-1965; Riessman-1964; Tisdel -1942; Trewarthi-1969).

Determinants

Urbanization is the function of socio-economic changes that take place through time. The determinants of urbanization have three categories: economic, social and demographic. The economic base of urban places is very much different from that of the countryside. The economic factor is the determinant factor of the nature and magnitude of urbanization. Contrary to the agrarian societies with subsistence economy, small and dwindling agricultural land-holdings, primitive technology and very little diversification of economy—the urban places are small-sized and widely spaced administrative headquarters. The stage of economic advancement along scientific and technological advancement is the crucial determinant of the degree of urbanization.

The degree of development transportation and communication

is also vital for urbanization. Inter-regional mobility has a two-way effect upon the process of urbanization. In the initial stages the availability of means of transportation and communication may break the rural isolation resulting in increased urban concentration. At a later stage, this may help in accelerating commuting activity between metropolitan cities and small towns as also between the countryside and the urban places.

Urban awakening is an important determinant of urbanization. This reflects the desire for urban living standards and benefits and urban value system. The technological advancement acts as a catalytic agent in the process of urban awakening.

The demographic factors including growth of population, pressure of population upon agricultural resources and the migration trends also determine the magnitude of urbanization. The five-staged model of urbanization process envisaged by Gibbs emphasized on the roles of rate of natural increase and migration in determining the degree of urbanization (Gibbs—1966). The regional differences in the rate of natural increase and the consequent migratory trends give a particular direction to the process of urbanization in any area. Increasing population pressure on agricultural activities lead to overcrowding of the urban settlements.

Urban Hierarchy in India

Towns have been classified according to a number of criteria. These include site characteristics, historical background (ancient, medieval, modern etc), cultural traits (temple towns, pilgrim centres, university towns etc), economic base (trade centre, commercial towns, industrial towns, mining towns, administrative towns etc) and size of population. The census of India from its very inception has used a particular concept of town and village for presenting population statistics and classifying urban places. In the case of urban places, it has used two terms: towns and Urban Agglomeration (U A). An UA denotes a continuous urban spread and normally consists of a town and its adjoining urban outgrowths or two or more physically contiguous towns together with contiguous and well-recognized outgrowths if any, of such towns.

To be classified as a town, an urban place should meet the following criteria:

- It must have a statutory municipality, corporation, cantonment board or notified town area committee etc, or it should have at least 5000 population;
- At least 75 per cent of male population be engaged in non-agricultural activities;
- It should have a density of population of at least 400 persons per Sq. Km.

The Directors of Census Operations in States are authorized to include some places having distinct urban characteristics though not conforming to any of the above criteria. All towns and UAs are then classified into six-size classes: Class I (100,000 and more population); Class II (50,000 to 99,999 population); Class III (20,000 to 49,999 population); Class IV (10,000 to 19,999 population); Class V (5,000 to 9,999 population), and Class VI (less than 5,000 population).

The distribution of various classes of towns among the States in India is uneven. In line with the socio-economic development of the country, there have been considerable changes in the size and class distribution of towns in India. Large cities have multiplied while the number of small towns has declined or stagnated. These towns have grown so fast that they have jumped their class to join intermediate and large cities. In the absence of any major diversification of rural economy, large villages, which ought to have become small towns, have failed to move up the urban hierarchy. Most of the Class III and IV towns are former Class V and VI towns.

Meghalaya

Meghalaya emerged as a full-fledged State within the Union of India on 21st January 1972. The State of Meghalaya was carved out of two hill districts of Assam—the erstwhile United Khasi and Jaintia Hills District area and the Garo Hills District. At present Meghalaya is divided into seven administrative districts, two sub-divisions and six special administrative units.

From the social perspective, Meghalaya may be characterized as a tribal state. The present day Meghalaya is characterized by yawning gap between the rich and the poor and the urban and rural sections of the population. One of Meghalaya's advantages is Shillong—the capital town. Though once known as the biggest hill station in India, today Shillong is fast developing into a city.

Trends of Urbanization in Meghalaya

An important feature of Meghalaya's urbanization is the economic push of surplus labour from rural areas and not the economic pull of labour scarce urban sector. This has been the main reason behind growth of urban population. Meghalaya is a backward state. Because of the low level of agriculture production, there is no surplus in farm product to feed agro-based industries. There is no significant employment generating activities, small scale and cottage industries. This causes surplus labour in rural areas. Seasonal unemployed or chronically disguised unemployed people rush to the urban areas in search of livelihood. This is how the economic push became a strong force behind the state's urbanization.

Under the impact of different development measures, a number of growth centers, new offices, institutions, industrial establishments, commercial centers, urban infrastructure and private construction works, etc. have come up. These opened up some scope of employment for the unskilled and semi-skilled rural workforce. The schemes of subsidy and loan assistance for commercial and industrial ventures and self-employment programmes caused in-flow of workers from rural to the urban centres.

There have been streams of immigration of people from other states of India and also from across the international borders. The influx of people from the East Pakistan (Bangladesh) and from Nepal brought about huge settlement areas of the immigrant population in the State. These immigrants got engaged in various occupations and also settled in various urban areas of the State.

Many rural families feel that they should have additional houses in the urban areas and in large towns particularly for children's education. Most of the best schools and colleges are situated in large towns and cities. The children when educated in the urban areas do not generally like to go back to the villages. They settle down in cities and towns. Moreover those who are educated in the rural areas do not find job opportunities in villages. Therefore there is a heavy rush of educated young people either for admission in higher educational institutions in the urban areas every year. This is an important reason behind growth of urban population in the State.

Generally when the young people get jobs in urban areas they remain unmarried. Normally, educated people marry after they are occupationally established. Subsequently when they marry, they generally live near their places of work. Those who leave behind other members of family also bring them to their urban residence. The growth of family size adds to the urban population. Moreover, when married people from rural areas come for jobs in trade and other occupations, they subsequently bring their families to the urban settlements. This is also an important reason for growth of urban population in the State.

Another reason for growth of urban population is attraction of colourful life, better amenities, social, economic opportunities, IT Access etc. Thus most of the well-to-do people of rural areas build houses in the cities and towns.

Urbanization has caused slum, deviance, anomie, unemployment, underemployment and misemployment. The problem of unemployment is more acute among the educated urban youths. Urban logistics for recreation, sports, arts, culture and health & educational infrastructures are poor. Over-population, road traffic and unplanned urban centers have created serious urban problems like traffic congestion, pollution and anomie.

Urban Growth Scenario in Meghalaya

The State of Meghalaya has a population of 23,06,069 persons, of which 452612 live in urban areas and 1853457 live in rural areas. The total male and female population in the State is 1167840 and 1138229 respectively. As far as the districts population is concerned, the East Khasi Hills district has the largest population in the State with 660994 persons. It is followed by West Garo Hills with 515813 population. The total number of child population in the age-group of 0-6 years in the State is 457442, of which 231571 are males and 225871 are females. The rural-urban breakup of child population in the State shows that 392305 are in rural and 65137 are in urban areas. Sex-wise breakup shows that the male child population is 198408 in rural and 33163 in urban areas and the female child population is 193897 and 31974 respectively. Seeing the child population of the age-group 0-6 years among different towns of the State, the highest population is found in the Shillong Urban Agglomeration. It has 32874 persons with 16556 males and 16318 females. East Khasi Hills district has the highest number of child population in urban as well as in rural areas.

In the 1991 census there were 30 C.D. Blocks. With the creation of two more new C.D Blocks namely, Tikri Killa in West Garo Hills and Ranikor in West Khasi Hills after 1991, their number has increased to 32 in 2001. In West Garo Hills district there are 7 C.D. Blocks, in East Garo Hills there are 4, in South Garo Hills there are 3, in West Khasi Hills there are 5, in Ri-Bhoi there are 2, in East Khasi Hills there are 7 and in Jaintia Hills there are 4 C.D. Blocks. Among the C.D. Blocks in the State, Mylliem C.D. Block under East Khasi Hills district has the highest number of urban population. The Shillong Municipality, the only class I city of the State falls under the jurisdiction of Mylliem C.D. Block. The constituent towns are Malawi, Nongthymmai, Madanrting, Pynthorumkrah, Nongmynsong, Shillong Municipality and Shillong cantonment. The other town of the district is Cherrapunji, known as Sohra Town that is under the Shella Bholaganj C.D Block. Thus, in East Khasi Hills out of 7 C.D. Blocks, 2 C.D. Blocks are having the urban areas.

In West Garo Hills district, only Rongram C.D. Block has the urban population. Tura town being the Headquarter of the district is the only town of the district and falls under the jurisdiction of Rongram C.D. Block. South Garo Hills district is having only one town known as Baghmara that falls under the jurisdiction of Baghmara C.D. Block. Jaintia Hills and Ri-Bhoi districts have one town each known as Jowai and Nongpoh respectively. East Garo Hills and West Khasi Hills district have two towns each. These are Resubelpara and Williamnagar in East Garo Hills and Mairang and Nogstoin in West Khasi Hills.

Table 22.1 shows the growth rate of urban population in each class of town from 1981 to 2001. From the table it is seen that the number of towns of all classes are same both in 1981 and in 1991 but in 2001, it is noticed that 4 new towns were added. There is only one class I town in the State whose status remained the same in 1981,1991 and 2001. The percentage decadal growth rate slightly increased from 36.76 in 1981-1991 to 37.14 in 1991-2001 for all classes of towns.

Table 22.1 Growth of Urban Population, 1981-2001

Size class of UA/city/town	*Number of UAs/Town*			*Population*			*Percent of population in each size-class*			*Percentage decadal growth*	
	1981	*1991*	*2001*	*1981*	*1991*	*2001*	*1981*	*1991*	*2001*	*1981-91*	*1991-01*
1	2	3	4	5	6	7	8	9	10	11	12
All classes	12	12	16	241333	330047	452612	100.00	100.00	100.00	+36.76	+37.14
Class I	1	1	1	109244	131719	132876	45.27	39.91	29.36	+20.57	+0.88
Class II	—	—	1	—	—	58391	—	—	12.90	—	—
Class III	3	4	5	77220	124569	141584	32.00	37.74	31.28	+61.32	+13.66
Class IV	2	4	8	23634	51101	111118	9.79	15.48	24.55	+116.22	+117.45
Class V	3	3	1	18882	22658	8643	7.82	6.87	1.91	+20.00	+61.85
Class VI	3	—	—	12353	—	—	5.12	—	—	-100.00	—

Source: Census of India

Percentage of urban population in Class I town is also decreased from 39.91 in 1991 to 29.36 in 2001. It has been noticed that there is no Class II town in both the decades of 1971-81 and 1981-91. In 2001 one Class II town emerged as a result of upgradation of Tura town. According to the population criteria of Class size it is found that Class III and Class IV towns have increased in number by 1 (one) and 4 (four) respectively in 2001. The percentage of urban population as recorded in these two categories of town is 31.28 per cent and 24.55 per cent respectively. The growth rate for Class III is 13.66 per cent in 1991-2001. A slight gain of growth rate of 1.23 per cent is noticed in Class IV towns in this decade. In case of Class V towns, it is seen that the population growth rate has declined considerably. It is also seen from the table above that there is no Class VI town in the State in 1991 and 2001.

Table 22.2 Number of Statutory and Census Towns, 1991 and 2001

State/District	*1991*			*2001*		
	Statutory Towns	*Census Towns*	*Total*	*Statutory Towns*	*Census Towns*	*Total*
1	2	3	4	5	6	7
Meghalaya	7	5	12	10	6	16
West Garo Hills	1	—	1	1	—	1
East Garo Hills	2	—	2	2	—	2
South Garo Hills	—	—	—	1	—	1
West Khasi Hills	1	—	1	2	—	2
East Khasi Hills	2	5	7	2	6	8
Ri-Bhoi	—	—	—	1	—	1
Jaintia Hills	1	—	1	1	—	1

Source: Census of India.

Table 22.2 displays the number of statutory and census towns between 1991 and 2001 in the State of Meghalaya. The total number of statutory towns has increased from 7 in 1991 to 10 in 2001. The census towns in 1991 were 5 and in 2001 they were 6. Thus the total number of statutory and census towns increased from 12 in 1991 to 16 in 2001. It is also noticed that the number of statutory towns of East Khasi Hills district remains at 2 whereas one more census town i.e. Nongmynsong, a new constituent unit of Shillong Urban Agglomeration is designated as a new census town in 2001. Ri-Bhoi and South Garo Hills districts are the newly created districts after the 1991 census. These districts have one town each in 2001. Each of East Garo Hills and West Khasi Hills districts has two towns and all of them are statutory towns.

Table 22.3 Ranking of Districts by Percentage of Urban Population, 1991 and 2001

Rank in 2001	*District*	*Percent Urban Population*		*Rank in 1991*
		2001	1991	
1	2	3	4	5
1.	East Khasi Hills	42.05	34.75	1
2.	East Garo Hills	14.50	6.36	5
3.	West Khasi Hills	11.40	6.51	4
4.	West Garo Hills	11.32	10.82	2
5.	South Garo Hills	8.72	—	—
6.	Jaintia Hills	8.46	9.34	3
7.	Ri-Bhoi	6.83	—	—

Source: Census of India.

Table 22.3 shows the percentage of urban population between 1991 and 2001 and the ranking of districts in terms of per cent of urban population in Meghalaya. East Khasi Hills district dominates over all the districts in urban population both in 1991 and 2001. There is an increase of 7.30 per cent of urban population in this district from that of 1991 census. West Garo Hills district occupied 2nd position in 1991. It has dropped to the 4th position in 2001. East Garo Hills district had 5th position in 1991. It has got 2nd position in 2001. Jaintia Hills district had 3rd position in 1991. It has gone down to the 6th position in 2001. But West Khasi Hills district has occupied 3rd position in 2001 against the 4th position in 1991. South Garo Hills got the 5th position in 2001. Ri-Bhoi with the least percentage of urban population had the last position.

Table 22.4 shows the trends in urbanization from 1901 to 2001. From 1901 till 1921 there was only one town in the State without any outgrowth and urban agglomeration. In 1931 an urban agglomeration was formed in the State capital with Shillong Municipality and Shillong Cantonment as constituent units. Two more towns namely Nongthymmai and Mawlai were added in 1961 and the area of the Shillong Urban Agglomeration was expanded. In 1981, two more census towns namely

Pynthorumkhrah and Madanrting were added to the Shillong urban agglomeration and the total number of the constituent units of Shillong Urban Agglomeration (U.A.) increased to 6. There was no new town in 1991 census. In 2001 a new census town named Nongmynsong came up and it formed a new constituent units of Shillong U.A. bringing altogether 7 towns within its jurisdiction. So from 1931 to 1951, there was only Shillong U.A. without independent town.

Table 22.4 Trends in Urbanization, 1901-2001

Census Year	Total Number of UAs/Towns	Total Population	Total Urban Population	Percent Urban Population	Decennial growth		Annual Exponential Growth Rate (urban)
					Absolute	Percent	
1	2	3	4	5	6	7	8
1901	1 Town	340524	9621	2.83	—	—	—
1911	1 Town	394005	13639	3.46	4018	41.76	3.49
1921	1 Town	422403	17230	4.07	3564	26.13	2.32
1931	1 U.A.	480837	26536	5.52	9335	54.26	4.33
1941	1 U.A.	555820	38192	6.87	11656	43.93	3.64
1951	1 U.A.	605674	58512	9.66	20320	53.20	4.27
1961	1 U.A. & 2 Towns	769380	117483	15.27	58971	100.78	6.97
1971	1 U.A. & 2 Towns	1011699	147170	14.55	29687	25.27	2.25
1981	1 U.A. & 6 Towns	1335819	241333	18.07	94163	63.98	4.95
1991	1 U.A. & 6 Towns	1774778	330047	18.60	88714	36.76	3.13
2001	1 U.A. & 9 Towns	2306069	452612	19.63	122565	37.14	3.16

Source: Census of India.

It is noticed that only from 1961 onwards that new independent towns started coming up. The independent towns that appeared in both 1961 and 1971 are Tura and Jowai. With the creation of new districts in the State after 1971 census, new towns such as Nongstoin, Williamnagar, Baghmara and Cherrapunjee come up. In 2001, again with the creation of two more new district, three new independent towns namely Nongpoh, Mairang and Resubelpara were formed in the State. Nongmynsong became another new census town in 2001 and became a constituent unit of Shillong U.A.

From the Table 22.4 it is seen that the total urban population in the state increased from 9621 in 1901 to 452612 in 2001 and the percentage of urban population increased from 2.83 in 1901 to 19.63 in 2001. It is observed that there is slight decrease in the percentage of urban population in 1971 as compared to 1961. In 1961, the percentage of urban population was 15.27 whereas in 1971 it was only 14.55. But again from 1981 till 2001 the increasing trend in the percentage of urban population is noticed in the State. Regarding the decennial growth rate of the urban population, it is seen that the year 1961 had the highest growth rate of 100.78 per cent. This is because of the fact that the two new independent towns, namely Tura and Jowai were notified in the two newly formed districts. It is also observed from the Table 22.4 that the annual exponential rate in the urban areas in the State was not uniform. In 1911 the annual exponential growth rate was 3.49 which fell down to 2.32 in 1921, again it went up to 4.33 in 1931 and came down to 3.64 in 1941. The annual exponental growth rate declined to 2.25 per cent in 1971 and raised to 4.85 per cent in 1981. A very negligible variation in the annual exponential growth rate of urban population is observed in 2001 as compared to 1991.

Impact of Urbanization

Large increase in urban population led to increased pressure and strain on the civic amenities. It created congestion, squatter and filth. It also produced social and political tensions. The situation got aggravated, as our urban centers were not geared up to face the load of massive immigration in the State. The consequences were proliferation of slums, degradation of the environment, degradation of civic amenities and widespread urban poverty.

Before Meghalaya become a full-fledged State, no effort for physical planning was made by the then Government of Assam. The hill area and autonomous areas were not even covered by the Town and Country Planning Act of Assam that was in force in the entire State of Assam since 1959. There was no officer to prepare even the outline of development plan for Shillong. The position in respect of other district towns was far worse. The first effort in this direction was made through the preparation of Shillong Master Plan in 1976. However in the absence of any legal backing the plan remained only in paper. The Town and Country Planning

Act was not extended immediately after the State was created, as the District Council's assent could not be obtained. The matter remained pending for quite sometime. In 1989 the State Government through a notification extended the Assam Town and Country Planning Act 1959 to the entire state which was adopted by Meghalaya in 1973. It is known as the Meghalaya Town and Country Planning Act, 1973.

By the time the Act was enforced the validity period of Shillong Master Plan was almost over. The Master Plan contained proposal up to 1991 but the Government decided to enforce the plan in October 1990. The plan since then is in operation. But the fact is that Shillong grew on its own momentum and not on the basis of any planned efforts. The trend is almost similar in all other urban centers in the State. At present the Master Plans for Shillong, Tura and Jowai are notified and steps are being taken to enforce and implement the same.

According to a study conducted by the National Institute of Urban Affairs, the supply of water in the State is highly inadequate. Even in the capital town Shillong the population served with piped water supply is only 56.2 percent. Water availability in Shillong urban areas is limited to 2.52 MGD (1988) while the estimated requirement being 12.39 MGD by 2001. The position in other urban areas is also more or less the same. Health and education facilities are adequate in the urban areas. But specialized medical facilities are not available. People have to go outside for special treatment. Further, in absence of any professional college in the State the number of technical hands is inadequate.

The economy in most urban centers of Meghalaya is tilted towards the commercial and service sector with very little diversification in the other sectors of the economy. The economy of the urban centers needs be strengthened through developing and enlarging the industrial base. Resources-based industries, agro and forest-based industries and electronic industries should be widely introduced. Development of these industries will generate good number of employment. Private sector investment should be encouraged and a review of all loss-running public sector undertakings needs to be made. The Government companies need encourage private sector participation. Meghalaya has many economic activities under the private sector such as transportation, mining etc. What is needed now is to encourage private agencies' involvement in urban sector planning and implementation.

In the process of economic development urbanization is not only inevitable but also desirable. Energy, essential for urban development, has faced critical challenges. Enhanced supply of energy and optimum use of energy in the Urban Areas are required for urban development. Meghalaya being surplus in power generation should take initiative for properly designed distribution system for all its centers and give better service to the consumers. The State could improve the financial position of the electricity board that could supply power to industries and commercial sectors. The urban infrastructure development and planning should match and be consistent with local skills, technology and resources.

Urban Policy and the State of Meghalaya

Urban policy needs to gear up productivity and employment. The metropolitan cities in the country in spite of their decay, filth and squalor are still the centers of attraction for the migrant communities from both rural and urban areas. So far in the field of urban development, the State Government has been providing funds for investment either directly or through its various agencies. The private sector is not involved at all in infrastructure building and in other services. With paltry finance of the State Government, the ever-increasing demand for better and costlier facilities could not be met. Though the size of urban areas in the State is small the volume of investment required for urban infrastructure and services is heavy. In order to make the urban areas economically viable necessary infrastructure should be provided. This would enhance the capacity of the urban areas to serve the people and to influence larger areas.

One important step is to mobilize the community initiatives in the process of urban planning and development. So far the people for whom the plans were meant were completely excluded from the process. Those who have the least information about the prevailing socio-economic conditions assess and plan for peoples' requirement. Civil administration is not free from bureaucratic inefficiency. In such situation the local bodies need to come forward and participate in urban planning and implementation process. A participant approach to urban planning needs to be adopted so that urban development becomes appropriate to the need of the people. Unlike the present trend of high-rise buildings in Shillong and in other urban areas, the proposed urban structure should reflect the architectural heritage with appropriate local technology. It should conserves local environment. The height of building should be restricted to the minimum acceptable so as to achieve low-rise high-density urban form. One of the problems in the city areas is non-availability of housing facilities and reduced supply of administrative land. The emphasis has to be laid on supply of developed land at right places at right time and at right prices. The urban land policy should aim at achieving an optimum social use of urban land. It should also encourage co-operative effort and bona-fide individual builders. The policy should be such that it can prevent concentration of land ownership in a few hands and can safeguards the interests of the poor and under-privileged sections of the urban society.

Thus there is a need to have a new approach to urban planning in the State. The rigid Master Plans as per the Statutory Act needs to be replaced by a more flexible, participatory physical planning exercises with due concern for environmental protection, urban poverty and developmental sustainability.

REFERENCES

1. Berry, B. J. (1962). Some relations of urbanization and basic patterns of economic development, in F.R. Pitts(ed) urban systems and economic development. Eugene, Oregan.
2. Chandana, R.C. and M. Sidhu. 1980, Introduction to Population Geography, Kalyani Publishing, Ludhiana.
3. Chandna, R.C. (1986). A Geography of Population, Kalyani Publishers, New Delhi.
4. Childe, V.G. (1950). "The Urban Revolution", Town Planning Review, Vol. 21, April 1950.
5. Census of India, (2001). Series 18, Meghalaya Part-II.
6. Carter, H. (1979). The Study of Urban Geography, Arnold Heimemann, London.
7. Castells, M. (1977). The Urban Question, translated by Alan Sheridan, the MIT Press, Cambridge.
8. Dubey, S. M. Urbanization in Tribal Areas in North East India, (1971). A Project Report. Deptt. of Sociology, Dibrugarh University.

9. D' Souza. V.S. (1974). Urban Studies. A Trend Report' in a Survey of Research in Sociology and Social Anthropology, Vol. 1, Popular Prakashan, Bombay.
10. Dobriner, W.M. (1958). The Suburban Community, G. P. Putman's Sons, New York.
11. Duncan, O.D. and Resiss, A. J. (1956). Social Characteristics of Urban and Rural Communities, New York.
12. Goswami, B.B. (1978). Cultural Profile of Shillong, Anthropological Survey of India, Calcutta.
13. Ghurye, G.S. (1962). Cities and Civilization, Popular Prakashan, Bombay.
14. Ganguly, J.B. (1995). Urbanization and Development in North East India, Deep and Deep Publications, New Delhi.
15. Gopalakrishanan R. (2001). Meghalaya: Land & People, Omsons Publications, New Delhi.
16. Gibbs, J. P. (1966). Measures of Urbanization, Social Forces. Vol. 45 (2).
17. Houser, P. M. (1965). (ed). The Study of Urbanization, New York.
18. Lampard, E.E. (1965). Historical Aspects of Urbanization, in P. M. Houser and L. E. Schnore, The Study of Urbanization, New York.
19. Misra, R.P. (1998). Urbanization in India: Challenges and Opportunities, Regency Publications, New Delhi.
20. Prakasha, Rao, V. L. S. and V. K. Tiwari (1986). Urbanization in India in Urban Geography (ed), P. D. Mahadev, Heritage Publications, New Delhi.
21. Riessman, L. (1964). The Urban Process, New York.
22. Singh, J.P. (1980). Urban Land-use Planning in Hill Areas: A Case Study of Shillong, Inter India, New Delhi.
23. Sinha, A.C. (ed) (1993). Hill Cities of Eastern Himalayas, Indus Publishing Company, New Delhi.
24. Sen Gupta, Surojit (200 6). Urban Social Structure. A Study of a Hill City, Akansha Publishing House, New Delhi.
25. Sen Gupta, Surojit (2004). Shillong at the Turn of 21st Century, in Sutapa Sen Gupta (ed), Shillong A tribal Town in Transition, Reliance Publishing House, New Delhi.
26. Sen Gupta, Surojit (2002). A Sociological Study of Urbanization in Arunachal Pradesh, paper presented in National Seminar on Urbanization in Eastern Himalayas. Emergences and Issues, organized by the Center for Himalayan Studies, North Bengal University.
27. Tisdale, H. (1942). The Process of Urbanization, Social Forces, Vol. 20.
28. Trewartha, G. T. (1969). A Geography of Population: Worlds Patterns, John Wiley and Sons Inc. New York.

23

Urbanisation among the Tribals of Tripura

MALABIKA DAS GUPTA

Introduction

It is a well-known proposition of development economics that economic growth in most countries generally by-passes the disadvantaged sections of the population. If urbanisation is taken to be an indicator of economic growth, Indian data show that urbanisation has eluded the Scheduled Tribes (STs) who form a section of the disadvantaged people of the country in a relative sense, the percentage of the total tribal people living in urban areas being lower than the percentage of the total population of the country who are urbanised. This is shown in Table 23.1 for the year 2001 for India as a whole and for the States of India which have an ST population. As Table 23.1 shows, whereas 23.82 per cent of the total population of India was urbanised in 2001, the corresponding figure for the tribal population of the country was only 8.29 percent. Though tribals constituted 8.20 per cent of the total population of the country, they comprised only 2.44 per cent of the total urban population of India. Not only in India as a whole, but with the solitary exception of Goa, in every State and Union Territory of India with a designated ST population, urbanisation among tribals lagged behind urbanisation of the total population in 2001.[1] Comparing columns 6 and 8 of Table 23.1 shows that the gap between the two indices was quite considerable in 2001. This

Table 23.1 Population and ST Population India and Her States and Union Territories, 2001

Name	Population		ST Population		Urbanisation	ST Total Pop. as % of Total Pop.	Urbanisation among ST	ST Urban Pop. as % of urban Pop.
	Total	Urban	Total	Urban				
1	2	3	4	5	6	7	8	9
					(col.3/col.2)* 100	(col.5/col.2)* 100	(col.5/col4)* 100	(col5/col.3)* 100
India	1,028,610,328	286,119,689	84,326,240	6,987,643	27.82	8.20	8.29	2.44
Jammu & Kashmir	10,143,700	2,516,638	1,105,979	51,491	24.81	10.90	4.66	2.05
Himachal Pradesh	6,077,900	595,581	244,587	7,527	9.80	4.02	3.08	1.26
Uttaranchal	8,489,349	2,179,074	256,129	15,920	25.67	3.02	6.22	0.73
Rajasthan	56,507,188	13,214,375	7,097,706	379,876	23.39	12.56	5.35	2.87
Uttar Pradesh	166,197,921	34,539,582	107,963	12,135	20.78	0.06	11.24	0.04
Bihar	82,998,509	8,681,800	758,351	40,649	10.46	0.91	5.36	0.47
Sikkim	540,851	59,870	111,405	9,496	11.07	20.60	8.52	15.86
Arunachal Pradesh	1,097,968	227,881	705,158	98,880	20.75	64.22	14.02	43.39
Nagaland	1,990,036	342,787	1,774,026	230,004	17.23	89.15	12.97	67.10
Manipur (Excl. 3 Sub-divisions)	2,166,788	575,968	741,141	35,229	26.58	34.20	4.75	6.12
Mizoram	888,573	441,006	839,310	408,427	49.63	94.46	48.66	92.61
Tripura	3,199,203	545,750	993,426	25,429	17.06	31.05	2.56	4.66
Meghalaya	2,318,822	454,111	1,992,862	310,192	19.58	85.94	15.57	68.30
Assam	26,655,528	3,439,240	3,308,570	154,024	12.90	12.41	4.66	4.48
West Bengal	80,176,197	22,427,251	4,406.794	270,428	27.97	5.50	6.14	1.21
Jharkhand	26,945,829	5,993,741	7,087,068	587,054	22.24	26.30	8.28	9.79
Orissa	36,804,660	5,517,238	8,145,081	446,723	14.99	22.13	5.48	8 10
Chhattisgarh	20,833,803	4,185,747	6,616,596	351,761	20.09	31.76	5.32	8.40

(Countd.)

Name	Population		ST Population		Urbanisation	ST Total Pop. as % of Total Pop.	Urbanisation among ST	ST Urban Pop. as % of Urban Pop.
	Total	Urban	Total	Urban				
1	2	3	4	5	6	7	8	9
Madhya Pradesh	60,348,023	15,967,145	12,233,474	787,026	26.46	20.27	6.43	4.93
Gujarat	50,671,017	18,930,250	7,481,160	614,523	37.36	14.76	8.21	3.25
Daman & Diu	158,204	57,348	13,997	2,809	36.25	8.85	20.07	4.90
Dadra & Nagar Haveli	220,490	50,463	137,225	9,815	22.89	62.24	7.15	19.45
Maharashtra	96,878,627	41,100,980	8,577,276	1,090,739	42.43	8.85	12.72	2.65
Andhra Pradesh	76,210,007	20,808,940	5,024,104	377,181	27.30	6.59	7.51	1.81
Karnataka	52,850,562	17,961,529	3,463,986	529,456	33.99	6.55	15.28	2.95
Goa	1,347,668	670,577	566	376	49.76	0.04	66.43	0.06
Lakshadweep	60,650	26,967	57,321	25,112	44.46	94.51	43.81	93.12
Kerala	31,841,374	8,266,925	364,189	14,170	25.96	1.14	3.89	0.17
Tamil Nadu	62,405,679	27,483,998	651,321	100,178	44.04	1.04	15.38	0.36
Andaman & Nicobar Islands	356,152	116,198	29,469	1,013	32.63	8.27	3.44	0.87

Source: Census of India.

Note: Data given only for States and Union Territories with ST population.

gap existed even in tribal-majority States like Arunachal Pradesh, Nagaland, Mizoram and Meghalaya and tribal-dominated Union Territories like Dadra & Nagar Haveli and Lakshadweep.[2]

Table 23.2 compares the all-India situation with that of the eight States of North-East India with respect to their level of urbanisation and urbanisation among the tribals in 2001. It measures the level of relative urbanisation of the tribals of the States of the North-East and of India as a whole in 2001 where by relative urbanisation we mean the level of urbanisation of the tribals of any unit vis-a-vis the level of urbanisation of its population at a given point of time which is measured by the gap between the latter and the former. The gap between urbanisation and urbanisation of the tribals is lower in the States of the northeast than in India as a whole. Among the States of the northeast, the gap is the highest in Manipur and the second highest in Tripura.

Table 23.2 India and the North East—Urbanisation and Urbanisation among Tribals, 2001

Name	*Urbanisation*	*Urbanisation among Tribals*	*Gap between col. 2 & col. 3*
1	2	3	4
India	27.82	8.29	19.53
Sikkim	11.07	8.52	2.55
Arunachal Pradesh	20.75	14.02	6.73
Nagaland	17.23	12.97	4.26
Manipur (Excl. 3 Sub-divisions)	26.58	4.75	21.83
Mizoram	49.63	48.66	0.97
Tripura	17.06	2.56	14.50
Meghalaya	19.58	15.57	4.01
Assam	12.90	4.66	8.24

Source: Table 23.1

Theme of the Paper

The present paper has a very limited agenda. Taking Tripura as a case in point, it attempts to (1) understand why the relative urbanisation of the tribals of the State was low in 2001 and (2) suggest measures for increasing their level of urbanisation.

This topic is considered to be important because it is a special case of growth by-passing the disadvantaged as urbanisation is an accepted index of growth and tribals constitute a disadvantaged group. The probable reasons for the low level of relative urbanisation among the tribals of India have not been adequately explored in the existing literature on urbanisation in India.[3] Though it has been noted in the 2001 Census that the share of the scheduled tribe population in urban areas is a meagre 2.4 per cent and there are only 57 Urban Agglomerations or towns in the country which have more than 50 per cent scheduled tribe population, the explanation given for this empirical phenomenon is that 'the Scheduled Tribe population prefers to live in groups in the rural surroundings which seems to be very simplistic and one dimensional.[4]

Justification for Choosing Tripura as the Focus of the Study

Tripura has been singled out for study from among the eight States of the northeast because (a) as is evident from Tables 23.1, among all the Sates of the northeast where the ST population exceeded 20 per cent of the population of the States in 2001, the level of urbanisation among the STs was the lowest in Tripura.[5,6] (b) another reason for singling out Tripura for study is that as shown in Table 23.2, if Manipur is excluded from the purview of the study because the Census Data on the State excluded three sub-divisions of the State in 2001, the gap between the level of urbanisation of the total population and the level of urbanisation of the ST population among the remaining seven States of the northeast was the highest in Tripura in 2001. (c) The other reason for singling out Tripura for study is evident from Table 23.3. It shows that the gap between urbanisation of the total population of the State and the level of urbanisation among the STs has increased over time in Tripura between 1961 when the STs were first designated in the Census in the State in 2001, when the latest Census was conducted in India. (d) Table 23.4 shows that the gap between urbanisation among the general population[7] and the tribal population and urbanisation among the SC population and the tribal population in Tripura increased steadily between 1961 and 2001 with the solitary exception of the gap between urbanisation among the SCs and STs of the State for the year 1971. The SCs are a disadvantaged community like the tribals but barring the year 1971, their level of urbanisation outstripped that of the tribals in Tripura, indicating that tribals have been excluded to a greater extent from urbanisation than the people belonging to the Scheduled Castes in the State and their greater exclusion from urbanisation merits the attention of researchers.

Table 23.3 Tripura—Urbanisation and Urbanisation among STs, 1961-2001

Year	Population			ST	Population	Urbanisation among Tribals	Gap between col. 4 & col.7
	Total	Urban	Urbanisation	Total	Urban		
1	2	3	4	5	6	7	8
2001	3199203	545750	17.06	993426	25429	2.56	14.50
1991	2757205	421721	15.30	853345	14081	1.65	13.65
1981	2053058	225568	10.99	583920	7668	1.31	9.67
1971	1556342	162380	10.43	450544	5485	1.22	9.22
1961	1142005	102997	9.02	356372	3698	1.04	7.98

Source: Census of India.

Table 23.4 Relative Urbanisation among Tribals, Tripura, 1961-2001

Year	Urbanisation Among			Gap Between	
	General Pop.	SC Pop.	ST Pop.	cols. 2 & 4	cols. 3 & 4
1	2	3	4	5	6
2001	25.46	18.01	2.56	22.90	15.45
1991	21.65	15.83	1.65	20.00	14.18
1981	17.12	6.29	1.31	15.81	4.98
1971	16.07	5.29	1.22	14.85	4.07
1961	13.98	5.63	1.03	12.95	4.60

Source: Census of India.

Data Sources Used for the Study

Our attempt will be restricted to trying to find an answer to research question (1) mentioned in the preceding paragraph mainly with the help of Census Data for 2001. More specifically, we shall use the relevant data from the SC, ST Primary Census Abstract of India and the Primary Census Abstract for Tripura, the Migration Tables and the Household Amenities data generated by the Census authorities for the State for 2001. The policy prescriptions for increasing the level of urbanisation among the tribals of Tripura will be based on the findings emerging from the attempt to answer the question regarding the relatively smaller level of urbanisation among the tribals of the State. Ideally, for dealing with the research questions more thoroughly, a field survey should have supplemented the use of secondary data mainly from the Census, this task will be taken up in the future.[8]

Finding of the Study

Introduction

Table 23.1 shows that Tripura had a total population of 31.99 lakhs out of which the urban population was 5.45 lakhs in 2001 so that the level of urbanisation in the State was 17.06 percent. The ST population of the State in 2001 was 9.9 lakhs comprising 31.5 per cent of the total population of the State. Out of this a mere 4.66 per cent lived in the urban areas of Tripura. Urban Tribals constituted only 2.56 per cent of the total ST population of the State in 2001. Table 23.5 gives the district-wise figures for the total and urban population of the State as well. It shows that the West District was most urbanised while Dhalai, the newly-formed district of Tripura was the least urbanized in 2001. The percentage of tribal population in the total population of the four districts shows that Dhalai had the largest percentage of tribals and West Tripura District the smallest. The urban tribal population as a percentage of the urban population of the corresponding District was the highest in Dhalai and the lowest in North Tripura District. What emerges very dearly from the Table is that tribals had a limited urban presence in Tripura and its Districts in 2001. Urbanisation among tribals, measured by the ratio urban ST population as a percentage of the total ST population of the State and its four districts was very low in 2001 except in the case of Dhalai which is a newly-formed district and has a large percentage of tribal population. The district also has two new census towns in 2001 from which tribals have probably not yet moved out as an inevitable consequence of urbanisation. There was a considerable gap between urbanisation and urbanisation among the tribals in all the four districts of Tripura.

Reasons for the Gap between the Level of Urbanisation in Tripura and Urbanisation Among the Tribals of the State

Many reasons seem to be responsible for the relatively low level of urbanisation among the tribals of Tripura in 2001. A part of the reason for the relatively low urban presence of tribals in Tripura and its districts in 2001 seems to lie in the demographic profile of the households of the State. As Table 23.6 shows, the average family size for urban households in Tripura and its districts was higher than the average family size for urban tribal households. This, coupled with the fact that the number of urban households exceeded the number of urban tribal households must have been a factor in the low urban presence of tribals in Tripura in 2001. The migation tables of Tripura for 2001 also show that marae migrants outnumbered females, the latter constituting 44.66 per cent of the tribal migrants from the rural to urban areas of the State. This indicated that entire tribal families did not migrate to urban areas so that the average family size of tribal migrants was low. In contrast, for the total population, the female migrants from rural to urban areas in Tripura outnumbered the males. Female migrants from rural to urban areas constituted 58.51 per cent of the total migrants from rural to urban areas and it is likely that many of the female migrants brought their children along with them, increasing the average family size of the migrants.

The number of migrants from rural to urban areas must have also had a part to play in the difference between the level of urbanisation in the total population of Tripura and the level of urbanisation among the tribals of the State. The level of urbanisation was low among the tribals of Tripura as compared to that of the total population because whereas urban migrants from rural areas as a percentage of the total ST population of the State in 2001 was 1.10 percent, as far as the total population of the State was concerned, migrants into urban areas from rural environs constituted 2.61 per cent of the total population of the State if all migrants irrespective of their years of stay in urban areas in 2001 were considered.

The lack of employment opportunities for tribals in the urban areas of the State as compared to the population of the State provides another reason for the difference in the level of urbanisation in the State and the level of urbanisation among the tribals of Tripura and its districts. Table 23.7 shows that with the exception of Dhalai district, a very small percentage of the total workers of urban Tripura and its districts is engaged in agricultural activities either as cultivators or as agricultural labourers. This percentage is relatively high in Dhalai because it is a new district with small new Census towns like Ambassa and Kanchanpur that have still retained a lot of their rural characteristics. Table 7 also shows that a very large percentage of the ST urban workers of Tripura and its districts comprises cultivators and agricultural labourers. This percentage is considerably higher than the percentage of cultivators and agricultural labourers in the total workers of the State. With this occupational pattern of the ST population of Tripura and its districts, it is quite natural that they have failed to secure a berth in urban areas as predominantly non-agricultural occupations prevail in the urban areas of the State and its districts. It is obvious that literacy is required to secure employment in urban areas. Table 23.8 shows that the percentage of literates in the total ST population of the State and its districts is smaller than the corresponding percentage of literates in the total population. This leads to a limited opportunity for employment of tribals in urban areas and results in the low urban presence of tribals in the urban areas of the State. Though the policy of reserving a certain percentage of jobs in the public sector for people belonging to the Scheduled Tribes is in operation in the State and is rigidly followed, the lack of suitably qualified candidates has often led to the posts remaining vacant at least till recently.

Another factor that has probably had a part to play in the large gap between the level of urbanisation in Tripura and among the STs of the State is the poor amenities that the urban tribals enjoy in Tripura compared to the amenities enjoyed by the urban population of the State as a whole. The disparity between the two groups is very obvious in terms of amenities available like housing, drinking water facility, sanitation, lighting, banking, fuels used for cooking and availability of assets. It is also questionable if rural tribals make decisions regarding migration to urban areas on the basis of the amenities and assets available to urban tribals even if it can be assumed that the prospective migrants have perfect knowledge about the amenities and assets available to their urban counterparts.

Though these figures culled from the 2001 Census data are revealing, there are other factors to be considered that are equally important for explaining the low level of urbanisation among the tribals of Tripura as compared to the level of urbanisation in the State in 2001 that are not captured by the Census data. For example, there seems to be a low urban presence of tribals in Tripura and its districts because the tribals live mainly in the hilly areas of the State while the towns of the State are located mainly in the plains. The lack of connectivity between the hills and the urban centres could probably explain why their level of urbanisation vis-a-vis that of the population of Tripura is low because rural people living in the plains find it easier to move to urban areas.

Secondly, the urban presence of a particular community in a particular year is a product of a historical process which has evolved over time. Agartala, Tripura's only town till 1951, had very few tribals in the late nineteenth century. These tribals were either members of the royal household who were related to the royal family and lived in the vicinity of the palace in Agartala or they were people who served the tribal king and his household. The urban tribals of Agartala owned property in the State capital or exercised control over urban lands granted to them informally by the Maharaja. A good many of them alienated these properties to the migrants form erstwhile East Pakistan and Bangladesh and retreated to the rural areas of Tripura so that there was a move towards the ruralization of a certain section of the urban tribal population over the years also.

There was a noticeable deurbanisation of tribals in Tripura in Udaipur and Belonia in 1981 as compared to 1971 as is shown in Table 23.9 because of the ethnic violence that rocked the State in 1980. There was a fall in the number of tribals living in Sonamura and Kamalpur between 1981 and 1991 and in Teliamura between 1991 and 2001 probably as a result of the Bengali Backlash to the extremist threat by tribals faced by them in the interior areas of the State. The tribals who were in a minority in the urban areas were under threat and probably there was an exodus of tribals from these towns because they felt insecured in the urban environment where they were surrounded by Bengalis. The urban tribals felt threatened in the towns as they were numerically outnumbered by non-tribals there and were sometimes under attack by the dominant community. A large number of them retreated to the villages in the interior where there was safety in numbers. In contrast, the population of these towns increased in 1981 as compared to 1971 probably because many non-tribals living in rural areas with a considerable tribal presence felt threatened and moved to urban areas in search of security.[10]

In addition to these factors, the relatively small presence of STs in the urban scene of Tripura may be due, partly at least, to the fact that the tribals themselves opt out of the urbanisation process from their own free will. They do not wish to become a part of the urban scene because they live in closely-knit hamlets in the interior of the State that they do not want to abandon, they do not wish to give up their symbiotic relationship with the forests and jhuming and have no fascination for urban life and its glamour. They consider the urban atmosphere to be an alien and exploitative one for them and stay away from urban centres.

Policy Measures for Increasing the Level of Urbanisation Among the STs of Tripura

The basic premise of the study is that urbanisation is a desired goal as ideally, urbanisation leads to greater and more varied employment and other opportunities for people and the enjoyment of urban amenities though it leads to a loss of the tribal way of life which may seem to be more desirable , however difficult it may be to sustain in this day and age.

In order to increase the level of urbanisation among the STs of Tripura, the Government should follow a more inclusive policy by improving the educational and urban employment opportunities available to the tribals of the State so that they can become more urbanised. Special attempts should be made to improve the amenities available to urban tribals and connectivity between the interior tribal areas of the State and the urban centres should be improved. Attempts should be made to set up urban centres closer to the tribal-inhabited interior areas so that tribals can take advantage of urbanisation. The psychological impediments to becoming urbanised which prevail among tribals should gradually be overcome. To combine the best of both the worlds, a conscious attempt should be made to ensure that urbanisation among tribals does not lead to a loss of the enviable aspects of the tribal and the rural way of life to the extent possible.

Table 23.5 ST Population as Percentage of Total Population & ST Urban Population as Percentage of Urban Population Tripura and its Districts, 2001

	Percentage of ST Population	*ST Urban Population as Percentage of Urban Population*
Districts and States		
West	25.25	4.85
South	37.72	3.15
Dhalai	54.03	11.43
North	25.47	2.64
Tripura	31.05	4.66

Source: Census of India.

Table 23.6 Number of Households and the Average Size of Households in Urban Areas of Tripura and its Districts and among the Urban Tribals, 2001

Urban Areas of State/District	*Total Urban*		*ST Urban*	
	Households	*Average Family size per Household*	*Households*	*Average Family size per Household*
Tripura	124.621	4.38	6700	3.80
West Tripura	92.679	4.42	5200	3.83
South Tripura	13.495	4.01	482	3.54
Dhalai	4.297	4.39	547	3.94
North Tripura	14.150	4.43	471	3.51

Source: Census of India.

Table 23.7 Agricultural Labourers and Cultivators in Tripura, 2001

	Agricultural Labourers and Cultivators		
State/district	As percentage of Urban Workers	As percentage of Total Workers	As percentage of ST Workers
Tripura	3.30	50.83	77.84
West Tripura	2.72	61.29	74.36
South Tripura	3.63	64.59	85.27
Dhalai	22.17	64.29	79.12
North Tripura	3.05	43.60	68.29

Source: Census of India.

Table 23.8 Literacy of Total and Tribal Population, Tripura, 2001

State/District	*Percentage of Literates in Total Population*	*Percentage of Literates in Tribal Population*
Tripura	63.21	47.22
West Tripura	67.54	57.61
South Tripura	59.87	41.81
Dhalai	51.45	37.20
North Tripura	62.42	42.00

Source: Census of India.

Table 23.9 ST Population and ST Population as a Percentage of the Total Population of Towns and City, Tripura, 1961-2001

Town/City	*ST Population*				
	2001	*1991*	*1981*	*1971*	*1961*
Agartala	15616 (8.22)	8601 (5.47)	6100 (4.61)	3655 (6.13)	3346 (6.10)
Khowai	1443 (8.16)	532 (4.24)	306 (2.85)	221 (2.37)	102 (1.16)
Udaipur	528 (2.43)	308 (1.64)	102 (0.63)	173 (2.55)	88 (1.00)
Belonia	202 (1.28)	75 (0.57)	72 (0.59)	106 (0.93)	62 (0.71)
Kailashahar	845 (4.17)	481 (2.98)	290 (2.24)	86 (0.81)	53 (0.62)
Dharmanagar	232 (0.75)	358 (1.38)	182 (0.87)	77 (0.46)	47 (0.35)
Sonamura	154 (1.53)	77 (0.95)	178 (2.79)		
Kamalpur	429 (8.34)	133 (3.09)	158 (4.28)		
Amarpur	503 (4.63)	253 (2.96)	162 (2.54)		
Sabroom	471 (8.17)	248 (5.20)	118 (3.35)		
Badharghat	1136 (2.38)	675 (1.90)			
Pratapgarh	275 (1.02)	147 (0.04)			
Barjala		72 (0.42)			
Singarbil		136 (1.48)			

(*Contd.*)

(*Contd.*)

Town/City	ST Population				
	2001	*1991*	*1981*	*1971*	*1961*
Gandhigram	93 (0.87)	55 (0.72)			
Jogendranagar	57 (0.16)	34 (0.13)			
Kumarghat	578 (4.47)	1120 (7.65)			
Teliamura	118 (0.60)	776 (2.81)			
Narsingarh	117 (1.72)				
Kunjaban	236 (3.21)				
Ranirbazar	6 (negligence)				
Indranagar	65 (0.36)				
Gokulnagar	598 (6.19)				
Kanchanpur	965 (12.57)				
Ambassa	762 (12.60)				

Source: Census of India.

Note: Figures within brackets show the percentage of tribals in the total population of the town/city.

NOTES

1. For the purposes of this paper, the level of urbanisation is defined as the percentage of the total population of a country or its constituent States or Union Territories that live in urban areas while the level of urbanisation among tribals is defined as the percentage of the total tribal population of the country or its constituent States or Union Territories that live in urban areas. The former is measured by (Urban population/Total population)* 100 while the latter is measured by (Tribal urban population/Total tribal population)* 100.
2. Tribal majority or tribal-dominated States or Union Territories are defined as States or Union Territories of India in which tribals constitute more than 50 per cent of the total population.
3. The research questions for which answers are being sought in the research work have not been examined by economists before. Quite

a substantial body of anthropological and sociological literature exists in India on tribals in the urban setting but these studies deal mainly with urban development taking place in tribal areas as a result of industrialization and its impact on the socio-economic impact of the industrialization and its impact on the tribals living in these areas. Hassan and Ahmad: 1988, Sacchidananda and Mandal: 1985, Banerjee 1981, Bidyarthi 1970, Das and Banerjee: 1964, Das Gupta : 1964, Orans 1959 are a few of them. Gare's Work (1973, 19760) deals with tribal migrants in the industrial setting of Puna, a city that is located far away from tribal areas.

4. Office of the Registrar General & Census Commissioner, India, Census and You: Basic Results from Census 2001. page 20.
5. By this 20 per cent ST population criterion, the State of Assam can be excluded from the list of the States of the North-East that are considered though in Assam urbanisation among tribals was only 0.58 per cent.
6. Table 23.1 shows that among all the States of India where tribals constitute 20 per cent or more of the population also, the level of urbanisation among the tribals was the lowest in Tripura in 2001.
7. By general population is meant the total population minus the SC and ST population.
8. The author hopes to make up for the lacuna in the present study when she completes her ICSSR Senior Fellowship Research Project entitled 'Urbanisation among the Tribals of Tripura'.
9. These data are available from the 2001 Census Tables on Houses, Household Amenities and Assets for Tripura but for the sake of brevity, no tables have been given to prove the point.
10. This trend seems to have been reversed somewhat with the migration of tribals from rural areas to urban areas in the recent past in search of jobs either in the urban informal sector or in the formal sector where jobs are now available to tribals because of their improving educational status and strict observance of the policy of job reservations for tribals. Tribals have also started migrating to urban areas of the State in order to avail of the greater opportunities available in urban areas and also in order to escape from the depredation of the extremists in interior areas and find a safe haven in the towns of the State. However, as far as the overall figures for the State and its districts show, this trend has not been powerful enough to lead to a narrowing of the gap between the urbanisation of tribals and urbanisation of the total population of the State though in certain pockets of the State a reversal of this trend could have occurred that could possibly be captured through an analysis of data at a more disaggregated level. This also will be attempted in the author's ICSSR Senior Fellowship Research Project entitled, 'Urbanisation among the Tribals of Tripura'.

24

Some Aspects of Urbanizations and Economic Development in Bodoland: A Perspective of Kokrajhar Town

SUJATA BHADRA

Introduction

After the economic reforms in 1991 there have been significant changes in Assam both in economic and administrative spheres. In order to make rapid development of the tribal areas, the special administrative set up known as B.T.A.D (Bodoland Territorial Areas District) came into existence comprising the four districts viz. Kokrajhar, Chirang, Baksa and Udalguri.

This rapid transformation is taking place in the socio-economic structure of the area under the initiative of B.T.A.D with emphasise upon the emerging urbanization process in the region along with new economic programme for improvement of the tribal population. As we know, urbanization has direct impact on economic advancement. The urban centres are hubs of increased production, service and marketing infrastructures for the organized economic activity. It also pledges better social status and social opportunities. In this context, the Kokrajhar town, the head quarters of B.T.A.D, is undergoing sharp transition. Importantly, in recent days the characteristics of urbanization such as transience, superficiality, anonymity, individualism etc. are more prominent to the life of people of Kokrajhar town. Today, it is a fast growing town and has come under tremendous pressure on the basic urban amenities and infrastructure like housing, sanitation, supply of drinking water, transportation, electricity, health etc. In fact, the massive upheaval in the life style of urban population of Kokrajhar town is the result of the development environment in Bodoland area. Moreover, the development discourses and the consequent development gains are not uniform in every parts of Bodoland, rather in many cases this new phase of development has adversely affected the traditional norms of life of the tribal people. Few such things like violence against women, trafficking, increasing trend of migration, corruption etc. are found to have emerged.

Therefore, in this paper the nature of urbanization in this tribal belt of Bodoland is examined. The study emphasises that if the urbanization process can be hastened as a priority programme in the development agenda, the socio-economic development of the Bodoland would be rapid and sustainable. We also suggest the key areas of work that would accelerate the process of urbanization and development of the tribal land. Again, the study attempts to highlight the functioning pattern of some of the key socio-economic activities and its impact on the urban growth, urbanization, and development in the Kokrajhar Municipal Area.

Physical Demarcation of the Study Area

Kokrajhar town is the headquarters of newly formed Bodoland Territorial Area Districts (B.T.A.D). Kokrajhar Municipal Board comprises of 10(ten) wards constituted within an area of 4651Bigha-3Katha-0 Lecha. As per the 1991 census, the total area of Kokrajhar (M.B.) is 8.24 sq.kms. Today, Kokrajhar town forms an important part of North-East region and serves as an important gateway to Assam, Bengal and the rest of India. It is situated almost in a flat terrain with some low lying areas and is bounded by the river Gaurang and a tea gardens on the western side and river Tarrang on the eastern side.

Kokrajhar town has the potential advantage of inter-connection by means of roads and communication. Four P.W.D. roads have connected Kokrajhar town. Many D.R.D.A. and Municipal constructed roads (34 in numbers) have connected the town with adjacent village areas and the roads. Also, the Kokrajhar town is well connected by the two National Highways N.H.-31(C) and NH-37 on three sides towards Karigaon on the North, Bahalpur towards the East and Bilasipara towards the South which cater bulk of inter-district and inter-state traffic and freight.

Objective of the Study

Following are the objectives of the study:

1. To study the pattern of demography, agriculture, industry, education, land use, employment, trade and commerce etc. in the Kokrajhar Municipal Area.
2. To study the trend of vehicular growth in Kokrajhar District.
3. To suggest various measures by which the problems of urbanization in the town can be addressed.

Methodology and Data Base

The study is based on data and information collected from the Office of the Deputy Director of Economics and Statistics, Kokrajhar, Office of the Executive Engineer, P.W.D. (Roads); Kokrajhar, D.T.O. Kokrajhar, Kokrajhar Municipal Office, Office of the Town and Country Planning; Kokrajhar, Office of The Circle Officer; Kokrajhar Revenue Circle, Kokrajhar and from Kokrajhar Thana. The views of many people and senior citizens are considered while studying the existing problems and prospects of the town. The survey was conducted during the period of June-July, 2006. The data thus obtained are presented in tables, analysed and interpreted.

SECTION-I

Analysis

Today urbanization is the greatest concern and its gravity has gained momentum with the intervention of liberalization, privatization and globalization. For urbanization, the concentration of population in cities and towns, the pattern of transportation, industrialization, land use pattern, agriculture, working population, educational activities, physical lay out of the town or cities, centre of economic and social institutions etc. are major indicators. In this process of urbanization, there are witnesses of different problems in the urban centres. Some of these obvious problems are alarming in Kokrajhar town such as high rate of population growth, growth of vehicular population, unplanned and haphazard land use, pollution, congestion, inadequate road length, high accident rates, defective drainage and sewage system, lack of industrialization, absence of provision of children parks, libraries, recreation centres, cinema and theatre halls etc.

The status of few relevant indicators of the research enquiry is as follows:

(i) *Demographic Pattern*: As per 1961 census, the population of Kokrajhar town was 9, 489 as against the 1971 Census figure of 17,060. This indicates a growing rate of 79.79% during the decade. The density of population of Kokrajhar Municipal area in 1971was 8 P.P.A. (approx.); in 1988 it was 13 P.P.A. Like other urban centres, Kokrajhar town also has a composite pattern of population with religious and community diversities. Kokrajhar as a town and district has shown a steady increase in population in the past few decades especially after the formation of B.T.A.D. The variation of growth rate appears to be mainly because of migration of people from urban to urban and from rural to urban area of the town in search of employment, education, health care, better living etc. According to 1991 Census report, the population of Kokrajhar town was 28,267, the total number of households was 4993 and total number of occupied residential houses was 4988. As per the 2001 Census, the order of population in Kokrajhar town is 31,164.

Table 24.1 Distribution of Households and Population in Kokrajhar Town (2001 Census)

Household/Population	*Total (in numbers)*	*Male (in numbers)*	*Female (in numbers)*
1. Households	6,233	—	—
2. Total Population	31,164	16,352	14,812
3. Population in the age group of (0-6)	3,228	1,672	1,556
4. Scheduled Caste	3,246	1,673	1,573
5. Scheduled Tribe	7,398	3,690	3,708

Source: Census of India, 2001.

Table 24.2 Growth of Population: Kokrajhar Master Plan Area

Year	*Municipal Area*	*Percentage of Increase*	*Total Master Plan Area*	*Percentage of Increase*
1961	9,489	—	24,623	—
1971	17,060	79.79	39,375	59.59
1988	26,775	56.95	60,808	54.43

Sources: 1. Census of India, Assam.

2. Town and Country Planning, Government of Assam.

Table 24.3 Decadal Variation in Population of Kokrajhar District Since 1951

Year	*Persons*	*Decadal Variation*	*Percentage*
1951	200807	17005	9.25
1961	293540	92733	46.18
1971	452919	159379	54.30
1981	Census	Not	Conducted
1991	808730	355811	76.78
2001	930404	121674	15.05

Source: Directorate of Census Operation, Assam.

(ii) *Agriculture*: It is the main source of livelihood of the people in this region. The total agricultural land under Kokrajhar Master Plan Area, 1988 is 10,260.34 acres and it is 48.67% of the total land area, in the Municipal Area it is very meagre i.e. 214.52 acre and it is 10.54% of the total area. The agricultural production in Kokrajhar Master Plan Area is very much meagre as it is a town where very little production of major crop is traced. Especially, bettle nut, areca nut and vegetable are the main items of agricultural production in the study area.

(iii) *Industrial Structure*: A few service industries are there in and around Kokrajhar town. These are auto repair shops, saw mills etc. Due to lack of physical planning, these industries have come up indiscriminately even in the residential areas which create obvious inconvenience. The total area under industrial use is only 14.03 acre which is only 0.69 per cent of the total Municipal Area. This clearly reveals that industrially Kokrajhar town has not made much progress though there is ample scope for development of cottage and small-scale industries especially of handloom and textile industries etc. that can create more employment in this sector.

(iv) *Educational Facilities*: Besides the Government institutions, many private and semi-Government institutions are coming up at Kokrajhar Municipal Area to meet the need of the local people. In Kokrajhar town area, the educational facilities are moderately satisfactory. There are 2 Higher Secondary Schools, 7 High Schools, 10 M.E. / M.V., 25 L.P. schools along with number of private (English and Bodo Medium) schools in Kokrajhar town like other urban centers of the State. For higher education, there are four (04) degree colleges (one of them is a Government College), one B.Ed. Government College, one Basic Training Centre, one Law College, one Fine Arts and Music College, 5 Nursery Schools, 2 numbers of Art Schools,4 Dance and Music Schools which offer the quality education/training to the pupils of the entire region. The Gauhati University campus, the Kokrajhar Centre of Post Graduate studies accommodates students from different parts of Assam.

Table 24.4 Existing Land Use (Municipal Area), 1988

Land Use	*Area in Acres*	*Area in Hectares*	*Percentage of Total Area*	*Percentage of Developed Area*
Residential	874.97	345.09	42.99	60.88
Commercial	113.98	46.13	5.60	7.93
Industrial	14.04	5.68	0.69	0.98
Public and Semi-public	189.28	76.60	9.30	13.17
Park and Playground	24.63	9.97	1.21	1.71
Roads	130.05	52.63	6.39	9.04
Railways	90.36	36.57	4.44	6.29
Developed Area	1437.31	581.67	70.62	100.00
Agricultural Land	214.52	86.81	10.54	
Vacant Land	377.34	152.70	18.54	
Water Bodies	6.11	2.47	0.30	
Total Land	2035.28	823.65	100.00	

Source: The Assam Gazette Extraordinary, June, 2001.

(v) *Land Use*: Proper uses of lands have immense importance in urban areas. A land use survey was conducted for the planning area of Kokrajhar in the year 1985 and the survey reveals that the present municipality area of Kokrajhar is 8.24 sq .km. against the proposed planning areas of 85.35 per cent comprising of 46 adjoining villages (three of them in parts). The developed area of the town within the Municipal limit is 1437.31 acres giving a town density of 19 P.P.A. As per the 2001 Census, the total urban area in Kokrajhar district is 18.26 Sq. Kms.

Table 24.5 Existing Land Use (Master Plan Area) 1988

Land Use	Area in Acres	Area in Hectares	Percentage of Total Population	Percentage of Developed Area
Residential	3,134.81	1,261.61	14.87	49.86
Commercial	260.00	105.0	1.24	4.15
Industrial	223.46	90.43	1.06	3.55
Public and Semi-public	581.85	235.97	2.76	9.25
Park and Playground	456.39	184.60	2.17	7.26
Roads	1032.87	417.00	4.88	16.43
Railways	596.60	241.43	2.84	9.50
Developed Area	6286.49	2544.04	29.82	100.00
Agricultural Land	10260.34	4154.21	40.67	
Vacant Land	1768.70	715.78	8.39	
Water Bodies	1831.98	741.38	8.69	
Forest	543.90	220.61	2.58	
Tea Garden	390.00	157.83	1.85	
Total Land	21081.45	8535.35	100.00	

Source: The Assam Gazette Extraordinary, June 14, 2001.

(vi) *Employment Projection*: Employment structure under Kokrajhar Master Plan Area, 1988 depicts the characteristics of a typical urban area. The table shows that percentage of workers in primary sectors has decreased from 66.37 per cent in 1961 to 48.98 per cent in 1971; worker in tertiary sector has increased from 24.54 per cent in 1961 to 39.45 per cent in 1971. The Government Offices seem to have saturated with working hands and there is much scope of employment generation in the field of small scale industry such as manufacturing of wooden furniture and bamboo craft, weaving, footwear, candles, soap, allied agriculture based industries, food processing units, hotel industries, tourism etc. Also, in recent days, construction work, trade and commerce etc. are involving a good number of people in the town area. In the Kokrajhar town area, as per 2001 Census, the participation of people in economically productive activities is categorically distributed in the following tables.

Table 24.6 Distribution of Workers in Kokrajhar town (2001 Census)

Category of Workers	*Total (in numbers)*	*Male (in numbers)*	*Female (in numbers)*
1. Marginal Worker	691	377	314
2. Cultivator	110	14	96
3. Agricultural Labourers	53	26	27
4. Household Industry Workers	30	11	19
5. Other Workers	498	326	172
6. Non-Workers	21,079	7,902	13,177

Source: Census of India, 2001.

Table 24.7 Occupation Pattern: Kokrajhar Master Plan Area

Sector	*Total Area*		*Total Number of Workers Village Master Plan Area*		*Master Plan Area*	
	1961	*1971*	*1961*	*1971*	*1961*	*1971*
1. Primary Sector	822 (24.89%)	707 (13.96%)	6277 (84.35%)	4667 (78.94%)	7159 (66.37%)	5374 (48.96)
2. Secondary Sector	585 (16.50%)	1018 (20.10%)	395 (5.30%)	254 (4.30%)	980 (9.09%)	1272 (11.59%)
3. Tertiary Sector	2007 (58.61%)	3339 (65.95%)	770 (10.35%)	991 (16.76%)	2647 (24.54%)	4330 (39.45%)

(vii) *Trade and Commerce*: Kokrajhar has developed as an important commercial and trade centre. Shopping activities, new commercial centres, show rooms especially meant for handloom and textile product like typical Bodo Costume Dokhna, Jwmgra, Aronai etc. have widely grown in the town area. A recent trend is entrepreneurship development and self employment especially through SHG's. In fact, the work participation of women in respect of trading is in a trajectory as compared to the past decades in and around the Kokrajhar town. Under Kokrajhar Municipal Area, only 113.98 acres of land are used for commercial use which is 5.60 per cent of the total area that is greatly inadequate and congested. The trade infrastructure, warehouse, cold storage etc. are the urgent need of the hour to overcome the shortcomings in this respect.

SECTION-II

Traffic Intensity and Transportation Network

Transportation is fundamental for overall development. Transportation plays a key role in upgrading the quality of human life, development of industry infrastructure, expansion of trade, agricultural marketing, better health services etc. In Kokrajhar, town there is no established road network. Road transport scenario has become highly chaotic and pollutant because of the galloping growth of auto vehicles. There are no organised parking areas. The main traffic terminals of the town are bus stand and railway station. The parking space is very inadequate and as such a good number of the buses are parked on the road side creating havoc to the town dwellers. The roads within the town are mostly narrow, uneven and treeless. Furthermore inadequate provision of footpath and wrong use of it makes the pedestrian horrified especially in the peak hours of the day. In some cases the footpaths are occupied by the vendors and are treated as parking zone of bicycle and motorbikes. The things become worse where there is cloud of dust and clumsy movement of vehicles on the road. Again, lack of proper drainage and sewage system, unplanned construction of houses and commercial centres almost on the roads interrupt the normal flow of both pedestrians and vehicles of all sorts. During monsoon, road patches, road caving, inundation after a single spell of shower have been a common feature for several years in most of the part of the town.The plight of the people under such circumstances hardly needs any mention. There are a number of defective road junctions which retard the speed of the vehicle, making the points highly accident prone. Also there are many level crossings in Kokrajhar town and the most critical one is in front of the Kokrajhar Railway Station, commonly known as rail gate on Bibekananda Path(road). One over bridge at this point is the urgent need of the hour. The Kokrajhar town has the advantage of rail communication—Broad Gauge as well as Metre Gauge lines. Both the railway lines pass through the main town connecting Guwahati and upper Assam on the east and Dhubri and other parts of the country on the west. Hopefully, the B.T.A.D Government has been attending these problems very seriously.

Table 24.8 Number of Motor Vehicles on Road in Kokrajhar District

Year	Bus	Motor Car	Motor Cycle & Scooter	Auto-Rickshaw	Jeep	Private Carrier	Public Carrier
1995-96	303	602	4283	09	181	01	389
1996-97	317	635	4485	12	188	01	461
1997-98	327	666	4644	18	190	01	498
1998-99	317	632	4819	30	190	01	507
1999-00	329	657	4969	38	192	02	570
2000-01	470	669	5056	41	192	02	590
2001-02	410	648	5056	41	160	—	—
2002-03	201	702	5969	65	96	—	259
2003-04	165	740	6030	70	96	—	270
2004-05	163	750	7090	75	96	—	265
2005-06	165	740	7270	74	90	—	266
2006-07	271	890	7174	135	50	—	560
2007-08 (Up to Aug'07)	04	129	680	27	—	—	21

Some Measures

(i) There should be diversion of agricultural working force and land to other sectors to foster balanced economic development.

(ii) The unplanned settlement in the Municipal area should be strictly controlled.

(iii) Road width, separate lanes for fast and slow moving vehicles, speed breakers, street lighting, roadside plantation etc. are the essential needs of today.

(iv) Major road junctions should be improved, road safety education, training of drivers, public education and traffic education should be imparted to all road users.

(v) Truck, bus terminals, off street parking sites, provision of footpath in all roads of the town require special emphasis.

(vi) Infrastructure should be developed that can reduce the problems of over crowded buses and increasing journey time with least comfort, safety etc.

(vii) Construction of bridge on river Gaurang is the urgent need of the hour to connect the western part of the town with the region.

(viii) Infrastructure of secondary and tertiary sectors should be developed.

(ix) There should be appropriate land use and facilities for education, tele-communication service, recreational purpose, proper health care etc. which should be attended on priority basis.

(x) Introducing organised marketing facilities, setting up of warehouses and storage spaces will be of immense use.

Table 24.9 Number of Motor Vehicles on Road in Kokrajhar District

Year	*Govt. Vehicle*	*Tracker*	*Tractor & Trailer*	*Ambulance*	*Light Commercial Vehicle*	*Total Table VIII (a) + Table VIII (b)*
1995-96	40	17	76	—	—	5971
1996-97	45	22	88	—	—	6324
1997-98	45	23	93	—	—	6575
1998-99	109	27	100	—	25	6764
1999-00	120	30	108	—	23	7055
2000-01	124	30	108	—	23	7323
2001-02	124	30	138	—	69	6676
2002-03	105	10	140	—	69	7616
2003-04	108	N.A.	115	07	64	7665
2004-05	150	60	110	05	70	8834
2005-06	220	70	110	06	116	9127
2006-07	272	115	124	08	286	9885
2007-08 (Up to Aug'07)	45	02	16	—	71	995

Source: District Transport Office, Kokrajhar, Assam.

Concluding Remarks

This paper establishes that Kokrajhar town Municipal Area has got several evils of urbanization such as high population growth, haphazard growth of commercialization, poor industrialization, unplanned land use, spectacular vehicle growth and its resultant congestion, pollution, high accident rates etc. We know that the infrastructure failures reduce the community's quality of life and improved infrastructure services enhance welfare and foster economic growth. The availability of adequate and high quality infrastructure facilities provides the enabling environment for rapid overall development.

Lastly, there is realisation that there should be well co-ordination amongst different sectors for all round development of the region. Physical and social infrastructure should obviously ensure decent living in the society. Farsightedness of the planners should be there so as to ensure how far the town would grow for the quality living of the people.

REFERENCES

1. Patankar .P.G. Urban Transport (in India) in Distress, published by CIRT, Pune.
2. Dhar, P.K. (2001). The Economy of Assam, Kalyani Publishers.
3. District Statistical Hand Book, Kokrajhar, 1996, 1998, 2005.
4. District Statistical Hand Book, Assam, 1995, 1997.
5. The Assam Gazette Extraordinary, June 14, 2001.
6. The Assam Tribune, 10th, 20th July and 25th August, 2002.
7. Indian Journal of Transport Management, Vol. 23, No. 10. October 97, pp. 575-645.
8. Primary Census Abstract, Part II-B, Series 4, Census of India, 1991, Directorate of Census Operation, Assam.
9. Primary Census Abstract, Census of India, 2001, Directorate of Census Operations, Assam.

25

A Glimpse at the Distribution and Concentration of Farm Land Holdings in North Eastern India

A.K. NEOG

Introduction

Factor endowments play a key role in generating economic well-being of an individual, a farmer, household, society, region, and a country. Land is an original factor of production like labour. In an agrarian economy, it is a source of livelihood and employment. The pattern of distribution of land holdings among the farmers, more particularly its eveness or otherwise, is of prime importance. Land is, however, only one form of endowments. In fact, *a priori*, a relationship of the type stated below can be visualized among endowments, farm size and practice:

Endowments	*Farm size*	*Farm Practice*
(A/N) < 1	Marginal and Small	Labour intensive crops
(A/N) > 1	Semi-medium to Large	Capital intensive crops

In the above, A denotes (percentage of) area operated and N denotes (percentage of) number of holdings. It may be mentioned that farm size of below one hectare is classified under agriculture census as marginal holdings, 1 to 2 hectares as small, 2 to 4 hectares as semi-medium, 4 to 10 hectares as medium, and above 10 hectares as large holdings. Usually, in a non-egalitarian economy, the percentage of area operated by marginal and small farmers are lower than their share in total number of holdings. The converse holds good in the case of semi-medium, medium and large size farmers. Labour intensity tends to be high in respect of marginal and small size farms, while in the other size groups capital-intensity tends to rise.

It is to be noted that the distribution of land holdings among farm households is intimately related to the distribution of economic well-being. Hence inequality in the distribution of land holdings can be at the core of development of an agricultural economy. It, however, needs to be mentioned that inequality in land distribution is only one dimension of inequality. 'Zero-inequality' can be an optimum solution for an 'all-inclusive' growth and an economic desideratum. But it can also be Utopian if the necessary and sufficient conditions do not exist. On the other hand, high and rising level of inequality may adversely impact future growth and development prospects. It may, therefore, suggest that relatively smaller farmers are not getting proportionate share of agricultural development, and growth is not broad-based. Unequal endowment means unequal wealth or low incomes. Those with low incomes hardly have surplus, and are unable to invest in wealth-creating activities, thereby, dampening the chances of future growth for them. Hence higher land inequality can lower growth. Lower inequality is necessary for growth to be high not only vertically but also horizontally, i.e., all-inclusive. It may be mentioned that in a situation when land is inelastic and land ceilings can not be lowered further without sacrificing farm viability and efficiency, the surplus manpower would have to move to non-farm activities.

The aim of this paper is to examine the trend of inequality in farm land holdings in the States of the North-Eastern region of India in particular, with tangential reference to some other States of the country, and test selected hypotheses.

2. Methodology, Data, Coverage and Reference Period

The implicit methodology introduced in this exercise is an identity to measure the endowment in terms of area operated by the farm size groups, which can be enunciated as follows:

$$(A/N) = (A/a)(m/N)(a/m)(A/b)(s/N)(b/s)(N/A)(h/c)(c/h), \quad \ldots (1)$$

Where A denotes total area operated by all groups of farm holdings; a, b and c denote area operated respectively by marginal, small and other (higher) farm groups (i.e., semi-medium, medium and large). N denotes the total number of holdings; m, s and h respectively denote the number of marginal, small and other (higher) holdings (i.e., semi-medium, medium and large).

The ratio (A/N) denotes the average size of all holdings. It is an outcome of several other ratios, as shown on the right hand side (RHS) of the identity. The RHS states that average size of total holdings is a cross product of the ratio of total area operated to area operated by each farm groups (marginal, small and others), share of each farm group in total number of holdings, average size of holdings in each group, reciprocals of average size of total holdings and of other holdings. The identity can be verified, as for instance, with the help of data given in Table 25.1 on the characteristics of 2000-01 agricultural census.

As already stated, the aim of the paper is to examine inequality. The Gini coefficient or concentration ratio, which is one of the most commonly used measures, is used here. It may be mentioned that there are different versions of the Gini concentration ratio, which may yield different results. The formula used to calculate the Gini ratio (G) here is similar to the one available in Fuller & Lury (1977). In our notation, it is as under:

$$G = (1/100)\,[(N_1A_2 - N_2A_1) + (N_2A_3 - N_3A_2) + (N_3A_4 - N_4A_3) + (N_4A_5 - N_5A_4)], \qquad \ldots (2)$$

where N_i and A_i are respectively the cumulative percentages of number of farm holdings of, and area operated by the i-th size class (I = 1, 2, 3, 4, 5). It may be mentioned that, in general, the five size classes in our study are the marginal, small, semi-medium, medium, and large farm size groups. Since the values of number of holdings and areas are taken in cumulative frequencies (percentages), $N_5 = 100 = A_5$.

The value of the Gini coefficient, theoretically, ranges between zero and unity. When it is zero, there is perfect equality i.e., everyone has the same size of area operated. When it is one, there is perfect inequality i.e., one farm household takes everything. In reality, the ratio lies between the two limits.

Agricultural data used in the exercise are official data, which are published by the Ministry of Agriculture, Government of India. Such data are available with five year interval from 1970-71 onwards. However, the reference period in this paper pertains to 1990-91 onwards. It may be mentioned that other than Assam, the other seven States are categorized as non-land record States in the Agricultural Census, where there is no village revenue agency for collection of data on a regular basis. Of course, at the All-India level Goa, Kerala, Orissa and West Bengal are also included in the non-land record States. In the non-land record States, for the purpose of agricultural census a stratified two-stage sampling is followed. This is, therefore, a limitation on the census results of such States.

Another official source of data on operational holdings is the National Sample Surveys (NSS) on land holdings, which are usually carried out with decadal interval. The results of first such survey data available are for the year 1953-54 (NSS 8th round) and the latest for 2002-03 (59th round). In this paper, data from this source are not used except for reference.

3. Analysis of Farm Holdings and Area Operated

As per Agricultural Census 2000-01, there are 1208.22 lakh number of total holdings in India (excluding Jharkhand for which data are not available). These holdings operate upon 1599.03 lakh hectare of agricultural land. In Assam, the corresponding numbers are 26.07 lakh number of holdings (i.e, 2.16 per cent of All-India) and 31.15 lakh hectares (i.e., 1.95 per cent of All-India). The marginal farmers account for 63 per cent of the holdings operating 18.82 per cent of the land at the All-India level. In Assam, these figures are 59.05 per cent and 19.49 per cent respectively. The small farmers at the All-India level account for 18.88 per cent operating upon 20.17 per cent of the land. As against this, in Assam the figures are 21.97 per cent and 23.05 per cent respectively. The marginal and small farmers together account for 81.88 per cent at the All-India level operating upon 38.99 per cent of the land. These figures for Assam are 81.02 per cent and 42.54 per cent. This shows the inequality in the shares of holdings vis-à-vis area operated. It may be mentioned that though the percentages of marginal and small holdings are not significant in Nagaland, the area operated by such holdings is very small i.e. 9.72 per cent holdings operating 1.24 per cent area, while in Arunachal Pradesh 32.71 per cent holdings operate 8.63 per cent area. These show inter-class unequal distribution of holdings. The percentage of marginal and small holdings in Tripura at 96.04 per cent is one of the highest operating 74.72 per cent area. These figures including that for the other States of the region are given in **Table 25.1.**

Table 25.1 Number of Holdings and Area Operated by All Groups and Percentage of Operational Holdings and Area by Farm size, 2000-01.

States	*All Groups*		*Marginal (%)*		*Small (%)*		*Semi-Medium to Large (%)*	
	No. of Holdings	*Area Operated*	*No. of Holdings*	*Area Operated*	*No. of Holdings*	*Area Operated*	*No. of Holdings*	*Area Operated*
Assam	26.07	31.15	59.05	19.49	21.97	23.05	18.98	57.46
Arunachal Pradesh	1.07	3.94	14.02	1.78	18.69	6.85	67.29	91.37
Manipur	1.49	1.72	50.33	23.26	32.89	36.63	16.78	40.11
Meghalaya	2.14	2.73	53.74	22.66	26.64	29.86	19.62	47.48
Mizoram	0.76	0.94	44.74	23.40	36.84	38.30	18.42	38.30
Nagaland	1.44	10.47	3.47	0.19	6.25	1.05	90.28	98.76
Sikkim	0.52	0.80	53.85	14.63	23.08	20.73	23.07	64.64
Tripura	4.79	2.70	84.58	46.84	11.46	27.88	3.96	25.28
All-India *	1208.22	1599.03	63.00	18.82	18.88	20.17	18.12	61.01

NB: * Denotes excluding Jharkhand. Due to rounding, figures may not aggregate 100.
(%) Denotes percentages to all Groups.

Source: Ministry of Agriculture, Govt. of India.

4. Degree and Trend of Inequality in Distribution of Holdings and Area Operated:

Existing literature (G.S. Bhalla, 2007) shows that the degree of inequality in the distribution of area operated by the operational holdings in the country as per the various rounds of NSS, as measured in terms of Gini concentration ratio, stood at 0.621 in 1953-54, 0.583 in 1960-61, 0.588 in 1971-72, 0.624 in 1981-82, 0.641 in 1991-92 and 0.624 in 2002-03. Further, the concentration ratio of ownership holdings in the above years stood at 0.751, 0.717,

0.706, 0.708, 0.71 and 0.74. In other words, the concentration ratio is higher in respect of ownership holdings than operational holdings.

The All-India Gini concentration ratio (**Table 25.2**) as per our estimates from agricultural census data on operational holdings stood at 0.5778 in 1990-91, 0.5685 in 1995-96 and 0.5534 in 2000-01 showing declining trend. It may be mentioned that during the period 1990-91 and 2000-01, the ratio has been falling for Assam (0.5281 in 1990-91, 0.5258 in 1995-96 and 0.5050 in 2000-01), Meghalaya, Mizoram, Nagaland, Tripura and Sikkim. The same has been fluctuating for Arunachal Pradesh and Manipur. It is seen that the degree of concentration is lower in the region than the All-India average. It may be mentioned that the Gini ratio for State like West Bengal had been gradually declining from 0.4125 in 1990-91, 0.3664 in 1995-96 to 0.3275 in 2000-01. For Kerala, the ratio during the corresponding years also showed a declining trend i.e., 0.4575, 0.4153 and 0.3964. For Punjab also, the ratio registered a declining trend i.e., 0.4898, 0.4599 and 0.4223 during the said three points of time. **Table 25.2** presents the Gini concentration ratio for the North-Eastern States.

Table 25.2 Estimated Gini coefficients of concentration of operational holdings based on data of Agricultural Census: 1990-91, 1995-96 & 2000-01.

States	*1990-91*	*1995-96*	*2000-01*	*Remarks*
Assam	0.5281	0.5258	0.5050	Falling
Arunachal Pradesh	0.4291	0.4481	0.4295	Fluctuating
Manipur	0.3491	0.3369	0.3467	Fluctuating
Meghalaya	0.4067	—	0.3922	Falling
Mizoram	0.3126	—	0.2926	Falling
Nagaland	0.3227	0.3091	0.2149	Falling
Sikkim	0.5729	0.5596	0.5377	Falling
Tripura	0.4540	0.4005	0.3979	Falling
All-India	0.5778	0.5685	0.5534	Falling

NB: Due to anomalous data for 1995-96 in respect of Meghalaya and Mizoram Gini coefficients could not be calculated.

Source: See Table 25.1 above.

5. Limitations of Gini Coefficient

Though Gini coefficient is a popular measure of concentration of wealth, it suffers from some limitations which are mentioned below. Different distributions may yield identical Gini ratios. The Gini ratio is insensitive to small percentage changes which may represent large shifts in wealth and assets like land. The boundaries of perfect inequality (G=1) and equality (G=0) are so extreme that changes in the Gini ratio over time would tend to understate any actual gains towards equality. The Gini coefficient is more sensitive to asset differences in the middle of the frequency distribution. It is also likely to understate inequality if the number of class intervals in the frequency distribution is less. To give an example, the Gini coefficient for Nagaland (in whose case size classes were compressed to four instead of five) is 0.2149 for 2000-01. We know that the lower the value of the Gini coefficient, the more equally distributed is the asset (land in this case). But the distribution of land holdings in the State is such that 29.16 per cent (i.e., marginal, small and semi-medium) of total holdings own/operate only 8.12 per cent of the total area under operational holdings, while 70.84 per cent holdings own/operate 91.97 per cent (**Table 25.1**) reflecting a glaring inequality. Hence, the summary result of Gini ratio may reflect 'pseudo' result.

6. Concluding Remarks

From our short study, the following inferences can be drawn:

- At the all-India level, as per agricultural census 2000-01 about 82 per cent of the total farm holdings are marginal and small, operating about 39 per cent of the area.
- For States like Assam, the above figures are about 81 per cent and 42.5 per cent, respectively.
- The inter-class unequal distribution of land holdings is evident.
- The degree of land inequality during 1990-91 and 2000-01, as measured by the Gini concentration ratio, is declining both at the all-India level and regional level except in Arunachal Pradesh and Manipur.

- Generally speaking, the degree of concentration is lower in the region than the all-India average.
- The period from 1990-91 and afterwards in Indian economy is characterized by economic reforms, though not dealt in our study and agriculture is not directly touched by reforms.
- A lower Gini concentration ratio with glaring inter-class inequality in land distribution can lead to misleading inference. The result in respect of Nagaland is a case in point.
- The States in the region, other than Assam, are categorized as non-land record States. Their figures are based on sample estimates.
- The ownership of land rests with the community in the hilly tribal areas and hardly with the individual. Farming practised is called 'Jhumming' i.e., shifting cultivation.
- In formulating policy, the planners and policy-makers need to keep the above scenario in view.

REFERENCES

1. Fuller, M.E. & Lury, D.A. (1977). Statistics Work Book for Social Science Students, Philip Allan Publishers Ltd. Oxford.
2. Bhalla, G.S. (2007). Indian Agriculture Since Independence, National Book Trust, India.
3. Neog, A.K. & Bardoloi, G. (1991). "A Study on the Impact of Land Reforms in Assam" in Dasgupta, M(ed): Impact of Land Reforms in North- East India, Omsons Publication, Guwahati.
4. Ministry of Agriculture, Agricultural Census Reports (2000-01, Government of India: 1995-96 & 1990-91).
5. Directorate of Economics & Agricultural Statistics at a Glance (2006, Statistics, Ministry of Agriculture, Government of India, 2004 & 2002).
6. Asian Development Bank (2007). Key Indicators 2007, Volume-38.

NOTES

1. G.L. Beckford, *Persistent Poverty: Underdevelopment in Plantation Economies of the Third World*, Oxford University Press, London, 1972

2. Sidney W. Mintz, *Caribbean Transformations*, The Johns Hopkins University Press, Baltimore and London, 1974, 54.
3. W. Robinson (1841). *A Descriptive Account of Assam*, London, p. 217
4. This has been discussed at length in my article, 'Plantation Economy and the Land Tenure System in the Brahmaputra Valley: 1839-1914', *Economic and Political Weekly*, July 16, 1983.
5. Clifford Geertz, *Agricultural Involution: The Process of Ecological Change in Indonesia*, University of California Press, Berkeley and Los Angeles, 1968, 84
6. Thompson, E. (1959). 'The Plantation as a Social System', in *Plantation Systems in the New World*, Washington D.C.
7. Beckford, *Op cit*, 37.
8. *Ibid.*, 38.
9. W. Robinson (1975). *A Descriptive Account of Assam*, (London, 1841), Imprint, Sanskaran Prakashak, Delhi, p. 245
10. E.J. Taaffee, R.L. Morrill and P.R. Gould, (1963). 'Transport Expansion in Underdeveloped Countries: A Comparative Analysis', *Geographical Review*, Volume. 53.
11. This has been discussed in my article, (1995). 'Urban Centres in the Spatial Structure of the Brahmaputra Valley under Colonialism', Proceedings of the North East India History Association, Fifteenth Session, Shillong.
12. The model is analysed in detail in Boudhayan Chattopadhyay and Moonis Raza, *The Indian Journal of Regional Science*, Volume VII, No.1, 1975. This has been discussed in Moonis Raza and Atiya Habeeb, 'Characteristics of Colonial Urbanization: A Case Study of the Satellitic "Primacy" of Calcutta', Occasional Paper No.1, Centre for the Study of Regional Development, School of Social Sciences, New Delhi, 1976, p. 7.
13. See for details, Hugh Tinker, (1974). *A New System of Slavery: The Export of Indian Labour Overseas: 1830-1920*, Oxford University Press, London, p. 136-137.
14. Adrian A. Graves, (1986). 'The Structure and Organisation of the Wage Labour Plantation in Queensland, 1862-1900, in Sue Eakin and John Tarver (Eds), *Plantations Around the World*, Louisiana State University Agricultural Center, Louisiana.
15. For a detailed discussion on this see Doreen Massey, *For Space*, Sage Publications, London, Thousand Oaks, New Delhi, 2005.

26

Centrally Sponsored Schemes for Upliftment of Rural Economy of North East India: An Analysis

A. RAJMANI SINGH

I. Introduction

The North East India, with a landmass of 2, 55,059 sq. km. (9 per cent of the country's total) hosts a population of 38, 539 million as per 2001 census. Urbanization in the seven sisters of North Eastern India has gradually increased over the last few decades. The urban population of North East India has increased significantly during the last two decades from 18.47 lakhs in 1991 to 59.72 lakhs in 2001 with the growing rate of 223.34 per cent spreading over 200 different urban centers of the region. But in comparison to all-India percentage of urban population to total population, the North East India's percentage is very poor. It accounts for only 15.51 per cent of the total population of the region against all-India percentage of 27.78.

Among the seven sisters of North Eastern India, Mizoram stands as the highest urbanized State with 49.5 per cent of its total population living in urban areas, followed by Manipur with 23.88 per cent, Arunachal Pradesh with 20.41 per cent, Meghalaya with 19.63 per cent, Nagaland with 17.74 per cent, Tripura with 17.02 per cent and Assam with 12.72 per cent as per 2001 census. It is very interesting to note that except Mizoram the remaining six states of the region are below the national average of 27.78

per cent of urban population. The highly urbanized State Mizoram which accounts 49.5 per cent of urban population is placed at 5th position among the different States and union territories of the country as per the 2001 census. Delhi, the capital of the county has the highest urban population with 93.01 per cent and Himachal Pradesh has the lowest urbanized state with 9.79 per cent of urban population.

The table given below represents the overall demographic features of the northeastern States. These include levels of literacy, density of population living in per sq. km, sex ratio of female, rural and urban distribution of population etc. The total area of seven north-eastern States is 2,55,028 sq. km. (2001) with habitation of about 38.539 million persons in 2001 supporting 3.75 per cent of India's population. N.E States' share of rural population is 4.38 per cent which is higher than the share of total population. Except Assam, in all the other States, their density of population is less than the national average which is an index of backwardness. In case of urbanization, all the north-eastern States except Mizoram are behind national average. Assam is the most populous State with least urbanization and Mizoram is the least populous State with highest urbanization. By literacy rate, N.E. States are more or less approximate to the national average. But Mizoram outshines with nearly 91 per cent male and 86 per cent female literacy with 88.8 per cent in total literacy rate, followed by Tripura. As per the report of CMIE, the selected indicators of development of all States and districts of India with all criteria taken together, India is given the value of 100. Developed States exceed 100 marks and less developed States fall below 100. The N.E. States show remarkable uniformity showing the values ranging between 54-55 marks only. However Arunachal is the only state having a little higher value with 66 marks.

The table also shows the trend of rural-urban settlements among the states of north eastern region of India for the last three decades. Mizoram was the most urbanized State in the region. Once, Mizoram state was second in position as urbanized during 1981 census after Manipur by a margin of 1.75 per cent. But it rose to 1st position during 1991 census and 2001 census. One of the main reasons behind the sudden improvement of urbanized during 1991 and 2001 census was returning of peace and normalcy in the

State. It is further shows that the difference in urbanization rate in both the decades was a big margin of 18.58 per cent in 1991 and 25.62 per cent in 2001. It is also seen from the table that except Mizoram and Manipur all the remaining states of the region are below the national average rate of urbanization. One very interesting figure is noticed from the table that except Manipur all the remaining States have improved their level of urbanization decade by decade. But for Manipur it was 26.42 per cent in 1981 rose to 27.52 in 1991 and again declined to 23.88 per cent. One of the basic reason behind the increasing and decreasing trend of urbanization in Manipur was delimitation of Churachandpur district which was recognized as urbanized in 1991 but it recognized as urbanized during 2001 census.

Table 26.1 Demographic Profile of North Eastern Region of India 2001

States of N-E India	Area Sq.km.	Population			Population		Literacy	Density per sq. Km.	Sex Ratio Per 1000 Males
		Total	Male	Female	Urban	Rural			
1	2	3	4	5	6	7	8	9	10
Arunachal	83743	10.98	5.80	5.18	20.81	79.19	54.30	13	893
Assam	78438	266.55	137.77	128.78	12.92	87.08	63.30	340	935
Manipur *	22327	23.89	12.07	11.82	23.88	76.12	68.80	107	978
Meghalaya	22429	23.19	11.76	11.43	19.63	80.37	62.60	103	972
Mizoram	21087	8.89	4.59	4.30	49.60	50.40	88.80	42	935
Nagaland	16579	19.90	10.47	9.43	17.24	82.76	66.60	120	900
Tripura	10486	31.99	16.42	15.57	17.12	82.88	73.20	305	848
NE Total	255079	385.39	198.88	186.51	15.51	84.49	68.77	149	936
All India	3287263	102.87	53.22	49.65	27.78	72.22	64.80	325	933

Sources: (i) Census of India, Series Manipur 2001.
(ii) NEDFi Data Bank Quarterly, Vol. Issue 1 July 2002 p. 2.
(iii) India's population is in crore.
(iv) * as per 2001 census provisional figure.

Over the last few decades a plethora of poverty alleviation programmes in various forms have been implemented in the country and a huge amount of social and financial investments have been made for poverty eradication. Most of the programmes have been top-down in approach that did not consider needs and requirements of the people and the pace of rural development remained far behind the expectation. The main reason behind the slow pace of development in rural economy is inability of the benefits to reach the direct beneficiaries at the grassroot level. It was rightly pointed out by the former Prime Minister Rajiv Gandhi, "that hardly 10 paisa is benefited out of Re 1 spent for rural development project". Thus, it is true that unless we change the strategy of top-down to bottom-up strategy for rural economy, we can not lessen the burden of poverty nor can we solve the problem of unemployment.

Various centrally sponsored schemes and area-based and beneficiary oriented programmes were undertaken by the Government over the last few five year plans such as Command Area Development Programmes (CADP) 1974, Integrated Rural Development Programme (IRDP) 1980, District Rural Development Agency (DRDA), National Rural Employment Programme (NREP), Rural Landless Employment Guarantee Programme (RLEGP) 1983, Jawahar Rojgar Yojana (JRY) 1989, Training of Rural Youth for Self Employment (TRYSEM) 1979, Development of Women and Children in Rural Areas (DWCRA) 1982, Prime Minister Rojgar Yojana (PMRY) 1993 and so on. After successfully implementing the above centrally sponsored schemes for the upliftment of rural economy, the pace of rural development in the region still remains standstill.

Many of the schemes have already closed down and a few of them have merged with the newly launched rural development programmes. One of the main reasons behind the slow pace of rural development in India in general and north eastern region in particular is lack of effective and efficient utilization of fund allocated for development, lack of transparency from the policy makers and lack of people's participation at the grassroot level.

In the late 1990s evaluation reports of the Integrated Rural Development Programme (IRDP), a major programme for creating self employment opportunities in rural areas reflected the flaws in implementation of the programme. This led the Central Government to announce a holistic programme called Swarnajayanti Gram Swarozgar Yojana (SGSY) 1999, Pradhan Mantri Gram Sadak Yojana (PMGSY) 2000, Sampurna Gramin Rojgar Yojana (SGRY) 2001 and very recently the National Rural Employment Guarantee Schemes (NREGS) 2006.

Thus, the present paper makes the performance appraisal of these centrally sponsored rural development programmes in North

Eastern Region of India on the basis of various secondary data published by the Government of India. Since the rural development schemes are large in number, it will be difficult task for the researcher to cover all the schemes, hence the present study is devoted to few selected schemes such as SGSY, PMGSY, and NREGS. An analysis of the above schemes implemented in the seven north eastern states are made in the present study. Efforts have been made to find out the reason behind the slow pace of rural development and the remedial measures are suggested.

II. Centrally Sponsored Rural Development Programmes

Improvement in the quality of life of the economically weaker sections of the society is one of the basic objectives of development planning. In order to achieve this a number of programmes viz. SGSY, PMGSY, and NREGS etc. have been under implementation in the seven States of the region. These programmes ensure minimum wage to rural workers and enable them to acquire assets and income through self employment ventures. In this context, it would be appropriate to evaluate various developmental schemes and programmes launched in the region to uplift the standard of living of the rural population and rural economy of the region. Some of the important selected rural development programmes are:

Swarnjayanti Gram Swarozgar Yojana (SGSY)

The Integrated Rural Development Programme (IRDP) and its allied programmes such as TRYSEM, DWCRA, MSW, SITRA and Ganga Kalyan Yojana have been restructured in a new rural development programme called the **Swarnjayanti Gram Swarozgar Yojana (SGSY)** in April 1, 1999 with the main objectives of (i) poverty alleviation, (ii) capitalizing advantages of group lending and (iii) overcoming the problems associated with multiplicity of numerous programmes. The scheme aims at establishing a large number of micro enterprises in rural areas of the country. This programme was based on a group (community) approach to rural development where the rural poor were organized into Self-Help Groups (SHGs), provided training, credit, technology, infrastructure and marketing support through viable economic activities on their own on a sustained basis with government subsidy and bank credit. It is financed on 75:25 cost sharing basis between the Centre and States. Since inception of the scheme up to November 2005, a total allocation of Rs. 8,067 crore was made available by the Centre and States. Total fund utilized were Rs. 16, 433.66 crore up to 31st December 2006 benefiting 73.20 lakh Swarozgaris.

Table 26.2 Financial Performance of Swarnjayanti Gram Swarozgar Yojana (SGSY) in North Eastern Region during 2005-06

States	*Central Allocation*	*State Allocation*	*Central Release*	*State Release*	*Misc Receipts*	*Total Funds*	*Utilization of Funds*	*%age of Utilization to Total Fund*
1	*2*	*3*	*4*	*5*	*6*	*7*	*8*	*9*
Arunachal Pradesh	2.91	92.30	143.24	0	0.00	143.24	53.65	37.45
Assam	7195.18	2398.39	3517.00	15.18	3336.67	6868.85	4571.55	66.55
Manipur	482.36	160.79	67.61	2.82	0.00	70.83	12.06	17.02
Meghalaya	540.42	180.14	128.77	51.29	1.97	182.03	129.93	71.38
Mizoram	125.06	41.69	117.83	34.12	0.27	152.22	96.80	63.59
Nagaland	370.70	123.57	117.27	—	0.00	117.27	—	—
Sikkim	138.45	46.15	67.68	30.00	15.98	113.66	106.03	93.29
Tripura	870.92	290.31	546.82	228.98	4.39	780.19	655.08	78.33

Source: Basic Statistics NEC, Shillong 2006 p. 443.

The above table representing financial performance of Swarnjayanti Gram Swarozgar Yojana in Northeastern Region of India shows that the overall performances of North Eastern States are quite encouraging in terms of utilization of funds allocated and release of fund by both Central and State Governments. Except Manipur and Arunachal Pradesh all the other State's performances were more than 50 per cent. It is also found that the Nagaland State has allocated and released the fund but was unable to utilized the said amount under SGSY.

The table 26.2 shows the physical performance of SGSY in North Eastern Region of India. As on 2005-06 28,768 members were covered under the SGSY scheme. Of this 829 individual Swarozgaris were assisted. Among the different States of the region Assam had the highest number of SHGs and Swarozgaris followed by Tripura and Manipur with 641 and 635 SHGs respectively.

Table 26.3 Physical Performance of Swarnjayanti Gram Swarozgar Yojana (SGSY) in North Eastern Region during 2005-06

States	*Members Covered Under SHGs*	*Number of Individual Swarozgaris Assisted*
1	2	3
Arunachal Pradesh	21	121
Assam	26305	212
Manipur	635	5
Meghalaya	488	11
Mizoram	290	87
Nagaland	0	0
Sikkim	388	393
Tripura	641	0

Source: Basic Statistics NEC, Shillong 2006 p. 443.

Pradhan Mantri Gram Sadak Yojana (PMGSY)

Pradhan Mantri Gram Sadak Yojana a 100 per cent Centrally Sponsored Scheme was started on 25th December 2000. The main objective of this scheme is to provide connectivity to all unconnected habitations in the rural areas having population of more than 500 persons, through good all-weather roads. In case of North East States and other Hilly States of the country, the habitations with a population of 250 and above are the criteria to provide road connectivity. Since inception, project proposals for Rs. 14,417 crore have been cleared. Up to 31st March 2006, project proposals amounting to Rs. 26,490.82 crore have been approved against which a sum of Rs. 16,120.10 crore has been released for 47,643 roads covering a length of 153938.46 km. Against these, 31251 road works having road length of 89758.66 km. have been completed with a cumulative total of Rs. 13,574.23 crore.

The table 26.3 highlighted the rural connectivity through Pradhan Mantri Gram Sadak Yojana in Northeastern Region of India. There were 2103 different roads connecting one rural area with another rural area under PMGSY in the region up to November 2005. To construct and connect the above roads in the region a total sum of Rs. 1100.06 crore have been spend against the Rs. 1344.41 crore released by the Central Government which account 81.82 per cent. Performance of this rural development programme in the region is quite encouraging with 99.74 per cent performance in Arunachal followed by 92.85 per cent performance in Nagaland, and by 62.95 per cent in Tripura.

Table 26.4 Rural Connectivity through Pradhan Mantri Gram Sadak Yojana in North Eastern Region during 2005-06

States	*Value of proposal cleared*	*Amount released*	*No. of road works completed*	*Expenditure up to Nov.05*	*% of Expenditure to amount released*
1	2	3	4	5	6
Arunachal Pradesh	233.68	127.46	330	127.13	99.74
Assam	1601.11	564.46	553	432.50	76.62
Manipur	120.71	98.00	451	82.05	83.72
Meghalaya	145.72	115.67	285	91.26	78.90
Mizoram	211.24	164.51	60	144.52	87.85
Nagaland	124.23	106.95	168	99.30	92.85
Sikkim	149.37	70.97	51	62.62	88.23
Tripura	116.19	96.39	205	60.68	62.95

Source: Basic Statistics of NEC 2006.

Special Accelerated Road Development Programme for North East India

The SARDP NE envisages widening of 3228 km. of National Highways and widening of 2500 km. of State roads and 2 lining of 1888 km. roads of strategic importance in the north-eastern region. This programme will provide at least double lane road connectivity to all State capitals and District Headquarters of the all the eight States of the region. This programme will be implemented in two phases as follows:

Phase–A consists of 1110 km. of National Highways and 200 km. State roads with an estimated expenditure of Rs. 4618 crore.

Phase–B involves improvement of 2118 km. National Highways and 4188 km. State Highways. Government approved implementation of phase–A on September 22, 2005 and gave approval for preparation of DPRs for Phase–B on May 18, 2006.

National Rural Employment Guarantee Scheme (NREGS)

National Rural Employment Guarantee Scheme (NREGS) was

launched on February 2, 2006. The two rural development programmes of Sampoorna Grameen Rojgar Yojana (SGRY) and National Food for Work Programme (NFWP) are sub-sumed within the NREGS in 200 districts identified in the initial stage. It is also proposed to cover all the districts of the country under the scheme within five years. In one year of NREGS 1.47 crore households were provided with employment against the demand from 1.51 crore households in 200 districts of the 27 States in the country. Of the 53.65 crore person days of employment generated out of which 21.13 crore were the women. The programme had a total available fund of Rs. 9,856.92 crore and the total expenditure was so far Rs 5,033.48 crore, which is 51.07 per cent of the available funds. While 64 per cent of the 5.81 lakh works taken up were water-based, roads construction work was 23.2 per cent and other works like land development was 12.7 per cent.

The NREGS is yet to yield desired results. Not only the scheme could not provide employment to all the eligible people, in many cases the labourer did not get the stipulated rate of wages too. According to a survey, in 2006-07, only 6 per cent of households registered in the scheme in the country got 100 days of employment as prescribed by law. NREGS was initially applicable to only 200 districts in the first phase and it subsequently extended to 330 districts in the second phase and now it is proposed that it will be applicable to all the 595 districts of the country which are classified as rural. (Prime Minister Dr Manmohon Singh 28th September 2007). The allocation for the NREGA for 2006-07 was Rs. 11,300 crore (200 districts) and Rs. 12,000 for 2007-08 (330 districts) and Rs. 20,000 crore for 595 districts from April 1, 2008. However, against this allocation, only Rs. 8,800 crore was actually spent in 2006-07 and this year the expenditure is likely to touch Rs. 10,000 crore at the most. "The programme has legal backing, so whatever money is required for the demand-driven NREGA will be provided by the Government," Mr. Singh said. It will provide an employment to 2.10 crore rural households in 200 districts in 2006-07, creating 90.5 crore man-days. Of this, over 60 per cent belong to scheduled castes and scheduled tribes and 40 per cent of those employed are women.

Contrary to the statement given by the Honourable Prime Minister, the NREGS did not yield the desired results. The lackluster attitude of the Government machinery to implement the scheme properly was evident as the survey showed that 4 states—Bihar, Orissa, Gujarat and Haryana out of 14 states did not even constitute State Employment Guarantee Council thought more than a year has passed.

Table 26.5 Financial Performance under NREGA in North East India during 2007-08

Rs. in Lakhs

States	*No of Districts Phases-I & II*	*OB as on 1st April of the year*	*Fund Release by the Centre*	*Misc Receipt*	*Total Funds*	*Total Cumulative Expenditure*	*%age of Exp. Against Total Funds*
Arunachal Pradesh	1+2=3	—	105.38	—	105.38	—	—
Assam	7+6=13	15377.26	35091.87	7047.58	57516.71	10887.64	18.93
Manipur	1+2=3	—	1088.13	—	1088.13	—	—
Meghalaya	2+3=5	509.14	3687.12	23.13	4219.39	2109.91	50.01
Mizoram	2+2=4	1211.10	652.96	4.50	1868.56	1517.76	81.23
Nagaland	1+4=5	140.33	2166.59	—	2306.92	36.14	1.57
Sikkim	1+2=3	710.98	—	—	710.98	94.58	13.3
Tripura	1+2=3	711.89	12451.45	637.37*	13800.71	2479.49	17.97
NE Total	15+21=36	18660.70	55243.50	7712.58	81616.78	17125.52	20.98

*(i) Rs. 421.77 lakhs release of last year but received during current year.
(ii) Rs. 185.60 lakhs release from state government during current year.
(iii) Misc. recived Rs. 30.00 laskhs.

Source: www.nrega, nic.in

Table 26.5 depicts the financial performance of National Rural Employment Guarantee Act in North Eastern Region during 2007-08. Out of 200 rural districts identified in first phase, 15 districts from Northeast India have been selected of which Assam has 7 districts Mizoram and Meghalaya have 2 districts each and the rest have one district each. In the second phase another 130 districts have been identified of which 21 district are selected from the North East.

Finding of the study

In the foregoing discussion the different aspects of rural development programmes have been examined and analyzed at length. However, some of the main observations emerged from the analysis are briefly stated below:

- Improper selection of beneficiaries due to absence of baseline surveys. Involvement of political leaders and bureaucratic red-tapism in the process of selection of beneficiaries.
- Coordination among the functionaries of rural development at various levels has been found weak. Horizontal and vertical linkages among functionaries at different levels have not been satisfactory. Moreover, in some cases, staff for implementation of the programme has been found to be inadequate.
- Bank branches are located far away from the village. Most of the nationalized banks are concentrated in urban areas. A few regional rural banks and Grameen Banks function in the remote places of the region.
- Admissible financial assistance for the promotion and development of rural areas were inadequate.
- Law and order situation of the region affect the smooth sailing of rural development programmes. There is wide variation in law and order front but a volatile situation in one state is perceived as a problem in the entire region.
- Most of the rural development funds released by the Central Government were delayed. Again loan sanction procedure is time consuming and it disables the beneficiaries in the process of rural development.
- Good governance is lacking in the region. This leads to lower growth and investment for economic development of the region.
- We need better public administration to maximize the impact of public expenditure.
- Rural infrastructure is poor and hinders implementation of rural development programmes. The money spent by the Centre has no reflections in infrastructure development.
- Inability to utilize the allocated fund and improper use of allocated fund is another concern. "Considering the volume of expenditure, nothing much is visible on the ground" said Jairam Ramesh, the Union Minister of State for Commerce.
- Among the three rural development programmes selected for the study the performance of Pradhan Mantri Gram

Sadak Yojana is found to be the best followed by Swarnjayanti Gram Swarozgar Yojana.

- The objectives of self reliance and peoples participation is very much lacking under SGSY schemes. Most of the SHGs under the scheme were established without understanding the vary concept of SHG and its significance role in the formation of micro-enterprise units.

Suggestions

Inspite of all these shortcomings, it would be fair to say that rural development programmes such as SGSY, PMGSY and NREGS were instrumental in laying the foundations for the rural economy and employment opportunities in the region. To lessen the problems of rural development programmes following suggestions are made:

- A well thought out plan for rural infrastructure is the basic and urgent need of the hour in the region to faster attainment of rural development.
- Harnessing of the central non-lapsable pool for supporting projects to build infrastructure and to undertake other economic development programmes in more viable and transparent manner.
- Harnessing of the Central grants for development of info-tech infrastructure and utilize them in right direction.
- Development of agro-based, horticulture-based, forest based small scale industries and eco-tourism to boost up the rural economy of northeast India.
- Development of floriculture and mushroom culture for direct and indirect employment opportunities to rural masses with minimum investment and less gestation period.
- Use the export development fund for setting up marketing infrastructure. More Special Economic Zones should be established in addition to the one for Nagaland. This will again provide employment opportunities to large chunk of rural unemployed youth of the region.
- Change in educational policy and technical education should replace conventional form of education to create

self employment opportunities for the unemployed educated youth of the region.

- Entrepreneurial development education is the need of the hour. This will provide job not only to the entrepreneur but also to the job-seekers of the region.

Conclusions

The skeptics would always apprehend that all the State Government machineries of the region would be neither capable of nor free from corruption in implementing the projects drawing resources from the Centre. The Union Minister of State for Commerce Jairam Ramesh stated "corruption, siphoning and black hole is present inspite of massive funding by the Centre". But the different State Government of the region must disillusion such skepticism. Moreover it is necessary that before implementation of any strategy for rural development either SGSY, PMGSY or NREGS, evaluation must be made so as to choose best strategies for best possible outcome. For attaining these, a firm commitment, strong will of the people, transparency of the local government specially the Panchayati Raj institutions and district administration and a long-term policy vision of the State Government, North Eastern Council, Department of North Eastern Region (DONER) and Central Government are necessary.

27

Women Development & Sex Ratio: Treading between North and North East India

PAULAVI DAS

Social norms, religion, religious ideologies, eco-system, class position and development generally determine women role and status all over the world. The social system exhibits such grave disparities in each of these aspects that it is almost impossible to depict women's role and status in a single statement. The traditional role is not identical in all societies. The position accorded to women in a particular culture or community differs across the region, culture and level of socio-economic development. One of the most trustworthy and reliable indexes of the state of a society is the position that women occupy. The role of women is determined by their role as wives and mother, the institution of marriage together with that of the family do offer a most genuine opportunity to define their position.

Veena Majumdar (1986) says that the question of women as an issue started in India from 19th century onwards when social reformers questioned the growing inequalities and the major evils of social customs like prohibitions of widow remarriage, child marriage, discrimination of women in education, purdah system, dowry etc.

In 1990 Amrtya Sen coined the term "missing girls and women" to refer to the millions of girls and women who are missing from the world due to sexual violence and discrimination. The 2001 census of India indicated there were over 35 million fewer females than males in India and the sex ratio had dramatically widened in northern India. If we compare between 1991 and 2001 census reports, it reveals an increasing 'masculinization' (i.e. a disproportionate number of males to females in a given population) in sex ratio. The 2001 census of India also reflects that the phenomenon has reached high proportion in states that had no prior history or practices of female discrimination against girls. The alarming nature of the report is the drastic decline of the sex ratio due to several reasons.[1]

The killing of women exist in various forms in societies the world over. However, the Indian Society displays some unique and particularly brutal versions, such as dowry deaths and sati. Female feticides are extreme manifestations of violence against women. Female foetuses are selectively aborted after pre-natal sex determination to avoid the birth of girls. Because of selective abortion between 35 and 40 millions girls and women are missing from the Indian population.[2]

The adverse sex ratio has been linked with the low status of women in patriarchy communities. The status of women in a society can be determined by their education, heath, and economic role, presence in the professions and management, and decision-making power within the family. Patriarchy in both Hindus and Muslims communities gives very low right to women. In Hindu society, preference for the male child is deeply enshrined in belief and practice.[3]

Ramayana and Manu Smriti represent the ideal women as obedient and submissive, and always needing the care of a male: first father, than husband and than son. The birth of a son is regarded essential in Hinduism and many prayers and lavish offerings are made in temples in the hope of having a male child. Modern medical technology is used in the service of this religion-driven devaluing of women and girls.

Abortion was legalized in 1971 (Medical Termination of Pregnancy Act) to strengthen humanitrain values. (Pregnancy can be aborted if it is a result of sexual assult, contraceptive failure, if the baby would be severally handicapped or if the mother is incapable of bearing a healthy child). But soon it began to used for determining the sex of the baby. This technology gained popularity and is now available in some of the most remote rural areas. These techniques are now being used for sex determination with the intention of abortion if the foetus turns out to be female. The women are frequently presuerised to undergo such procedure. Many women suffer from psychological trauma because of forcibly undergoing repeated abortions.

India is one of the few countries in the world where males out numbered females. The sex ratio of Indian population in the country has shown a secular declining trend except some marginal increase in the Census of 1951 and 1981.

The sex ratio in 2001was 933, six points higher then the sex ratio of 972 recorded in 1991. If we consider the Census Reports in 1921 it was 955, 1931-950, 1941-945, 1951-946, 1961-941, 1971-932, 1981-945, 1991-927, and in 2001, it was 933.

As per the Census Figures of 1921–1951 accross different geographical zones the sex ratio is found very low particularly in North West Zone in India. In 1921, the sex ratio at all-India level was 956, but in North West Zone, it was 853.

Table 27.1 Sex Ratio

Zone	*1921*	*1931*	*1941*	*1951*
North India	909	904	907	910
East India	986	967	951	945
South India	1011	1010	1001	999
West India	941	941	941	938
Central India	972	968	966	973
North West India	853	863	871	883
India	956	951	946	947

The above table shows that there was a marginal increase in the general sex ratio, it continued to be significantly adverse to women. According to 2001 Census Report, the sex ratio has gone down to 933.

Now if we concentrate on the situation of North East India, we find there is a vast change in sex ratio, which is much better than all-India average. The following table shows the ratio of North East India according to 2001 Census Report.

In North East India, the influence of Christianity is much more pervasive than in Northern part of India. The most important and interesting social system that exist in Meghalaya is matrilineal system. This system is prevalent among the tribes of Meghalaya. This Matrilineal system is also found in Malabar and in some parts of South India. Three features characterize matrilineal Societies. First, Inheritance is traced through the mother. Second, Matrilocal residence in which the groom has to stay with his wife after marriage. Third, Inheritance of the property through the female.[4]

Table 27.2 Population Data Sheet in Respect of North Eastern State of India: 2001 Census of India including Sikkim

Sl. No.	*States*	*Total Population*	*Males*	*Females*	*Sex Ratio*
1.	Arunachal Pradesh	1,091,117	573,951	517,166	901
2.	Assam	26,638,407	13,787,799	12,850,608	932
3.	Manipur	2,388,634	1,207,338	1,181,296	978
4.	Meghalaya	2,306,069	1,167,840	1,138,229	975
5.	Mizoram	891,058	459,783	431,275	938
6.	Nagaland	1,988,636	1,041,686	946,950	909
7.	Sikkim	540,493	288,217	252,276	875
8.	Tripura	3,191,168	1,636,138	1,555,030	950
	Total	39,035,582	20,162,752	18,872,830	7,458

(DIPR of Meghalaya Shillong for providing me the data).

Matrilineal system is one, which traces linage through the mother. It is an important contributor to the cultural pattern and social system of the tribes in Meghalaya. The entire tribe has it's decent from a common ancestress, similarly, the member of a clan are supposed to be the off springs of one ancestress, strictly matrilineal one who have a common right over ancestral property. It is also a religious unit. The property is handed over to the nearest matrilineal kin. The youngest daughter is theoretically the repository of the property. She is supposed to shelter its young, orphans, the sick and the handicapped. Therefore, the youngest daughter has many obligations both social and economical. The woman manages the property and on her death, the clan makes the decisions regarding the management, transfer of property etc.[5]

The North East women are more developed then other States. Women are more in trade than men are. These trends are not only observed in rural areas but also in urban areas. A recent study revealed that 57.5 per cent of rural tribal women are actively involved in economic activities. The picture of women in trade is in sharp contrast to the picture we usually see in non-tribal areas or among tribal women in the patriarchal system. In a tribal community, women enjoy a relatively high status and role compared to the non-tribal counterparts. They are treated more humanly. There is virtually no female infanticide. There is no bride burning. They play more active role in rituals, economy and in family affairs.

The scheduled tribes are generally socio-economically more back word. Naturally women are also quite back ward. However, North East women are busy in different economic activities and provide a good economic support in the family. Women enjoy a position of unusual dignity and importance in the society.

The Northern part of India is purely dominated by patriarchy, which is define as "the system of social structure and practices in which men dominate, oppress and exploit women". In this system, women are unequal to men. It is a system in which masculinity confers a privileged position of power and authority in the society. In this model of patriarchy, old men held authority, younger males were subservient, and women were excluded. Early feminist theories used the term strategically to highlight men's dominance over women in the private (the family) and the public (work, politics, culture) spheres. Now, however, it is generally used to refer to the structural dominance in the cultural, economic and social position of men in relation to women.

The Northern States of India like Punjab, Chandigarh, Haryana, Himachal Pradesh, Rajasthan, Delhi, Bihar, and Uttar Pradesh follow patriarchy and have a very low rate of sex ratio. Prejudice against daughters is a very common form of subjugation. Pre-natal sex selection, selective abortion of female foetus, female infanticide and systematic neglect and ill-treatment towards daughters, wives and mothers are also very common in patriarchal societies. Every wife must be able to present a few children to her husband and one of the children must be a son, so that the male line may continue. Thus, the blessing comes to her as *'shata putra bhava'*(may thou be the mother of hundred sons).

The inhabitant of Punjab, who pioneered the green revolution in the last century, are now heading for a devastating economic and social fall in the near future due to sharply declining sex ratio. The reasons of 'son mania' are socio-cultural, economic and political ones. The predominant cause is the agrarian set up associated with the male ownership of land and the social infrastructure sustained by Punjab. The beautiful Chandigarh city is also having the lowest sex ratio in the country despite its high literacy rate of 81.76 per cent. The worst situation is also found in some other places like Ludhiana (824), Fategarh Sahib (851) and Patiala (864).[6]

Haryana, is a North Indian developed state but the sex ratio has gone down from 879 to 820, and in many areas it has gone down to dismal 640 women per 1000 males. In many villages young men do not find women to marry which has resulted in polygamous marriages. The Hindustan Times recently reported that young girls from Assam and West Bengal are being kidnapped and sold for marriage in neighbouring states. Teenage suicide among girls have gone up and resulted in violence against women.

The economics of son preference has a major role in low valuation and neglect of female children in Rajasthan. Every woman must produce a male child who would be the future head of the family. Women are either less keen to bear girl child, or are goaded, coerced and encouraged by their families to flush the female foetus down the drain. As a result, number of girls are decreasing day by day. In a marital situation, the groom's families are now offering to bear the cost of finding a suitable bride for their sons. "There are no girls. If there is one in a house, the father is like a king. He can demand anything," said Prahlad Singh, the head of Bhorki village in Rajasthan.

The above fait clearly shows that the North-Weastrn Zone has a very low sex ratio. Prof. Ashish Bose gave a new acronym to brand the above mentioned states where there is a sharp decrease in the sex ratio of the child population as DEMARU—daughters killers (D stand for daughter, E for Elimination in English and MARU for killing in Hindi).

Table 27.3 Population of India 2001

States	*Total*	*Male*	*Female*
	1,027,015,247	531,277,078	495,738,169
Bihar	82878796	43153964	39724832
Haryana	21082989	11327658	9755331
Himachal Pr.	6077248	3085256	2991992
Madhya Pradesh	60385118	31456873	28928245
Maharashtra	96752247	50334270	46477977
Rajasthan	56473122	29381657	27091465
U.P	166052859	87466301	78586558
Uttaranchal	8479562	4316401	4163161

After comparering the sex ratio of North India and North East India, I found, women are more developed in North Eastern region. One of the biggest reasons is Matrilineal culture, where female babies and daughters get adequate attention of the parents with respect to education and health care. Women enjoy more autonomy not only when compared to Northern India but also compare to all women in India as a whole. All the tribal societies of Tripura are patriarchal in nature and though the mother has no legal right to property, the opinion of the mother is held in high esteem.[7]

Today North-Eastern women participation in outdoor socio-economic activities is gradually increasing. Their participation in social services has also gone up. Greater participation of women in social services encouraged the establishment of various organizations among women. In recent years, the need to involve women in the National development processes has been increasingly recognized. Many women organizations are now working towards achiving this goal, and specific programmes for improving the condition of women have been undertaken by both National and International Agencies. There has been a fairly rapid expansion of skill and professional training facilities for women. Attempts are also being made to involve rural women in cottage and handicraft industries through co-operatives and to give them an opportunity to earn. Now it is the duty of the activist, social reformers, NGO and the Governoment to take initiative for the protection and progress of the women and the Matrilineal system of North East India should not be excluded from such initiative.

NOTES

1. IDRC Contribution, Project No. 101429-2005-06.

2&3. International Humanist & Ethical Union/Female Foeticide in India-2004.

4&5. 'Women & Society' M. Vishwanathan. Printwell Pub. Jaipur

6. "Skewed Sex ratio in Punjab: A demographic catastrophe" Singh D., Kumar A., Vij. K., GMC. Chandigarh.

7. 'Tribal Women in India—Sharma'. S.P, Mittal A.C. Radha Pub.

BIBLIOGRAPHY

1. Low Aline and Tremayne Soraya, (2001). "Secred Custodians of the Earth" Berhahn Books New York, Oxford.
2. N. Ruwanpura, Kanchana (2006). "Matrilineal Communities, Patraichal Realities" Pub. Zubaan, New Delhi.
3. Das, Gupta Pranab Kr. (1984). Life and Culture of Matrilineal Tribe of Meghalaya, Inter-India Publication, New Delhi.
4. Vishnanathan Maithili, Women and Society vol-III, Printwell, Jaipur 1994.
5. Ghaadially Rehana, (1988). Women in Indian Society Vol-III, Sage Publication, New Delhi.
6. Goswami, U.S. (1993). Woman in Man's World, M.D. Publications Pvt. Ltd., New Delhi.
7. Bhattacharjee J.B., (1989). Sequences of Development in N.E. India, Pub.-Omsons, New Delhi.
8. Bhandari, J.B. (1996). Kingship and Family in the North East, Cosmo Publication, New Delhi.
9. Chattopadhay, (1985). Tribal Institution of Meghalaya, Spectrum Publication, Guwahati.
10. Shadap Namita Catherini, (1981). The Orgine and early history of the Khasi Synteng People, Pub. Firma KLM Pvt. Ltd., Kolkata.
11. Roy Kalpana, Encyclopedia of violence against Women and Dowry Death in India.
12. Anmol Publication Pvt. Ltd. New Delhi (1999).
13. Ahnja, Ram (1998). Violence against Women, Rawat Publication, Jaipur, New Delhi.
14. Kahol Yudhislatir, (2003). Violence against Women, Refree Press, Delhi.
15. K. Sinha, (2003). Meghalaya Publication Division Daryaganj, Delhi.
16. H. Bareh, (1967). The History of Culture of the Khasi People, by the Author.
17. Ehrenfels, Matrilineal Civil in India, *The Hindu*, April 27 1952.
18. Ehrenfels, The comparative study of Matrilineal Civilization in India. Mimeographed.
19. Pathak Manisha, Commission for Gender Sensitization.
20. Tharbhai. L., Women studies in India, Pub. APH, Corp. New Delhi.

28

Empowerment of Women Through Information and Communication Technology

JAHITHA BEGUM and M. VAKKIL

ICT encompasses all those technologies that enable the handling of information and facilitate different forms of communication among human actors, between human beings and electronic systems and among electronic systems (Hamelink:1997). This definition entails two parts: 'technology' and 'information and communication'. Technology is the means to serve the goals of information handling and communication. Now we call this age as information age and the society as information society. Various apparatuses, including those for handling information and communication are the mechanisms for the 'circulation and accumulation' of knowledge. It is the new asset, new source of power and a new imperative. ICT can immensely contribute to empowerment of the women in all aspects. This paper deals with the issue of women empowerment through ICT.

Empowerment of Women

There are various ways to define empowerment, but we focus on several aspects most relevant to information and communication. It is the transformation of consciousness that seeks to cultivate women's sense of control over their own lives. Secondly, it is the collective strength emerging through organization and strengthening of networks and alliance among women on the basis of shared interest. Finally, it is the ability to mobilize the women themselves around self-defined concerns and priorities. (Kabeer:1996). More and more women are getting involved in career building in the communication sector, but few have been able to reach the position of decision-making level or to serve on governing boards and bodies that influence media policy. This leads to lack of gender sensitivity in media. Women should be empowered through enhancing their skills, knowledge and access to information technology. Bringing in more women into decision-making, programming, research and promoting women media will undoubtedly progress the nation.

The establishment of local, national and international women's media networks has contributed to global information dissemination, exchange of views and support to women groups active in media work. The development of information and communication technologies, specially the internet, has provided improved communication opportunities to the women and girls and has enabled an increasing number of them to knowledge sharing and networking. Electronic platforms can also be combined with other communication medium to improve the lives of the grassroots women in the society. It includes strategic alliances with women's radio, video and print media networks.

The role of women is key to socio-economic development and, therefore, their participation in all spheres of life has to be promoted. ICT could be used to empower women, improve gender equality, enhance women's participation in development and narrow down the gender gap. Increasing education and literacy and creating employment in the ICT sector can make a change in the scenario. ICT can also be used as a powerful tool for mobilization and organization of women. It can be used in the primary and secondary levels of education for girls. Many developing countries are beginning to understand the positive role of ICT in poverty reduction in the rural and urban areas. Using ICT to create small and medium enterprises has resulted in numerous Internet cafes, phone shops and community radio stations. However, these small and medium enterprises are owned and operated largely by men. The women are excluded from this. Access to ICT can provide easy access to market for the products of the women entrepreneurs. But unfortunately, large section of women in the developing countries has still limited access to ICT. Efforts need to be made for increasing the women in policy, regulatory bodies and in advocacy in effective and powerful ways to achieve competitive advantage in the ICT sector. With increased participation women can reflect the gender issues in ICT resource planning and administration. Some nations, such as India, have been able to successfully empower the poor including the women and children through increased ICT use. As a result of implementing ICT at all levels of the Indian Government, citizens now enjoy increased income, better health-care, improved education and training and better access to job opportunities. ICT has also enabled better access to government services, enhanced communication both within and without the countries, maximized private sector opportunities, increased agricultural productivity and improved better-access to markets.

Ways to Enhance Women Participation in the ICT Sector

Women are getting lesser advantage in the process of building information and knowledge in society. Structural inequalities in the society (including lack of income, social opportunities, time constraint and bias against girl-child education) and other gender based discriminations are responsible for this. These should be resisted. In the developing countries such inequalities are very conspicuous.

ICT can be used as a tool to promote broader equity by increasing women's access to the democratic institutions and the political resources, education, business and income generation opportunities. Gender equity should be explicit in ICT policy. Gender awareness should be built into the entire policy process—from development, implementation to evaluation. The policy makers need to be aware of the different social contexts in which men and women live. Data need to be in place to measure the desparate impacts based on gender. Gender equity in ICT goes beyond women's access to ICT to include wider economic opportunities, new innovations and decision-making.

ICT can be a powerful engine for increased participation of women in the democratic process and can ensure greater representation of women in the institution of governance, in private sector companies and in the civil society organizations. At the same time ICT can be promoted for better economic development and income generation activities. Location-neutral ICT can offer women greater opportunities for work without leaving their communities. (In the Indian social context, women working in the internet café's is considered socially undesirable). Credit and digital payment facilities and online business opportunities for women business owners need be created. For this, women focused campaign is required. Intellectual capabilities of the women in the field of ICT should be harnessed and gender component in ICT education in classrooms and in educational institutions need be incorporated. Female role models in training and instruction need be encouraged. Affirmative action is needed in order to bring the women in the senior management roles and in the regulatory bodies. The policy makers should build an inclusive information society promoting full and active participation of women.

Strategy building for extension of ICT and ICT connectivity in the rural areas have been stipulated in the 'Bharat Nirman' project of Government of India. The task is now to make it inclusive and target the rural women leaders who can effectively work for poverty eradication and improved governance.

ICT and infrastructure in the Northeast India is yet to strengthen and spread widely. Weak infrastructure and restrictive ICT connectivity in this region needs be addressed adequately so as to mainstream the women of this region and empower them. Northeastern India has quite a number of vantage points. The youth community of the region is better equipped with English language, communication skill in English language, the girls of this region are more exposed to public sphere and corporate sector like NASSCOM is interested to promote this industry in the region. The DoNER Ministry has earmarked a good budget for promotion of ITC. Concerted efforts need be done to tap the dormant human resources of this region and to bring the women at the forefront of ICT boom in this region.

BIBLIOGRAPHY

1. Chen, M.A. (1995). 'Engendering World Conferences: The International Women's Movement and United Nations'. Third World Quarterly, Vol 15 (3).

2. Fortier, F. (1999). "Virtual Community, Real Struggle—Seeking Alternatives for Democratic Networking. Unpublished.
3. Hamelink, C. (1997). 'New Information and Communication Technologies, Social Development and Cultural Change' Discussion Paper 86, UNRISD, Geneva.
4. Henwood F., (1993). 'Establishing Gender Perspectives on Information Technology: Problems, Issues and Opportunities in Green, E., Owen, J. & Pain D (eds), Gendered Design? Information Technology and Office Systems, Taylor Francis, London.
5. Herman, C. (1999). Women and the Internet, in Liberating Cyberspace—Civil Liberties, Human Rights and the Internet' Edited by The National Council for Civil Liberties, Pluto Press, London.
6. Kabeer, N. (1996). Empowerment from Below: Learning from the Grassroots, Revised Realities, Gender Hierarchies in Development Thought, New Delhi.
7. Kole, E., (1998). Whose Empowerment? http://www.yorku.ca/research/dkproj/crit-ict/ek1.html.
8. Kole, E., (2000). Connecting Women from Developing Countries to the Internet: Searching for an Appropriate Paradigm, Faculty of Social and Behavoural Sciences, Univessity of Amsterdam,
9. Schiller, H., (1996). Information Inequality : The Deepening Social Crisis in America, New York, Routledge.
10. Wacjman, J., (1991). Feminism Confronts Technology, Polity Press, Cambridge.
11. Women Action 2000 (2000a). Alternative Assessment of Women and Media Based on NGO Review of Sec. J., Beijing Platform for Action', Coordinated by ISIS International—Manila on Behalf of WomenAction-2000. http://www.womenaction.org/csw44/44/altrepeng.html.

29

Ecosystem Enrichment and Livelihood Management: An Endeavour for Synthesis towards Symbiotic Sustainability

KAUSTUBH LAHIRI

Introduction

Sustainable Development is basically an approach that *inter alia,* permits continuing improvement in the present quality of life at a *negotiated intensity* of resource use, thereby allowing future generation's access to functional stock of productive natural capital. This can enhance opportunities for improving their quality of life. Symbiotic Sustainability is a planning effort for building community confidence to adapt to the *negotiation* for an alternative form of resource utilization either by *Proliferation* or by *Substitution* for Sustainable Development. ' Sustainable development requires meeting the basic needs of all and extending to all the opportunity to satisfy their aspiration for a better Life' (WECD 1987)

Here the emphasis is laid on identifying the Ecological Components of a particular geographical region for exploring their potentiality towards discerning the objectives for development planning. It is believed that a harmony between communities and the Ecosystem can only be procured and secured if their livelihood is not threatened due to the conventional Conservation Policies.

Environmental Sustainability: A Profile of Thematic Concepts

The Ecological Dimension of Sustainability focuses on the overall viability and health of ecosystem, in terms of a comprehensive, multi-scale, dynamic, hierarchical measure of resilience, vigor and organization of Ecosystem. (Costzana 2000).

Resilience

Resilience is critically Important (Holling 1973). It implies ability of an ecosystem to persist despite external shocks. Resilience is determined by the amount of change / disruption that causes an ecosystem to switch from one system to another. Petersen, Allen and Holling (1998) stated that resilience of a given ecosystem depends on the continuity of related ecological processes at both larger and smaller spatial scales.

Vigor

Vigor is associated with the Primary Productivity of an Ecosystem. It is analogous to Output and Growth as indicators of dynamism in an economic system. **Organization** depends on both complexity and structure of an ecological and biological system. The different paradigms of 'Weak' and 'Strong' sustainability stem from two different perspectives. **Strong Sustainability** is rooted to the assumption that the economy is an open subsystem of the finite and non-growing global Ecosystem. It implies the strong requirement of balancing the depletion of non-renewable resources and therefore underlines the emergency of strengthening the ecosystem foundations. **Weak Sustainability** is an integrative approach. In principle it is related to ' Solow Sustainability'. Here the emphasis is laid on maintaining the total value of aggregate Livelihood Activity and Ecological set up and subsequently assume a constant value for generations to come. Weak Sustainability requires that a suitably defined value of the services of Ecological and Economic stock be maintained.

For all practical reasons the concept of 'Weak Sustainability' is affordable in grassroots Indian realty because the nation can not harbour a ' Stationary – State' Economy as perceived by Strong Sustainability. Notwithstanding preservation of ecosystem resilience, the physical stock of Ecological components at the level of regeneration potentiality can be abandoned altogether, particularly for the North East India. Planning for sustainability is required to incorporate a method for appraisal of stress on Ecosystem Resilience and here the adopted purpose is Resource valuation in Utilization Perspective.

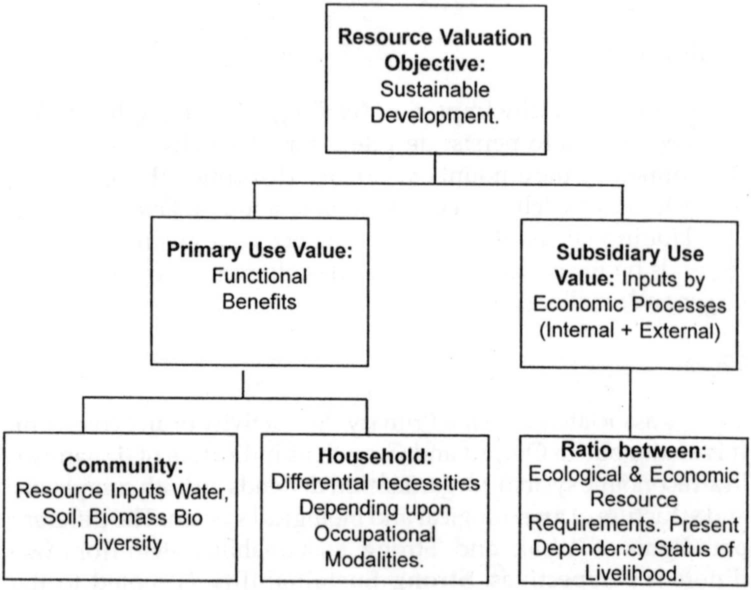

Fig. 29.1 Resource Valuation in Utility Orientation Perspective

Implicit in this framework is aggregate Natural and Man generated Capitals and their comparative roles in producing the existing Land Use Pattern. Natural Capital or Ecosystem Support System is associated with Nutrient Cycle & Climatic Parameters determining the Resilience & the stability of the Vigor and Organization of the Ecosystem. The distinction between 'Recurring Resources' that are being utilized regularly and that are being occasionally harvested is also critically significant. Man Generated Capital is rooted in Skill Formation driven by level of technological infusion and social organization.

Physical transformation of rural livelihood by directing planning towards sustainability dimension can involve both production and consumption. In Indian context the concept of Common Pool Resources is a dependable indicator for this purpose.

Common Pool Resources: [CPRs]

In order to evaluate resource potentialities in broad perspective of Resource availability provided by Ecological attributes, the concept of Common Pool Resource is significant in the context of rural communities. The essential components of CPRs are fuel wood, fodder, crop wastes, cow dung, organic manure, small timber and other products that are derived from the bark, seeds, flowers, fruits of trees as well as water for drinking, cooking, and irrigation and local fisheries. The existence of imperfect factor markets results in an intimate link between the rural economy and it's natural resource base [Vira 2007]. The Common Pool Approach in resource evaluation assumes additional importance to organize a safety-net program in the case of natural disaster.

NSSO has adopted following Dimensions for a survey of 78,990 Rural Households in 5114 Villages (54th Round):

- de jure - legal status of the land ; the boundary of the villages held by Panchayats or a community of the Villages.
- de facto –the extent to which rural households use such Resources, actual utilization Pattern.

Common Pool Resources [CPRs]: NSSO, 1999.

The Broad Indian Frame.

1. Share of CPRs in total Geographical area - 15%

Table 29.1 Common Pool Land Resources { Selected states }

(Total CPR land / Total Geographical Area)

Serial No.	*States*	*Ratio*
1.	Sikkim+	0.14
2.	Tripura+	0.01
3.	Nagaland+	0.08
4.	Assam+	0.07
5.	West Bengal*	0.02
6.	Himachal Pradesh±	0.12
7.	Punjab±	0.01
8.	Orissa*	0.11

+North East States; * Eastern India States; ± for Comparison Purpose.

2. Common Pool Land Resource/ Household - 0.31ha.
3. Common Pool Land resources / Persons - 0.06 ha.
4. Reduction in CPR land in last 5 years (per 1000 ha) – 19ha (0.38% / annum)

Table 29.2 Information on the utilization pattern of CRPs by Households. Category: Fuel wood.

Population Size of Villages.	*% of Households*	*Common Land/ Household [Ratio]*	*% of Household reporting*		
			Fuel Wood Collection	*Fuel Wood Use*	*Fuel Wood Sale.*
< 100	1.4	6.28	87.7	93.7	8.0
101 – 200	1.1	0.56	71.3	78.9	0.6
201-600	11.2	0.55	52.8	66.5	2.3
601-1200	19.7	0.31	48.4	64.9	1.3
1201-2000	19.6	0.19	44.8	61.7	0.9
2001-5000	32.3	0.15	40.8	60.9	0.6
5000+	14.7	0.09	37.0	55.3	0.3

NSSO (1999)

The First Two categories are important in the context of North East India but the striking distinction is associated with the sharp fall in availability of common land/household from first to second categories. The selection of fuel wood posses the rationale that its is still the reliable source of rural energy. Table 29.3 provides ample evidence to it.

Table 29.3 Percentage Share of total Household energy consumption in rural area in India.

Source of	*Income Group (Rs. Per annum per Household)*				
Energy	Upto 3000	3001-6000	6001-12000	12001-18000	>18000
Traditional	86	85	83	84	82
Modern	14	15	17	16	18

Ramsey (2000)

For North East the numerical national value associated with traditional category in all certainty is bound to rise due to poor accessibility if not poverty.

Table 29.4 Growth Dynamics of North East : Assessing Macro spatial Economic Impact on Ecology Infra Structure.

Criterion I : Implied Annual Growth Rate [Rural & Urban] for North East States.

States	*Implied Annual Growth Rate (%) [2002]*					
	Overall		*Rural*		*Urban*	
	TA	*NW*	*TA*	*NW*	*TA*	*NW*
Arunachal Pradesh	0.5	0.5	0.1	0.1	0.0	6.1
Assam	2.7	2.7	2.7	2.7	1.4	1.5
Manipur	3.0	2.9	1.3	1.2	6.1	6.1
Meghalaya	7.8	7.8	8.0	8.0	8.1	8.1
Mizoram	10.8	10.8	6.3	6.2	11.1	11.2
Nagaland	14.8	14.9	17.6	17.6	9.3	9.5
Sikkim	0.1	0.0	-1.2	-1.3	9.8	9.7
Tripura	0.7	0.7	-0.1	-0.1	0.0	-0.1

TA? Total Asset; NW? Net Worth. Source: 2002 AIDIS.

The anomaly between Rural and Urban growth in terms of TA & NW is potentially alarming as rapid urbanization implies enormous pressure on natural ecosystems depriving rural habitats from ecosystem sponsored livelihood sources.

Table 29.5 *Criterion II* : A Comparative Annual Growth Rate of Employment and Enterprises. In North East India[1998-2005]

States	*Annual Growth Rate (Employment) %*⁺			*Annual Growth Rate (Enterprise) %*		
	Urban	*Rural*	*Combined*	*Urban*	*Rural*	*Combined*
Arunachal Pradesh	3.07	6.02	4.17	3.65	7.08	4.74
Assam	2.08	5.61	3.19	6.62	6.46	6.57
Manipur	3.24	1.28	2.25	4.46	2.92	3.96
Meghalaya	5.05	3.02	4.12	6.48	5.05	5.98
Mizoram	4.96	3.45	3.91	8.40	10.39	9.60
Nagaland	1.95	0.02	0.75	6.05	1.22	3.64
Sikkim	6.41	4.32	5.52	8.39	1.16	5.83
Tripura	5.84	3.71	5.07	9.85	6.37	8.79

Source: Fifth Economic Census 2005.

⁺ in Agricultural (excluding Crop Production and Plantation) and Non-Agricultural Enterprises.

Criterion II becomes self-explanatory in substantiating Criterion I and in reinforcing the uncertainty in preserving the resilience of North East Ecosystem particularly the precious and delicate Biodiversity components. Criterion III would provide an insight to certain key indicators exhibiting the Economic Status of Rural Communities in the North East.

Table 29.6 *Criterion III* : Selected Key Rural Indicators.

States	*Poverty Status Rural*	*Cultivators as % of Total workers*	*Av size of Operational Holding(in ha)*
Mizoram	*Moderately Poor 10-20%*	*77.8 (4.96)*	*1.4*
Manipur	Poor 20-30%	53.5 (3.24)	1.2
Arunachal Pradesh	Very Poor > 30%	68.3 (3.07)	3.7
Assam		44.0 (2.08)	1.3
Meghalaya.		54.5 (5.05)	1.8
Nagaland		73.0 (1.95)	6.8
Tripura		31.4(5.84)	1.0

( )Annual Growth Rate of Rural Workforce.

Source : Professor (Dr) **T.B. Lahiri.** (2004) & Fifth Economic Census.

The Vulnerable Ecosystem

An appraisal of Criterion II and III shows that farming as an occupation has attained a stationary level. As discussed, unlike farming, the non farming enterprise depends on non recurring elements of Ecosystem. Therefore both the recurring and auxiliary new Ecosystem elements are depleting.

The condition is turning more precarious by renewed thrust of urbanization. Urban Culture, essentially not consistent with traditional rural socio – ethnic tradition, demands those bio-ingredients promising much higher return would inflict new multi dimensional strains on already stressed Ecosystem. For North East States, insulated in historical perspective, Social Ecological contradictions can engulf along with Physical Ecological disturbances.

In a regime of Climatic Uncertainty, either appearing from Global warming or Global Dimming, Rainfall regime in North East India is suffering from regular deficiency. The map below shows the rainfall status of a designated day within High Monsoon Phase.

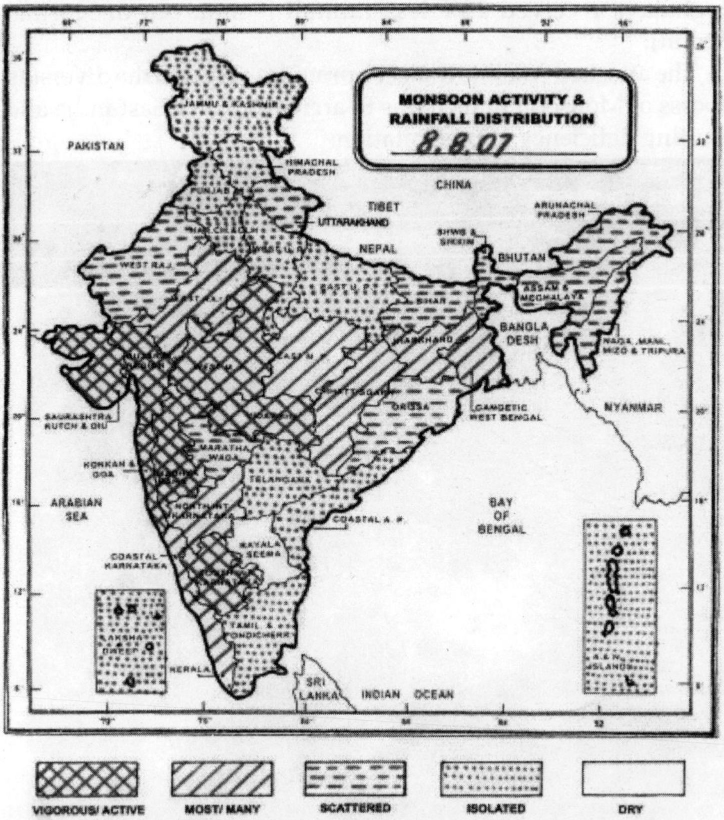

Data source: IMD, Government of India.

Rainfall Distribution

Percentage of Departure of rainfall from June 01, 2007 to July 03, 2007.

Region Wise Departure:

- North Western India (+19),

- Central India (+ 43),
- Peninsular India (+50),
- North East India (- 23).

In this deemed High Monsoon activity Phase, Assam and Meghalaya received 28% less rainfall [96mm out of Normal 132mm].

The attached Satellite Imagery provides access to the diversion process of Monsoon Branch due to arrive to North East India and resulting deficiency in precipitation.

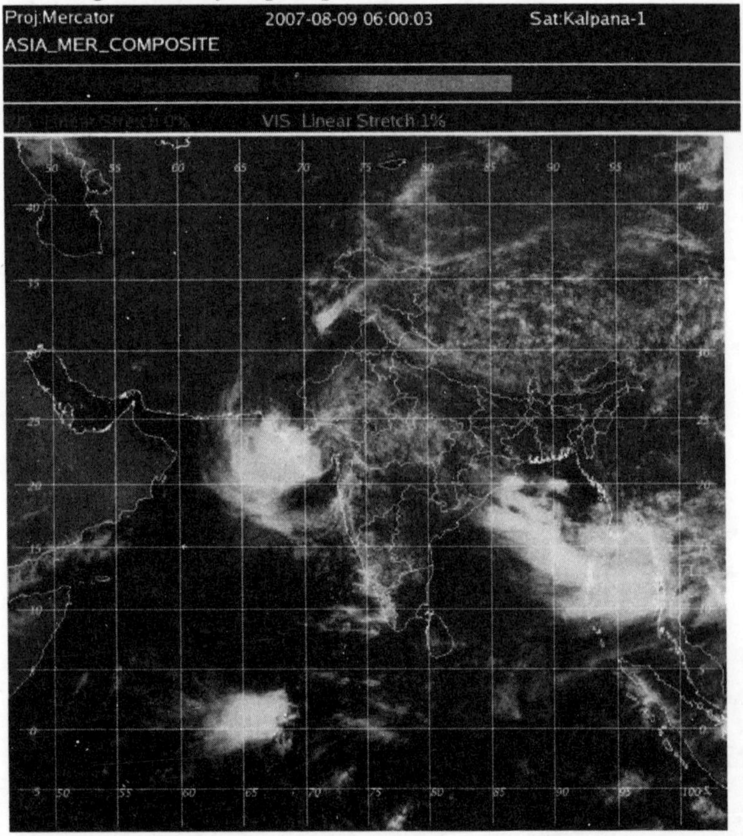

Source: IMD, Government of India.

One of the plausible reasons behind such diversion may be attached to growing Petrochemical and Chemical Industries in the

Bengal and Orissa Coast along with function of the existing refineries.

Recommendations

Priority I

Appraisal of land as a utility resource in the context of their production capability in comparison to their potentiality status to serve the spiraling demand pattern. In a study on Jhum cultivation in Meghalaya, Subhas Chandra Srivastava has shown that though the net area under Jhum has increased, the size of plot / family has declined and there exists a striking anomaly between the largest (1.5 ha) to smallest (0.25ha) Jhum plots. Consequent upon the contracted size of Jhum plots [average 0.50 – 0.98 hectare], regular reduction in Jhum Cycle has become a reality [from Previous 10 - 15 years to 4-5 years] resulting in the increase of Cropping Intensity and also growing dependency on market for foodgrains brought from outside.

Priority II

The much higher rate of Non farm Employment indicated in Criterion II in proportion to Annual Growth of Workforce in Criterion III clearly demonstrates that the process of Decentralization in Rural Economy has already set in. *The Dimensions of Decentralization need to be mapped with their impact on the elements of Ecosystem.* The Future Demand on Common Pool Resources is also to be projected for securing ecosystem following the concept of Weak Sustainability.

Sikkim deserves the primary attention because of its easy accessibility in comparison to other North India states and it's attraction as favourite tourist destination. Impact is that Villages after villages are adopting Urban facilities molding their economy and Land Use Mosaic [as evident from *Criterion II*]

Criterion I substantiates this contention as Urban Total worth & assets is galloping ahead whereas the Rural Counterpart in the same category is reeling under recession. Similar contradiction though in lesser quantum prevails in **Nagaland**. But in contrast to Sikkim in **Nagaland**, rural assets and worth are increasing in tandem with urban counterparts coupled with extremely limited annual growth rate in rural employment & enterprise. These demonstrate a highly skewed concentration of possession. In Future this condition may encourage a drastic transformation of Ecosystem Mosaic resulting in collapse of Ecological system. Mizoram is poised better for sustainability due to attained balance both in Criterion I and Criterion II. Meghalaya possesses similar status in these two fronts but in poverty perspective they are distant cousins. Assam & Arunachal Pradesh have reverse condition but this can be designated relatively appropriate for attaining sustainability. But strikingly higher rate of Non Farm workforce in both these states indicates growing extraction of non-recurring ecosystem elements.

Priority III

Energy & Water Management. Present Status.[GOI 2005]

Table 29.7

States	*Rural Households (%)*	
	Fetching drinking Water from far away.	*With no Drainage & Latrine*
Arunachal Pradesh	19.79	73.93 & 52.66
Assam	24.47	85.00 & 40.43
Manipur	33.58	67.21 & 22.50
Meghalaya	32.30	73.69 & 59.90
Mizoram	37.92	75.21 & 20.26
Nagaland	33.45	61.42 & 35.36
Sikkim	20.87	68.40 & 40.65
Tripura	31.42	76.83 & 22.07
India	19.54	65.82 & 78.08

The exhibited figures are to be coupled with requirement for farming and non-farming enterprises. With North East is becoming more arid, as evident from represented Met. Data, securing water for each purpose would be delicate in the days to come.

On 'Common Pool Resources', a couple of Non Conventional Substitutes affordable for North East is presented below with their All India Estimation and future projection.

Priority III: Ecosystem Demarcation: Utilization mode and Possible Vulnerabilities are to be taken into account in the broad

Table 29.8

Agricultural Crop Residue	Production 1994	Projected 2010	Processing based Residue.	Production 1994	Projected 2010
Rice Straw	214.35 mt	284.99 mt	Rice Husk	32.57 mt	43.31 mt.
Jute Stalks	4.58 mt	5.21 mt	Rice barn	10.13 mt	13.46 mt.
Maize Stalks	18.98 mt	29.07 mt	Maize Cob	2.59 mt	3.97 mt.
Soybeans	12.87 mt	34.87 mt	Maize Husks	1.90 mt	2.91 mt.

Iyer *et al* (2002)

perspective of resource identification valuation. These properties are going to determine the Resilience and Vigor of Ecosystem and a hierarchical categorization of the ecosystems in accordance to their Organization potentiality has to be ascertained. For this purpose the following conceptual method can be adopted.

The Habitat Index by L. Hannah, J.L. Carr and A. Landerani

The Habitat Index is aligned to Weak Sustainability. It is a direct measure of land cover/land use concentrating on the degree of disturbance of natural land cover. The minimum area mapped was 40×10^3 ha . The method for calculation of Habitat Index adopted by Hannah is as follows.

$$\text{Habitat Indes} = \frac{\text{Undisturbed Area} + 0.25\,(\text{partially disturbed area})}{} \times 100$$

The value of 0.25 can be changed in accordance to the prevailing situation. The Method of Geographical Information System can be utilized for identifying disturbed area.

Conclusion

This has been an endeavour to represent a profile of scopes how ecosystem oriented Management can cultivate Livelihood Prosperity for North East India. Coupled with Participatory Planning Approach, a cohesive ambience can ensure Sustainable Development.

REFERENCES

Economic & Political Weekly: Various Issues.

Fifth Economic Census: Government of India.
India Infrastructure Report : 3 i Network. Oxford University Press.
India Development Report : IGIRD. Oxford University Press.
Lahiri, Professor Taun Bikas : Macro Economic Development of North East India, with an Overview of North Eastern Region.
NSSO : Report of Various Rounds.
Twenty First Century India: Ed. by Tim Dyson & Robert Casseen.
Yojona :.Various Issues.

Index

Adivasi, 48
Agrarian
  economy, 221, 223, 307
  sectors, 22, 23
  society, 265
Agricultural communities, 264
Agricultural cultivators, 291
Agricultural data, 310
Agricultural economy, 76, 181, 308
Agricultural growth, 194, 219
Agricultural labourer, 224, 288
Agricultural life, 41
Agricultural operation, 65, 196
Agricultural policy reforms, 169
Agricultural production, 185, 299
Agricultural resources, 266
Agricultural sectors, 181, 194, 222, 240
Agricultural situation, 195
Agriculture and allied activities, 231
Agriculture crops, 223
AIDS, 132, 135-36, 166, 212
American Folklore society, 19
Ancient Meiteis society, 82
Anemia, 135
Angamis, 117
Animal husbandry, 223-24
Anthropological Survey of India, 39, 51, 58
Anthropologists, 25
Anxiety, 20-22, 24, 90
Archaeological sites, 6, 7
Archaeological Survey of India, 39
Armed Forces Special Power Act, 104-05
Artisan households, 252
ASEAN markets, 152
Asian Highway, 253-54, 258
Assam Gazette Extraordinary, 300-01
Assam Land and Revenue Regulation, 199
Assam Town and Country Planning Act, 275-76

Bamboo, 68, 69, 71, 230
Basic training centre, 300
Basketry, 64, 65
Bengal Alluvion and Dilluvion Regulation, 197-99
Khasi Hills, Bhoi region of, 8
Bilateral agreements, 171
Bio-diverse region, 245
Bio-social diversity, 139
Bodo movement, 56
Border states, 108
Brahmaputra valley, 12, 175, 177-78, 180, 183, 185, 187-88, 195-96, 245
Bride price, 81, 85
British period, 101
Buddhism, 5, 7, 9, 10, 12, 255

Cadastral survey, 202, 204
Casteless society, 116
Ceasefire agreement, 106, 160
Central sponsored scheme, 132
Challa temples, 10
Cheap labour, 162
Christianity, 33-34, 74, 94-95, 97, 125, 331

Civil society organisations, 167, 339
Civil society space, 159
Colonial administrators, 192-93, 195
Colonial economy, 176, 183, 186
Colonial period, 197, 200-01
Colonial states, 180, 192, 201
Colonialism, 48, 176, 185-88
Colonisation, 48, 168, 175
Commercial agriculture, 177
Common pool resources, 344-46, 351-52
Communist Party of India, 22, 23
Community health centres, 218
Composite society, 49, 59
Concerning Land Legislation and Revenue Administration, 201
Conflict resolution, 109, 172
Contexualists, 18, 19
Contraception, 238
Contractual theory, 118
Credit deposit ratio, 234-35
Cultivable lands, 100
Cultural attainments, 45
Cultural autonomy, 94
Cultural contacts, 4
Cultural distinctiveness, 33
Cultural diversity, 46
Cultural education, 45
Cultural exchanges, 68
Cultural hybridization, 30
Cultural markers, 26
Cultural milieu, 11
Cultural myopia, 26
Cultural pluralism, 120
Cultural resources, 259
Cultural space, 27
Cultural symbols, 22
Cultural system, 25
Cultural tensions, 250
Cultural tradition, 41, 77
Customary law, 22, 99, 100, 109, 258

Decadal variation in population, 299
Democratic society, 49
Dendrogram, 140, 142
Development of women and children, 319
Divine theory, 118
Domestic pillars, 168
Domestic tourists, 256, 261
Dual citizenship, 159-61

East Khasi Hills, 269-70, 272-73
Ecological components, 342-43
Ecological niches, 51
Economic disparities, 239, 243
Economic practices, 51
Economic rationality, 151, 154, 160
Ecosystem resilience, 343-44
Educated elites, 92, 125
Educational institutions, 44-45, 90, 102, 269, 340
Electronic system, 337
English folklore society, 16
Ethnic cousins, 153-54, 161
Ethnic identity, 26, 30-31, 94, 105, 159, 161

Family planning programmes, 238
Farm land holdings, 307, 309-10
Farm-settlers, 195-97
Female infanticide, 333
Female migrants, 287
Female participation rate, 133-34
Financial centers, 185
Folklore scholarship, 15-16, 18-19
Folklore studies, 17, 19
Foreign tourists, 244, 253, 256-57, 259, 261
Formal education, 50, 91, 95, 124-26
Formal schools, 124

Garo Hills of Meghalaya in India, 154
Gender equality, 109, 128-29, 131, 338
Gene differentiation, 139, 141
Gene diversity, 140-41

Gene frequencies, 139-41
Gini coefficient, 309, 311-13
Gini concentration ratio, 309, 311-13
Girls dormitories, 66, 69, 74
Global economy, 170
Globalisation, 23, 97, 149, 154, 162-63, 166-68, 170, 173, 212, 297
Governance reforms, 167-68
Group marriages, 78
Growth theory, 166-67, 173

Habitat index, 353
Hajo centering, 4
Handloom industries, 229-30
Harnessing, 327
Head hunting, days of, 68, 74
Health centres, 218
Heterogeneous society, 100
Heterozygosity, 140-41
Hijam Irawat, 102
Hill areas of Manipur, 105
Hilly region, 244
Hindu society, 330
Hindu Vaisnavite culture, 101
Hinduism, 10, 12, 103, 330
Hinterlands, 185-86
Historical materialism, 17, 18
History of Manipur, 83, 100
HIV, 135-36, 212
Homeland, 3, 12, 106, 157, 159
Homogeneous society, 33
Homogeneous states, 34
Horticulture, 152, 223
Housing shortage, 215
Human resource development, 39, 125, 256
Hydel, 225-27

IMD, 349-50
Immigrant prone districts, 196
Immigrants, 155-56, 158, 162, 193, 195-96, 268
Inbuilt mechanism, 26, 27
Indenture system, 180
Indigenous communities, 41
Indigenous peasants, 194
Indo-Burma region, 155
Industrial growth, 119, 227, 229
Industrial sectors, 229-30
Industrialization, 20-21, 23-25, 93, 129, 228, 297-98, 305
Inequalitarian society, 108
Inequality, 124, 308-11, 339
Infant mortality rate, 135
Inhabitants, 3, 48, 224, 333
Institutional arrangements, 175, 256-57
Institutional reforms, 166-68, 170-71, 173
Integrated Rural Development Programme, 319-20
Intensive crops, 307
International Centre for Settlement of Investment Disputes, 168
International routes, 253-54
Inter-regional mobility, 266
Inter-state traffic, 297
Intra-regional tours, 258
Investment disputes, 168
IRDP, 319-20

Jharkhand movement, 56
Jhum plots, 351
Jong, 66, 70, 73, 74
Jowai, 270, 274-76
Jungle creeper, 69, 70

Kachari, 4, 9, 10, 85
Kaibarta, 142
Kaireima, 80
Kartikeya, 6-8
Kham, 66, 68, 69
Khasis, 23, 97, 122-25
  families, 123, 125
  society, 125-26
Khiatham, 71
King of Manipur, 100-01
Koch, 142
Kokrajhar, 295-98, 301-03, 305

Kokrajhar Centre of Post Graduate Studies, 300
Kokrajhar Master Plan Area, 299, 301-02
Kokrajhar Municipal Area, 296-97, 300, 302
Krishna Leela Dance of Manipur, 245
Kuki, 33, 62, 99, 105-06
  -Chin descent, 155

Lallup system, 109-10
Land-based resources, 190
Land holdings, 92, 258, 307, 310, 313
Land inequality, 308, 313
Land Legislation Concerning, 197
Land legislation, 197, 201, 204
Land mass, 244-45
Land ownership, 117, 190, 258, 278, 314
Land reforms, 22
Land revenue, 177, 194
  administration, 198, 200
  payment of, 204
  policies, 194, 204
  settlements, 202-04
Land settlement, 178, 202
Land tenures, 22, 177, 198
Landmasses, 245, 316
Lang, 17
Lauden festival, 67
Life expectancy, 130, 135, 213
Linguistic group, 55, 56
Livelihood Prosperity for North East India, 353
Locus-by-locus analysis, 143
Look East Policy, 150-53, 157, 163, 169-70
Low-density region, 180
Lower Siang District, 5, 6
Lowest urbanized states, 317
Luwang girls, 83, 85, 86

Maharaja of Manipur, 102-03
Male dormitories, 62, 66, 68, 74
Male participation rate, 133
Malnutrition, 135-36
Manipur AIDS Control Society, 136
Manipur Budget, 131
Manipur Nupi Marup, 111
Manipur Students Federation, 95
Manipur Students Union, 95
Manipuri princess, 85

Marriage
  institution of, 76-78, 329
  love, 81-84
  system of, 82-84, 117
Marxist concept of dialectical, 17, 18
Marxists, 18, 19
Matrilineal
  society, 79, 332
  system, 331-32
Matrilocal society, 77
Matrimonial relations, 65
Mediaeval Eastern Indian art tradition, 6
Mediaeval period, 6-8, 10
Meira Paibis, 105
Meitei society, 79, 86
Mezzadra, 161
Migration, 3, 4, 7, 12, 51, 142, 176, 212, 215, 266, 288, 296, 298
  illegal, 155
  inter-state, 94
Millennium Development Goals, 128, 131, 212, 276
Ministry of Agriculture, 310-11
Ministry of Power data, 225-26
Ministry of Tourism, 251, 253
Mizo society, 24, 95
Mizo-inhabited areas of India, 155
Monogamy, 76, 78, 81
Morphology, 185-86
Morungs, 62, 66, 69-71
Mud fort, 6, 11
Multi-culturalism, 120
Multi-cultural
  demographies, 179
  nature, 120

Multiethnic plural society, 47

Naga negotiators, 156-57
Naga Regional Council, 158
Naga-inhabited areas, 156-57
Naga-Kuki conflict, 105
Naothingkhong, 80, 83
Nascent stages, 230
Nation state society, 53
National highways, 112, 261, 296, 323
National parks, 25
National Rural Employment Guarantee Schemes, 319, 323, 325
National Socialist Council of Nagaland, 160
Natural habitats, 191, 193, 195
Nepotism, 239-40
Newly-formed districts, 286
Non-agricultural
  activities, 267
  communities, 264
  enterprises, 347
  occupations, 264, 288
Nongda Lairen Pakhangba, 79
Non-land record states, 310, 314
Non-traditional society, 191
North East Indian Tribal Values and Culture, 115
North Eastern Council, 169, 328
North-East India History Association, 92
NREGA, 324
NSSO, 345-46
Nungbal Pombee Luwaoba, 83

Operational holdings, 310-13
Oral tradition, 65
Outbound tourist countries, 247
Ownership holdings, 311-12

Pacha-Loishang, 79
Patriarchal society, 77, 333
Patrilocal society, 77
Peace negotiations, 156-57
Perpetuation, 22, 23
Philanthropologist, 25
Pilgrim centres, 5, 266
Pisciculture, 249
Planning Commission, 213
Plantation
  enterprises, 175, 180
  region, 175
  society, 179, 187
  system, 175-77, 179, 188
Plural society, 45, 49, 53
Political Agent, 101, 109-10
Political Change, 102, 104
Political regime, 153
Political system, 99
Polyandry, 78-80
Polygamy, 78, 80, 81
Poorest region, 219
Population
  density of, 122, 212, 214, 267, 298, 317
  elderly, 238
  indigenous, 55, 180
  labouring, 181
  niche, 51, 52
  non-tribal, 95
  rural, 317, 320
  tribal, 95, 280, 284, 286, 292, 295
Post feudal societies, 190
Post-colonial period, 92, 201, 204
Power generation, 225, 227, 277
Pradhan Mantri Gram Sadak Yojana, 319-20, 322-23, 327-28
Primary agency of education, 122
Promiscuity, 76-78
Protest movements, 110

Quality of life, 131-32, 136-37, 212, 249, 305, 320, 342
Quit India Movement, 93

Rainfall regime, 349
Rape, 105, 110-11
Recreation centres, 298

Regional context recognition, 131
Regional economy, 170, 175
Regional finance institutions, 169
Regional identity, 93
Regional imbalances, 215
Regional insurgency, 170, 173
Regional interests, 169
Regional political parties, 96
Regional routes, 253
Regional tourist potentials, 249
Regional trade agreements, 170
Regional trade cooperation, 168
Regional trading circuits, 181
Regional trading networks, 177
Religious rites, 100-01
Revenue
  administration, 200-01, 204
  settlement, 200-01, 204
Rice-beer, 69-71
Rich cultural heritage, 246
Rural communities, 345, 348
Rural development programmes, 320, 322, 324-27
Rural households, 225-27, 324, 345
Rural poverty, 112
Rural society, 49
Rural-urban fringes, 264-65
Russian folklorists, 17, 18

Safe drinking water, 136, 211-14
Salvage operation, 18, 19
Satellite centers, 186
Sauria Paharias, 51
Scheduled commercial banks, 234
Sculptures, 5, 8, 9, 11
Self-help groups, 113, 173, 302, 320-21, 327
Sericulture, 223, 230, 249
Sex-gratification, 77, 78
SGSY, 319-22, 327-28
Shared cultural practices, 36
Shifting cultivation, 116, 219, 222, 314
Shillong Master Plan, 275-76
Shillong Urban Agglomeration, 270, 272-74
Social hierarchy, 50, 64, 142
Social life of Manipur, 106
Social movements, 95-96, 104
Social norms, 71, 99, 100, 109, 123, 329
Social organizations, 179, 187, 190, 344
Socialization, 41, 74, 123-24
Societal problems, 126
Socio-cultural
  division, 56
  life, 41
  roots, 203
  situation, 25
Socio-economic development, 260
South Asia Sub-regional Economic Cooperation, 255
South Asian Regional Economic Zone, 169
South Garo Hills, 270, 273
Sovereignty, 35, 106, 171
Special Accelerated Road Development Programme 323
Sponsored schemes, 227, 319
Stable society, 99, 101
State patronage, 182
Stratified society, 216
Sub-Regional Plan, 258
Surplus labour, 268
Swarnjayanti Gram Swarozgar Yojana, 320-22, 327
Swarozgaris, 321
Symbiotic Sustainability, 342
Symbolic identity, 23

Tai culture, 11
Taothingmang, 82
Tea Association, 183
Tea Industry, 214, 232
Tea plantations, 176-80, 187
Territorial integrity, 31, 33, 36, 106, 158

Terrorism, 168
Textile-producing region, 246
Thangbi Lanthaba, 83
Third World Countries, 211, 250
Tirap district, 63
Tour operators, 257, 260-61
Tourism
  domestic, 253, 256
  mass, 250
  regional, 253
  sustainable, 255
Town and Country Planning, 275, 297, 299
Trade, regional, 170
Trading centers, 122
Traditional
  crops, 178
  cultivation, 177-78
  society, 191
Tribal
  identity, 30, 31
  states, 267
Tribalism, 30, 31
Tribal-majority states, 283
Tribes of Manipur, 33
Tributaries, 183, 195, 202, 204, 245
TRYSEM, 319-20

ULFA, 155-56
Underground organizations, 104, 107
Unused land, 191-93
Urban agglomerations, 266, 273, 284
Urban awakening, 266
Urban centers, 264, 275-76, 300, 316
  growing, 185
  unplanned, 269
Urban development, 277
Urban hierarchy, 266
Urban planning, 277-78
Urban population, 220, 269-73, 275, 286, 288, 291, 296, 316
Urban tribal households, 287
Urbanisation, 280, 283-87, 290-91
  degree of, 265-66
  level of, 283-84, 286-90
  magnitude of, 265-66
  relative, 283-85
Urbanism, 264-65

Vaishnavite
  culture, 245
  Hindu culture, 101
  Hindu Manipuri, 101
Value system, 117-18, 120, 129
Village council, 64, 72

Wancho society, 62-63, 65-66, 69, 72-75
Wangham, 63-64, 67, 71, 74
Wangpans, 63-64, 74
Wangsa, 63-64, 67, 74
Wastelands, 177-78, 191-93, 196
Weberian thesis, 119
West Garo Hills, 269-70, 273
Widow remarriage, 109, 329
Women
  movements, 109-10, 112-13
  organizations, 110, 335
  Social Movement, 108
Womenfolk of Manipur, 105
Woodcarving, 72
Work culture, 126
Work Participation Rates, 133-34
Work permit regime, 162-63
World Tourism Organization, 170, 247, 252

Yoiren Tompokpi, 83
Youth movements, 89-91, 93-94, 96, 97

Zama, 24, 26
Zipsam, 62, 66, 69, 71-74